Mustin

Mustin

A NAVAL FAMILY OF THE
TWENTIETH CENTURY

A UNITED DEFENSE, L.P.
BOOK BY JOHN FASS MORTON

NAVAL INSTITUTE PRESS
ANNAPOLIS, MARYLAND

Naval Institute Press
291 Wood Road
Annapolis, MD 21402

Library of Congress Cataloging-in-Publication Data
Morton, John Fass, 1947–
Mustin : a Naval family of the twentieth century / by John Fass Morton.
p. cm.
ISBN 1-59114-492-2 (hardcover : alk. paper)
1. Mustin, Henry Croskey, 1874–1923. 2. Mustin, Lloyd Montague, 1911–1999. 3. Mustin, Henry A. 4. Mustin, Thomas Morton. 5. United States. Navy—Officers—Biography. 6. Mustin family. I. Title.
V62.M87M67 2003
359'.0092'273—dc21
2003005264

Printed in the United States of America on acid-free paper ♾
10 09 08 07 06 05 04 03 9 8 7 6 5 4 3 2
First printing

For Margaret Virginia and Emily Anne,
that they too may respond to the call to serve

Contents

PART III. THE SURFACE WARRIORS

Acknowledgments

Thanks to Col. John G. Miller, USMC (Ret.), for the referral that led to my writing this book. To Rick Snider, Russ Schuler, and United Defense Limited Partnership, for sustaining the project during research and writing. Thanks also to Julie Olver, managing editor of *Proceedings,* Paul Stillwell, director of the USNI History Division, and Jeanne Pinault, for their assistance in its editing. To Prof. Barton C. Shaw of Cedar Crest College for a historian's professional critique, Danielle and Darlene Tate for assistance in research, and Debbie Madigan for transcription. Thanks especially to Dave Winkler of the Naval Historical Foundation, who generously allowed me to rely on material from his interview with Hank Mustin and on his edited version of Lloyd Mustin's *Atlanta* diary. Thanks in addition to the extended Mustin family, who made themselves available for interviews and innumerable phone calls, and also to the many others who consented to interviews, including Adm. Thomas H. Moorer, USN (Ret.), Adm. Worth H. Bagley, USN (Ret.), Vice Adm. James H. Doyle Jr., USN (Ret.), Vice Adm. Ted Parker Jr., USN (Ret.), Vice Adm. Douglas Katz, USN (Ret.), Rear Adm. Hugh Webster, USN (Ret.), Col. John Adams, USMC (Ret.), Jim Toole, Anne Howard Thomas, Cdr. Joseph Bowyer Howard, USN (Ret.), Lawrence C. Baldauf Jr., Marni Barrow Arnold, Neil Byrne, and Allan McMasters. Finally, thanks to my adored and adoring wife, Gail Bradshaw Morton, for cheerfully allowing me to put part of our life on hold as I worked on this project.

Introduction

I saw that war differs from all the other activities of men in one way only, in being the most important activity; and that the same qualities of foresight, preparation, and energy which affect success in all other activities affect success in war.
Bradley A. Fiske, *From Midshipman to Rear-Admiral* (1919)

"How long have you been in the Navy, mister?"

"All me bloomin' life, sor! Me mother was a mermaid; me father was King Neptune. I was born on the crest of a wave and rocked in the cradle of the deep. Seaweed and barnacles are me clothes. Every tooth in me head is a marlinspike; the hair on me head is hemp. Every bone in me body is a spar, and when I spits, I spits tar. I'm hard, I is, I am, I are."
Reef Points

Sometime in the late summer of 1985, a U.S. naval officer by the name of Neil Byrne was present at a crowded press conference aboard a ship in a Norwegian fjord. The commander of the NATO Striking Fleet, Atlantic, an American vice admiral, had just conducted the largest allied maritime exercise since World War II. A somewhat mistaken notion had taken root in the minds of many that the operation purposed solely to rattle sabers against the Soviet Union. Byrne recalled a skeptical British journalist trying to belittle the operational achievement by commenting on the density of Soviet air defenses to the east that protected the Kola Peninsula. "Yeah," came the audacious response from the admiral, interrupting. "And they're gonna need 'em."

That officer was of the third generation of a family that had served the United States Navy throughout a period just prior to World War II that *Time* publisher Henry Luce labeled "the American Century." In that family, naval officers thought as warriors. For them, *defensive weapon* was no such term. If the soldier of antiquity was without his sword, he fought striking with his shield.

Three generations of men in this family were key participants in many of the major naval milestones of that century. Their stories tell the history of the U.S. Navy as it rose to be the preeminent maritime player on the international stage, for within the decade of the admiral's riposte the Cold War would be won, in part thanks to exercises like his that contributed to the bankrupting of the Soviet Empire.

This admiral's legacy dates from the late summer of 1892 when his namesake grandfather, Henry Croskey Mustin, raised his hand as a midshipman to join a sea service that would burgeon with the rise of the battleship. Mustin's inventive interest in ordnance and gunnery and prescient vision led him to naval aviation, where he is best remembered as one of its fathers—indeed, called by one World War II aviator commander its "brains."

Sharing his father's fascination with ordnance and gunnery, a second Mustin, Lloyd Montague, had a career that uniquely spanned the fullest range of accomplishment—from proficiency in small arms to the testing of nuclear weapons. His mid-century carrier, submarine, and missile navy grappled not only with the geostrategic consequences of the Cold War but also with the growth of the military-industrial complex and its impact on the fleet. During the Vietnam War, at the pinnacle of his career, this Mustin had to wrestle firsthand with the consequences of increased civilian control of the military in the context of the era's high policy predisposition to arms control and what became known as détente.

Lloyd Mustin experienced the conduct of that war as the Joint Staff's director of operations. His two sons, the second Henry Croskey ("Hank") and Thomas Morton, however, fought it as brown-water sailors in combat in the Mekong Delta. Hank advanced to flag lieutenant serving the commander in chief of the Pacific Command and immediately thereafter became a bold destroyer skipper on the gun line in the Tonkin Gulf.

This Mustin's post-Vietnam navy was a service whose military readiness was dramatically reduced and one that faced the new threat of the antiship missile in the context of the Soviet blue-water challenge to sea control. Hank Mustin was a high-profile spear carrier in 1970s fight to empower the surface navy and define its new requirements. In the following decade, he was that three-star admiral who first helped to develop and then executed the mature iteration of the Maritime Strategy with NATO partners in a way that accommodated the aviation, submarine, and surface communities. By leading his fleet into the fjords, Hank—in a personal sense and perhaps for his generation and his father's—did his part to finish the unfinished business of Vietnam.

For three generations, then, these Mustins applied a character of fortitude, intellect, and physical courage to their calling—the naval profession. Known to be cool under fire, they shared early in their careers close-quarters combat experience. Each put a premium on the operational and regarded ship-handling as a professional naval officer's fundamental skill and competitive training as the means to perfect that and other skills—notably the ability to command at all levels—both to achieve combat readiness and better to serve their country.

What follows is the story of this distinguished naval family and these four men for whom the Navy has rightly named its newest *Arleigh Burke*–class Aegis destroyer *Mustin* (DDG-89).

PART I

The Aviator

Chapter 1

The Academy Years

A PHILADELPHIAN JOINS THE TIDE

Henry Croskey Mustin was born in Philadelphia on 6 February 1874 at 3908 Spruce Street, the home of his father, Thomas Jones Mustin, and before him, his grandfather, John Mustin. The Mustins were descendants of a French Huguenot family, originally Mostyn, that had come to the United States via England in the late eighteenth century. Through most of the nineteenth century, the family had prospered in textiles, and they long had been active in the church life of west Philadelphia. The family patriarchs of the day were described in the local press as "all foremost in Church work" at Philadelphia's Fifth Baptist Church. Said one church member, Thomas Mustin was "one of the most active and useful of our Tabernacle members, a man whom we all held in high esteem."

Henry's mother was the former Ida Croskey, a very capable woman who herself came from a distinguished Philadelphia line through Capt. John Ashmead V, her great-grandfather and a first cousin to Benjamin Rush, a signer of the Declaration of Independence. Ashmead was a heroic, swashbuckling, but nonetheless religious naval commander of the Revolutionary War who later became Philadelphia's harbormaster.

Henry was the first of two sons. He and his younger brother, John Burton, were very alike in character, both possessing fierce determination. At a very early age, Henry applied himself to music, learning to play piano by ear and becoming a church

3

organist. Notwithstanding his father's deep involvement with the church, he credited his Episcopalian mother with having taught him how to pray, and he would carry both parents' faith with him throughout his career. Thomas and Ida instilled in their boys the belief that honor is a key attribute of a person's character, and that prized family value was a continuous inspiration.

Thomas Mustin was a vigorous man whose example clearly encouraged Henry and Burton. He prompted both to excel in athletics, and as they grew older they often competed together in track and field events in the Philadelphia area. Henry in particular devoted himself to what then was called physical culture. In the summers, Thomas would take his family to Atlantic City, which was easily accessible by train from Philadelphia. The boys enjoyed active summers in New Jersey and often sporting winters as well. An extraordinarily busy man who commuted to the city during the week, Thomas would dedicate Sundays to his sons, taking them sailing or fishing. Occasionally, they would accompany some of the local men, whom Henry later remembered as a "hard drinking and riotous crowd" who "loved and admired" his dad.

The boys were devoted to their father. On summer mornings, young Henry would walk his dad to the train station to see him on his way to Philadelphia. In the afternoons, he would wait seemingly for hours for his father's return. Some evenings, the elder Mustin would arrive early, and he and his son would head to the beach, where they would swim in the surf until dark. Henry later would recall one occasion, after he had put considerable effort into developing his young biceps, when he stripped for the sea and flexed his muscles proudly for his dad. His father smiled and removed his own shirt to reveal a powerful chest and stomach before diving into the surf, leaving the young Henry with the resolve to build for himself a body just like his dad's.

Thomas Mustin must have promoted in his sons a familiarity and self-reliance around water. Among his early memories, Henry would recall with pride his first "very wonderful day" as perhaps a ten-year-old, spent by himself in a sailboat. He also would recollect saving a boy from drowning a year or two later, for which the youth rewarded him with a large watermelon.

In January 1888, the elder Mustin had finished organizing the Stratford Knitting Mill, which would be his own family business. All that remained was to distribute samples, but before doing so, he wanted to take time with his sons, so the three repaired to New Jersey, probably to hunt. During their return, their train hit a ferocious blizzard and stalled on the track. The temperature inside the compartment dropped precipitously, and to keep his two sons warm, Thomas removed his coat and sweaters and wrapped them tightly around the pair. Rescue was not immediately forthcoming. Despite his vigor, the elder Mustin succumbed to the bitter cold, caught pneumonia, and died shortly thereafter. Henry was fourteen.

Years later, at sea with the Great White Fleet, Henry wrote to his new bride of the kind of father he aspired to be, observing that if his dad had lived, he would have made him a "better man."

So it was that Ida Croskey Mustin was left with two young sons and a mill to open and run. Fortunately, she was well connected in Philadelphia circles, within which was John Wanamaker, the nation's preeminent department store magnate and probably also a customer of Mustin textiles. The leading light of the city's Young Men's Christian Association, Wanamaker also was a prominent Republican.

Ida did not remain a widow for long. Within three years, she married William S. Lloyd, another prosperous Philadelphian, who proved to be a devoted and generous stepfather to Henry and Burton. Lloyd subsequently bought and improved the Stratford Mill.

In early 1891, Henry turned seventeen. Drawn perhaps by adventure, he was interested in a Naval Academy appointment. Ida petitioned directly to John Wanamaker, who, with the 1888 election of Benjamin Harrison, had become postmaster general, then a key cabinet position. In February, Wanamaker arranged for Henry and his mother to meet with Secretary of the Navy Benjamin F. Tracy, while he continued to work in Washington on their behalf.

The Republican Party was the party of the navalists at a time when the U.S. Navy was entering an era of expansion. Benjamin Tracy, a retired army general and wounded Union veteran, had little naval background, but he proved to be a great naval proponent. Largely through the influence of the famed Civil War commander Rear Adm. David Dixon Porter and the up-and-coming naval strategist Capt. Alfred Thayer Mahan, Tracy valued forward-looking naval strategy as a means to enable an expansionist-minded United States to flex its muscles overseas. Perhaps his greatest achievement in office was driving the 1890 legislation that provided for the U.S. Navy's first true battleships—the *Indiana, Massachusetts,* and *Oregon*—arguably the act that launched the so-called new navy.

In spite of the Wanamaker entree, Henry's middling career as a student undid his chances for an 1891 Naval Academy appointment. At the time, appointments to the battalion-sized academy were especially competitive, and sons of naval officers often had the advantage. Fearing the lad might be discouraged, Wanamaker urged Henry to keep him informed of his progress in school. Henry needed no encouragement to stay the course, for events abroad told him that the U.S. Navy offered a heroic life of challenge and adventure, more to his taste than running a family textile business.

American jingoism was at fever pitch in 1891. Revolution in Chile had prompted a U.S. naval presence in Chilean waters. On 16 October, several sailors got into a drunken brawl with locals and police at the True Blue Saloon in Valparaiso. Two Americans died, and several suffered serious injuries. Through the winter and into 1892, President Harrison and Secretary Tracy blustered for war.

For Henry, naval heroes were front-page news. One of the sailors killed, Boatswain's Mate Charles W. Riggin, came home to lie in state at Philadelphia's Independence Hall. The press wrote profiles of such naval officers as Capt. Robley "Fighting Bob" Evans, commander of the units off Valparaiso. These were the larger-than-life celebrities of the day, embodiments of valor, strength, and independence. Henry knew what he wanted to be—an officer in the U.S. Navy. He would continue his studies and persist in his quest for admission to the Naval Academy.

Late that summer, on 6 September, he attained the prize: an appointment from Secretary Tracy. He would go as a naval cadet (the term *midshipman* was not revived until 1901) from the First District of Tennessee, a fact that reflected some political doing as, of course, he was Pennsylvanian.

The year started officially on 1 October 1892, and Henry entered as a member of the seventy-seven-man class of 1896. The popular Civil War commander Capt. Robert L. Phythian was superintendent. Among his staff was Lt. William S. Benson, who would advance to be the first chief of naval operations. Henry would find the U.S. Navy a close and very small world of men, with whom, for whom, and later over whom, he would serve. Reputations and friendships were made early, beginning in Annapolis, and would form the foundation on which he would build his career.

Mustin was one of the latecomers. Part of the class of 1896 had taken the three-month summer cruise and thus entered the academic year with some firsthand knowledge of leadership and matters naval. It would be a challenging year of adjustment for Mustin. He and the rest of his class soon were knocked into shape by the colorful sword master of the day, A. J. Corbesier of the Ordnance and Gunnery Department. Evidently, however, Henry had a lot of stuffing left, for the record shows he got into plenty of trouble his plebe year: whistling loudly during study, skylarking on drill, throwing water in corridor, creating disturbance after taps, talking in ranks, careless in performance of duty as section leader, crossing grass, and the more serious offense, smoking.

Although not a large youth, Mustin soon become known for his physical strength and great interest in athletics. On 20 May 1893, at the academy's spring athletic meeting, Mustin and another cadet tied in the pole vault at 9'¾", setting an Annapolis record.

After his plebe year, Mustin took his first summer cruise on the forty-year-old *Constellation,* the U.S. Navy's last all sail–powered warship. She had served as training vessel for the Naval Academy since 1871, and this cruise would be her last at the Yard. Leaving Annapolis on 6 June, 123 cadets headed first to Old Point Comfort, Hampton Roads, Virginia—where they got the chance to "spoon" with the belles of Norfolk for two nights—and then across the Atlantic to Horta on the island of Fayal in the Azores. Mustin and his classmates participated in drills of all kinds, notably the dangerous ones aloft in the rigging, where, rain or shine, they handled the sails. In this work, Henry could draw on his sailing experience with his father on the Jersey shore. He may have been too full of himself, however. During the cruise, he received demerits for "unwarranted assumption of authority."

The *Constellation* arrived in the Azores on 2 July, another "very wonderful day" for Mustin, who marked it as the first time he had "set foot in a foreign land." For four days, the cadets sampled the local wine in quantity before sailing to Funchal, Madeira. They arrived on 11 July and left on the nineteenth for a "three-day windjammer" to Hampton Roads, the *Constellation*'s last run under sail before being towed to Newport to serve there as a naval training station and receiving ship. The ship remained off Fort Monroe for several days before arriving in Annapolis on the twenty-ninth and debarking her cadets for well-earned leave.

By the time Mustin returned to the academy on 1 October 1893 as a third classman, his class had defined itself, having been both to sea and on liberty, and had formed impressions of each of its members. The class of 1896's fiftieth anniversary book speaks tantalizingly of "fast riding" at Bay Ridge, then a major regional resort on the Chesapeake Bay, five miles from the academy. The editors—speaking for their class— wrote that "they also indulged in spooning, as far as was permissible, and at that early stage showed evidences of the very great development they have later reached in that most important part of their functions." They tagged Henry as "Corkscrew Mustin, Baltimore street pilot, and man with the gold plated smile, open for all engagements."

Unfortunately, his plebe year academic achievements had been unimpressive. Among a class that had dwindled to fifty-eight, Mustin stood forty-ninth in order of merit and fifty-fifth in discipline. Yet, he continued to make his mark in athletics, and in his youngster (third-class) year became quarterback of the class football team.

Academy football was building momentum and was especially magnetic for a feisty cadet such as Mustin. The 1893 season was noteworthy for a particularly intense grid-iron clash between the two service rivals, Army and Navy. It was the fourth such contest, and Navy went into the game with a series record of two to one. After a hard fight, the Navy team won a narrow victory with a score of six to four. As was characteristic of the time, the intensity spread to the fans.

In the excited aftermath, a retired brigadier general and a rear admiral got into a fistfight that reportedly escalated into a duel with firearms at Washington's Army and Navy Club. Following a letter from the West Point superintendent to the secretary of war, Army–Navy football and the duel were discussed at cabinet level. In the interest of good order and discipline, the War and Navy Departments decided to prohibit any further Army–Navy football games. The rivalry did not resume until 1899, at Franklin Field in Philadelphia, thought to be a less provocative venue than the playing fields of either academy.

Off the football field, Mustin would have a boisterous year. Significant demerits during his youngster year included those for pitching a football against a building, fighting, snowballing in the vicinity of Old Quarters, using insulting language to another cadet, breaking a window with a snowball, and "throwing water from a window of Number 4." Among his cohorts in a number of these high jinks was his classmate and close friend Amon Bronson Jr. Mustin and Bronson had much in common. Raised by his widowed mother, Bronson also was a less than satisfactory student and a smoker. The two of them were put on report by a number of different officers, most frequently by Lt. De Witt Coffman, one of the drill officers in the commandant's office. On 29 May, Coffman caught Bronson smoking in Mustin's room. In July, both were on report for food fights at dinner.

In the spring of 1894, the academy published the first *Lucky Bag* yearbook, and Mustin's class moved from Old Quarters, the nine pre–Civil War attached dormitory buildings along Stribling Row, to the postwar New Quarters. These quarters would remain the cadets' primary residence until 1904, when Bancroft Hall was completed.

At the end of his youngster year, Mustin's class had dropped to fifty-one cadets, and Mustin stood twenty-ninth in order of merit and forty-fourth in discipline, with 210 demerits. His one great academic achievement was in mechanical drawing, taught by the legendary Lt. G. F. Colvocoresses: Mustin stood first in the course.

That summer, for the practice cruise, the academy replaced the *Constellation* with two ships, the gunboat *Bancroft,* a new and specially built steam training ship, and the sloop *Monongahela,* veteran of the Battle of Mobile Bay, which had arrived at the academy in

1892. The battalion split into two units that rotated across the ships halfway through the cruise. Mustin was assigned first to the *Bancroft.* On 7 July, the night before his departure, he received demerits for having civilian clothes under suspicious circumstances and for being out of room after taps, adding to his growing reputation as a ladies' man.

The *Bancroft*'s first cruise took her along the East Coast, allowing Mustin and his fellow cadets to enjoy a succession of onboard dances. They romanced the local belles, from Hampton Roads and Norfolk to New York and Newport, and spent six days in Mustin's hometown of Philadelphia, which he reportedly "painted red." Returning to Hampton Roads, Mustin's unit transferred to the *Monongahela* on 3 August. The sloop went to sea four days later, and the cadets turned to, applying themselves seriously to their drills. They returned to the Roads on 18 August and spent a few more nights on the town before arriving to anchor off the South River just below Annapolis on the twenty-fourth. Six days later, they were back in the Yard and ready for leave.

In November, Henry spent two days in sick bay with a contused leg, but quickly recovered. He participated in a number of sports through the year. In the spring he rowed bow oar on the crew. With him, rowing three, was his classmate and admiral's son Thomas T. Craven, who later would serve as director of naval aviation from 1919 to 1921. In addition, Mustin was a member of the fencing and baseball teams and manager of field, track, and gymnasium athletics. According to one Philadelphia news clip, he proved himself "adept in wrestling and use of the sword—in fact, a good all-round athlete." On the academy field day, Saturday, 25 May, Mustin got medals in a number of events, scoring 19' 5" in the running broad jump, 10'¾" in the pole vault (breaking the academy record), and fourteen seconds in "running the bases," beating a world record in an obscure contest that had stood since 1868. With all this athletic activity, he apparently had little time to get into trouble. His worst offenses for the year were having his cap visor turned up, laughing (and later inattentive), and hair not closely cut.

The summer cruise for 1895 was on the *Monongahela,* the *Bancroft* having proved too cramped for a training ship. On 9 June, the cadets began their run to Madeira, arriving in Funchal on 13 July. By now, Mustin felt himself an accomplished sailor. On the return run to Hampton Roads five days later, he frequently could be seen off duty reading in the foretop. Presumably as a result of his accumulated exploits ashore, he also had earned the nickname that was to stay with him a lifetime: "Rum."

That autumn, the class returned for first-class year, now numbering forty-two. Mustin stood thirty-second and, with 170 demerits, was thirty-third in conduct. He remained in the lower half of his class in all subjects except mechanical drawing, in which he stood first. Leadership also eluded his grasp; he was not a cadet officer. He was, however, quarterback and captain of the 1895 Navy football team, leading the cadets to a four-to-two record. He also played on the class football team, which he led to an academy championship. In the spring, he captained the track team.

Throughout the year, he continued to test Yard discipline. In December, his smoking got him sent to the *Santee,* the academy's Civil War veteran station ship that served as a brig. In April, he was charged for breaking branches from trees in grounds. To graduate, he had to retake the electricity examination.

At the end of the year, twenty-six cadets of the class of 1986 elected to become line officers, with the balance opting to specialize in engineering. The anchorman of the line division was his scrappy cohort Bronson; Mustin was twenty-fifth. Craven managed to graduate fourth. Notably, Mustin stood number one in mathematical and geometrical drawing—the academy even kept models of his work on exhibit—an achievement on which he would capitalize during his first duty with the fleet.

On 25 May, Mustin was graduated, and the June Week that followed brought pageantry, family, dances, and the ladies. His belle of the moment was Mary Randall, and their romance led to what was perhaps a rum-induced marriage proposal the week before he left the academy. As to whether the proposal "should count," Mustin later wrote that it had occurred "before he was on the water wagon." How Mary received the entreaty remains a mystery. It was his stepfather, however, who capped Henry's June Week. "Father Lloyd," as Mustin always would refer to him, generously hosted a 4 June graduation dinner at the Hotel Maryland in Annapolis, following which Henry was away to the fleet for his required two-year service as a passed cadet.

Mustin's orders were to the *New York,* flagship of Rear Adm. Francis M. Bunce and the North Atlantic Squadron and the U.S. Navy's first armored cruiser, commissioned on 1 August 1893 in Philadelphia. It was an auspicious start, especially for a cadet who finished next to last in his class. Not much is known about Henry's prewar years on the *New York,* although, later in his career, he did mention one incident. Recalling in a 1908 letter what he called "his very wonderful days," he wrote that one "was spent as a Midshipman boarding a schooner flying the ensign union down and dragging ashore on the reefs outside of Dry Tortugas in the Gulf of Mexico."

The *New York*'s skipper, Capt. French Ensor Chadwick, probably recognized early and encouraged Mustin's command initiative. Chadwick was a well-connected officer, very close to former Secretary of the Navy Tracy. Mustin also would have benefited from his exposure to Bunce, a veteran commander of the Union blockade, who emphasized training and readiness. As a ship department head and commander, Mustin later would make these emphases his own.

In the autumn of 1897, the *New York* and her sister cruisers were in port at the Brooklyn Navy Yard. For the second year in a row, the North Atlantic Squadron, known familiarly as the White Squadron because of the ships' peacetime hull color, fielded a football team to challenge the Naval Academy. Mustin was assigned to play, and on Thanksgiving Day, 25 November, the rivals met at Annapolis, playing before a frenzied crowd of two thousand fans. Mustin, as captain and quarterback, led the team, with Thomas Craven as his preferred receiver. A *Baltimore Sun* press account described the contest as "the most spirited and exciting game since the Army Navy game five years before." The hard-fought duel continued to halftime without a score. In the second half, the cadets finally put eight points on the board, and they led to the end. Mustin made a fifty-yard touchdown run near the end of the game, but the play was not allowed, and the final score remained eight to nothing.

As the fans poured on to the field, a group of cadets plotted to steal one of the White Squadron flags from its cheerleaders. A second-class cadet named Dodd led the attempt, and according to the *Sun* report, a flag was "accidentally pulled from the hands of a lady." Mustin, nearby and still furious over the referee's call on his touchdown, hit Dodd as he grabbed the *New York* flag and broke the cadet's nose. It was an explosive performance, characteristically Mustin in its defense of honor. Suddenly, a melee was in the making. "Fighting Bob" Evans, the hero of Valparaiso, "quieted them down," said the report, which concluded by noting that "Mustin is popular and considered one of the best players the academy has turned out."

Soon the year turned to 1898, and the White Squadron returned to sea—once again to the Dry Tortugas and the diplomatically charged waters around Cuba. Honor would be suffused with jingoism on the national stage. For Mustin, it would be the year he would complete his naval apprenticeship and experience a baptism of fire as a commissioned ensign in a navy at war.

Chapter 2

An Ensign Goes To War

On 15 February 1898, an explosion sank the battleship *Maine* in Havana harbor, killing some 260 men and precipitating the U.S. decision to go to war against Spain.

The Cuban insurrection, a guerrilla war against Spanish rule that had persisted stubbornly for decades, had come to Havana with what Washington believed was unusually serious rioting. With contraband arms continuing to flow by sea to Cuban insurgents, the region was tense. The mood had not been helped by New York newspaper publisher William Randolph Hearst's "yellow" journalism that fomented support for the *insurrectos*.

In January 1989, the Navy Department had responded by sending the North Atlantic Squadron to conduct maneuvers in the Gulf of Florida—the first such exercises in two years. Not wanting the Spanish to interpret the deployment as a naval demonstration, Rear Adm. Montgomery Sicard, who had succeeded Bunce as squadron commander, selected as his base of operations Dry Tortugas, an island sixty miles west of Key West that was deemed to be less threatening to the Spaniards. Nevertheless, in February, Washington had sent the *Maine* to Havana to show the flag.

Accompanying the battleship was the torpedo boat *Cushing*. The Navy wanted secure communications between the mainland and any U.S. units in Havana, and the

Spanish authorities agreed to allow the vessel to serve as a dispatch boat. The courier service was to start on 15 February; however, the *Cushing* left Cuban waters that day in deference to Spanish sensitivity to having two U.S. naval vessels in the harbor. Then the *Maine* blew.

Immediately on hearing of the explosion, Cdr. James M. Forsyth, commandant of Key West, ordered the armed lighthouse supply ship *Mangrove* and the *Fern,* a small tender/transport loaded with doctors, to steam to Havana and provide assistance.

The crisis proved to be a career opportunity for Henry Mustin. By now, he certainly had made a good impression on Captain Chadwick, such that his skipper on the *New York* would have seen that he was made available for additional duties. On 17 February, Mustin received orders from Forsyth to act temporarily as ensign on the *Cushing* to take the cable about the *Maine* to Admiral Sicard at Dry Tortugas. Two days later, he returned to Key West with Sicard's cable ordering a court of inquiry. On the twenty-first, his relief reported, and Mustin resumed his duties on the *New York.*

Sicard selected Capt. William T. Sampson, the skipper of the battleship *Iowa,* to chair the court. Head of the Bureau of Ordnance and Gunnery from 1893 to 1897, Sampson was regarded as an ordnance expert and thus an appropriate president for the inquiry. Serving with him would be Captain Chadwick. On 21 February on board the *Mangrove,* Sampson convened his court in Havana harbor. On 19 March, the proceedings transferred to the *Iowa* as Sampson prepared the report for President William McKinley. Thanks probably to Chadwick, the court looked to Mustin to exercise his one outstanding academic achievement at the academy—his efficiency and accuracy in mechanical drawing. As credited in the published report, Mustin drew the "'projection showing present position of keel and bow of *Maine* redrawn from draft made by Ens. W. Y. N. Powelson' assisted by divers Olsson, Smith, Rindquist and Schluter." Mustin, therefore, was privy to much of what was *not* said in the report and perhaps knew the private conclusions drawn by Sampson, Chadwick, and other senior Navy officers on a matter that was about to direct the course of U.S. naval history.

On 21 March, officers from the *Maine* conveyed the documentation—with Mustin's drawing—to the *New York,* where the flagship's junior officers guarded it closely. On 22 March, Sicard approved the report, including the key but questionable finding that a mine had caused the explosion. Under guard, the document went by train to Washington and President McKinley. On the twenty-eighth, the president presented the report and his message to Congress in advance of congressional hearings on the disaster.

While the administration and lawmakers wrestled with the legal mechanics of going to war, Key West became the focus of naval preparations for war. Sicard had shifted his headquarters from Dry Tortugas to Key West, whose shallow harbor, among other things, presented a logistical challenge to the squadron. The *New York* and other capital ships had to lie seven miles offshore and take their coal and ammunition from lighters. The island also was becoming home to the swarms of war correspondents clamoring for stories and vessels to follow the ships into the anticipated action.

The course of larger events continued to be fortuitous for Mustin. Admiral Sicard had been ill for some time, and it was clear he was not fit to command the squadron in time of war. On 26 March, Sampson relieved him by right of rank within the squadron. Looking ahead to the challenges posed by modern naval gunnery, Sampson's first act was to order the use of lead instead of black for his ships' war paint to frustrate accurate sighting by Spanish gunners.

Mustin was about to complete his requisite two-year cruise following graduation from the Naval Academy. Having performed well for Chadwick on the *New York,* he soon would examine for ensign and go to war as a commissioned officer. Whatever his glorious imaginings, Mustin got orders to an auxiliary, the *Mangrove.* Judging by his later responses to what he considered bad orders and the way he would call on seniors to go to bat for him to get them changed, he probably took advantage of his service to Sampson to request the commander in chief's intervention. Mustin wanted to sail into harm's way on a man-of-war. Sampson must have been impressed with the young cadet's zeal and got the order revoked. In addition, he retained Mustin on his flagship, the *New York,* to serve as his aide and signal officer.

To be assigned to the staff of a fighting commander in chief was, in itself, a great opportunity, but given Sampson's own deteriorating health, it was momentous. Some, notably Capt. Edward L. Beach, have suggested that Sampson might have suffered a series of small strokes, with physical effects that got progressively worse during the war. Thus his staff played a key role during the various campaigns and, according to Captain Beach, did everything in Sampson's name. If that indeed was the case, Mustin would have gained an awareness of wartime decision-making at every level of the operational Navy, including insights into planning and politics far beyond what could have been expected at his rank. As it transpired, this duty on the *New York* put Mustin in one of the naval theaters of the Spanish-American War and gave him experience in operations from blockade to bombardment, search, amphibious landing, and fleet engagement.

Congress authorized armed intervention on 19 April 1898. Drawing from his experience in the Union Navy blockade of Confederate Atlantic ports, Sampson wanted to initiate hostilities by bombarding Havana, but the Navy Department said no. On 21 April, the president ordered only a naval blockade of Cuba, an act of war, which Congress formally declared on the twenty-fifth. At 4:30 A.M. on 22 April, the *New York* and her squadron left Key West for Cuban waters, and Sampson was promoted to acting rear admiral.

They arrived off Cuba at three o'clock that afternoon, and Mustin was at war. His station as the admiral's aide was on the bridge with Sampson and Chadwick, at the center of the action. On the twenty-third, lookouts sighted smoke on the horizon, and the *New York* entered chase. It was a Spanish merchant steamer, the *Pedro,* trying to sneak from Havana harbor; the *New York* took it as a prize. Until abolished by Congress in 1899, prize money was one of the side benefits that naval officers received in wartime. The next day, lookouts spotted a warship, and the *New York* went to general quarters. The ship turned toward the *New York* and appeared to commence firing. Quickly, it was ascertained that it was the Italian cruiser *Don Giovanni Bausan*—firing a salute.

Recognition would be a problem throughout the blockade and was worse at night. U.S. naval units operated with lights extinguished. Night maneuvering was further complicated by the presence of the innumerable newspaper dispatch boats that continually jostled amid the ships on station to be positioned for the best story in the event of action.

Blockade duty soon settled into a monotony, but it did lead to some engagements against targets ashore. Spanish batteries at Matanzas, east of Havana, had fired on the torpedo boat *Foote.* In the early afternoon of 27 April, the *New York* arrived to fire its first shots against the offending shore fortifications on Point Rubalcaya. The ship lobbed a nineteen-minute barrage of three hundred shells but caused little damage— the first evidence of the questionable effect of ship fire against land targets. A second minor exchange occurred in the early evening of the twenty-ninth at Cabanas, some twenty-five miles west of Havana. A dismounted Spanish cavalry ashore peppered the *New York* with small-arms fire, prompting a response of fifteen 4-inch shells. Further excitement came later that night when the *New York* got under way and, while at sea, almost engaged the U.S. torpedo boat *Porter.* On 1 May, she left her station for Key West for coal and instructions.

At that time, the U.S. East Coast was alarmed by news that the Spanish Atlantic Squadron commanded by Adm. Pascual Cervera y Topete had sailed from Spain to augment naval forces in the Caribbean. Cervera presented a potential bombardment threat to U.S. coastal communities, but his intentions were not clear. On 2 May, Sampson led a force to Puerto Rico, thinking that the fortified San Juan might be the Spaniard's destination. En route, the crew ripped the planking off the deck and the trim from the bulkheads, throwing everything wooden overboard to clear the ship for the expected action. On 7 May, word came of Dewey's victory in Manila Bay, and Sampson's force readied for what they hoped would be an equally decisive engagement with Cervera.

Four days later, as the force arrived off San Juan, Mustin received official word that he had passed his examinations and was an ensign as of 6 May. He thought he soon would see his first action as a commissioned officer, but Sampson had guessed wrong. Cervera was not at San Juan. Nonetheless, he elected to bombard the fortifications. During the three-hour operation on the twelfth, Spanish shore batteries scored hits on both the *Iowa,* which was temporarily carrying Sampson and his staff, and the *New York,* killing one and wounding four. On the sixteenth, the U.S. force departed for Key West. En route, the *New York* captured another prize, the Spanish barque *Carlos F. Rozes.*

Later in the month, Washington received reports that Cervera was heading for Santiago de Cuba. Commo. Winfield Scott Schley's Flying Squadron arrived on station off Santiago and on 29 May determined that Cervera was in the harbor. At six o'clock on the morning of 1 June, Sampson arrived to assume command. The Spanish ships were bottled in the harbor, the entrance to which was mined and guarded by fortified gun batteries on both sides. Since the *Maine* explosion, mines were taken very seriously, and Sampson had no intention of fighting his way into the harbor to engage Cervera. Instead, his plan was to put a cork in the bottle by sinking the collier *Merrimac* in the channel. The mission was led by a young officer who served on board the *New York* with Mustin and who, two decades later, would be an important ally of the Navy and naval aviation as a congressman and House of Representatives committee chairman—Assistant Naval Constructor Richmond Pearson Hobson. On 3 June, Hobson and his volunteers sank the *Merrimac* in the channel; however, the hulk settled out of position, and the channel remained open.

On 6 June, Sampson decided to bombard the fortifications. The barrage was intense. Mustin's station during the firing was below the forward bridge. At one point, a loud report shattered the charthouse above him, sending down a shower of glass and wood. By one account, Sampson casually leaned over the rail and asked, "Was that a shell?" It was in fact the result of concussion from one of the ship's guns. Ten days later, the *New York* renewed bombardment.

By now, however, the emphasis was shifting from blockade and occasional bombardment to preparations for an amphibious operation. On 20 June, thirty-two steamers loaded with the Army's hastily assembled expeditionary force arrived off Santiago. Sampson and his staff went ashore to confer with Maj. Gen. William R. Shafter, USA, the expeditionary commander, and the insurrecto leader, Gen. Calixto Garcia. The amphibious landing, they determined, would occur eighteen miles to the east at Daiquiri.

The operation began on 22 June with a bombardment. The landing itself was intended to be an entirely Army affair. As ships' bands on the steamers played "There'll Be a Hot Time in the Old Town Tonight," six thousand troops attempted to get ashore amid heavy swells and rough surf. It was soon obvious that they needed Navy boats to help. Although the *New York* was not at Daiquiri, she sent some steam cutters to serve as transports. Fortunately, the landing was unopposed. A second landing came the next day at Siboney, eight miles closer to Santiago. As the Army progressed along the coast and inland toward Santiago, it began to meet with fierce resistance, and the *New York* struggled to stay in communication with the front—a challenge not lost on Mustin. On 1 July, the ship bombarded Aguadores in support of Army units, but farther inland that day was a bloodbath. Shafter lost a thousand men, and suddenly the joint operation was in jeopardy.

On 2 July, Sampson again bombarded the forts at Santiago, but it did little to resolve what had become a flag misunderstanding between the Army and the Navy. In Shafter's mind, the plan was to march on Santiago, and he assumed that Sampson understood. Sampson thought Shafter was attacking the harbor batteries and fortifications that had to be put out of action before the Navy could clear the mines. Shafter claimed that his decision was dictated to a member of Sampson's staff. Since his land campaign was going awry, he was now asking Sampson to enter the mined harbor to provide fire support.

At 8:30 A.M. on 3 July, the *New York* left her blockade station to steam east to Siboney. Sampson was planning to land and consult with Shafter to resolve their mutual misperceptions. Meanwhile, in Santiago harbor, Cervera thought it an opportune time to surprise the U.S. units during their Sunday morning inspections and fight his way to freedom. At 9:35 A.M., the Spanish naval force emerged from the harbor entrance. Out of position to the east, the *New York* was going to play a significant role in the battle only if the Spanish turned toward her. Cervera turned west. Now well behind the fleeing Spanish combatants, Sampson raced to join the engagement. In the end, the battle was a rout, and the *New York* suffered no injuries. At the close of the day, the ship engaged in one last operation—saving Spain's helpless *Colon* by giving the sinking armored cruiser two or three nudges with her ram to position her on the shelf off the beach.

Mustin reckoned 3 July 1898 as another of his "wonderful days." For Sampson, however, the day was bittersweet. His decision to leave his station would add one more element to what was to be an acrimonious postwar fight with Schley, who on his flagship the *Brooklyn* had remained on station and thus had reason to claim credit for the subsequent victory.

Into July, Sampson continued to bombard Santiago with his secondary batteries to hasten the capitulation, which came on the seventeenth. He then transferred his forces to Guantánamo in preparation for a possible expedition against Spain, but finally suspending operations on 13 August when word came of the 12 August protocol that ended the war. The *New York* hosted a peace jubilee, capping a number of shipboard social events. On 14 August, she and other warships headed north for a review in New York City. Arriving off Sandy Hook at eight o'clock on the morning of the twentieth, the *New York* led the *Iowa, Brooklyn, Oregon, Massachusetts,* and *Indiana* up the Hudson and past the forts on Staten Island, which fired a salute and detonated mines that had been defending the harbor. Tugs, police boats, fire tugs, sailboats, ferries, scows, and excursion boats packed with people—and film crews—joined the review, sounding their sirens and whistles as the line of ships steamed past the crowd-covered Riverside Park on the Upper West Side of Manhattan. As the ships passed Grant's tomb, they responded to salutes from the shore and continued upriver to anchor off Tompkinsville late in the afternoon.

Among the many lessons of the Spanish-American War, the Navy had learned a great deal about operations in the tropics, such as the problem of disease and the importance of distilled water—lessons it would apply soon to its operations in the Philippines. Sampson addressed several issues immediately after the war, notably the need for better communication systems within and between ships and the urgent requirement for range finders. The dirty secret of Santiago and Manila Bay that the U.S. victories obscured was the Navy's abysmal gunnery. One record has it that at Santiago, the Navy fired 170 guns and scored 163 hits, less than one hit per gun. Another statistic is more telling: Those 170 guns fired more than nine thousand rounds. The story from Manila Bay was somewhat the same—141 recorded hits out of 5,859 rounds.

As far as the public was concerned, however, the Spanish-American War was America's "splendid little war." The national press gave a lot of attention to its naval officers who served at Manila Bay or at Santiago, thanks to the steady stream of reports from war correspondents such as Richard Harding Davis and others who managed to get on board U.S. warships. On the *New York* during the blockade, Davis had mess with the officers, and the Associated Press correspondent and Ralph Paine of *The World* and

Press of Philadelphia ate "with the middies." These fellow Philadelphians certainly did their part to introduce Mustin as the one of the war's hometown heroes. One report quoted Sampson describing him as "an intelligent officer, capable of performing the duties assigned to him with the utmost zeal."

The once primarily physical Mustin had discovered in battle an intellectual element that would drive him to study the art of war. The obvious ineffectiveness of naval gunnery and the inefficiency of ship-to-shore communications were a catalyst, pushing him to marry his mechanical drawing ability with his natural inventiveness. As a passed cadet on the *New York,* he already had applied himself to the design of a mechanical semaphore attachment to use in signaling when electricity failed or was not obtainable. This early invention had come to the attention of a mid-career naval reformer, Lt. Cdr. Bradley A. Fiske, whose genius moved along a path Mustin now sought to follow. Yet, before he would give himself to the more contemplative pursuit of invention, he was to experience shots fired in anger once more—this time as a combat commander in the capricious waters of the Philippine Insurrection.

Chapter 3

Command in the Philippines

FROM OYSTER TO PIRATE

As the nineteenth century gave way to the twentieth, prescient navalists saw that the United States' maritime future would be in the Pacific, where soon the U.S. Navy would replace the Royal Navy as mistress of the seas. Presence in the region would have to increase dramatically to cope with the U.S. acquisition of the Philippines in particular and with duties on the China station more generally. Here lay the opportunities for young naval officers.

With most of the new battleships, the Atlantic Squadron still might have been the prestige squadron. It certainly offered the billets for junior officers who stood high in their classes at the Naval Academy and consequently had the better "numbers," but Henry C. Mustin did not fit this profile. Now ambitious for both action and advancement, he resolved, therefore, to set his course westward.

After the New York victory review, Mustin was able to secure orders to report on 18 September 1898 as a watch and division officer to the collier *Scindia,* bound for the Pacific. As a unit in the Special Service Squadron, the *Scindia* would be going around South America with the battleships *Oregon* and *Iowa,* the distilling ship *Iris,* and another collier, the *Justin.* Recently celebrated for her daring sixty-seven-day voyage from California eastbound through the Magellan Strait to join Sampson's units off

Santiago, the *Oregon* was returning to the Pacific to provide battleship muscle in the Far East and to serve as flagship of the Asiatic Station.

The westbound voyage would be long and tough for the *Scindia*. Some legs were forty days from port to port. Somewhere near the equator on the southward leg, she broke down and drifted for two days before the crew could repair the engines and continue to Bahia on the coast of Brazil.

Mustin did enjoy some respite. During the transit of the strait, he was able to spend some liberty ashore at Punta Arenas, the Chilean coaling stop and maritime crossroads of the hemisphere. With his classmate Thomas T. Craven, who was serving aboard another ship, he ventured into the uplands to hunt fox and puma. New Year's Eve found him in Callao, Peru. At a Callao Club dance he fell in love with a seventeen-year-old belle who was half-American and half-Spanish. He gave her a "grand rush" and, as every good sailor does when parting, promised her he would return someday.

Troubles returned to the *Scindia* on the crossing to Hawaii, when she broke down again and had to be towed into Honolulu for repairs.

When Mustin arrived in Hawaii, action in the Philippines was imminent. On 4 February 1899, as the U.S. Senate was moving to ratify the Treaty of Paris, which ceded the Philippines and other former Spanish colonies to the United States, the U.S. Army attempted to disperse the insurrectos around Manila. These events ignited Filipino patriot Emilio Aguinaldo's fight against U.S. occupation.

Stranded on the *Scindia* in Honolulu, knowing the collier would have to return to San Francisco, Mustin was eager to get to what had become another theater of war. Billets were unlikely to be available on the *Oregon* or any other combatants going to Philippine waters, so he stood a better chance of getting there on another auxiliary. The recent experience at Santiago had highlighted the importance of water to military and naval operations in the tropics, and U.S. authorities had become aware of an insurgent plan to contaminate Manila's water supply. The Navy ordered the *Iris* to join units operating in the Philippines.

After several days, a determined Mustin somehow got orders from Rear Adm. Albert Kautz, commander of the Pacific Station, to make an exchange with Ensign James J. Raby, who was on board the *Iris*. He began his duties on the distiller on 17 February, and on 18 March, the *Iris* and the *Oregon* arrived in Manila. By spring, Mustin was involved in the bloodiest conflict in Philippine history—including World War II.

Emilio Aguinaldo was president of the insurgent Philippine Republic, declared a month after Dewey's 1898 victory in Manila Bay. Aware of the political debate over the Philippines in Washington, his objective initially was to survive in the field until—he hoped—the more noninterventionist and anti-imperial Democrats won the 1900 election. For the U.S. Navy, a key military objective was to blockade the islands and strangle the flow of rifles and cartridges from smugglers to Aguinaldo's units. The U.S. plan was to occupy and garrison port cities and to control trade into the islands, thereby asserting sovereignty.

For most of 1899, the U.S. Army struggled to organize itself and win insurgent territory within a sixty-mile radius of Manila. As had happened at Santiago, the service frequently wrangled with the Navy over the conduct of joint operations and who was responsible for what. In February 1899, an Army general proposed to capture the Philippines' second largest city, Iloilo, on the island of Panay. The more mobile Navy and Marine Corps got there first. Led by Cdr. James Wilde, captain of the protected cruiser *Boston* and later captain of the *Oregon,* the operation led to a series of bitter exchanges between the Army and the Navy that colored the services' attitudes toward each other in succeeding operations.

Once the Army took the offensive into northern Luzon, however, logistics would prove to be a serious challenge and would necessitate considerable naval support. The Army also benefited from offshore naval gunfire support in the campaign around Manila. In a testament to joint operations, the monitor *Monadnock* successfully provided enfilade fire on insurgent lines from within half a mile of the shoreline. Vital ship-to-shore communication often had to be jury-rigged, with Army units ashore indicating the forward position of their lines with red flags. On board the *Monadnock* was the rising naval reformer Bradley Fiske, who used this operational experience in an attempt to refine the use of telescopic sights for fire control and electricity for the training and elevation of guns.

Directing the war from his headquarters in the Manila "Palace" was Maj. Gen. Elwell S. Otis, military governor of the Philippines. Dewey's relief, Rear Adm. John C. Watson, commander in chief of the U.S. naval force on the Asiatic Station, was headquartered on board the *Oregon,* homeported nearby at Cavite. The social epicenter—even for junior officers such as Mustin—was the swank Manila Army and Navy Club overlooking the bay, but the Navy also hosted various gatherings on board the *Oregon* when she was in port. War correspondents were ever present, and Otis endeavored to run a strict and unpopular press censorship. The news was not exactly good.

By the summer of 1899, the Army's Manila campaign had resulted in two thousand casualties, not counting sickness and disease. Brig. Gen. Lloyd V. Wheaton, a Civil War

Congressional Medal of Honor recipient, had the job of extending the occupation to the south; however, his task soon became one of withdrawal to garrisons after search-and-destroy missions. On 15 August, Otis had to ask for sixty thousand more men for the autumn offensive planned for northern Luzon. His objective would be to destroy the insurgent army in the field, capture Aguinaldo, and complete the occupation of Luzon. The Navy, therefore, turned to increase its tempo of operations in Luzon waters to interdict the rebel army's supplies.

On board the *Iris,* Mustin must have performed his duties well and pressed his case for assignment to a combatant. His efforts finally were rewarded on 9 August, when Admiral Watson ordered him transferred to Manila to report for duty as a watch and station officer on the *Oregon.* On 17 August, Mustin reported to her skipper, Captain Wilde.

In September, the *Oregon* again was off Iloilo. In addition to blockade activities, the Navy began operating close to shore, at times striking with landing parties in sweeps to interdict insurgent supplies. The *Oregon* and other larger combatants supported the real workhorses of the blockade: a score or more of small shallow-draft gunboats, formerly Spanish, that performed the actual capture and destruction of insurgent bancas, most often loaded with rice and other foodstuffs. Gunboat command was a prize opportunity for a fighting junior officer.

Command of a gunboat was for only the most intrepid. The waters around the Philippines were tidal and essentially uncharted—especially dangerous for maneuvering close inshore. On 17 September, the steam launch *Urdaneta,* one of two gunboats assigned to the *Oregon,* was performing routine duty in tidal and uncharted waters off Orani, across the bay from Manila. In command was a naval cadet. The *Urdaneta* grounded and was attacked by insurgents who killed the young captain and a number of his crew and took several others prisoner.

Such was the theater of war in which Mustin would play a command role. Probably on the night of 25 September, somewhere near Iloilo, Mustin led a number of *Oregon* crewmen on a swim ashore with knives in their teeth to cut loose the insurrecto steamer *Taaleno,* taking her into the river to anchor. Placed in charge of the salvage, Mustin then oversaw an eight-man work party to shift the berth of the captured vessel and kedge the stern on a downstream flat to do repairs. His crew of carpenters, machinists, and Filipino workers went over everything from the ship's bottom, to fire pumps, boiler, and engines. Two days later, they made way to the Iloilo seawall for further repairs. With the vessel now reasonably seaworthy, Mustin was able on 3 October to proceed on engines farther upriver to coal. The *Oregon* provided fresh provisions, as well as a Colt gun and a full range of small arms and ammunition. Later that day, Wilde ordered Mustin to assume command of the *Taaleno* and take her to Cavite, with instructions to "overhaul" (overtake) any suspicious craft en route. Mindful of the fate of the *Urdaneta,* he advised, "If you anchor, be sure to secure an anchorage safe from sudden attack, and keep a sharp lookout at all times with armed watch on deck, and with ammunition near guns ready for instant use to repel attack."

Arriving in Cavite, Mustin reported to Admiral Watson on 10 October. Refitting the *Taaleno* for blockade duty probably was too great a challenge, and when the *Oregon* was assigned another gunboat, the *Samar,* Mustin reportedly asked to command her. Captain Wilde approved the request, and on 13 October, Watson ordered him to shift himself, the bulk of his crew, and all stores and provisions to the *Samar.*

Mustin's primary mission was blockade enforcement and interdiction, but the real near-term action was in support of the coordinated three-pronged Army offensive northward from Manila. On 15 October, Watson ordered him to Lingayen Gulf to relieve the gunboat *Paragua.* The next day, he already was bombarding a harbor and trenches.

Between 17 and 29 October, Mustin was enforcing the blockade along the so-called Kings Highway, running from the east coast ports of San Fernando to San Fabian and northward to Vigan. Sometime during this short period, he was operating with the gunboat *Bennington* off Candon Harbor, just south of Vigan. The approaches to the harbor were too small for him to enter safely, but, seeing three rebel schooners inside, he opened fire from a distance and sank all three. Just as he was sending the ammunition below and backing away, he sighted a sail to seaward, turned, and started in chase. It was an insurgent banca (a large, flat-bottomed canoe) that went about as soon as the *Samar* cleared Cape Candono. The wind was fresh, and it looked for a short time as if she might get away. The *Samar,* however, was able to draw close enough to open fire. After three shots across her bow, the banca hove to, and Mustin drew up alongside. She was his first capture.

Recalling the event years later, he wrote, "I'll never forget the feelings of excitement that took possession of me then, although I probably stood all the time on the bridge, looking as dumb as an oyster! She had a rebel flag (which I am sorry to say I gave to the captain of the *Bennington*), a rebel license and other insurgent papers. So we set her afire, and with all the kerosene on board she made a tremendous blaze, and I felt very much like a pirate." For this and later actions against the insurgents, he earned a price on his head—five hundred Mexican dollars.

In late October, the *Samar* and other naval units operating in Lingayen Gulf readied for tactical operations in support of the army offensive. The initial Navy role would be to transport, land, and support a force of 2,500 men of the Thirty-third Volunteer and Thirteenth Regular Infantry Regiments and a platoon of the Sixth Artillery led by General Wheaton. The force would sail from Manila around Bataan and northward up the western coast of Luzon to San Fabian in the Lingayen Gulf.

The main U.S. force was a division commanded by Maj. Gen. Henry W. Lawton. Like Wheaton, he was a Civil War Medal of Honor recipient, but he was better known as the man who captured the Indian warrior Geronimo. Lawton had arrived in the Philippines in the spring of 1899 as commander of the First Division.

Along the east side of the Luzon plain, Lawton's force would move up the Rio Grande de Pampanga. Maj. Gen. Arthur MacArthur, father of the World War II five-star commander Douglas MacArthur, would lead troops along the railway up the central plain of Luzon to drive the enemy to the Lingayen Gulf. Wheaton's force was to seize Dagupan at the railroad's terminus, occupy the coast road and port towns, and link with Lawton to block Aguinaldo's retreat from MacArthur and prevent his escape by sea.

Geography would complicate the plan and communications among the commanders. The coastal range stood between MacArthur and Wheaton. The Candaba swamp separated MacArthur and Lawton. The rebels slowed MacArthur's advance by destroying the rail lines. The river from San Isidro northward was either flooded or too shallow, and Lawton's food and ammunition became bottlenecked at San Isidro. He was stalled until the rains came on 27 October, and the river finally rose. To catch Aguinaldo's forces, which had forged well ahead, Lawton unleashed a mobile 1,100-man force of artillery, two cavalry squadrons, and a battalion of the Twenty-second infantry. In command was Brig. Gen. Samuel Young, the former commander of the III Corps in Cuba and a resourceful and aggressive soldier.

On 6 November, Wheaton's force of transports sailed from Manila. When it arrived in Lingayen Gulf, Mustin and his fellow commanders, by now all familiar with the east coast of the gulf, met on board the light-draft gunboat *Helena* with Wheaton and Cdr. Harry Knox, captain of the barkentine gunboat *Princeton* and the Navy's senior officer present, to select a place for the Army to land. The next day, after giving Mustin the plan of action and his orders, Knox then led his six-ship squadron—the *Princeton, Helena, Bennington, Manila, Callao,* and *Samar*—into San Fabian. The *Callao* and *Samar,* the only shallow-draft combatants in the force, steamed virtually to shore to bombard insurrecto trenches, fortifications, and the city. While the Army landed 2,500 troops, Mustin maneuvered between the insurgents and the head of the lead column of *cascos* to take the brunt of and return enemy fire. Seventy-five yards from the insurgent trenches, he actually ran the *Samar* aground, firing at point-blank range, driving the enemy from their positions.

Mustin's audacious action enabled the Thirty-third Infantry, led by Col. Luther R. Hare, to land without further opposition and push the last of the defenders into San Fabian. As a brigadier general, Hare later wrote of Mustin's "splendid capacity and daring in action." The young ensign's conduct went some way toward bridging the gulf that had opened at Iloilo between the two services in regard to joint operations. "I saw him very closely at San Fabian," wrote Hare, "and his coolness coupled with his daring management of his vessel excited not only my highest respect but ardent admiration as well. His picture as he walked the decks and concisely, emphatically, and intelligently directed his command will remain as a pleasant feature of my pleasant association with our Navy."

Several times during that day and the next, Mustin shuttled the commanders back and forth to confer on the evolving situation, taking Knox to meet with Wheaton and then to Wilde on the *Oregon*. Reporting from Manila on 9 November, Watson commended Mustin and the *Samar,* which he said was struck several times.

Nevertheless, Aguinaldo and his forces were able to make a quick escape northward along the coast road. Wheaton consolidated his position in San Fabian and was slow to pursue. Young and his advance force were in the vicinity but unable to close the trap. They had been through an arduous, 120-mile campaign through hard terrain for more than five weeks. Now, surviving on half-rations for two weeks, they were continually hungry and fearful of being butchered.

On 14 November, when a column encountered Aguinaldo's rear guard, Young's cavalry informed Wheaton of the situation. Young and one of his battalions were at Alava. He could see that only the Navy could secure the coast road to the north to block Aguinaldo's retreat and communicated to Otis his desire to have naval units "examine all ports from San Fernando . . . northward."

Not knowing the whereabouts of Young, Wilde in the *Oregon* ordered Mustin on 15 November to support Wheaton (actually Hare and his battalion of Thirty-third Infantry). Mustin quickly found it difficult to communicate with the Army units ashore. Young still was inland, leading a battalion of three hundred Maccabebe scouts and a troop of the Third Cavalry toward Alava, about thirty miles north-northwest of Dagupan and hard by the Benguet range. On the eighteenth, Young finally reached Aringay on the coast.

Young knew he was hot on the trail of Aguinaldo. Moving north along the coast highway to Booang, he had as his objective the provincial capital of San Fernando. He needed to know the disposition of forces. Eager to help, on 19 and 20 November

Mustin led an *Oregon* whaleboat through the surf to establish communications between Hare and Young. In his operation report, Young noted that on the twentieth Mustin established for him flag communication with Hare at Aringay. At San Fernando, along the road to the north, Young also asked Mustin to open fire on some three hundred insurgents behind earthworks that he and his thirty-seven-man force were assaulting. From the hills beyond, the insurgents were keeping "an annoying fire" on his exhausted men until Mustin's guns "frightened them away."

Sensing that Aguinaldo still was close, Young sent a message via Mustin to have Hare's men join him. Hare unfortunately met stiff resistance on the road, and Wheaton ordered him to return to San Fabian. On 21 November, Young sent another message via Mustin to Wheaton, saying his forces were "much depleted and worn out." He now hoped Wheaton would provide fresh troops for Mustin and the Navy to land farther north at Vigan, blocking Aguinaldo's continuing retreat up the coast road. With Mustin was one of Young's aggressive staff officers, Lt. Col. James Parker, who was to execute the plan to capture Vigan. Wheaton refused the request. Parker then secured approval from Wilde and the Navy and tried again to get Army support from one of Wheaton's battalion commanders in San Fernando. After a "sharp discussion," Parker again failed to win troops and left with Mustin for Vigan on the *Samar,* in company with the *Callao* and *Oregon.*

Young, who was leading his column up the coast road, needed to know what Parker was attempting at Vigan. On 22 November, Mustin made contact with Young north of San Fernando, but surf conditions were too rough to land a boat. Mustin dove into the water and body surfed to shore to convey word of the situation. Two days later, the *Samar, Callao,* and *Oregon* made a show of "bombarding" Vigan, that is, firing in a way to minimize civilian casualties. On the twenty-sixth, the *Samar* towed to shore *Oregon* boats loaded with 201 men, including Parker, Lieutenant Commander McCracken, their staffs, and a battalion of 50 marines and 142 sailors.

After the action, Wilde reported that the *Samar* "covered the landing of the same by an incessant fire upon the trenches so that the battalion landed without a single casualty." The *Oregon*'s commander noted, "After Vigan was captured I ordered Ensign Mustin to proceed south and find Gen. Young's column and to communicate with him. He did so, but finding the surf too heavy to risk the lives of his crew in a boat, he sprang overboard, swam through the breakers, carried out his orders and then swam back to his vessel. This he did twice. He commands his vessel with splendid judgment and is indefatigable in his attention to his duties, working day and night without sleep. He is a most promising young officer, and it is with pleasure I commend him to the attention of the Navy Department."

Admiral Watson approved Wilde's report, adding his own testimony "to the zeal and efficiency of this gallant young officer."

The capture of Vigan forced Aguinaldo to turn to the northeast into the Benguet Mountains and northern Luzon. He would not be able to leave the island.

With this phase of the campaign over, Mustin and the *Samar* returned to Manila, in part to overhaul engines. On 9 December, Mustin received orders to assist Young, who had moved his headquarters to Vigan. In addition to pursuing Aguinaldo, Young, Hare, and other units were hoping to find and release U.S. and Spanish prisoners of war, including some of the survivors of the *Urdaneta* incident.

On 13 December, Mustin took Young and some men on board the *Samar* and made way to Luoag. In his report, Young noted that on the fifteenth he was "unable to receive sufficient reinforcements of troops and supplies from [his] military base, or from Manila, notwithstanding the urgent need of them." To terminate the campaign successfully, he needed the Navy to cooperate with reinforcements and provisions "for the half starved men, clothing and shoes for the naked and bare-footed."

Mustin and others were zealous in assisting him and anticipating his needs. Testifying to the success of his joint operation, Young wrote that "the difficulties and dangers of my situation could not have been appreciated better or the aid given more freely by any one, than was done by the officers of the Navy." Mustin and other naval units enabled him to pursue "Aguinaldo's forces rapidly, without giving him time to concentrate them, and with a comparatively small force, to complete the dispersion of his command, which had been for months keeping a large American army in check along the railroad." Young concluded that he would "gladly accord to them the share to which they are entitled for assisting me in bringing to a successful termination a campaign which had for its object the dispersion of Aguinaldo's army and the liberation of the American and Spanish Prisoners held by it."

At year's end, the insurgents released the prisoners. It was clear that Aguinaldo's forces were exhausted in the field. Having all but lost Luzon, the Filipino chieftain ordered guerrilla tactics, and the insurrectos continued resistance.

On 16 December, Mustin took the *Samar* to Cavite for repairs, and he stayed there through the holidays, to 4 January 1900. He would remain in command for another two months, operating mostly in waters around Vigan. He conducted an occasional landing, but generally he wrestled with more mundane tasks—taking soundings, provisioning a lighthouse, vaccinating his crew against smallpox, coping with a grounding, conducting target practice.

On 17 February while at Vigan, Mustin got orders for the armored cruiser *Brooklyn,* which, as the new flagship of the Asiatic Squadron, would fly the flag of Rear Adm. George Remey when he relieved Watson in April. Mustin's last log entry on the *Samar* was on 28 February. Relieved on 3 March by Lt. G. C. Day, he reported for temporary duty on the cruiser *Newark,* whose skipper was the redoubtable Capt. Bowman H. McCalla. An experienced amphibious commander, McCalla later would lead the advance Navy–Marine Corps component of the international China Relief Expedition that lifted the Boxer siege in Beijing.

On 15 March, Mustin left for Manila on board the steamer *Gloria.* On the nineteenth, he reported to Watson on the *Brooklyn* as watch and division officer. The ship was fresh from an expeditionary action at Piris in the Gulf of Ragay that liberated a number of Spanish prisoners of war. In May, she went to the China Station and was at the Royal Navy's Kowloon Dry Dock in Hong Kong for overhauls.

Also on board was the dauntless reformer of the Naval Academy class of 1880, Lt. William Snowden Sims, an officer who was to be a great friend and example to Mustin in the next phase of his career. Sims was the *Brooklyn*'s intelligence officer and soon would be in the midst of a close study of British efforts to improve gunnery, a sensitive issue at the time. U.S. naval officers were especially touchy over any suggestion that their recent victories at Manila and Santiago were the result more of luck than of skill.

Between 8:00 and 9:00 o'clock on the evening of 20 May, Mustin was carousing with his brother officers, possibly at the Royal Naval Canteen at Kowloon. According to Mustin family legend, a British officer made some disparaging remarks about the poor performance of the U.S. Navy at Manila Bay. "What a ragtag bunch of no goods they were," he allegedly said, challenging the Americans. According to one eyewitness, Mustin responded by displacing the Brit's nose "around the side of his face."

After the fracas, Mustin returned to the *Brooklyn* to stand watch. According to Navy records, at about 12:30 A.M. he asked Naval Cadet Charles H. Fischer, who also was on duty, to relieve him because he did not feel well. He later claimed to have been ill the previous week, too. Fischer relieved him, and Mustin went below. At 12:45, a crewman attempted six times to wake him. Finally, Mustin returned to his station at 2:15. For his actions that morning Mustin would face a court-martial.

This personal footnote occurred as China was primed to explode into the Boxer

Rebellion. The U.S. Navy now had forty-two ships in the Pacific, compared to six in the North Atlantic, and Remey wanted the bulk of his naval forces to be on station in the Philippines to deal with the continuing insurrection. The *Brooklyn* thus left Chinese waters before the real action commenced.

So instead of high adventure in Beijing, from 4 through 6 June, off Cavite, Mustin endured three days of court-martial—case #8821. He faced two charges: leaving his station without being regularly relieved (on watch, he was unauthorized to be relieved by a junior officer) and sleeping on watch.

Mustin pleaded not guilty. Referring elliptically to his stand for the honor of the U.S. Navy, he said his exhaustion was a reaction to an extraordinary amount of violent exercise from 8:00 to 9:00 o'clock on 20 May 1900. In his defense, he stated that he feared falling asleep on watch and that he was accustomed on the *Oregon* to having a junior officer relieve a senior officer. He did not consult with the ship's doctor or the executive officer, he explained, because it was midnight, and he preferred not to disturb them.

Mustin was found guilty on both charges and sentenced to a loss of ten numbers in grade. Because he had no previous convictions, however, the court decided to reduce his loss of numbers to five.

In no time, Mustin obtained character references from Young, Hare, and other senior commanders with whom he recently had served. Writing from Vigan on 7 June, Young said Mustin "rendered me auxiliary assistance of the highest importance while in command of the gunboat *Samar*. I always found him ready, obliging, energetic, reliable and efficient. My staff has been intimately associated with him on many official occasions and they always found him a most reliable officer in every respect."

The support was helpful. The court reconvened twice, and on 11 June, Cdr. W. H. Everett, president of the general court-martial, and Rear Admiral Remey both pardoned him. On 23 July, Remey would receive news that Mustin had been unconditionally pardoned by the president, but evidently his loss of numbers remained. Review of the case would continue in Washington.

In the meantime, Remey must have felt that Mustin would be better served by returning to the fray. On 13 June, he ordered him to take passage on the Army transport *Pennsylvania*, bound for Cebu, for duty on the unarmored steel gunboat *Isla de Cuba*. Arriving in Cebu waters, Mustin transferred to the gunboat *Pampanga*, and on 29 June he continued his passage on the gunboat *Concord*, with duty while on board. On 6 July he finally reported to the senior officer present and the communications officer on the *Isla de Cuba*.

Rigged as a two-masted schooner, the *Isla de Cuba* operated in support of smaller naval units throughout the Visayas and south to Mindanao. At the time Mustin reported, she was off Samar, where the fighting was heavy and very ugly. Ashore, the Army had few troops on the mountainous island, which was extremely wild and difficult to penetrate; thus, its units were deployed defensively in port garrisons at Katbalogan and Kalbayog. The U.S. troops faced a notoriously ruthless insurgent leader, Lukban, whose bolo-wielding tribesmen slaughtered with merciless abandon.

Army and Navy cooperation was good in Samar. Under the joint service understanding in operation throughout the Philippines, gunboats had the right to take on coal, oil, and water at any Army post. The *Isla de Cuba* and other naval units were active intercepting rebel bancas and lorchas (sailing barges) involved in gun running and illicit trading in consumables. Samar produced hemp but was lacking in rice and other foods, so insurgent supplies were coming across the narrow channels and straits that separated Samar and Leyte.

Often, the gunboats would have to organize shore parties to suppress illicit trade. On 10 August, the *Isla de Cuba* skipper ordered Mustin to lead one such landing party "fitted out in a steam launch and whaleboat" for the Libukan Islands, an important transit point for rebel supplies. His instructions illustrate the dangers: "You will guard against any of your party being surprised on shore, and to this end will not allow them to struggle and see that their arms are ready for use, that the Colt Gun is kept trained on any village or landing place you may land at. Only one Officer will land at a time, the other having charge of the covering party. You will see that you are provided with rockets, and the firing of one or more rockets will be considered as a call for aid. Endeavor to return to the ship before nightfall. In case you discover any boats without proper papers or engaged in illicit trading you will destroy them, or see that they proceed at once to Kalbayog to get proper papers. Any boats destroyed will be appraised by the Officers and Petty officers. Asst. Surgeon J. J. Snyder, USN, will accompany you and be under your orders."

Mustin returned to his ship from this excursion to an ironic reward. A 16 August letter from Washington informed him that he had been awarded prize money for the *New York*'s capture of the *Pedro* and *Carlos F. Rozes*. His "piratical" cut was $407.58.

By 27 August, the *Isla de Cuba* was in Cebu with the gunboats *Concord, Marietta, Panay,* and *Pampanga.* In late September, however, insurgents in Leyte began assaulting the seventy-five-man Army garrison at the hitherto peaceful port of Ormoc, and the *Isla de Cuba* rushed to assist the *Panay* in providing fire support and additional machine guns and crews for defense of the town. Arriving on the third day of attacks, she provided valuable support to Army units ashore with her main battery of four 4-inch guns and secondary battery of four 6-pounders and four Colts. As weather allowed, from 30 September well into October the two gunboats alternated on station.

In August Brig. Gen. Luther Hare assumed command of the Fourth District, which included southern Luzon and Samar, hotbeds of insurgent activity. Having had a good rapport with naval officers in northern Luzon in late 1899, Hare was sure that by working with the Navy he could engage the insurrectos aggressively from the water and thereby pacify his region. He increased the garrison at Katbalogan and readied his troops for another autumn offensive. U.S. forces went into action in late October. On 28 October, they received fire support from *Isla de Cuba* against snipers ashore at Katbalogan. Mustin's ship then proceeded to Kalbayog, transferring ammunition from the *Panay.*

Further operations were suspended when two typhoons rolled into the region, hitting on 31 October and again on 15 November. Two days after the second storm passed, Hare was on board the *Panay* planning an Army and Navy assault up the Gandara River to attack Lukban and his headquarters. The *Panay* was to provide transport and artillery support. On 24 November, however, with malarial fever raging through the region, Hare canceled the operation.

Hare planned another assault for December and requested Mustin to serve on his staff for both the preparation and execution. Mustin was detached temporarily from the *Isla de Cuba* and assigned to serve on the gunboat *Mindoro* until the twenty-first. On 16 December, Mustin joined Hare's landing party at Guian on Samar, and Hare later reported that he was very pleased with his help. Unfortunately, this excursion also was unsuccessful in eliminating Lukban, and it would be well into 1902 before the Army could mount a larger campaign to assert U.S. authority.

Mustin's continued duties on the *Isla de Cuba* took him ashore throughout the Philippines and inspired many sea stories, for which he would become well known. On one notable occasion, he met Pedro Cuervas, the notorious *daito* (warlord) of Basilan, an island southwest of the Basilan Straits in Mindanao and a former Spanish naval station. In June 1900, the U.S. Navy had assumed responsibility for Basilan, and the main challenge was keeping order among the rival Christian and Muslim Filipinos and others who vied for regional leadership. Recalling the encounter eight years later as an officer with the Great White Fleet, Mustin wrote,

> One day I gave him a lump of ice, something he had never seen before, and when he took it in his hands he dropped it saying "mucho calor" (very hot). Then he turned it over to a slave to keep for him and of course in a few minutes it had melted away. The old man was furious when he found the slave had lost his keepsake and would have chopped off his head there and then if I hadn't explained. He didn't value his slaves very highly. . . . I bought a campilan (a beheading sword) from him but before closing the deal I asked him if it was sharp; before answering he looked over five or six slaves with him in a meditative way and then I told him I would be satisfied if it could cut in two a Mexican dollar which I supplied!

After almost two years in the Philippines, it was time for Mustin to return "to the world." Rear Admiral Remey ordered him relieved on 23 March 1901, and when Ensign J. S. Graham reported to the *Isla de Cuba,* Mustin took passage on 12 April on the steamer *Zafiro* bound for Cavite. On 25 April in Hong Kong, he reported for duty on the *Newark,* which departed for Boston shortly thereafter for decommissioning.

The summer of 1901, Mustin was back in the United States at Boston's Charlestown Navy Yard. On 9 July, he was ordered to Washington for the examining board for lieutenant junior grade; he was examined on 13 July and returned to his ship on the sixteenth. On 27 July, he was ordered home to await new orders from the Bureau of Navigation. When a twenty-seven-year-old Henry Mustin finally arrived at the Lloyd residence at 4110 Spruce Street, Philadelphia, he was no more the rambunctious son, full of callow longing for a life at sea, but a tried and tested warrior of audacity and promise.

Chapter 4

The Gunner Finds His Mascotte

On 9 August 1901, Lt. (jg) Henry C. Mustin got orders to report on 1 September to the Norfolk Navy Yard for duty with torpedo boats. Whether by accident or design, it would begin almost a year of shore assignments that would expose him to developing warship technologies and warfighting concepts a generation ahead of the current naval icon, the battleship. The Norfolk assignment perhaps reflected the Navy's acknowledgment of his combat command experience in smaller combatants such as the *Samar.*

Five days after Mustin reported, President McKinley was assassinated, and the vice president and Mahanian navalist Theodore Roosevelt assumed office. Roosevelt's presidency would galvanize the Navy and complete the United States' transformation into a world-class naval power. Mustin would play a significant supporting role, but it would not be in Norfolk. Stricken with an illness perhaps acquired in the tropics, he was detached from duty at the yard and sent home to Philadelphia for a two-month sick leave. Doctors at Philadelphia's Presbyterian Hospital treated him until early December, when he received orders for "duty under instruction" at the Naval Academy.

During his time ashore, Mustin readdressed the matter of his court-martial and loss of numbers. On 14 March 1902, Admiral Watson wrote to Secretary of the Navy John

D. Long asking for his "special consideration" of Mustin's war record and urging Long to do all in his power to secure a pardon that would restore Mustin's numbers. He cited Young, Hare, and McCalla specifically as having "all endorsed this gallant and efficient young officer in the highest terms." Watson concluded his letter by quoting Hare: "'I bespeak for him the indulgence of the authorities and am a willing bondsman that should his country place him where courage, firmness and splendid judgment in action are required he will fully meet every demand.'"

The issue went all the way to the new president. When Roosevelt asked for the story behind the official report, his aide is said to have replied, "Well, Mr. President, this Brit insulted the U.S. Navy, and Mustin took exception and beat him up." "He won, did he?" Roosevelt asked. "Yes, Mr. President." "Well, the court-martial is canceled, and his numbers are restored by order of the president."

While the fate of his numbers was being determined in Washington, Mustin received further orders to report for instruction on board the Navy's first submarine, the *Holland,* then stationed at Annapolis. "This duty," read the orders, "will continue until you consider yourself thoroughly familiar with this type of boat." A proviso noted that "making submerged runs in the *Holland* is to be voluntary on your part." After a little more than two months of training with the submarine, Mustin began temporary duty in charge of the naval tug *Standish,* which in July convoyed the *Holland* to the New York Navy Yard. He then returned to Annapolis with the tug to await orders that would take him to sea once again.

Mustin's next orders would place him at the center of the most important warfighting developments of the day—the rapid advances occurring in ordnance and gunnery. In 1902, under Roosevelt's direction, the Navy consolidated the North Atlantic and other squadrons into fleets and put all its battleships under the command of Admiral of the Navy George Dewey. The United States now would be a full participant in the grand and glorious fleet reviews. More important from a readiness standpoint, Roosevelt saw that Dewey had the authority to establish a program of large-scale naval maneuvers to institute new training techniques and competitive exercises fleet-wide. Roosevelt was aware of the need to correct a critical deficiency that even the size and power of the modern battleship could not conceal—the inability to put ordnance on target.

The president had gained this awareness thanks to Lt. William Snowden Sims. In November 1901, while on the Asiatic Station, Sims had written a letter to Roosevelt calling attention to the U.S. Navy's shortcomings. He had been studying the British efforts to improve gunnery during their annual competitions on the China Station in 1899 and 1900. The Royal Navy had been getting hits at distances of fifteen hundred yards. Observing the competition in 1901, Sims reported that British hits were 80 to 85 percent at a rate of four per minute. The man behind this achievement was Royal Navy captain Sir Percy Scott, who used telescopes and pointers to support a technique called continuous aim firing. Sims had learned Scott's methods, prompting him to relay to the president his concerns over U.S. battleships' deficiencies. In turn, Roosevelt saw to it that the Navy relayed Sims's reports to every officer in the service.

Mustin received his orders to report on 31 July 1902 to the battleship *Kearsarge*. Home-ported at the New York Navy Yard, she was flying the flag of the commander of the North Atlantic Squadron. Mustin had drawn duty on his fourth flagship and into 1903 would qualify as a turret officer. In October 1902, Sims became inspector of target practice in the Bureau of Navigation, a position from which he could champion the continuous aim technique and shortly thereafter a systematic approach to fire control. Mustin found himself at the business end of these developments, toward which he would devote all his professional energies for the next eight years.

His direct participation in Sims's initiatives began in earnest in the winter of 1902–3 with the Atlantic Fleet exercises at Culebra in the Caribbean. Aside from his brief tour on the *Brooklyn*, Mustin's initial link to Sims probably was via Lt. Ridley McLean of the Naval Academy class of 1894. McLean was a key member of Sims's staff and assisted his boss in proselytizing the British approach to gunnery during the exercises. In the spring, the pair prepared and issued a drill book that set standards for dotters and Morris Tube Targets—devices rigged before the muzzles of a gun battery to record the aim points of simulated fire. For continuous aim firing, the latter device was superior because it used a subcaliber rifle inserted into the bore instead of a pencil to mark the target. After Sims's introduction of continuous aim and Morris Tubes and dotters, the Navy achieved a somewhat improved accuracy of 40 to 73 percent for large guns and 55 percent for small guns.

By the time of the 1902–3 exercises, Mustin was becoming a first-rate turret officer. During the exercises, the magazine *Collier's* featured him prominently in a well-reported and -photographed story on six-pounder target practice. Mustin saw that the gathering pace of technology presented a major challenge to capital ships and the fleet— accuracy at increasing ranges—and he decided to combine his current responsibilities and his mechanical drawing skills to address that challenge.

Initially, Mustin would design telescope gun sights. The importance of this quest was expressed best by Sims's classmate, Professor Philip Rounseville Alger, a strong gunnery advocate. Sometime after Sims and McLean's efforts at Culebra, Alger wrote, "The most successful application of the telescope sight to naval guns is perhaps the most important improvement tending to the accuracy of gunfire at sea since the introduction of rifled canon." Sims wanted an improved sight, and Mustin had gotten the message.

In the summer of 1903, the *Kearsarge* served briefly on the European Station as Rear Adm. C. S. Cotton's squadron flagship during reviews at Kiel and Portsmouth. Mustin was witness to two noteworthy official ship visits, by the Kaiser and the Prince of Wales, but more significant for his career was his trip to the British Gunnery School at Whale Island. There, he was privy to the Brits' work in gun-sight development and the particular problems they faced with exposed sights.

Whale Island provided useful food for thought that Mustin would apply as soon as he returned to the United States. In early August, he got orders as executive officer to the *Culgoa,* the supply ship that supported Atlantic Squadron battleships. The orders upset him greatly. Given his combat experience and recent work in gunnery, he considered service on another auxiliary as "unjust and humiliating." Once he discovered the potential of *Culgoa*'s machine shop, however, he saw that the otherwise grindingly routine duty could allow him to experiment with gun-sight prototypes. In fact, as he commented several years later, his time aboard enabled him to do his "biggest work in optics."

His reference was to his gun-sight designs for twelve-inch turrets. By the end of the summer, the *Culgoa* machine shop had built his first design for the *Kearsarge.* Mustin then got authorization from the Bureau of Ordnance to build the second sight for the battleship *Missouri.* In a 23 October letter to Capt. William S. Cowles at the Bureau of Navigation, the *Culgoa*'s skipper, Lt. Cdr. James H. Oliver, noted the completed drawings for the second sight promised a marked improvement over the *Kearsarge* design. Oliver wanted the bureau to allow his young designer to supervise installation personally. With Mustin's sights, he said, the *Missouri* could get advantage over all battleships in the Navy. Identifying him as "one of the most competent turret officers in the Navy," Oliver went on to recommend Mustin for command of a turret division. "I am aware that this is somewhat against the tradition of the Service," Oliver wrote, "but that is rapidly passing away, as Commanding Officers are now assigning their officers according to their special capabilities for certain kinds of work. Mustin's bent is strongly mechanical and scientific, and he is, I believe, the only officer assigned to the *Missouri* who has had any experience in turrets, under the new system of training and firing, though there are, I understand, two other watch officers senior to him."

On 26 October, the chief of the Bureau of Ordnance replied to Oliver granting permission for Mustin to construct and supervise the mounting of his turret sight on the *Missouri*. Oliver would be delighted with Mustin's work. In a 7 April 1904 letter to a fellow commander, he praised Mustin as "a very valuable officer, practical and so brilliant. . . . No country on earth can boast of a finer officer than he."

Sometime during this period, Mustin had "another wonderful day . . . when the Commanding General of the Army introduced me to the President and I took luncheon and spent the whole afternoon with him." (The introduction probably came through his Army comrade in arms in the Philippines, Samuel Young, who had risen to lieutenant general. Although not commanding general of the Army, Young was serving from 15 August 1903 to 8 January 1904 under the successor title, chief of staff—the Army's first.) Alike in temperament, the commander in chief and the young lieutenant probably used the opportunity to take a sounding from the fleet and to make the case for gun sights, respectively, and to swap war stories.

Mustin's scientific bent would not transform him into a strictly cerebral naval officer. He always would embrace the physical aspects of his career. While on the *Culgoa*, he once again came to the Navy Department's attention for an act of personal heroism. His ship was at anchor in the Hudson River at a time when heavy rainfall upstream had produced an unusually strong current. The force capsized a steam cutter that was alongside, throwing a crewman overboard. Dressed in heavy oilskins and rubber boots, the man was helpless against the current, which rapidly carried him astern. Without hesitation, Mustin jumped overboard and assisted the struggling man, for which he received a Navy Department commendation for his "courage and prompt action."

Mustin was building a reputation as a man of both action and invention. It was time to capitalize on it. In 1904, he sought to patent his gun sights and in particular an indirect vision prism and focusing cap for the Navy's Mark XIII telescope. In April he filed what would be his first lucrative telescope patent.

Mustin wasn't the only serving naval officer patenting inventions, then a customary pursuit. Innovative naval officers, keen to advance both their careers and the technologies that were beginning to revolutionize the Navy, had an added incentive: a patent royalty. This object was a major element of Mustin's career strategy, although initially he drew satisfaction purely from seeing fleet gunnery exercising and excelling with his inventions.

Mustin's example in this regard was Bradley Fiske, who since the 1890s had been patenting with an industry partner, Western Electric. Known initially for his work with electricity and its application to training and elevating guns, Fiske would become aware of his gifted young competitor while working on semaphore signal devices. In 1896, Fiske had a design for a semaphore system installed on the battleships *Kearsarge* and *Alabama* that led to installation of an electric-power semaphore signal system aboard the *New York*. The latter device failed when water got into one of the solenoids that moved the semaphore arms.

At the time of the testing, Mustin was a cadet on board the *New York*. Observing where Fiske failed, he saw an opportunity to design a less sophisticated but operationally reliable semaphore device. In his autobiography, Fiske credited him for inventing an "ingenious and effective" hand-power apparatus—the first recognition of Mustin's inventive work.

Fiske's main work was in gun-sight technologies. In the 1890s, he had patented a telescopic sight and optical range finder. It was manufactured by the American Range Finder Company, but Fiske later found that the Bureau of Ordnance had allowed the then Washington-based German inventor George N. Saegmuller and Newport News Drydock Company not only to acquire his telescope design but also to manufacture devices based on the design. Fiske sued in 1899, and the bureau settled for $10,000.

Five years later, Mustin and Saegmuller—always on the lookout for partners inside the service—found each other. The German also had joined with Bausch & Lomb, the Rochester, New York, manufacturer of astronomical, engineering, and other precision instruments. Mustin and Saegmuller would be design partners for almost a decade, sharing equally patents for a number of gun sights, including Mustin's indirect vision prism and focusing cap for the Mark XIII telescope.

The initial partnership married Mustin's design for prismatic telescopes and ordnance sights with Saegmuller's gun-sight telescopes. In their 1904 contract, the two men agreed to split the costs of patent filings, with Saegmuller paying Mustin for the difference until then. On 23 June 1904, Mustin transferred one-half interest of his foreign patents to Saegmuller. Two years later, he would get $1,000 from Saegmuller for all U.S. rights for improvements to his ordnance sight, in which he had a half-interest. Saegmuller also would get British royalties for the device and would forward half those sums to Mustin while he was at sea.

From early 1903 and well into 1904, Sims had attempted to get the Navy to develop new sights for continuous aim. Eventually, he was able once again to put his case directly to the president, and Roosevelt put his weight behind Sims's efforts. Encouraging individual officers to work their own ordnance and gunnery solutions, Sims got many to rise to the challenge. Both his office and the Bureau of Ordnance received submissions from a number of naval officers, including Robley Evans and Mustin's future aviation nemesis, Mark Bristol, with ideas for telescopic sights, the location of fire control stations, communications links from the stations to the guns, and other improvements.

Sims's efforts ran counter to Fiske's emphasis on range-finding. In 1900, Fiske had patented a turret range finder, although his device did not have support from the Bureau of Ordnance. Undeterred, in 1903 he got installed on the battleship *Maine* a design for a turret sight mount. When tested, however, the sight failed. Retested in 1905, it could not stand the concussion from the gun. In addition, because the device was mounted on top of the turret, hot gases and smoke from each firing interfered with accurate sighting. Finally, the Bureau of Ordnance and it new chief, Rear Adm. Newton E. Mason, refused further testing.

Mustin, on the other hand, was by now a Sims disciple and was designing for continuous aim firing. Continuous aim was not really possible if the gun crew had to remove a telescope before firing the gun, so Mustin was working on a sighting system that could remain in place. Through his and others' work, Sims would get his new sights in the fleet by 1906.

Realizing that, once past the challenge of sight improvements, Sims would next seek solutions for centralized control of fire from all the ship's batteries, Fiske moved in 1905 to tackle the complexities of fire control. He believed the Navy was not spending enough on range-finding and that Sims's approach therefore would arrive at a fire control system that relied almost wholly on spotting, that is, determining aim by narrowing the gap between the splashes of the rounds in the water and the target.

If Fiske thought that the advanced calculus of fire control was beyond the ken of the next generation, he underestimated Mustin, who moved right with him. On 6 February 1905, Mustin submitted to Sims his own "Memorandum on Fire Control." In it he advocated continuous aim and telescopes for all sizes of gun, while arguing the need to treat the whole battery as a unit. "The fire control," he wrote, "is now reduced to the determination of two elements: range and deflection, by the operator of the unit, the fire control officer. And the transmission of these elements to the gun platform." Basing his argument on the operational challenge, he agreed that in fleet engagements fire control could not rely on splashes—it is difficult for anyone except the gun pointer to tell which splashes are from which guns. Significantly, he argued for opening fire at 4,500 yards, well past the previously accepted 1,600-yard range, because of the higher probability of hits enabled by fire control.

Mustin's submission was one of many that Sims incorporated in a 21 December 1905 report. Issued after the autumn target practice and the 21 November establishment of a Navy fire control board, the report set general principles for spotting, range-finding, and fire control. The Navy thereafter moved to implement fire control in the fleet. On 19 March 1906, an experimental system went on the battleship *Virginia.* In late 1907, fire control systems went on the battleships that would participate the following year in the Cruise of the Great White Fleet.

In 1905, Mustin had played hard on all fronts, including in signals. During the Culebra exercises in January of that year, he tested an electrical signal keyboard that he invented while on the *Culgoa,* thus venturing again onto Fiske's turf. Mustin now had versions of his device on the *Culgoa* as well as on the battleships *Missouri* and *Kentucky.* The system proved so efficient that it would allow 180 signal displays a minute, which critics said was too fast to read and record. Mustin agreed, reporting that doctrine should limit the speed to 120, a rate he said the *Culgoa* had established as a "habit" and that was readable at one mile.

Returning from the Caribbean in June 1905, Mustin received orders to the Washington Navy Yard and its Gun Factory, the Navy's center for research and development in ordnance and gunnery. The powers that be had recognized his creativity and finally rewarded him with a key shore billet in which he could focus on his work in optics and the design of gun-sight telescopes. He would dedicate himself to improving the "very unsatisfactory condition of turret sights for heavy guns."

In addition to working on bore sights at the yard, Mustin took as his primary challenge the design of a telescope and mounting that would reduce the pointer's exposure during battle, an issue the British were addressing during his visit to Whale Island in 1903. He also wanted a system that would not involve so many lenses, which would make the telescope unsuitable for night firings.

By August, Mustin had begun testing a system that called for two right-angle prisms. The prism construct absorbed too much light, however, so he designed a double right-angle telescope that doubled the amount of light coming into the sight. To reduce further obstruction of light through the lens, he replaced the cross wires that went diametrically across the entire sight with tiny cross lines only at the very center. Not wanting to repeat Fiske's mistake, he mounted the pointer's telescope on the side of the turret, clear of rising smoke from the muzzle. Last, he fashioned the unit to be easily replaceable if damaged by shrapnel. Under Mustin's system, the gun pointer would sight the telescope on the bull's-eye while the turret trainer completed the vertical line using cross-connected sights.

In the midst of this work, Mustin was commissioned a lieutenant on 1 October, ad interim from 21 March. It was time for Mustin, now fully in grade, to look at what life had to offer beyond the walls of the Gun Factory.

The Washington Navy Yard of 1906, when the nation's capital was still a very small town, was a colorful center for society. In the yard sail loft, a dance committee hosted balls that attracted many of Washington's eligible belles. Mustin participated fully in these social events, along with Ridley McLean and a rising star in the Marine Corps and commander of the Marine barracks at Eighth and Eye, Lt. Col. George Barnett. A class behind Sims at the Naval Academy, Barnett was well connected outside the yard. His social set included his Naval Academy roommate, Massachusetts Representative John W. Weeks (later senator, Republican nominee for president, and secretary of war); Capt. Archie Butt, Roosevelt's military aide; and Col. Blanton Winship, USA, then in the judge advocate general's office and much later the controversial governor of Puerto Rico.

The Washington social scene of the time included a flamboyant newcomer named Lelia Montague Gordon, who eventually would reign as "Lady of the Marines" and be remembered, among many other things, for being the first American woman to enter Germany after the Armistice of 1918 and an advocate for a marriage and divorce law as the twentieth amendment to Constitution. Her journey to the Navy Yard would bring with it a love that would change Henry C. Mustin's life.

Born in 1871, Lelia was a wealthy young widow from Baltimore. Her husband, Basil Gordon, had died in 1901, leaving her four children and Wakefield Manor, a large Virginia estate nine miles south of Front Royal. After Gordon's death, she spent time in Europe, and returning to America in 1905, she and her young children took a house at 1334 Nineteenth Street, N.W.

As a result of an introduction from her late husband's family, Lelia received a house call from one of Washington's haughtiest social arbiters, Mrs. John R. McLean, wife of the owner of the *Cincinnati Enquirer* and the *Washington Post.* Mrs. McLean introduced her to some of the younger Washington belles, including by Lelia's account the "fascinating" Winifred Mattingly and the "brilliant and talented" Eleanor Terry.

In their search of eligible bachelors, Winifred and Eleanor were keen to attend one of the Navy balls and asked Lelia to chaperone. Together, the three piled into a carriage and headed for the yard. As they passed through the receiving line, they met Barnett, who was serving as the chairman of the dance committee. The marine was immediately taken with Lelia, prompting her to return to join him for other dances and excursions to the Naval Academy and Annapolis, a social mecca in its own right.

Moving in this circle of young naval officers, Lelia immediately recognized the social potential for her youngest sister, Corinne, who was sixteen years her junior and fresh from Hannah More Academy in Baltimore and Stuart Hall in southern Virginia. Corinne soon joined her at the house on Nineteenth Street.

The Montague girls were predisposed to the military and to the Navy in particular, given their maternal Sinclair family heritage. That lineage was Scottish, from the Earl of Caithness, grandson of King Robert II of Scotland. Arthur Sinclair Sr. was one of the first navigators to sail around the world. Commo. Arthur Sinclair II served as a midshipman on the *Constellation* during the Revolutionary War and later was known as a gallant officer of the War of 1812. He helped to found and then supervise the first naval school in the United States on board the frigate *Genevieve* in Norfolk. Cdr. Arthur Sinclair III served with Commo. Matthew Perry in Japan. He later resigned his commission to serve as a captain in the Confederate Navy and was lost at sea off the coast of Scotland while commanding the blockade runner *Lelia*. His daughter, Lelia Sinclair, was nineteen and living in Richmond when the Confederate capital fell in April 1865. After the war, she married Walter Powhatan Montague, whose Virginia family was of genteel, agricultural, pre–Civil War wealth.

Born in New York City on 28 May 1887, Corinne was the youngest of the Montague children and grew up in Baltimore. Standing with Barnett in one of the many receiving lines at Navy Yard events, Mustin happened upon her with a passing glance. The two were introduced. She made an impression on him but no more. He was thirty-two; she, nineteen.

Late in the summer of 1906, Ridley McLean and his wife hosted a dinner party that included Mustin, Lelia, Corinne, and others who, by Mustin's account, were somewhat older and a good deal more raffish. Feeling Corinne was misplaced among the more worldly crowd, Mustin was protective. Seated by her at dinner, he listened attentively as she "gushed" about the many midshipmen she had met. Finding himself attracted to her, he later went calling to the Nineteenth Street house. Mustin continued the liaison and the relationship deepened into the autumn.

Shortly thereafter Lelia decided on Barnett, and the sisters began to chaperone each other. When the marine temporarily took to his bed with illness, Lelia was a frequent visitor. Upstairs in Barnett's quarters, she would fuss over the patient. Downstairs, Corinne would sit in the parlor while Mustin wooed her, playing the piano "gloriously."

This romantic interlude came to an end on 25 September, when Mustin got orders to the *Brooklyn,* home-ported at League Island, in Philadelphia. He spent two months on the armored cruiser off Cuba, providing support to a Marine landing in Havana. In November, the *Brooklyn* returned to Philadelphia and went into reserve, and Mustin received orders as the ordnance officer on the battleship *Indiana.* On its face, this seemed a prize opportunity, but Mustin did not think so. Although the ship was based in Philadelphia, she was serving with the Naval Academy Practice Squadron and hence, in his mind, was not a front-line ship. He wanted to remain at the Navy Yard, where he could continue to promote his inventions and court Corinne. Mustin battled with the Bureau of Navigation, saying later that he had "an awful fight to get the orders revoked." He succeeded, and before the month was out, was once again in Washington.

In December, he took as his task circulating his telescopic findings throughout the Navy, but he met with resistance. On 31 December, Admiral Mason refused to allow Mustin's notes on the Mark XI telescope to be printed as a confidential circular. Said the Bureau of Ordnance chief, "The Bureau is making all possible efforts to confine to the Naval service all detailed knowledge of the gun sights and telescopes now in use and these efforts would be largely nullified by printing for distribution, even confidentially, the notes prepared by Lieut. Mustin."

By now, Lelia's whirlwind social pace was getting her into the newspapers. The Washington press identified her as "a dashing woman," "notable for her social activity and the beauty and number of her gowns." In time, they would come to describe her and her sisters as famous for their wit and charm. Her Nineteenth Street house had become a salon of sorts. Barnett, Mustin, and their crowd would be there, as would senators and congressmen. The as yet undiscovered muckraking journalist and author Upton Sinclair, a cousin, was a frequent visitor whom Lelia delighted in introducing to lawmakers.

Mustin and Barnett continued to host the Montague women at the Navy Yard dances and escorted them to Annapolis for academy functions. Often, they would spend the weekend at Annapolis's celebrated Carvel Hall Hotel, today restored to its original colonial state as the Paca House and Gardens.

Around Corinne, Mustin was sensitive about his age. In the company of younger midshipmen, she could be coquettish with him. At one Saturday night Naval Academy dance, she spurned him and dallied with a second classman. Angry and despondent, Mustin returned to Washington. Corinne remained for the rest of the weekend to share a Sunday walk with the mid. Later, Mustin "got even" at a Navy Yard dance, and afterward, at the house on Nineteenth Street, "scarcely spoke to her." In their discussions about marriage, he pretended that he would remain a bachelor permanently.

They were now under each other's skin. Mustin was in love with Corinne, and he knew that if he did not declare his feelings, events would intervene, for he would soon get orders to sea. On 5 February, he "stole his first kisses." For the next month, the couple basked in feelings for each other now expressed.

On 3 March, Mustin spent the evening with Corinne and Lelia at the Nineteenth Street townhouse. Although Lelia retired early, he remained to converse with Corinne. Their banter drifted into longer and longer periods of silence during which kisses were stolen. Suspicious of the quiet below, Lelia summoned Corinne upstairs. She returned apparently somewhat chagrined, and Mustin this time masked their activity by discussing loudly his theories on optics. At 10:00 P.M., he finally proposed. He wrote later that her response was "so sweet and so astonished." "Do you really mean it?" she asked. He declared himself again, and she said yes. He offered later that her response had surprised him, as the form of the time called for the lady initially to reply no. Immediately, Corinne went upstairs to tell Lelia, and all was well. For the next two weeks, the couple spent virtually every evening together .

On 15 March, Mustin received his orders: On 20 March he would report to the Navy's newest battleship, the *Kansas,* to serve as ordnance officer on her commissioning crew, a distinction for any officer. Mustin was happy. The first Sunday after he was detached from the Gun Factory, he and Corinne had the whole day in Washington, together "nearly all the time without anybody else!"

The *Kansas* was commissioned on 18 April with Capt. Charles B. Vreeland in command. The ceremony was somewhat disappointing for Mustin and his fellow officers, who included Ens. William F. Halsey and Lt. Edward C. Kalbfus, who would rise to ranks of five- and four-star admiral, respectively. It was a dry occasion, in deference to the sensibilities of a dry state: At the ship christening, instead of striking the bow with the customary bottle of champagne, the sponsor had instead used Kansas River water.

Immediately, the *Kansas* left Philadelphia for shakedown training off Provincetown, Massachusetts. By the end of the month, she and other capital ships were in Virginia waters at the Jamestown Exposition, along with warships from the British, German, and other international navies. In mid-May, the *Kansas* joined fleet exercises in northern waters.

Secure in his engagement, Mustin was buoyant. He wrote that Corinne was his "mascotte" and that she had brought him luck in practices and inventions. He was indeed now making progress in the implementation of his telescopes. The ordnance officer of the *Missouri* reported results of his four Mark XI telescopes that the ship received for trial. During the recent record practice, he wrote, Mustin's instruments received "unanimous and enthusiastic recommendations of all officers that these telescopes be furnished for all 6-inch sights." In an 8 May letter, Mason said Mustin would get fifty dollars royalty for each Mark XIII telescope, for his work done prior to his assignment to the Gun Factory.

In the meantime, Lelia and Corinne left Washington and moved to Wakefield. In mid-May, Mustin was able to join his fiancée for some very happy days there. Twice, he got leave from the *Kansas* and took long and expensive train rides for the sake of spending a day or two with his sweetheart. In the manor visitors' book, he would write that he "came with Basil" (Lelia's son) and "left with Basil's aunt." The engaged couple would sit close on the steep bank of the trout stream, walk through woods and up and down hills in the pleasant sunshine. At times, he would lift her and carry her across a little stream where she had not the slightest need of assistance. They would spend evenings on the porch and put off "saying goodnight and reluctantly going to different bed rooms."

On 10 June, the *Kansas* and the other ships had returned to the exposition for the presidential review, and Mustin began to hear rumors of ambitious plans for an Atlantic Fleet cruise into the Pacific. In mid-July, the ships went north again for exercises with target practice off Cape Cod. Then in late August, after they participated in the exposition's closing ceremonies, Mustin was able to get leave to join Corinne at Wakefield before returning to sea for full battle maneuvers. When the exercises finished on 24 September, the *Kansas* headed for Philadelphia for alterations in preparation for what now was whispered as something more than a transit through the Magellan Strait to California—an epic circumnavigation under steam.

Chapter 5

With the Great White Fleet

ALMOST BETTER THAN MY HONOR

Teddy Roosevelt, an ardent navalist, certainly was the driver behind an around-the-world cruise of the Atlantic battleship fleet, or what history now calls the Great White Fleet, in 1907–9. A confluence of factors supported the idea, the most obvious being the ongoing naval expansion and rivalry among the world's great powers, including the United States and Japan.

The naval arms race of the new century perhaps originated with the German ambition to challenge the British Empire. In 1898, Germany introduced its first *Flottengesetz,* or naval law, that called for significant naval appropriations for a fleet of battleships. It prompted a British response, championed by Adm. Sir John Fisher, who became First Sea Lord in 1904. Fisher put his weight behind the battleship *Dreadnought,* commissioned in 1906, whose main battery of ten 12-inch guns made the U.S. battleship fleet obsolete even before it left Hampton Roads.

In the U.S. Navy, the General Board also had determined that the German fleet would be the main threat to the Western Hemisphere. The greatest fear was of bombardment of the East Coast, and battleships, symbols of international power and ultimate instruments of sea control, were seen as deterrents to that threat. Indeed, the motto of the Navy League, founded in 1903, was "Battleships are cheaper than battles."

Senior U.S. naval officers also envisaged a scenario in which they might have to defend Culebra and the approaches to the Isthmus of Panama against a German threat. In 1905, Admiral Fisher, responding to Germany's burgeoning battleship program, had decided to concentrate his naval forces in the North Sea, and the Royal Navy abandoned the Caribbean to the U.S. Navy. The stakes were high because, after the Spanish-American War and acquisition of the Philippines, the United States was driving for a canal to reduce steaming times between the Atlantic and Pacific. Construction began in early 1904, and in February 1908, the Army–Navy Joint Board, whose focus was on war scenarios involving Japan, would institute a swing strategy that depended on a completed canal through which Atlantic forces would move into the Pacific and vice versa, as required.

When the Navy looked toward the Pacific, it saw a naval power vacuum that Japan was eager to fill. In 1906, Britain had begun a second round of naval withdrawal, moving its Pacific units to exercise scenarios against the Germans in the North Sea. The U.S. Army and Navy had no plan to defend the Philippines, only an agreement to retreat to Pearl Harbor. Although some naval officers still were suspicious of the Brits, others felt that the Royal Navy could bottle the Germans in the North Sea. Thus freed from the German threat, the United States could move the Atlantic Fleet battleships into the Pacific and thereby fill some of that vacuum.

In July 1907 at the Jamestown Exposition, Roosevelt supported the latter view and decided to transfer his battleships to the Pacific under the command of Rear Adm. Robley Evans. The Navy then had twenty-six battleships. Roosevelt wanted twenty to make the cruise, but four were not seaworthy. In the end, sixteen deployed, with substitutions in California, along with a scouting force and a number of auxiliaries. Fearful of antagonizing Japan, the Navy called the redeployment merely an exercise for naval contingency planning and for training modern capital warships and their supporting auxiliaries to operate as a fleet.

At the time, it was a real engineering challenge to keep battleships at sea longer than a week, and the Navy had questions about whether its Pacific facilities could support a battle fleet. The only dry dock on the West Coast was in Washington's Puget Sound. The Mare Island Yard in San Francisco Bay would need an upgrade to handle battleships. In addition, the real industrial and political clout to support shipyards was on the East Coast.

By the time the fleet arrived in California, Washington had concluded that the cruise had demonstrated the Navy's capability to maintain the Monroe Doctrine and that the second half thus would be more of an exercise in naval diplomacy in the Pacific and Mediterranean. In the end, the cruise perhaps was really about national prestige. To reinforce the grandeur of his fleet, Roosevelt insisted that the battleships remain white until after the cruise, even though most fleets were painted gray.

The cruise also helped divert national attention from the 1907–8 depression. High unemployment certainly helped recruiting. To encourage clean-cut Midwestern farm boys to enlist to represent the United States, the cruise launched the now famous slogan, "Join the Navy and see the world." It also was the first time the service issued toothbrushes as a standard item in a sailor's ditty bag. Shipshape appearances were so important that the fleet refused liberty to members of the "black gang," the men who shoveled the coal and could never get entirely clean. As a result, a few firemen reportedly went mad.

Roosevelt had to muzzle a number of naval officers who criticized the cruise as a nuisance that would take time away from the serious business of practice and exercise. As an ordnance officer, Henry C. Mustin certainly held to that position and would voice it continually in letters to Corinne. The older admirals and captains especially dreaded the year of grueling diplomatic duties that lay ahead. Despite the grumbling, most of the best men in the Navy went to sea on the cruise, including many officers who rose to command and to senior command positions in World Wars I and II.

Lelia did not return to Washington in the autumn of 1907. As her sister finalized her own wedding plans, she prepared for her marriage to George Barnett. She still owned a home in Baltimore, at 909 Charles Street, near Christ Church Episcopal, the Montague family church. Lelia and Corinne decided to hold their weddings there amid their own social set.

Closer to Philadelphia and his family and not too far for his Washington cohorts, a Baltimore wedding worked well for Mustin. He and his wedding party gathered at the Hotel Belvedere, a number of them carousing late into the night. The groom restrained himself and awoke early on his wedding day. Relieved to find the weather clearing, he went to prayer, solemnizing the occasion. Barnett was his best man. His six ushers were his brother, Burton, two shipmates who would join him on the world cruise, and three academy classmates. The couple exchanged vows at 1:10 P.M. on Tuesday, 29 October. Following the service, they mounted their carriage, but Corinne's veil tangled in Mustin's face. Remaining composed, she calmly sat on his one derby hat.

Through November, the couple honeymooned in New York, staying in midtown Manhattan's Gregorian Apartments off Sixth Avenue. The *Kansas* and six other battleships were homeported at the Brooklyn Navy Yard, getting provisioned and fitted out for the upcoming cruise. A number of accounts have it that the fleet loaded on board between twenty-four and sixty grand pianos and sixty phonographs. Mustin, ever the piano player, paid $90 toward a piano for the *Kansas*.

The Navy provided the honeymooners plenty of hoopla. To bolster support for the cruise, the yard extended hospitality to huge crowds of New Yorkers, with ship visits, hops, and receptions. The newlyweds, however, were just as interested in enjoying the theater. They went to see such new fare as *The Merry Widow* at the New Amsterdam. Another night, they went to Madison Square Garden, taking a hansom cab and arriving late. The highlight of their activity perhaps was hearing the Met's great soprano, Geraldine Farrar, sing the title role in *Madame Butterfly*. Their last adventure was on 30 November, when they joined other Navy couples and took the train to Philadelphia for the Army-Navy game. In an closely fought contest played before thirty thousand fans at Franklin Field, Navy upset Army six to nothing.

In early December, the *Kansas* and other ships left New York and headed south to rendezvous with the rest of the fleet at Hampton Roads. Corinne and the other wives and sweethearts joined them there to continue the party during Navy Farewell Week. The festivities culminated on Friday, 13 December, with a grand ball at the Chamberlin Hotel. On Monday, under a clear morning sky, sixteen battleships and their escorts and auxiliaries passed in review before their president on board his yacht, the *Mayflower,* and steamed toward the Atlantic. The *Kansas* had the distinction of serving as the second ship in Evans's First Battleship Division.

Mustin was once again at sea, and Corinne returned to 909 Charles. Fresh off their honeymoon, he was eager to communicate with her as often as possible. The couple wrote frequently and at length throughout the cruise. A more immediate mode was by telegram, by now a worldwide, albeit expensive, means of ship-to-shore communication. Mustin's shipmate Keating had devised a code book for his wife that reduced lengthy sentences to a few words and thus made such contact more affordable. Mustin told Corinne to use the Keatings' code whenever she wired.

The impact of telegraphy extended beyond personal communications. Because of diplomatic sensitivity and the internal controversy over the effort, much information regarding the cruise was censored. The declared destination was San Francisco; however, sixty miles off Hatteras, Evans signaled to his fleet that the cruise would in fact be worldwide. Unfortunately, his wireless message was monitored and leaked to the press—the first example of a radio intercept that made its way into the media.

On 23 December, the fleet made the Gulf of Paria near the British colony of Trinidad. Entering the gulf, the ships executed a complicated and impressive maneuver, but it was for naught. The colony officially shunned them, apparently expressing concern for the sensitivities of Britain's Japanese allies. As a result, the officers and men had to fend for themselves. Mindful of the diplomatic purpose of the cruise, the Navy ensured that no incidents would mar the visit: Trinidad saw the first use of a U.S. shore patrol to police liberty. The fleet spent Christmas in Port of Spain and left on the twenty-ninth, after coaling.

One of the key issues on the cruise was coal. Having too few of its own colliers, the Navy had to charter forty-one British ships. Coaling took place about every two weeks, and to boost morale, the ships' bands played on the after bridges throughout the operation. The fear of sabotage was real. Several times, inspectors found dynamite sticks in the coal bunkers. It was never clear whether they were blasting sticks from the mines that accidentally found their way into the coal stocks or were placed by saboteurs or anarchists involved in domestic industrial disputes.

Into January, Mustin already was longing for Corinne, who had returned to Baltimore to help prepare for Lelia's 11 January wedding to Barnett. On his way to Rio, the fleet's next port of call, he grumbled about being separated from his wife of three months as well as over the operational questionability of the cruise. On the ninth, he wrote, "I have just crossed off the 25th day on my calendar and that means I am just 25 times as much disgusted with this cruise as I was on the day it began."

The sea had become smooth, and Mustin's gun crews were able to remove the shutters from the 7-inch gun ports for the first time since they left Port of Spain. "As I expected, the elevating and training gear of that battery is so badly rusted that the guns won't move at all; it will take weeks to get them in working order." He feared the problem would recur on the runs from Rio to Punta Arenas in the Magellan Strait and from there to Callao. "Naturally we can't teach the men of the crews of these guns anything. It's disgusting; I wish George Barnett had been here today; the idea of his sitting up at the lunch table there in the Belvedere and saying this cruise was the finest thing that has happened to the Navy for years! As a matter of fact it simply means that we will lose a solid year, if not more, in our progress in gunnery."

Pondering the effects of the sea on his guns, Mustin worked on designs for spray protectors and also began to reflect on how to better provide for his wife. For the first time in his life, money was a consideration. As a soon-to-be lieutenant commander, he anticipated earning $4,900 a year on shore if he and Corinne didn't live in quarters.

It now occurred to him that he had neglected the income potential of his inventions. "There were some things that, if I hadn't been so uninterested in money, I could have patented. Every ship in this fleet has more than one unpatented invention of mine on board. The only reason I patented the Mark XIII telescope, and the things after it, was because I was 'sore' at not getting enough 'feathers' for the things that went before it; I knew that by taking out the patents I could protect my name, but I had little idea of making money out of them."

The long leg to Rio also exposed engineering difficulties, especially the matter of coal supplies for the older ships. The *Maine* was burning vast quantities to maintain the speed of the newer ships. Slowing the pace to keep formation at the prescribed four-hundred-yard interval between ships, the fleet arrived in Rio two days behind schedule.

The Brazilians were extremely hospitable, giving Evans a fifteen-gun salute, appropriate for a vice admiral. The gesture highlighted the irony that the U.S. Navy now had a fleet and a fleet commander but the antimilitary Congress refused to promote Evans beyond two stars. After an eventful visit, the fleet left Rio on 22 January and continued steaming south into Argentine waters. Not to be outdone by the Brazilians, the Argentineans arranged for their navy to rendezvous with the fleet at sea and gave Evans a seventeen-gun salute, appropriate for a full admiral.

The fleet entered the Magellan Strait beginning the 350-mile passage from the Atlantic to the Pacific, and on 1 February dropped anchor at Punta Arenas for coaling. A British cruiser, the *Sappho*, had been shadowing the battleships. One of Mustin's friends from his days on the China Station, a Royal Navy commander named Townsend, was on board and invited Mustin for dinner. "It was a very pleasant evening of reminiscences, but I guess Townsend was rather disappointed to find the wild Indian he had known in the East had become very tame." Fishing for intelligence on his gun sights, the *Sappho*'s gunnery officer questioned Mustin about the Navy's new Mark XIII telescope, knowing it was his invention, but Mustin bobbed and weaved, frequently changing the subject.

Under way again, the fleet emerged from the strait and steamed past the Evangelistas Islands Light House, marking the first transfer of U.S. naval power from the Atlantic to the Pacific. Passing the uninhabited and gray, windswept landscape, Mustin grew pensive, and wondered whether he could ever be the lighthouse keeper in such a place. He said he would—if Corinne were with him. She recently had written that she was suffering from headaches and taking phenacetin, and he worried that she was relying on a painkiller, feeling she had gotten the idea from Lelia, whom he regarded as weak-willed. Writing back, he noted that he had used willpower to overcome his appetite for strong drink, adding that one needs faith in self as well as in God.

As the fleet turned north and headed up the western coast of South America, Mustin reapplied himself to professional tasks. The fleet target practice in Mexico's Magdalena Bay was upcoming, and he began planning how his fire control system could give the *Kansas* an advantage over the other battleships. His solution was organization: Taussig in the crow's nest as spotter; Keating operating the range clock for deflection correction for speed of passing; and Mustin as the range finder, with an assistant to telephone the readings to the sight setters at all the 12-inch guns.

After a ceremonial sweep past the Chilean harbor at Valparaiso, where they received an enthusiastic greeting, the *Kansas* and company made for Callao. Mustin recalled his visit ten years before. Writing to Corinne, he confessed to having been a wild man then, but declared himself changed—as evidenced by his disapproval of ragtime. He was more interested this trip in planning to meet his wife while his ship was on the West Coast. Corinne was asking for a "honeymoon" in California, and having heard rumors the fleet would make a number of stops beginning in San Diego, Mustin proposed that he take leave there and rejoin the ship in San Francisco. His new idea was for Corinne then to follow the fleet in the Orient and to travel there with Lelia and her children, who were joining Barnett in Beijing. Another potential traveling companion who met his approval was the wife of a young shipmate, Midshipman S. Danenhower. Fearful of bad influences on his young bride, he cautioned her to avoid the company of two other wives of shipmates, regarding them as too adventurous and given to mingle with questionable characters. Most Caucasians in the East are "a pretty bad lot straight through," he wrote. "Every man a villain and every woman crooked until they prove themselves otherwise."

Seeking to reassure her husband, who had seemed anxious over her doings, Corinne had written that she was taking communion and going to church frequently. The news prompted him to respond that although he was not a regular churchgoer, his faith was firm and that he was saying the prayers he learned from his mother. Mustin continued with a revealing insight into the nature of his faith: "How can a man or woman go through life's work without a belief and confidence in a supreme being?" he asked.

Many do, and as a rule men of a scientific turn of mind are usually agnostics. But I don't see how a man can be cool and brave in the face of death if he thinks that he is on the verge of oblivion. Always before going into action I have asked God, in a silent prayer, to make my brain clear, to let me behave as a brave and honorable Christian, and to forgive my many sins if he sees fit to take my life. And there are other occasions that I have asked him to give me wisdom and strength to battle with the angry sea. But darling, I have never been a believer in putting the whole responsibility in God.

On the night of 21 February, Mustin was toastmaster for a *Kansas* wardroom evening for Henry Reuterdahl and Frederick Mathews, two of the correspondents accompanying the fleet. In the first of his two-volume chronicle of the cruise, Mathews described the evening's "good natured raillery" among the officers. After nearly every course, someone sang and played piano. The correspondent found the evening especially memorable for Mustin's singing of "rare English ballads," in particular, one he sang "half a dozen times, that old gypsy song 'Dip Your Fingers in the Stew.'"

Mustin also used this period to push the Navy for remuneration for his inventions. In a 28 February letter from Callao to the Bureau of Ordnance, he wrote that he wanted royalties for sight mountings being constructed for turrets on the *Michigan* and *South Carolina* and vessels of later design. He had invented the sight and made patent application, he noted, while on the supply ship *Culgoa,* which was in no way connected with ordnance duty. The sight made possible the arrangement of turrets in tandem, which was "impossible with sights requiring hoods on the turret roof like those now in service. Furthermore, this sight eliminates all the inherent difficulties now experienced with turret sights containing a parallel motion mechanism, like those now in service, and this account provides a sight mounting that can be relied on to remain indefinitely in proper adjustment."

In early March, the *Kansas* was off the coast of Ecuador, and Mustin was desperate to hear from Corinne, "like a hungry tiger waiting for the keeper to bring him his food." The next mail delivery would not be until after the fleet arrived at Magdalena Bay, however, so he continued to absorb himself in the upcoming gunnery exercises. Writing on 3 March, he said, "This afternoon I finished all the deductions for my spotting system, so now I can let my assistants do the work of calculating. I have found out some very surprising things in working out this scheme and now I see an explanation for a good many of the misses we made with our small guns last practice. We ought to do very much better this time." Despite his dedication as an ordnance and gunnery officer, his final words revealed how much his young bride had influenced his priorities. "Good night my own darling; I love you better than ambition, health, wealth or riches; almost better than my honor. God bless you dearest."

Mindful of resentment over the canal and the U.S. role in the 1903 Panamanian declaration of independence, the fleet did not put into Colombia. The focus was shifting from diplomacy toward training as the column approached its Mexican practice waters, and on the final run to Magdalena Bay, the fleet held its signaling championship. During each individual contest, two ships would leave the column and steam on parallel courses about three thousand yards apart. Midway between them and in advance, the hoisting ship would signal for the competitors to repeat. Signalmen would snap signal flags to halyards and hoist them to the yardarms. The *Kansas* won the First Squadron championship, and the *Kentucky* won for the Second Squadron. On 10 March, the *Kansas* defeated the *Kentucky,* but the following day, she lost, twenty-seven to twenty-six, to the fleet champion, *Georgia.*

The critical exercises, however, were gunnery. Magdalena Bay would host a month of record practice, during which each ship would fire every gun at a target placed at a known distance to qualify her gun pointers. In the autumn in Philippine waters, the fleet would conduct battle practice. In this second exercise, the target and its placement would simulate the size and distance of an enemy ship. Gunners would have to estimate range, and umpires would score each ship on the basis of speed and accuracy.

On 12 March, the fleet dropped anchor in the bay. His second day in Magdalena, Mustin left lunch to begin bore sighting. The painstaking process required absolute attention to detail. For each gun in his battery, he first inserted a bore-sight telescope into the gun, aligning it along the exact axis of the barrel. He then adjusted the actual sighting telescope on the gun mount to ensure it was in true alignment with the bore sight.

Mustin was working with a green gun crew on a new ship, and he knew some of the crews on the older ships had been together for as long as seven years. He had studied the gunnery problem for months, but he still had a few days to apply his brain power to optics and fire control in an effort to seize every advantage. It took five days for the exercise teams to survey and mark the four ranges, and he expected his ship to be out on or about the twenty-seventh. In the end, the *Kansas* joined the *Vermont, Alabama,* and *Maine* on the seventeenth for their first day on the range.

On 22 March, Mustin learned of the fleet's itinerary and excitedly wrote Corinne that he had only twenty-two days until their second honeymoon in California. He advised her to get a train ticket from the East Coast to San Francisco via Los Angeles, as well as a round trip ticket from Los Angeles to San Diego. That way, she could follow the fleet as it progressed northward, or better yet, they could write their own itinerary and spend time alone if he got leave. "I work hard in my profession," he wrote,

> simply that you may be happy in my achievements. Any selfishness that others may see in me is not real selfishness, for it is the determination to make your husband a man that you can be proud of. But in this I am a changed man for in former years I must confess that I have been selfish when any one stood between me and my ambitions. This great love has made me a new man in many ways and I look back with pity on the man Mustin that existed,—thinking he was living,—in the days before a gray-eyed angel kissed him and transformed his nature.

Corinne evidently had the money to get to the West Coast, but the extra money to get her to San Diego was a problem. Mustin assured her that Father Lloyd would supplement his income to get her to San Diego. Their plan was to meet at the Hotel Del Coronado on Tuesday, 14 April, at 2:00 P.M. On 1 April, he reiterated his desire for her to follow the fleet around the world after San Francisco. Again, though, he was despondent about his calling:

> Since the Navy is now nothing more than the pawn of politicians and is used as a means of advertising the self styled "Grand Old Party" I am getting mightily disgusted with it as a life work. Some one once said the mainspring of human existence is hope of reward and fear of punishment, or words to that effect. On this basis the mainspring of naval existence is incomplete for it certainly lacks hope of reward. There is little glory and practically no money in it. I doubt if any officer thinks of the latter until he has married, and finds that money affairs are serious considerations.

Record practice concluded, and Mathews reported that the Navy had improved with 100 percent accuracy and rapidity over 1903, the first year of the competition.

Leaving Magdalena Bay on 11 April en route to California, the ships spent many days painting and preparing for their arrival and the festivities awaiting at each port of call. His mixed feelings about his career notwithstanding, Mustin had worked hard during the cruise, and he got his leave. From the Hotel Del, the couple worked their way north by train, taking time to visit the redwood forests. They arrived in San Francisco, still in ruins after the earthquake and fire of April 1906, and spent Corinne's twenty-first birthday, 28 May, at Mare Island.

While in California, the fleet readied itself for the engineering and diplomatic challenges of the Pacific and Japan, and on 7 July, a modified battleship fleet finally set sail for Hawaii. Evans had recommended replacing the *Maine* and the *Alabama,* which clearly were not up to the challenge of a continued cruise. In their places sailed the newly commissioned *Nebraska* and *Wisconsin.*

The pressures of the cruise also were taking a toll on the senior commanders, a number of whom were relieved. Seriously handicapped by gout, Evans himself had reached his limit. His relief was his Fourth Division commander, Rear Adm. Charles Sperry, who proved to be a hard taskmaster. Right away, Sperry insisted that the ships do four hours of maneuvers daily during the crossing to Hawaii.

Mustin occupied himself working on ballistics and gunnery problems. His concern at the time was powder errors. A shot could fall either long or short, depending on the strength of the charge, which depended in turn on the density of the powder, which varied according to temperature—a significant factor in the tropics. Mustin's solution was refrigeration. On the evening of 13 July, two days from Honolulu, he argued his case with the fleet's chief constructor, R. H. Robinson. He wrote Corinne,

> I think I made him appreciate the need of refrigeration for our powder magazine. It seemed strange to be having a "heart to heart" talk with the man who is supposed to be the arch enemy of the line. I am mighty glad of it, though, for I have come to have a great respect for him. It seemed strange, afterwards, that a man with the rank of Rear Admiral was willing to argue with a young Lieutenant and not put himself on a different plane.

Corinne was at sea, too, en route to Honolulu. Along with nine other wives, she had gotten passage on the *Tenyo Maru,* Japan's first large, domestically built passenger liner. Once reunited in Honolulu, she and Mustin spent glorious mornings together dipping in the surf before breakfast. In the evenings, the social whirl would continue, highlighted by a reception and ball at Waikiki.

Mustin and the fleet left Hawaii to begin a seventeen-day run to New Zealand, at that point the longest leg of the cruise. On 24 July, Corinne and five of the wives on the *Tenyo Maru* followed, getting direct passage to Sydney on the *Marama,* of the Union Steam Ship Company of New Zealand. After stops at Fanning Island and in Suva and

Fiji, they arrived in Sydney ten days before the fleet. Mustin and his ships had encountered three days of heavy weather with twenty-foot swells before arriving in Auckland, where he was acutely disappointed to find no letters from his bride.

In Sydney, Corinne and her companions found the Australians wildly enthusiastic about the American visit. Many wives received free lodging in hotel royal suites, and some got to sit in the royal box at the opera. According to Mustin family lore, however, Corinne and some of her fellow wives had trouble finding a vacancy. When a hotel manager told them, "We have a card room, and you can have that during the day," Corinne replied, "We didn't come all the way to Australia to play cards with our husbands!"

The city opened its arms to the fleet. Many of the wives appeared as celebrities in a number of newspapers. Some were on postcards and in rotogravure sections specially issued by Australian government. Mustin wrote later that he often was identified as the "husband of Mrs. Mustin" and was secretly delighted at her breaking the hearts of the British Army. In Australia, Corinne was coming into her own. Mustin felt that at twenty-one she was among the most privileged young women in the world, having on one occasion the chance to row ashore with Lord Northcote, the governor general of Australia, to Thursday Island, the northernmost point of Queensland, and during their time in Sydney having made friends with the Lady Mayoress.

When the fleet left for Melbourne, Corinne followed by train. The two-and-a-half-day separation was a busy one for Mustin, who was angered by Sperry's insistence on double duty on the run. Soon the fleet and the attendant wives, now known as "the geese," would head northward. The thought prompted Mustin to address his concern over the effect the non-European world might have on his young wife. In a 27 August letter, he wrote:

> Advice for China
> 1. In China never eat anything uncooked that grows in the ground (Typhoid!)
> 2. In China, Japan or the Philippines always wash a cut (even the smallest scratch) with an antiseptic solution and don't leave a cut exposed. (Bubonic Plague!)
> 3. In the Philippines never leave anything valuable loose for a minute (Sneak thieves!)
> 4. In the Philippines disclaim any relationship to "el commandante del vapor Samar": (the insurrectos had a price on my head in '99 and they might take it out on you!)

5. In the Philippines avoid going in Native houses and always keep windward of a funeral (Small Pox!)

6. All through the Far East, put no trust at all in a stranger and very little in those that are not strangers.

7. Keep out of the sun when it is very hot, take plenty of exercise and be very regular in your habits.

   Now if you will memorize these seven tips and carry them out religiously you will be a good girl.

When the fleet left Melbourne harbor, one of its auxiliaries, the *Ajax,* rammed the British steamer *Laura.* The *Kansas* had to remain to represent the U.S. Navy at the court of inquiry into the accident. The hearings commenced on Saturday, 5 September. As with the *Maine* inquiry, Mustin lent his mechanical drawing talents to the presentation of the case. According to one account, he "prepared further drawings of the scene of the accident and the relative positions of the ships. The speed and efficiency with which he did this impressed the Australians present."

The court continued into a Sunday session. Nevertheless, the *Kansas* went ahead to host Melbourne VIPs at an onboard social. After the court adjourned, Mustin chose to forgo the party and instead made a frenzied dash to the train station to bid Corinne good-bye as she left for Sydney, to board the steamer that would take her to Yokohama.

"It was very satisfactory to be able to get to the station in time to kiss you goodbye," he wrote the next day,

for no one in the ship thought I could get there in time. It was 4:15 when the court adjourned and 4:20 when the boat shoved off; although I urged the fireman and engineer they couldn't make the run to Port Melbourne in less than 15 minutes and so I missed the 4:30 train—badly. Then it occurred to me that some of our guests might have motor cars on the dock waiting for them and I decided to steal one! There were two standing there, a little red one and a big fine looking green one. I dashed up to the driver of the Irish colored one and said, "Whose car is this?" "It's Mr. Manifold's, sir," he said. "Well, he won't need it for an hour, can you get me up to Spencer St. Station in ten minutes?" "I think I can, sir." "Well, let her go. I want to see my wife off to Sydney; I'll pay your fines for speeding!"

   It was 4:38 when we started and in just seven minutes he landed me at the station!

. . . My uniform evidently saved us from arrest and helped in getting through the
crowd as the "bobbies" on every corner gave us right of way. . . .

I risked a 10-pound fine in kissing you good bye as that is the penalty for jump-
ing on or off a moving train, but again the uniform did its duty!

The *Kansas* went to sea on 9 September, and after the rush of Melbourne, despon-
dency beset Mustin once more. "Sometimes I contemplate giving up all chances of
my flying an Admiral's flag, and making a bid for the retired list," he wrote on 11
September.

But then I don't believe you would love me quite as much if I turned myself into one
who didn't count; to become an idler who has no voice in the progress of events. . . .
It is disheartening to compare our service with the British Navy where a man doesn't
have to wait for dead men's shoes to get his place at the top if he has ability and
energy. . . . Well, after this round the world jaunt is finished I think the fleet will have
a hard time to get away from the Navy Yards and for the rest of my three years I
think it will hang in pretty close to home; then when I can get on shore duty, just you
watch me hold on to the beach!

Annoyed that the Navy was granting him only a $250 royalty instead of $500 for
his sights, he wrote, "According to law, they have no right to cut down the figures I
gave them, for they used the invention without my license. Saegmuller writes me that
for the present he has ceased operations on disposing of my foreign patents for the reason there is an agitation about Naval Officers' patents; my attorneys say the same thing
but think it will blow over as usual. For the present I'll take no steps in the disposal
of the spray protector, or I am likely to get myself disliked!"

The officer patents issue seemed serious, and Mustin feared he might be ordered
back to the United States to testify at a court of inquiry. His letters do not make clear
to what case he was referring, but it may have had to do with Bradley Fiske's problems
with the Navy, which had frustrated his efforts to keep his inventiveness in step with
the rapid advances in gunnery. The older reformer continued to work with Western
Electric on improved Morris Tube procedures, but in this area, he and Mustin clearly
were competitors. According to Fiske, the Bureau of Ordnance had in the winter of
1906–7 a "Lt. M——" (very probably Mustin) take up his sighting machine concept.
Fiske said "M's" 1908 blueprints were his and "M's dotter" was identical to Fiske's own

sighting machine. He protested and later wrote, "The bureau suppressed the name of M———, and not long afterward withdrew the machine from service."

Corinne was now heading northward on the *Kumano Maru*. It was not clear whether the steamer would stop at Manila, but Mustin expected her to put into Hong Kong, where she had a "date" with him on 17 October. On 15 September, the fleet was coaling at Albany, on Australia's west coast, and he was busy working on a mathematical problem. On the twentieth, he was at sea again, his mind drifting to Corinne, who, he imagined, was ahead of him passing through the Basilan Straits. He wrote,

This morning I fired the sixteen calibration shots from the 12" guns and enjoyed it exceedingly. Next to making love to you, I believe firing those great big guns is the most fascinating occupation I know of. It is most impressive: you stand in the turret hood, one hand on the electric controller which moves the gun up and down and with the telescope (*my* telescope) that shows you where that tremendous force is to be directed; your other hand is on the firing key where just a quarter of an inch motion of your forefinger will let loose 870 lbs of death and destruction at a good 2,700 ft a second. The turret trainer in the hood between the guns is swinging the telescope of your gun and with it the gun and the whole turret structure around towards the target. He moves his hand on his controller using no more effort,—probably not as much—as the cook does in grinding the coffee. Your one hand on the controller raises that 70 ton gun up and down with less effort than that. Then when you have the intersection of the crosshairs of the telescope on a bullseye that you can't see at all with the naked eye, the same amount of effort that you use in beckoning with your forefinger lets loose pandemonium! For a few seconds the whole field of view is obscured by a brown haze; then it is indistinct by reason of the heated gases, and finally it is clear again in time for you to see the splash of the projectile, a column of water a hundred feet high, apparently in exactly the same spot the last one struck.

As Corinne was making passage through Philippine waters ahead of him, Mustin worried she might put into Manila. He had gotten word of a cholera epidemic and confessed to getting "a little thrill of terror." The *Kumano Maru* bypassed Manila, however, and only touched at Hong Kong.

During Mustin's own journey through Philippine waters, it was "hot as the hinges of Hell," and he had to sleep with his "square port opened wide." The fleet did stop in Manila, but Sperry ordered no liberty for fear of introducing cholera to his ships. Mustin was one of the privileged few officers who managed to get ashore. In a letter written from Manila's Army and Navy Club, he proudly reported that he was "on the wagon." He further boasted that he had just captained the *Kansas* under way while all the senior officers were off ship, participating in a series of courts-martial for the fleet. He took the ship from Manila down to the mine field at San Nicholas and returned to the anchorage, rounding the bow of the *Minnesota* within twenty yards of her ram. He felt he was a "supremely confident ship handler" and ascribed his confidence to "re-incarnation."

On 8 October, three days before leaving Manila for Japan, Mustin organized his three ushers on board—Keating, Merriam, and Harding—to join him at 1:00 P.M. in his room for a champagne toast in honor of his first wedding anniversary.

The passage to Japan was tense and diplomatically stressful. Washington was not certain how the Japanese would react as the U.S. fleet steamed toward their waters. Japan's own sixty-ship fleet was on maneuvers, steaming toward Sperry's force. Whatever the Japanese intentions, the weather intervened. During the week of 11 October, the worst typhoon since 1867 hit the fleet as it made way through the China Seas. The U.S. battleships encountered sixty-foot waves and winds in excess of a hundred miles an hour. On 18 October, they arrived in Yokohama a day late with surprisingly little damage. The wives, who had been in Japan for the better part of the month, rented a boat and steamed into the harbor to greet them.

The Japanese in fact went overboard to be good hosts for the week-long visit. Washington now felt compelled to reciprocate goodwill, and Tokyo evidently prevailed on the State Department to downgrade the fleet's subsequent visit to China by sending only the Third and Fourth Battleship Divisions—in effect a diplomatic snub to Japan's regional rival. The issue put the State and Navy Departments at odds, as they often were. The Navy would have been happy for the fleet to bypass China altogether to return to the Philippines to prepare for its autumn target practice.

The China visit proved to be a diplomatic embarrassment all around. The Navy was especially fickle in deciding on a suitable Chinese port. Initially, it planned for the ships to go to Shanghai. Wary of the port's shallow waters, it changed to Chefu before finally settling on Amoy. The Chinese gamely struggled to make their own hasty preparations amid this chopping and changing. The awkward episode humiliated the Dowager Empress. On 15 November, two weeks after the fleet left China waters, she died, setting the stage for the collapse of the Manchu dynasty and the revolution of 1911.

The First and Second Battleship Divisions went directly to Manila. While Mustin and the *Kansas* awaited the arrival of the Third and Fourth Divisions, Corinne was in

Beijing for a two-week stay with the Barnetts, now ensconced in the Legation Quarter. The rumors of trouble in China worried Mustin and continued to do so until she caught a steamer and began the next leg of her trip, through the Suez Canal and into the Mediterranean. On 8 November, the four divisions finally reunited in Manila.

Battle practice ran from 10 to 18 November. Unlike the spring target practice at Magdalena Bay, these exercises simulated actual battle. Ranges varied from one to six miles. Night practice included attacks by torpedo boats. In the end, the fleet recorded a 50 percent improvement over the spring. Diplomatically, however, it was a trial. For the second time, Sperry ordered no shore visits, to prevent cholera infection. This time, the insult to Manila was too much. Roosevelt, buoyed by the 13 November election of Taft, his chosen successor, insisted on two days' shore leave to placate the Filipinos.

On 1 December, the fleet departed Manila. En route to the Suez Canal, the column made a pre-Christmas coaling stop at Colombo in Ceylon. With the serious business of range practice behind him, Mustin focused on his personal pursuits. On Christmas Eve, he wrote that he had memorized Chopin's Prelude in C Major. He also was considering his future. Homeward bound, he again was feeling upbeat about his naval calling. Immodestly, he wrote that his development of a system of training should be taken as an "authoritative standard" and that he had an offer for assignment to the Naval War College. As for his patents, he had decided to do business with Sub-target Gun Co. for his rolling indicator, so as not to be beholden to Saegmuller. He had hit his inventive stride and felt he could capitalize on a number of industry options. If the Bureau of Ordnance did not offer him a suitable billet when he returned, it would cost the Navy a lot of money, he reckoned. As he had in the past, he would do his inventing on his own time, file his patents, and have industry manufacture his devices— for which the Navy would have to pay him handsomely.

By the time the fleet reached the Mediterranean, the world had come to regard the cruise as a great feat; however, the wear and tear on the ships now was evident. It was clear to Mustin that when they returned in late February, the battleships would remain in the shipyards until May or June.

On New Year's Day 1909, the fleet received a telegram reporting that an earthquake and subsequent tidal wave had devastated Messina, Sicily, causing an estimated 150,000 casualties. The fleet would not reach the Suez Canal until 3 January, and the battleship commanders all realized that the clock was ticking on the cruise. The plan was to return to Hampton Roads to give Roosevelt his 22 February presidential review before he passed the White House reins to Taft. To stay on schedule, meet his diplomatic obligations with some of the European powers, and now provide assistance to the Sicilians, Sperry decided to divide his fleet. On 6 January, he sent the Second, Third, and Fourth Divisions to make a round of port visits throughout the Eastern Med and took the First Division to Messina.

Sperry's recovery force arrived in Messina on 9 January. However, the humanitarian gesture embarrassed the Italians, who were offended by implication that they could not manage the disaster themselves. Sperry thereupon sent the *Kansas, Minnesota,* and *Vermont* to Villefranche on the Riviera, where they remained for two weeks.

France was another social whirlwind, as well as an opportunity for Mustin to parade his football prowess. In an exhibition game, his *Kansas* football team beat the *Minnesota's* by a score of six to two. The athletic contest so fascinated the French that the city of Nice presented his ship with a prize of $6,000. During the visit, the Mustins joined other officers and wives on a trip to Paris, before the division left to rendezvous with the rest of the fleet at Gibraltar.

With the unexpected extra duty in the Med, the fleet found itself short of food and dependent on British largesse. After provisioning at Gibraltar, the ships departed, passing through the Pillars of Hercules to begin their westward voyage home. The crossing proved to be a final trial: The fleet had to endure two days of a severe Atlantic storm. On 22 February, the column arrived at Hampton Roads for the fanfare of Roosevelt's last presidential review aboard the *Mayflower.* Two weeks later, Roosevelt left office, and the Great White Fleet likewise passed into history.

For the most part regarded as a qualified success, the year-long cruise aroused Americans' interest in world affairs and put the Navy at the forefront of the public's mind. The Great White Fleet solidified the battleship as the embodiment of U.S. national power. The cruise still had its critics, even in the Navy. Most formidable was "Fighting Bob" Evans, who forcefully expressed the view that the voyage seriously compromised readiness. The Navy had lost a year of training and would lose several months more to costly overhauls.

As Mustin had predicted, the *Kansas* went into overhaul on 28 February at the Philadelphia Navy Yard and remained there officially until mid-June. When she emerged, she went straight to sea for drills against torpedo boat attacks off Hampton Roads. In July, she was on maneuvers in Massachusetts Bay. The rest of the year would be filled with more maneuvers, tactics, and battle practice that ranged from the Massachusetts coast and New York to the Virginia Capes. On 5 August, Mustin received his commission as a lieutenant commander, but he was full of the sea and had swallowed enough. He wanted a home. It had become his time to "hold on to the beach."

Chapter 6

Into the Air

In October 1909, Henry C. Mustin was detached from the *Kansas* to go to the Philadelphia Navy Yard at League Island, first as ordnance inspector and then in December as senior assistant engineer officer. League Island was the preeminent battleship yard in the country and was a choice billet for an ordnance and gunnery professional. In all probability, Mustin was there because the Navy recognized his already significant contributions to advancing gunnery in the fleet. With Corinne comfortably ensconced in quarters, he continued his work on gun sights.

Naval gunnery had been continuously extending range. In a few years, Mustin would begin to imagine solutions beyond meaningful visual fire control from the turret, that is, at ranges out to twenty-five thousand yards. Battleship fire control towers and ship-towed kite balloons were early fixes, but Mustin would be one of the first to see naval aircraft as a means to resolve this spotting challenge.

The battle fleet returned to a United States besotted with aviation. Mustin had come home to find members of Philadelphia society's Aero Club of Pennsylvania active on all fronts, from stunt flying to air meets. One stalwart was a twenty-four-year-old adventurer, Marshall Earl Reid, whose sister had married Mustin's brother, John Burton. Reid apparently learned to fly from Glenn Curtiss and became a friend of the Hammondsport, New York, aviation pioneer.

In mid-November 1910, the Aero Club sponsored an eight-day international exhibition that drew a lot of public attention. Some internationals, notably British aviator Claude Grahame-White, even demonstrated potential military capability. Grahame-White flew a Farman from Point Breeze to League Island and dropped a "stage bomb," thought to be a sack of flour, on the yard's administration building.

Reid and Mustin were kindred spirits, driven by challenge and adventure. Reid, who later would earn his naval aviator wings during World War I, introduced Mustin to the air. As part of the exhibition, he conducted two days of flight demonstrations in his own hydroplane. Delighting the crowds, Reid took advantage of a calm November afternoon to make seven flights, six with passengers. The flights lasted from seven to fifteen minutes, at speeds ranging from forty-five miles per hour just above the water to sixty-five miles per hour in the air at heights of 100 to 150 feet. Mustin took the third flight and reportedly was "thoroughly tickled." He told reporters that it was as steady as going to church and that he thought he would soon learn to fly.

As prophetic as that remark might have been, the next day the headlines focused on Corinne: "Woman, First Time, Makes Flight Here in Hydro-aeroplane." She had immediately followed her husband into the air, and hers was one of the longest flights of the day. Asked by a reporter for her reaction, she replied, "I liked it. It's as good a sport as I've ever experienced. Beats an auto ride."

Not long after, the Mustins learned that Corinne was expecting their first child. During her pregnancy, their life would settle into a comfortable routine of work and parties. For the Navy, 1910 was the year it began to take aviation seriously.

Taking its first organizational step in October, the Navy Department directed Capt. Washington Irving Chambers (U.S. Naval Academy class of 1876), an ordnance engineer and battleship skipper, to carry the brief for naval aviation. It was not a running start, however. Chambers's duty would be in addition to duties as aide for material to Secretary of the Navy George von Lengerke Meyer. The Navy gave Chambers no executive authority. His mission was simply to prove the practicality of aircraft for use as fleet elements.

Cdr. Hutchinson I. Cone, chief of the Bureau of Steam Engineering and a colleague of Fiske and Sims, had begun promoting the idea of a plane for the new scout cruiser *Chester*. The concept was endorsed by the General Board in August, but Secretary Meyer remained lukewarm. Assistant Secretary Beekman Winthrop was more inclined toward aviation and ordered Chambers to attend the first U.S. international air meet later that month at Belmont, New York. There Chambers met Glenn Curtiss, beginning a close relationship that was to shape the course of early naval aviation.

Curtiss already was an aviation hero of national prominence and had been making grandstanding statements as to the threat aircraft could pose to battleships. Chambers learned that he had arranged through the *New York World* to test the feasibility of a civilian plane service to deliver mail from a Hamburg-American ocean liner. This discovery prompted some in the Navy to speculate that the German Navy might have an interest in the experiment. Whatever the truth, Chambers knew naval aviation could benefit if the U.S. Navy were the first to launch a plane from a ship. Taking advantage of bad weather and technical delays in the *World* project, he got Curtiss to cooperate with his own hasty planning for an alternative demonstration.

Curtiss assigned to the task one of his exhibition flyers, Eugene Ely. Setting the stage for the first milestone in the development of naval aviation, Chambers and his Navy team quickly established themselves at the Norfolk Navy Yard and rigged a ramp on the forecastle of the cruiser *Birmingham*. On 14 November, while the ship was at anchor, Ely launched his Curtiss plane into the rain and sleet and flew two and a half miles through fog to Willoughby Spit.

Celebrating the experiment's success and wanting to capitalize on a potential business opportunity, Curtiss immediately offered free flight instruction to Navy and Army officers, fully aware that aviation training funds were nonexistent in the services. Chambers in December got orders for Lt. Theodore G. "Spuds" Ellyson to report for training at the Curtiss winter camp on North Island in San Diego. A submarine officer recently assigned to Newport News, Ellyson had put in a request for aviation duty earlier that month. He arrived on 2 January 1911; operations were scheduled to begin on the seventeenth. Curtiss, however, was engaged in the Navy's next high-profile aviation feat.

This time, Chambers had secured Ely to fly on and off a ship. Ely had suggested that he do it in San Francisco Bay to coincide with the California Aero Club's second major air meet, and on 18 January, he flew his Curtiss "pusher" from the old Presidio parade ground to a platform mounted on the stern of the anchored armored cruiser *Pennsylvania*. After a ceremonial toast below, Ely launched and flew back to the Presidio.

Following this celebrated success, the Curtiss group returned to North Island to prepare for a follow-on experiment. On 17 February, Curtiss flew a single-float hydroplane from Spanish Bight to the *Pennsylvania* in San Diego Bay, had it hoisted aboard and back to the water, and then flew back to base, all in the space of half an hour. With these three achievements, Ely and Curtiss proved that aircraft could operate from ships. With Ellyson's graduation from North Island on 11 April, Chambers now was positioned to press for funding.

The same month, Fiske, serving now as aide for inspections, suggested that naval aircraft stationed at and flying from a line of four island bases across the Pacific could solve the problem of how to defend of Philippines. With this senior ally, on 8 May Chambers got $25,000, which he applied to the purchase of the A-1 and A-2 hydroplanes from Curtiss and a land machine from Howard Wright. For the next several years, the Navy trained on Curtiss and Wright aircraft, each of which would have its own trainees. Ellyson went with Curtiss to Hammondsport and soon was joined by his 1906 academy classmate Lt. John H. Towers, a battleship fire control officer. Lt. John Rodgers, the fourth in a long line of distinguished naval officers, went to train at the Wright school and works in Dayton, Ohio.

In September, Ellyson, Towers, and Rodgers were joined by Ens. Victor D. Herbster to start work at the first naval air station at Greenbury Point on the Severn, across from the Naval Academy. The sixty-acre site was vulnerable to fire from the midshipmen's rifle range and was representative of how Ellyson and his aviators had to make do, largely ignored by the mainstream Navy.

This new generation of reformers and insurgents was attuned to the military potential of the century's new technologies. With allies such as Chambers, they wanted to integrate aviation into the fleet, and they were willing to fight the political battles to make it so.

In Philadelphia, Mustin found others in his service who were attracted by aviation. Naval constructor and aeronautical engineer Lieutenant Holden "Dick" Richardson had arrived in the yard in 1909. Another Pennsylvanian, he and the technically minded Mustin became fast friends. Mustin also began to spend more time with Reid, who by now was well into hydroplanes and attendant design issues—in particular, the one persistent challenge of pontoon design. A hydro needed a lightweight pontoon to reach altitudes of five hundred feet or more. At the same time, the float had to be strong enough to maintain impermeability and withstand the buffeting of takeoff and landing.

Mustin and Reid's preoccupation was shared by Richardson, who also lent his intellect to float design while at the yard. The work fascinated him and led him to request aviation duty. In mid-summer, Chambers would bring him to the Washington Navy Yard, where aviation experimentation was under way. There, Richardson not only would continue his pontoon work but also would team with Chambers, who was developing a catapult design.

As the birth of his first child approached, Mustin applied himself more to solving gunnery problems than to venturing with Reid on his aerial escapades, although the pair continued occasionally to fly together and work on various design issues. On 30 July, Lloyd Montague was born. If marriage to Corinne had compromised some of the sailor in Mustin, having a child prompted in him a desire to "hold on to the beach" even more.

All along, Mustin and other officers in Philadelphia witnessed the military potential of aviation, and usually it was demonstrated by the visiting Europeans. On 20 May 1911, British aircraft aviator-designer Thomas O. M. Sopwith, of Camel fame, had landed a Howard Wright biplane unexpectedly near the main barracks, making the Philadelphia Navy Yard's first landing. On 6 April 1912, Belgian aviator M. V. de Jonckhere, in a night demonstration of his Bleriot monoplane, simulated a spectacular attack on the battleship *Massachusetts*. His Marine friend 1st Lt. Alfred A. Cunningham was duly impressed and thereupon rented a biplane and kept it at the yard. He never got it off the ground, but by mid-year, he was in Annapolis for aviation training. Cunningham also was instrumental in getting the Aero Club to lobby for a Marine aviation facility at League Island.

By now, the Navy was eager to have the Annapolis contingent participate in fleet exercises off Guantánamo. Not yet ready to demonstrate convincing capability, however, they chose to winter again in early 1912 at North Island, this time establishing their own camp to house the Navy's Wright B-1 aircraft. On their return to Annapolis in the spring to a new site beside the Experiment Station, training fell into three competitive categories: the Curtiss camp, the Wright camp, and the Marine camp.

Chambers also was driving experimentation to prove that aircraft could be used with combatants. The battleship commanders certainly did not want planes on their ships or cruisers—platforms masked gun turrets and restricted firing arcs—and he feared they would relegate aircraft to auxiliary ships. Chambers was betting on the hydroplane, with the advantage that it could launch by monorail, taut wire, or catapult and be retrieved from the water. Hydroplanes also would not require additional funds for airfield construction.

Thus, Chambers put his full weight behind the catapult. Working for him at the Washington Navy Yard, Richardson and Lt. St. Clair Smith designed and built the first compressed-air catapult using torpedo tube components. On 31 July, Ellyson tested the device on the Severn, but it launched the plane into the river. Returning to the yard, the team on 12 November repeated the experiment successfully from a barge in the Anacostia River. On 17 December, Ellyson succeeded again, this time in the Navy's first flying boat, the C-1, proving that a cat could launch both types of planes.

The fleet commanders still questioned how much operational value aviation could provide. Ellyson's classmate and friend Lt. Chester Nimitz, the future World War II five-star Pacific commander in chief, at the time commander of Atlantic Fleet submarines, wondered whether aviators aloft could spot subs. In October, he brought his submarines to Annapolis, where they conducted submerged exercises at the mouth of the Severn while aviators flew reconnaissance above. The water was too murky, and the results were inconclusive. Nevertheless, the Navy allowed one participating submarine commander, Lt. (jg) P. N. L. Bellinger, to transfer to the aviation camp for training. That autumn, the General Board recommended that the Annapolis contingent operate with the fleet during maneuvers in January 1913. By mid-December, the aviation camp was readying for the move to Guantánamo Bay. Within months, the operating Navy would have some idea of aviation's practical worth.

In March 1912, Mustin started flying lessons with Reid on his own time and thus began to devote himself more and more to aviation. Officially, however, he still was very active in gunnery, notably the testing of the new bore sight. One of his issues involved prototyping an interference plate to mount a sight adjuster on the gun slide of a 14-inch gun. For the parallel interference plates, Mustin was testing varieties of glass and metal to find ones with the same coefficient of expansion. His contractor support came from his colleague George Saegmuller. Married with a second child on the way, Mustin pushed Saegmuller's firm and the Bureau of Ordnance harder than ever to forward the back royalties he felt they owed him.

Throughout the autumn, Saegmuller lobbied both the Bureau of Ordnance and his firm's attorneys to resolve the issue, but he had his own problem with the Navy. During a visit to the Washington Navy Yard, Saegmuller had seen a copy of his firm's bore-sight telescope identified as manufactured by the New York firm K&E Co.—a patent infringement. Evidently, the Navy was using the K&E device as a turret sight. He wrote that he was trying to settle their royalty issues before Mustin went to sea.

Mustin was getting impatient. He knew he soon would get orders to a ship, and he was not looking forward to it. His inventive spirit was drawing him to aviation, and he saw that aviation experimentation would remain on shore for the foreseeable future. He also passionately wanted to remain with Corinne, Lloyd, and the new baby that was due in the spring. It dawned on him that an aviation career could pull all the facets of his life together. In October, he decided to team with Reid in a highly risky aviation gambit.

Ever the adventurer, Reid was keen to establish a distance record for the hydroplane. For Mustin, pontoons still were a key design issue, and he was eager to prove to the Navy their worth, as well as the hydroplane's distance capabilities. After some effort, he was able to secure approval to fly with Reid in a semiofficial capacity and file a report. Mustin was hoping the flight would catapult him into the national limelight and consequently induce the Navy to assign him to a billet that would give him a voice in the progress of events.

The plan was to fly Reid's plane from Cape May Point, New Jersey, across the Delaware Bay and up the river to League Island in a daring attempt to capture both the hydroplane distance and altitude records. The pair took to the air at 1:42 P.M. on Saturday, 11 October. Leaving Cape May, they ascended to two hundred feet and ran about eighteen miles to the very wildest part of the bay. Half an hour into the flight and unable to see land on either side, Reid had to steer by the sun. Suddenly, the motor exploded, sending shards of metal past the aviators' heads. The hydro went down like a shot.

On the water, the shaken but unhurt pilots took twenty minutes to extinguish the fire started by the explosion. By then it was evident that the hard landing had caused a pontoon leak. Removing the air cap, they siphoned the water with their mouths, taking turns virtually nonstop.

When the plane failed to arrive in Philadelphia, wireless messages were transmitted to naval and commercial vessels all along the Atlantic coast. Late in the afternoon, Mustin and Reid sighted sails from oyster boats some two miles away. They yelled for an hour to no avail. Night fell quickly, and soon it was pitch dark and foggy. They were fortunate, however. On a flood tide, they made some headway up the bay toward land. At about 11:00 P.M., they bumped into a stake in the oyster beds. Securing the hydro to the stake with wire from the wing struts, they held fast as the tide flowed back to the sea.

About midnight, they sighted the lights of another sailing vessel and called for help. "What is it?" came the reply through the darkness. "Aeroplane adrift!" "What is it?" repeated the other half a dozen times. "Help! Help!" the aviators screamed. "We're wrecked in an airship!" "Oh, hell," a skeptical voice huffed, and the windjammer continued on her course.

Sunday at 5:00 A.M., the wind shifted with the flood tide, and they cast off. They were headed toward the mouth of the Maurice River on the New Jersey side. It still was dark at about 6:45 when they sighted and hailed a Jersey oyster police patrol boat, the *Lelia Boyle,* en route to Port Norris. Although Captain Bacon of the *Lelia Boyle* had caught one of the numerous wireless messages, his business was to guard the oyster beds. Hearing their cries for help, he believed them to be oystermen or even poachers. "Stop your kidding and show your light," he snapped. Once it became apparent they were the missing aviators, Bacon brought the pair on board, took the hydro under tow, and gave them breakfast and a couple of clay pipes of tobacco.

They had failed in their attempt to set hydroplane records, and that failure hit Mustin hard. He dutifully reported to the Navy his conclusion that hydroplane pontoons had to be absolutely seaworthy. Inside, however, he was despondent and feeling somewhat foolish.

On 15 October, he wrote to Sims, griping about the Navy's lack of interest in aviation. Sims replied promptly on the twenty-first, assuring him that the Naval War College was discussing it "in connection with scouting." Sims was displeased that Mustin had attempted to make a record flight when he could have just gathered performance data. He agreed that the Navy was not doing enough development and was dependent on private enterprise, but he did not think any officer was justified "either personally or officially, in taking part in flights, involving considerable danger, the purpose of which is advertising for the professional," that is, a private entrepreneur.

Responding to Mustin's worry over how his brother officers now viewed him, Sims wrote, "Concerning your particular adventure, I can assure you that nobody that I have talked with considers you anything approaching a 'fool,' much less an 'ass.' Some said: 'That's just like Musty; he's not afraid of anything.'

"I know what you are worth to the service better than most men, and my kick was that you are too valuable a man to take any *unnecessary* risk of having your light put out."

Sims wanted Mustin to continue "work in development of a practicable 'seagoing' (fleet-going) hydroplane for the service, and to make a cruise with it—but all the same, do not despise the regular work in the fleet." Those in the fleet, he noted, "are commencing to do real work there, and you will find heaps to interest you in developing fleet efficiency." Recognizing "Musty" was in need of a fillip, he lastly exhorted him to "Remain Cheerful."

Saegmuller, too, counseled caution upon hearing of the abortive flight and worried over Mustin's predilection for risk taking. He was also not the bearer of good news on the matter of their royalties. Mustin's position had been that his patent on his indirect vision prism for the Mark XIII covered the Mark XIV, XV, and XVII and that Saegmuller's firm owed him royalties for those telescopes as well. The firm's attorney maintained that Mustin's patent covered indirect sighting only: The firm did not regard sighting modifications to the latest telescopes as indirect. In a 15 October letter, Saegmuller explained the firm's position. Mustin's patent, he wrote, covered "mainly the combinations of the prisms at the eye-piece by means of which the image is erected, and when we abandoned the prism system the erection of the image had to be done by means of lenses, which, however, is nothing new, as it has been done long ago."

Saegmuller tried to reassure Mustin that he was endeavoring to enforce their earlier patents with the Navy. He asked what minimum he would accept and found that Mustin wanted a lot. Saegmuller observed in his letter of 19 October that he was asking for "a pretty stiff royalty." In the end, he succeeded in getting Mustin modest sums. As frustrating as these battles might have been, Mustin put the additional income to good use over the next year to ease the several moves Corinne would have to make while he was at sea.

By now optics clearly were no longer his primary interest. His failed attempt with Reid notwithstanding, Mustin knew he was an aviator at heart. He resolved to follow Sims's advice: Work on hydroplane development, and the next time he went into the air, do it in a Navy machine.

Before leaving Philadelphia, he made a public case for a flying field at the yard. When the German naval training ship *Hansa* was visiting later that autumn, the Navy hosted a gala review that generated a lot of press coverage. Among the statements reported in the papers were Mustin's carefully chosen words that Philadelphia was an ideal location for a naval air facility. He said he was forwarding a proposal to the Navy Department and that he envisaged "a great government central station for aeroplanes and hydroplanes of both the Navy and Army."

Mustin had concluded that Philadelphia was ideal for overland machines, as well as having water for hydros, an artificial beach that was immune to tidal fluctuations, floating hangars, up-to-date machine shops for both constructive and repair work, and air conditions favorable for both experimentation and actual flight. "They have a good course at Annapolis, but no shops," he told the press. "At Washington, they have good shops, but the course is not good. New York is out of the question because of the crowded condition of the harbor. So it goes. Norfolk, Portsmouth, all the other yards, have handicaps that are not encountered here. Skilled labor of the highest type is to be found in Philadelphia and supplies for every requirement."

His words were prophetic. In 1917, the yard would get the Naval Aircraft Factory, for nearly thirty years the nation's only government-owned and government-operated aircraft facility and for a time the only major aircraft plant that also manufactured engines. In 1926, it would dedicate Mustin Field in honor of Philadelphia's native son.

On 3 December 1912, Mustin was detached from the yard with orders to report for duty on the battleship *Minnesota* as first lieutenant. He joined the ship on 1 January 1913 and almost immediately went to sea in preparation for the winter fleet maneuvers off Guantánamo. In addition to readying the ship's departments for the tactical problems they would exercise, Mustin now was determined to qualify as an aviator. While the *Minnesota* was in Guantánamo, he planned to spend time with the Annapolis aviation contingent encamped at Fisherman's Bay.

The aviators had left Annapolis on 6 January. When they embarked on the collier *Sterling* with the Curtiss A-2 and A-3, the Wright B-1 and B-2, and the Curtiss C-1 flying boat, it was the first naval aircraft deployment aboard ship. Towers, Bellinger, Herbster, Cunningham, Ens. Godfrey de C. Chevalier, and 1st Lt. Bernie Smith, USMC, and their planes arrived in Guantánamo on the tenth and prepared for winter training.

The detachment also was charged with participating in the fleet exercises. At the outset, the commander in chief of the Atlantic Fleet, Rear Adm. Charles J. Badger, was skeptical, but Chambers was determined to get senior officers of the Atlantic Fleet into the air and converted to aviation proponents. Among his marks was Capt. William A. Moffett, who commanded the scout cruiser *Chester*. The initial overture was unsuccessful. Looking for an opportunity to proselytize, the aviators took Moffett duck hunting and broached the subject of aviation. Moffett's response was that an aviator was "either crazy or else a plain damned fool."

When Mustin arrived, no pitch was required. He logged his first flight on 30 January. His intent was to seek instruction to qualify, but no sooner had he gotten started than the *Minnesota* embarked for Panama. Mustin expected the hiatus to be brief; the ship was off Colon for only a few days, and on 9 February, got under way back to Guantánamo.

During this time, Mustin's inventive side was working overtime, impelled now by aviation problems. On 15 February, he wrote Corinne, "Today I nearly completed my drawings for a patent application on my 'seagoing' aeroplane, and it looks very good to me; the papers will be ready to send on to my attorneys inside of a week. Practically all my spare time is taken up with this invention."

Arriving back at Guantánamo, the *Minnesota* unexpectedly began all-night coaling, to ready for possible deployment to Mexico. In the latest chapter in the Mexican

Revolution, on 9 February, Gen. Victoriano Huerta had taken power in a coup that ousted Francisco I. Madero, who had won a reasonably honest election in May 1911.

Four days later, however, Mustin remained in Guantánamo. "Here we are still, in spite of rumors of Mexican trouble," he wrote to Corinne. "At present we are under sailing orders at 24 hours notice to go to Vera Cruz and occupy it with a landing force of seamen & marines, until the arrival of the army 3 weeks from the time we start from here. However, the news today is peaceful and the impression is gaining that we never will have to go to Mexico." Mustin was in no mood to be a hero, leading a contingent of bluejackets. His second child was on the way, and he hoped his deployment would finish in time for him to be present at the birth.

Events in Mexico played out without immediate U.S. intervention, and on 24 February the *Minnesota* began a week of fleet exercises, affording Mustin no time for either aviation training or seaplane design. Two days into the maneuvers, he wrote to Corinne, "On this trip I haven't been able to work very consistently at my inventions because the tactical problems keep me on deck a good part of the day and at night we steam without lights." He was not able to break from his regular duties and return to Fisherman's Bay for a second training flight until 5 March.

As the exercises progressed, the aviators continued taking senior officers into the air. Working around the fleet commander's initial skepticism, they lobbied to have their aircraft participate in fleet maneuvers. On 6 March, Badger ordered them to do an air search for a hostile fleet of battleships, the first tactical maneuver using aircraft. The aviation detachment dropped missiles and bombs, spotted Nimitz's submerged submarines, detected mines, tested radio transmissions, and took photographs.

Aviation was beginning to prove its capabilities, in particular to Admiral Badger. Aware that he still had contingency plans for a possible intervention in Mexico, the aviators pushed their reconnaissance scouting capability as support for a Vera Cruz landing. Badger was now convinced and began to plan for operations from both water and shore, prompting experimentation with attaching a rig for wheels to the hydros.

In Washington, the Wilson administration took office on 4 March, and Josephus Daniels assumed the helm at the Navy Department as secretary. A progressive and teetotaling southern newspaper publisher, Daniels did not engender great expectations in the fleet. Mustin was among the many pessimists. "We have just heard that Daniels is the new Secretary of the Navy," he wrote Corinne. "Some people here say he is a 'little Navy' man, others say he is not. In any case I am afraid the next four years will not be a prosperous one for the service,—any branch of it. . . . As for service aviation appropriations, I believe this government is now behind China!"

Daniels came into office wanting to dismantle the powers of the conservative officers in the bureaus. Ironically, this effort would make him an uncertain ally of aviation. As his senior administrative officer, Daniels inherited Bradley Fiske. A freshly minted rear admiral, Fiske was aligned with the younger insurgent reformers and publicly disposed to aviation. In service to his strategic plan for naval aviation to play a role in the defense of the Philippines, he was designing and would patent a torpedo-launching aircraft.

The prospects for naval aviation actually were encouraging. The deployment to Guantánamo had yielded results. In addition to their successful participation in fleet exercises, the aviators had fulfilled both their promotional efforts and their winter training mission. They had taken aloft more than two hundred fleet officers and had incurred no personnel injuries.

On 13 March, they were ready to conclude their last day of operations before striking camp and leaving for Annapolis. One of the last log entries of the morning was for Mustin, who wanted to complete his flight instruction. Bellinger gave him the up-check for his first solo, and before noon, Mustin had passed the test for his hydroplane pilot's license. He was now an aviator and poised to request aviation duty.

That month, the fleet got the news that Daniels was cleaning house, forcing the bureaus' conservative senior officers to sea by increasing the sea time requirements for promotion. In addition, word was out that Fiske was not happy with Chambers, who probably would be relieved.

With that intelligence, Mustin resolved to lobby for Chambers's job as head of naval aviation. With almost four years in grade as a lieutenant commander, Mustin reckoned he might have the seniority to qualify. On 1 April, Daniels directed that those naval officers who had soloed would get aviation duty and a 50 percent increase in pay. Mustin had gotten in just under the wire.

In late March, the *Minnesota* returned, but to Old Point Comfort, Norfolk, not Philadelphia. Mustin would not be there for the birth of his second child on 27 March—another boy, Henry Ashmead. Mustin was able, however, to make a quick trip to Washington to lobby for Chambers's job. Among the officers with whom he met was Spuds Ellyson. In his 5 April letter to Corinne, he wrote, "Much to my surprise I soon found out that Ellyson,—although he said he wanted me to be chief—had entertained hopes of getting the job himself." Mustin impressed on Ellyson that it would be in the best interest of his career to go to sea. He continued, "Several people there yesterday told me they had heard I was a candidate for the job so the matter has leaked out."

Mustin counted on Chambers's support, and by some accounts he had it. Unfortunately, he could not continue working his contacts in Washington. The *Minnesota* was returning to sea to observe a week of target practice and was due in Philadelphia for an inspection on 20 April. Once in his home port, Mustin was able to see his new son and family only very briefly. The Mexican crisis suddenly turned for the worse, and the *Minnesota* departed the Delaware Bay on 16 April, bound once again for Mexican waters.

Violence between rival Mexican forces was escalating, threatening U.S. interests, and relations between the Wilson administration and General Huerta had deteriorated. Although his Republican predecessors' policy was to recognize de facto governments in the interest of stability, Wilson wanted Huerta out. He would have the United States mediate a truce between the Constitutionalists and Huerta, if the latter would agree to hold elections.

The *Minnesota* made an eight-day run to Vera Cruz. This time, Mustin was unsure of his fate. Worried about the welfare of his family, he instructed Saegmuller to send his royalty checks directly to Corinne, and on 23 April, he made a will leaving her all.

The ship would remain on station to protect Americans from the revolutionary violence raging in the hinterlands. Mustin remained on board continuously, spending a great deal of his time on patent drawings of deep-sea flying boats. He still was working with Reid on concepts and while in Norfolk had seen his flying boat. Mustin claimed in a letter to Corinne that one of Reid's backers, the Washington Aeroplane Co., would give them a license. Evidently still believing he had a shot at the Chambers billet, he added, "but not a sole one because it would put him in an embarrassing position if he becomes chief of aviation."

On 9 May a frustrated Mustin wrote from his station in Vera Cruz. Huerta was trying to get U.S. recognition for his government. "There is no point in doing gunboat duty," he wrote. "There is no excuse for our having a lot of gunboats if they don't do their legitimate duty, which is just this sort of thing, and let the battleship fleet remain intact for drilling in battle maneuvers and all the other exercises it should be having and is sadly in need of before we can call it a real fleet; it is very much of a bluff at present and always will be as long as the State Department butts in on our regular work, which it seldom fails to do about once each year.

"However, I think Huerta has got a pretty good grip on the situation; the rebels are being driven back pretty well all through the rebellious states, and if the money does become entirely exhausted the rebellion will soon be over; then Bill Bryan [Wilson's secretary of state] will have to let us go home. So I am strong for Huerta, more power to him!"

Huerta refused mediation into the summer. On 27 August, Wilson went before Congress to urge Americans to leave Mexico. The president announced an embargo on arms shipments from the United States to Mexico and put in place his "Watchful Waiting" policy. Only the landlocked Constitutionalists in the north suffered from this naive gesture. Huerta still had the ability to get arms via his ports.

When the *Minnesota* finally returned home, she joined the fleet homeported for the summer in New England. Thanks to help from Sims and his wife, Anne, who still were in Newport, the Mustins took a cottage in Jamestown, Rhode Island. The fleet often was under way on maneuvers, however, so a sustained home life eluded Mustin once more. On 2 September, he wrote from Old Point. "Dearest, I am so homesick for you and my babies; I don't believe I have the proper disposition for a naval officer; a few weeks separation from my family makes me discontented with everything connected with the service; and so I am never happy when I am at sea." He could look forward to some recompense, however. Mid-month, he would serve as chief umpire on the battleship *Arkansas,* which was conducting target practice. For the first time, he would be able to witness his sights in use.

Mustin continued inventing, turning his attention now to catapults. In a letter of 7 September he wrote, "While I was at breakfast I conceived an idea for a machine for launching an aeroplane from a ship's deck. It was so simple that I was able to work out the whole thing before dinner this evening. It is very fine and I am quite sure it will be a success." He hoped the idea would help him on one of two fronts—in his quest to replace Chambers, or if he had to go to sea again, in getting him orders to the *Chester,* expected to be the first ship to operate with aircraft aboard. "I want to use this thing as a lever to get the job [of director of naval aviation], so I am going to submit plans and description to the Department, showing how nicely it can be applied to the *Chester.* (However, I will send copies of the same plans to the patent office first!)"

Evidently, Ellyson had told him that Chambers's catapult was a failure, for he added, "It seems kind of 'low down' to invent something that will knock out Captain Chamber's pet scheme, but as Ellyson says he wouldn't use that catapult from the deck of a battleship for any amount of money, and as something reliable of the kind is an absolute necessity for the Naval Aeroplane, I will have to go ahead. In the mean time I will have to suspend work on my flying boat plans, which I don't like to do; but that can wait a while, and any way this other thing is so simple,—comparatively,—that it will only delay me a few days from the other job."

By now, Europe clearly was pulling ahead of the United States in aviation. Although an American invention, the airplane was viewed by many as a toy for the wealthy, and thus the United States did not pursue development aggressively after 1910. In 1914, some twenty U.S. manufacturers would produce forty-nine planes annually. The Navy had just eight, five of which were Curtiss. By contrast, European governments were very involved in aircraft development and more aware of the plane's military potential. By 1911–12, they had spent millions, whereas the U.S. Navy and Army had authority to spend less than $100,000.

The summer of 1913 did not begin well. On 20 June, the Navy lost its first aviator in a mishap over the Chesapeake, when Ens. William D. Billingsley plunged to his death from a two-seater Wright B-2. On 1 July, Fiske finally retired Chambers, although the Navy kept him on board as a technical adviser. Daniels wanted the director of naval aviation to have two years' sea duty in grade, which Chambers did not have. As the Navy searched for his replacement, Fiske for a time considered quitting as aide for operations to take the post.

By late summer, events were moving in a more positive direction. On 30 August, Dewey and the General Board recommended establishment of a naval air service. In October, the Navy chartered a board to make a comprehensive plan for organizing such a service and placed Chambers in charge. Serving with him were Cunningham, Richardson, Towers (by now regarded as the best and most experienced aviator, teacher, and administrator of flying activities), and some nonaviators from the Bureaus of Navigation, Ordnance, and Steam Engineering.

The Chambers board reported in November, proposing to establish the Office of Naval Aeronautics (directed by a captain), test facilities, and an aeronautical center. It further recommended assignment of a training ship, the battleship *Mississippi,* along with fifty planes and lighter-than-air equipment. Annapolis was requested as the aviation center, but the board instead got Pensacola, which was somewhat dilapidated but good for year-round flying.

Mustin's shot at Chambers's job had missed its mark; on 23 November Capt. Mark L. Bristol assumed command of the Office of Naval Aeronautics as director of naval aviation. Having some idea that Bristol was a good administrator, Fiske had prevailed on him to take the post, notwithstanding his lack of aviation experience. A veteran of the Spanish-American War, Bristol was a battleship officer with ordnance, gunnery, and torpedo expertise. He also was known as an advocate of the Navy Department reorganization and consolidation efforts of former Secretary of the Navy Truman H. Newberry.

Bristol's distinguished record included one item that troubled traditional ship-handlers such as Mustin. In mid-1912, as captain of the protected cruiser *Albany* on the China Station, he had given the quartermaster at the helm a wrong course that grounded the ship off Lamock Island, southeast of Amoy. As a result, Bristol faced a court-martial and had to scramble to save his career. In the end, he escaped a reprimand but was admonished.

Thus, Bristol came ashore to Washington with a burning need to prove himself. He would spend the next year sharing Fiske's desk, and, like Chambers, he would find himself with no executive authority. In the minds of working-level aviators such as Mustin, he would prove less of an aviation advocate than a bureaucratic meddler. More often than not, they found a better ally for advancing aviation technology in Rear Adm. David W. Taylor, who was appointed to head the Bureau of Construction and Repair at same time Bristol took the helm as director of naval aviation.

Mustin would not direct the next chapter of naval aviation, but he did get a consolation prize: orders to be executive officer of the *Mississippi,* then in Philadelphia. On 31 December, Mustin reported to the venerable ship as executive officer with acting command, which he very much hoped to retain. The following day, the Navy put in place a new certification policy for aviators. According to the 1 January 1914 ranking, Ellyson was Navy pilot number 1; Towers was number 2; and Mustin was number 3.

On 6 January, Bristol directed Mustin to regard his primary task as training pilots and his secondary task as conducting experiments. However, the director designated Towers as the aviation detachment commander in charge of the actual flying, leaving Mustin to be in charge of the *Mississippi* and shore facility. Although the aviators were close friends, Bristol's delineation accentuated Mustin's competitiveness and made fuzzy the lines of authority.

Later in the month, Mustin brought the *Mississippi* and the collier *Orion* to Annapolis to transfer Towers's aviation detachment to Pensacola. Mustin's ship carried Towers and the largest assemblage of U.S. naval aircraft to date: five flying boats and two hydros. It was a tough passage, with two days of high winds and choppy seas, and Mustin handled the ship throughout. On a cold, overcast 20 January, the detachment of some nine officers and two dozen enlisted mechanics arrived a day late in Pensacola. Mustin conned the ship into the harbor and docked without a tug or a pilot. He was sure the feat would go a long way toward his retaining command. Immediately Bellinger and his crew began two days of unloading planes and supplies.

Pensacola was in shambles. The hurricane of 1906 had wrecked buildings and strewn debris all along the waterfront. Closed in October 1911 as an economic measure, the 1,800-acre base was reopened by Daniels in December 1913 in response to increasing tensions in Mexico. A detail of marines already was ensconced in those buildings onshore that still were serviceable. Mustin and his officers and mechanics remained on the *Mississippi*.

Getting the site ready for flight operations and training was a colossal undertaking. Mustin pushed the men hard and was able to begin operations within two weeks. The first flight was on 2 February.

Once Pensacola was up and running, Bristol arrived from Washington and remained through most of February. Regarded as an unpleasant person, he embittered many aviators, including Mustin, Bellinger, and Richardson.

It soon became apparent that Mustin and Bellinger would disagree with their boss on most operational and administrative matters. Bristol intended Pensacola to provide only training for the student aviators; Mustin and Bellinger wanted to conduct experiments as well. Bristol did not want the Navy beholden to one aircraft supplier; Mustin and the aviators were unhappy with the Wright machines. These so-called pushers had the engines behind the pilots—a hazardous construct in a crash. Moreover, the Wright planes' controls were complicated, compared with those of the Curtiss planes. The aviators felt that Curtiss was the only reliable seaplane operation left. Lt. (jg) James D. Murray and Herbster had specialized with Wrights and now were getting retrained in the Curtiss. On 16 February, some two weeks into flight operations, Bristol was still present when Murray crashed and died in the Burgess-Curtiss D-1 flying boat, an event that probably induced the DNA to want to exercise more oversight.

Administration was never ending. With six of his aviators having workloads aside from air duty, Mustin made requests to Bristol for all manner of support. In Washington, however, Bristol had trouble getting the requisitions past Louis Howe, the gatekeeper in the office of Assistant Secretary of the Navy Franklin D. Roosevelt.

Mustin and Towers pressed ahead, writing the formal training syllabus. Determined to train with an operational orientation, they included a section on mine spotting in offshore waters—a topic that would find application sooner rather than later in the Mexican port of Vera Cruz.

Chapter 7

A High Type in Vera Cruz

On 13 October 1913, General Huerta assumed dictatorial powers over Mexico. The Constitutionalists responded by increasing their offensive into the Tampico oil fields, threatening the extensive production facilities and vital U.S. interests. In an effort to compel them to cease their anti-Huerta operations, Rear Adm. Frank F. Fletcher, commander of U.S. naval forces off the east coast of Mexico, concentrated his ships off Tampico. An ordnance officer of distinction, Fletcher flew his flag on the battleship *Rhode Island,* remaining primarily off Vera Cruz. He assigned the Tampico duty to newly promoted Rear Adm. Henry T. Mayo, who had just arrived from assignment in Washington as Daniels's aide.

Not much happened for several months. U.S. naval units had been off the coast since 1912, and by early 1914, President Wilson had grown impatient with his efforts to thwart Huerta. On 3 February, he revoked the arms embargo. While his action may have pleased the Constitutionalists, it pushed the Mexican propertied classes into the dictator's camp and suddenly polarized the political situation.

On 9 April, Huerta's authorities in Tampico seized and held a number of U.S. sailors who had gone ashore to purchase gasoline. Although the Mexicans released the men after less than two hours, Mayo insisted on a gun salute to the U.S. colors. The local *commandante* refused. Presumably acting unilaterally but possibly acting on advance instructions from Daniels to take advantage of such an incident, Mayo threatened armed intervention. While the State Department wrestled with the diplomatic repercussions, Mayo and Daniels worked on a plan to seize Tampico. By now determined to oust Huerta, Wilson supported them.

On 10 April, Sims arrived in Pensacola on the cruiser *Birmingham,* flying his flag as commander of destroyer squadrons en route to Tampico. Armed with the knowledge that the Atlantic commander in chief, Admiral Badger, supported the use of their aviation unit in any Mexican intervention, Mustin and Towers went on board to discuss with Sims his requirements. Together, they secured Navy Department authorization for three planes for the ship.

Badger got orders on 14 April to concentrate his fleet off the Mexican coast with the expectation that a U.S. force would intervene in Tampico per Mayo's plan. On the eighteenth, however, Washington's attention shifted. The U.S. consul in Vera Cruz had sent word to the State Department that the *Ypiranga,* a Hamburg-American liner, was loaded with arms for Huerta and scheduled to arrive in Vera Cruz on the twenty-first. Wilson's new priority was to prevent his Mexican nemesis from getting those weapons. Mayo, however, was reluctant to redeploy his units, arguing that such a move would put U.S. citizens in Tampico at risk. Fletcher would have to proceed without him.

On Sunday, 19 April, Mustin was having lunch with Sims on board the *Birmingham* when the radio order arrived, sending the destroyers to Tampico. Mustin expeditiously rigged the ship with a derrick for the aircraft and assigned Towers, Smith, and Chevalier to go aboard with the C-5 and the A-4, with the C-4 and E-1 as spares. The *Birmingham* departed Pensacola later that day. Ever the tactician, Mustin anticipated possible aircraft operations ashore and had Smith make a land chassis for the A-4. He wrote Bristol the next day boasting that he had suspected an imminent intervention and had thought in advance what the *Birmingham* would need, based on drawings of her ship class.

Washington was ready for its naval forces to intercept the *Ypiranga.* The Navy could not seize the cargo of Remington rifles as contraband; the United States was not at war with Huerta. Instead, the plan was to confiscate the arms as they went through customs at Vera Cruz—thus requiring a landing. On 21 April, Daniels ordered the occupation of the customs house in Vera Cruz.

No sooner had the *Birmingham* left Pensacola than the Navy Department ordered

Mustin to assemble a second aviation section (Bellinger and three trainees), together with his five hundred marines, and to make way on the *Mississippi* for Vera Cruz. He quickly readied the ship and loaded aboard the C-3, the A-3, and four motors, plus instruments. He had Smith build another land chassis for the A-3.

The Vera Cruz operation would be the first U.S. employment of military aircraft in a hostile environment. The Italians and Spanish had flown aircraft in combat in their North African colonies, and Greek aircraft had seen action in the Balkans, but Mustin's operation would be a first for a major naval power. Competitive to a fault, he was keen to see his section fly into harm's way before Towers's.

Readied, Mustin virtually followed the *Birmingham*'s wake from Pensacola. The trip's first hours brought him another occasion to demonstrate his ship-handling abilities. Although there were some mechanical malfunctions in one of the engine-room telegraph systems, he was able to leave the dock "in fine style in spite of not having a tug." After a dozy pilot gave the wrong order to the helm, Mustin took the ship away from him "instantly" before the ship could go aground. "As it was, I don't believe we escaped by more than a foot, for it took all my knowledge of handling a twin screw ship to work her out of the corner of the channel against the ebb tide. . . . When we got into blue water I breathed a very large sigh of relief and vowed that was my first and last time for taking a pilot at Pensacola!"

During the passage to Vera Cruz, Mustin worked on his inventions to keep from being idle. For the other approximately nine hundred "souls" on board, he wrote, the ship's band was "a great help although its selections are mostly of the zoological class of music, suitable for the so called modern dances, most of which were well known by my bluejackets as far back as the Spanish War."

Writing to Bristol on 20 April, he asked, "Are we beating the Army to it?" He wanted the operational flexibility of the land chassis for his planes, if for no other reason than to prevent the Army from assuming tactical control. The nearest Army planes were in Texas and unable to get to Vera Cruz. Mustin saw that he could demonstrate operational capabilities for naval aviation that the rival service did not possess.

On 22 April, the Vera Cruz landing commenced with Capt. William Moffett, still in command of the *Chester,* bringing his ship into the harbor at 12:05 A.M. At sea, Mustin heard the report. "Our radio picked up the press news about the seizure of the Custom house at Vera Cruz in which five marines were killed and twenty wounded. It is too bad there has had to be bloodshed but it is a blessing in one way for now the

Administration can't postpone settling the Mexican question; the 'dove of peace' business is over now."

Mustin also wrote that the ship's radio intercepted a cipher from the Navy Department to Admiral Badger on the *Arkansas,* warning that the Mexicans had planted a mine eastward of the Vera Cruz breakwater. "If it is true, here is a job right away for my aeroplanes for we can locate it about 15 minutes. I am therefore hoping that we reach Vera Cruz before the *Birmingham* so this aeroplane section can steal a march on the first section!"

By then, Mayo had gotten all Americans out of Tampico and on board ships, away from the rioting in the city. On 23 April, a special train from Mexico City carrying U.S. embassy staff arrived in Vera Cruz. The next day, Friday, the so-called ABC (Argentina, Brazil, and Chile) powers offered to mediate the crisis, and Wilson accepted.

Both the *Mississippi* and *Birmingham* arrived on their stations late on 24 April. At 9:00 P.M. Mustin anchored his ship close to the Vera Cruz breakwater. With both his aircraft "assembled and hooked on ready for hoisting," he met with Badger, who briefed him on the situation and advised him to make no flights until he went ashore and reported to Fletcher, which he did at 5:30 the following morning. Fletcher instructed him both to search for mines and to scout the condition of the railroad bridges around Vera Cruz, which were important tactical factors for troop movements.

Mustin liaised with Col. John A. Lejeune, who commanded the brigade of marines the *Mississippi* had just reinforced, to get the first of his scouting flight assignments. Returning to his ship, he shifted berth to a point near the breakwater entrance and, within five minutes of anchoring, had Bellinger aloft in the C-3 flying boat to look for the reported mine. Naval aviators regard the flight as noteworthy because it was the first use of naval air in support of a military operation in a combat environment. It also would be the first in a record forty-eight days of continuous flying, in all kinds of weather. Bellinger was twenty-eight minutes in the air.

The water actually was too rough for Bellinger to make a satisfactory inspection for a mine; his effort was more effective over land. According to one newspaper account, which might have compressed separate events into one day, his flight

sailed over the city and out to the westward on a reconnoitering expedition to ascertain the location and number of troops now being gathered by General Maas to attack the city. . . . The navy flyers with their machines arrived this morning from Pensacola on the battleship *Mississippi.* . . . No time was lost in assembling the machines, and at 11 o'clock one was ready for flight. It rose slowly to a height of several hundred feet, and the aviator circled about over the city and toward the sand hill, in the hope of getting a glimpse of General Maas' position. . . . This first flight was a brief one, later two hydro-aeroplanes went up almost simultaneously and sped away to the westward to inspect the entire section which was being held by the Mexican troops. . . . The aviators were provided with a stock of bombs, so that if fired upon by the Mexicans they could return the compliment, the men were under orders to report back at intervals to Rear Admiral Fletcher with any information they might have obtained.

Bellinger returned, landed on the water, collected Ens. Melvin Stoltz, one of the trainees, and took to the air from inside the breakwater for a second fifty-minute flight at 1,200 feet. Mustin immediately recognized that to enable continuous air operations, he would have to take his ship inside the breakwater for smooth water. Operating from land would be even better, as he had anticipated when he insisted they deploy with the land chassis rigs.

Mustin shifted berth again and got an order to transfer his planes to the beach inside the outer breakwater, where they could get into the air no matter how rough the water. On Sunday, he ferried the C-3 and Bellinger took the A-3 to the beach. By midday, they had both planes assembled with land chassis.

In response to a request from Lejeune, Mustin sent Bellinger and Lt. (jg) Richard C. Saufley to scout in the A-3. Saufley used a military map to locate the railroad bridges to determine which were destroyed and what parts of the railroad had been removed. They first headed north at seven hundred feet for twelve miles along the coast before turning ten miles inland, following a river. The pair found seven cavalrymen and a railroad bridge intact but track removed for two hundred yards on either side. They then circled and returned to traverse the city and go beyond fifteen miles to the south before finally landing at the camp. During the reconnaissance, the aviators flew over half a dozen towns. Mustin wrote that they "spread consternation among the inhabitants who all fled indoors; the cattle also were stampeded!" The flight provided "very good information," he continued. "I have now arranged that two principal scouting flights will be made each day, one between 6 and 8 in the morning, the other between 3 P.M. and sunset." When the pair returned, Mustin ordered Saufley to report his observations to Lejeune and Fletcher.

On 27 April, calmer weather allowed Bellinger in the C-3 to make a more successful sweep over the water, to establish finally that the harbor and anchorage were clear.

Just before midnight, the Army transports arrived. The troops began landing in the early morning. Realizing the crisis had now seriously deepened, Huerta agreed to a mediation by Argentina, Brazil, and Colombia.

The U.S. Army had arrived without its airplanes. The following day, Mustin asked Fletcher to order Towers and Smith to join him with their A-4 and its land chassis and to issue orders to Ellyson, another land flier, then on the battleship *South Carolina*. His idea was to put together a land section of two land planes and three experienced land aviators, plus Bellinger, who "could very soon catch on."

In a larger sense, however, he had grown displeased with the Vera Cruz operation. He wrote Corinne that he and most of his shipmates were disgusted with the administration and Democrats. He believed the civilian leadership had been afraid to land the troops as it would mean a declaration of war.

Mustin also had become impatient with the operationally unsound guidance he was getting from Bristol. He had a particular beef with his superior's loyalty to the C-3, writing to him on 29 April that the "flying boat in a deep sea swell is worthless, on account of her long hull." He added, however, that the experience of operating the planes would help in the design of a suitable hoist. He stressed that he had said yes to every tasking and had made it a point to operate in all kinds of weather. Between the scouting, he continued to train his detachment, and he passed to Bristol an extensive report on the performance of the aircraft and engines.

For the next several days, Mustin continued the twice-daily scouting flights in all directions to ascertain any changes in situation on the ground. More would follow, initially for the Marines and later for the Army. His next priority would be to photograph the city and harbor. On the afternoon of 29 April, he made one flight himself in the C-3, to give Bellinger some "much needed rest."

Mustin was again a hometown hero. One Philadelphia puff piece read, "When the march from Vera Cruz to Mexico City is ordered—if it is ordered—it is certain that the van will be led by the airmen, and Commander Mustin is one who does not say to others 'go,' but himself sails the ambient atmosphere ahead of all others. It is not an enviable task, but it seems certain that the gallant Philadelphian will lead the way into Mexico City or fall victim to the accidents which have bereft army and navy of so many gallant men."

In fact, though the securing of Vera Cruz had been a bloody three days, neither Mustin's section nor any other U.S. unit would conduct offensive operations or march on Mexico City during the seven months of occupation. The press would not have much real combat action to report. In letter of 29 April to Corinne, Mustin offered that he was pleased to find in Vera Cruz a number of war correspondents who were his acquaintances during the Santiago campaign, Jack London, James B. Connolly, Henry Reuterdahl, Frederick Palmer, Richard Harding Davis, and Jimmy Hare among them.

On 6 May, Bellinger and Saufley made an observation flight in the A-3 to verify a report that a hundred men were massing at Punta Gorda, one mile north of Vera Cruz. They found no one, but naval aviation lore has it that during the mission the plane was hit by rifle fire—the first U.S. warplane to take hostile fire. Notwithstanding the extensive press reports, a few skeptics felt that the punctures in the plane's canvas might have resulted from a mishandled screwdriver.

Now settled into an uninspired routine, Mustin was cheered when Ellyson finally arrived on board the *Mississippi,* and he pressed him for news. Spuds briefed him on his recent experiences with Richardson's improved catapult, which had just come to Pensacola. It was a significant advance over the life-threatening device that the naval constructor had built with Chambers. Mustin thrilled to Ellyson's report. The catapult now seemed a viable launch technology, and this insight made him impatient to return home and participate in its testing.

On 10 May, Mustin reported to Corinne.

I have had two letters from Towers; the *Birmingham* outfit has had no flying at all and now they are under orders from Department to *not* fly over Tampico; they are crazy to come down here, and I don't wonder, for Tampico is an even worse place than this for discomfort; they can't go ashore at all, and the anchorage is always rough for a roller like the *Birmingham.* The newspaper accounts of Towers' flights are pure bosh of course, because he hasn't been here at all. Evidently he has a very good press agent, and that sort of thing makes me tired.

I could easily have gotten a lot of cheap notoriety by doing the scouting flights here myself, but it wouldn't count much with people who amount to anything. In fact, I think I am making more character by not taking risks when there is nothing to be gained. Every one here is surprised that the aeroplanes are up every day no matter how hard the wind blows; in that respect we are showing something of the future value of the naval aeroplane; as a matter of fact, no matter how hard it blows it is always easy flying air for it is the steady trade wind, the smoothest of all sea breezes.

But I am impatient at the standstill in Naval Aeronautics; it is now time for starting off the 1915 class of aviators, and besides every thing is ready to go ahead with the catapult tests. I am in hopes [of] the army aeroplanes, of which our last news is their [planes] at Galveston will soon arrive and relieve us of further work here.

Mustin and Towers were chafing at the use of naval aviation in a support role for ground forces. Their vision was far more ambitious. Within two years, they would be arguing aggressively that naval aviation had offensive capabilities in its own right.

In any case, the action in Vera Cruz was over. In a 6 May letter, Towers had written to Bristol from the *Birmingham* to say that he was wasting time, when he could be working with Mustin and back at Pensacola. Bristol replied on the fourteenth that Mustin wanted him to stay in Tampico, a somewhat debatable allegation.

In his letter of 14 May to his boss, Mustin wrote that he agreed with Bristol and Badger that they should not turn planes over to the Army or Marine Corps. The Navy needed them with the ships in case some foreign fleet might make a "demonstration." Again he noted for Bristol the shortcomings of the flying boat, adding that the non-stop operational tempo had put great wear on both his aircraft. He could not dismantle the A-3 engine because the plane had to remain on standby. He thus needed new machines. Inspired now by Ellyson's report, he wrote that he wanted to return to Pensacola and work on the catapult. "One of the best lessons of this trip is the absolute indispensability of the catapult for naval work."

On 18 May, however, Mustin received a Navy Department cablegram that cited "meager" reports of air operations. Was Bristol questioning him, covering his backside, or both? The next day, Mustin replied in a report that was "more elaborate than is customary." Reiterating his equipment worries, he wrote that the duration of flights into mid-May was down to fifteen minutes because of his concern over the A-3 falling apart and that, per the department's instruction, there had been no flying from the *Birmingham* off Tampico. He assured his masters, however, that he had ordered one or more flights every day, regardless of weather conditions. He concluded that the operation was valuable in supplying information about future requirements for aircraft and for maintenance spares aboard ship and ashore. If the detachment were to remain much longer, he cautioned, "relief aeroplanes will be required to replace these now in use, which will eventually become unsafe, due to fatigue of materials." Sensing that he and Bristol might be on a collision course, he was laying an audit trail.

Mustin got support from Admiral Badger. Writing on 20 May to Daniels and Fiske, the admiral said naval aviation had proven useful in short scouting expeditions for troop concentrations, mine detection, and spotting bombardment. The flying boat, however, was not suitable for operations distant from the sea. He endorsed the aviators' view that the hydro was preferable to the C-3, because the latter required two pilots, was slow, and could not reach high altitude quickly. If Navy planes were needed to work with the Army, Badger wrote, other types—that is, land planes—were required. He conveyed to Daniels, who concurred, that he was pleased with aviation and affirmed its role in the fleet. Two days later, Badger wrote a recommendation that the *Mississippi* return to Pensacola.

On 23 May, Bristol replied to Mustin with less enthusiasm for the flying boat. Instead, he lent support to the hydro and the catapult, although he continued to insist on the need for a plane that could launch from the water.

Towers arrived on the *Mississippi* the next day, having finally convinced Fletcher to transfer his unit to Vera Cruz. Also reporting were six new aviation students to train. Mustin now had his men conduct bombing practice in addition to scouting, but the action otherwise was slow. Exasperated with the vastly reduced pace of operations, he again wrote to Daniels on 29 May, asking him to withdraw the two sections. He argued that the Navy could pass the air work to the Army now that the occupation had become entirely a land operation.

Mustin was still in Vera Cruz in early June. He was now ill-humored, homesick for Corinne and the boys, and looking for distraction. He found it among the reporters. "Our water polo games in the late afternoon are making us all feel fit. Yesterday we had a match,—aviators against War Correspondents and we beat them badly: 5 to 0 first half, 3 to 0 second half. In the first half I made three of the 5 goals; in the second half I played goal keeper where under the circumstances there wasn't much to do. It was lots of fun. I have never played this game before I came here,—in fact never saw one, but find that my football knowledge is quite useful."

Despite his pretense about not courting the press, he wrote on 6 June, "I took 'Jimmy Hare' the *Collier's* photographer up last week and he got some good photographs; I enclose one or two samples, but will have a complete set when he gets them developed in New York; the facilities aren't very satisfactory down here."

He reassured Corinne that he had no eye for other pursuits, however.

I can't take any interest in the society here although there are a number of fine looking women among the refugees; every night at the Hotel Universal they have turkey trot parties but I have danced once. I as well as the majority of the men here are satisfied with the society of men only. Why is it that women can't get along together that way; they are never contented unless they have some men dangling around. . . . There are several American women here whose husbands are remaining in Mexico City and thereby risking their lives. One would naturally expect them to keep to themselves and avoid gaiety, for who knows when the news of death of one of their men will arrive? It may come when they are in the arms of some other man, dancing a sort of dance that in any generation but this would be considered lewd. You can see them every night at the Universal either at a dinner party or dancing every minute that the music plays. Perhaps they love their husbands but one wouldn't think so from appearances.

Mustin was working his ally Badger very hard.

On Monday I wrote a letter to the C-in-C that night to "start something." I said that, due to the damp climate here and lack of facilities for taking proper care of the material, the aeroplanes were deteriorating so rapidly that it was only a question of time when it would result in the death of one or more aviators. I asked that he send a telegram to that effect to the Department and ask them, if the *Mississippi* is to remain here, that delivery of new aeroplanes asked for in previous telegrams (more than two weeks ago) be expedited. The Admiral sent the telegram right away and added to it that he had ordered one of the machines withdrawn from service because it was in such bad condition. I had already given the order for "canning" it as the fabric in the tail has gotten so rotten you can poke a finger through it.

The inventor continued to look ahead.

Have made a little model of a scheme I have for a water brake which I believe is going to solve the problem of landing in rough water in a very simple way; I won't attempt to describe it to you because I would first have to explain some things in analytical mechanics which I couldn't very well do by letter. I tried the little model in my bath tub and found the principles involved are correct; now I am making a full sized one and will test it out partly by means of the speed boat. You can bet I have written up a patent application which I will send to Washington as soon as I am sure, which will be after

my tests with the speed boat. It is so simple and easy to make that I believe it is going
to be a great "hit"; the best part about it is that it can be applied to any kind of
hydroaeroplane without involving anything but very minor structural changes.

On 7 June, he wrote in impatience,

> I am in despair about getting any action out of the Navy Department; the Admiral
> sent the telegram I fixed up last Monday, but there has been no reply and it seems
> impossible that such a message should be ignored, for it plainly states that it is a mat-
> ter of life or death to continue working the aeroplanes in this climate.
>
> The Admiral has talked to me very freely about his own troubles in the same line;
> he told me the whole history of the landing of the ammunition from the *Ypiranga* at
> Puerto Mexico,—how he sent telegram after telegram warning the Dep't that she was
> sure to land it there and that he had two gun boats ready to stop it if they would
> only untie his hands.

This news further outraged Mustin. The *Ypiranga* had left Vera Cruz on 3 May after
embarking with some U.S. refugees. After dropping them at Mobile, she went to Puerto
Mexico and unloaded the arms. The liner then boldly returned to Vera Cruz, where a
Navy commander, acting as the U.S. authority in the port, fined the Hamburg-America
Line. In the end, Washington revoked the fine, fearing the penalty would provoke
Germany.

> As you know the *Ypiranga*'s cargo was the reason for the capture of Vera Cruz; all
> deaths here were caused by our efforts to prevent those arms from getting into the
> hands of the Federals; we must not only count our seamen and marines but also all
> the Mexicans that were killed. All those lives were wasted, for now we are no better
> off than if that cargo had been landed in Vera Cruz in the first place. Could anything
> possibly be worse than this Administration? If we only had some strong man among
> the Naval Officers in the Department like Evans who would not be afraid to speak
> his mind. The present Aide for Operations,—Admiral Fiske is a weak sister and
> besides he is trying to be Admiral Badger's relief as C. in C. of the fleet, so we are all
> decided that he is soft soaping the Secretary.
>
> Admiral Badger has been trying for weeks to get the fleet,—all except a small
> squadron of gun boats and one battleship—up north where the officers and men can

get in decent physical condition and the fleet can get back to its legitimate work. . . .
It is so ridiculous to see this great fleet of battleships blockading one port and then
the State Department lets about twenty million rounds of ammunition be landed a little over a hundred miles away from here! And Bryan, the unmitigated liar, has the
nerve to state he was given to understand the *Ypiranga* would not land her cargo.
Admiral Badger has caught Daniels in a lie with regard to the ships being ordered
out of the river at Tampico and wrote a letter of protest, which I suppose will be kept
pigeon-holed in the Navy Department.

Mustin wrote further, "This week I am going to cut the flying down to practically nothing; the Chief of Staff told me I could stop altogether if I wanted to, but I want to keep
our record of a flight every day, and I still have one aeroplane in first class order."

He was now in a rebellious and suspicious mood.

What Captain Bristol is doing, I can't understand; if he was looking out for us properly
he would have had us ordered back long ago, for I write to him every mail and keep him
fully informed of the situation. Two or three of the older officers here have told me not
to trust him at all,—that he is all for Bristol; you told me he wrote you a very eulogistic
letter about me, but I haven't noticed anything of that kind officially as yet! However, the
bulk of the Navy is right here, and from what a good many officers have said I believe I
have made good in this affair to the satisfaction of those who really count, the Captains
of the battleship fleet and the Admirals of a few years hence, and judging from the way
they all speak to me, I feel that I stand pretty well with them.

But after all, what is the use? I suppose there are thousands of men envious of me
for being down here in command of a battleship and the aeroplane squadron.

Last night Smith, Towers, Bellinger and I saw a man shot and killed by an army officer within ten steps of where we were standing and another man get his throat cut. I will
tell you all about it when I come home, for it is too long a story to write. It was quicker
gun-play than anything I have seen before,—even in a moving picture show.

I have been counting up some things: more than half my life—two years more—
has been spent in the service and about half that time has been spent in rotten parts
of the world like this.

In contrast to Mustin's inner discontent, the world was seeing him in almost heroic
terms. On 20 June, Connolly published in *Collier's* a profile of the aviators and their

role in the intervention. He wrote that they were "popular idols with natives and American colony where women watch from shaded veranda of waterfront club and bathhouse with protected salt pool." His portrait spoke of Mustin carrying his .45 and his fellow aviators living in four khaki tents and swimming with the ladies.

Mustin had taken the correspondent hydroplaning in the harbor in the C-3, "porpoising" on the swells. Mustin is a "high type," wrote Connolly. "He learns something from every new experience; and when a man of high intelligence, quiet courage, will power, imagination, backs that equipment with a wide experience, the world benefits. All these officers are seeking to better the service."

"If you knew Mustin," Connolly continued, "and he said, 'I think I can do so and so with an aeroplane,' you would probably prefer to try that thing, even though it looked hazardous, than to try a most ordinary thing with a most ordinary performer. The Mustin type will increase; and then we shall see most of the presently impossible things solved. These men who love adventure, but can forget the adventure for the sake of something more useful to the service and the world—they will be the men to do it."

Connolly finished his piece with a carefully worded insight doubtless planted by Mustin. Scouting is the great value to the fleet today, he wrote. A pilot flying at ten thousand feet can see a battleship fleet fifty miles away but cannot be seen by battleships. "How are the battleships ever to beat that game?"

Before publication of Connolly's article, the Navy Department on 11 June finally directed Mustin and the *Mississippi* to proceed to Pensacola, "to repair the aeroplanes and other aeronautic equipment which has been seriously damaged by continued use, under varying conditions, without ability to effect repairs." Said the official order, "The work of the Aeronautic Division is in keeping with the splendid accomplishments of our Navy in Mexican waters during the present unsettled conditions in Mexico. Great credit is due the personnel of the Navy's Aeronautic Service."

The work of Mustin and his aviators at Vera Cruz was done.

On 12 June, the *Mississippi* sailed for Pensacola. During her passage, on 13 June, the Navy went dry by direction of its teetotaling secretary, Josephus Daniels. Two days later, the battleship arrived home.

The *Mississippi* was to serve as aviation station ship for only a week, denying Mustin any extended time with his wife and sons. On 28 June, after being relieved as base commander, he was ordered to take the *Mississippi,* with Bellinger and an aviation section on board, to Norfolk. The ship was to be sold to Greece.

On 3 July, thirty miles off Norfolk, Mustin wanted to pull a stunt. Presenting Bellinger with an official correspondence, he had him lowered in the flying boat. Bellinger thereupon flew to shore, landing on a beach near Old Point Comfort, and mailed the letter—one of the first instances of such postal delivery. Three hours later, the *Mississippi* arrived in Virginia.

It was the summer of 1914. The concerns of the nation were shifting to Europe with a gathering awareness of the darkening clouds of war.

As for Mexico, the ABC powers who met at Niagara Falls to negotiate an end to the U.S. intervention had adjourned in failure at the end of June. Huerta resigned the provisional presidency on 15 July and later secured asylum aboard a German cruiser. Installing himself as president, Venustiano Carranza embarrassed Wilson by failing to call for elections and then demanded that the United States withdraw its forces from Vera Cruz. On 16 September, Washington announced the end of the occupation, but the last U.S. forces did not leave until 23 November, just as the Carranza regime turned its attention to the revolt of Emiliano Zapata. Mexico then descended into the next phase of civil war, prompting two years later another U.S. intervention across the border against Pancho Villa.

Chapter 8

A Warrior at War
Within and Without

On 28 June 1914, Mustin was on the *Mississippi* steaming south off the west coast of Florida on the first leg of the battleship's transit to Norfolk, her final run as a U.S. man-of-war. Earlier in the day, Archduke Franz Ferdinand of Austria had been assassinated in Sarajevo—putting a match to what has been called the long fuse that ignited the Great War. At the time, the event probably was just another news item for Mustin. He was at sea, absorbed with his own life and affairs.

Mustin arrived in Norfolk a few days later, hoping to remain there for the summer. After almost three months in tropical Vera Cruz, he was in no hurry to return to hot and muggy Pensacola, and his men were in need of a well-deserved leave. For the first week of July, he was involved part-time in the turnover of the *Mississippi* to Newport News Shipbuilding in preparation for her sale to Greece. The other half of his time he spent as acting commander of the armored cruiser *North Carolina,* outfitting her as Pensacola's next aviation station ship.

On 1 July in Washington, Bristol had assumed command of the newly created Office of Naval Aeronautics. Richardson continued his work on the catapult in Pensacola, developing a better means to achieve pressure sufficient to launch a hydroplane. Satisfied that he could rig Richardson's advanced catapult to the *North Carolina,* Mustin was ready to take aviation to the fleet. He would carry two hydros on the cruiser's rail and another two assembled aircraft—or four with folding or detachable wings—on the ship's aft superstructure.

On 10 July, Mustin completed the transfer of his aviation unit to the *North Carolina*. Afterward, he took just more than a week's leave to join his family at Wakefield. When the time came for his return to the ship, he said his good-byes to Corinne and the boys at the Front Royal train station, expecting to see them again in two weeks, after a brief trip to Boston, the ship's home port.

Mustin reported aboard on 21 July to find that the Navy had other plans. With war in Europe imminent, the State Department had prevailed on the Navy to divert the *North Carolina*. She was to join the cruiser *Tennessee* to form the American Relief Expedition to protect and bring home Americans stranded in Europe. With orders to sail from Boston, the *North Carolina* carried funds for the purpose in the form of a keg full of gold.

When the *North Carolina* arrived in Boston, Mustin was relieved of command but retained as executive officer. It was a slap. Among his additional duties on the grossly undermanned ship, he had charge of an aviation section that had no planes. Mustin reported on 4 August for duty in his new capacities and immediately cabled Bristol to have the section detached. The ship sailed on the seventh without a response. Mustin was livid. Without aircraft, the aviators became merely watch standers. Mustin, however, was thoroughly overworked, having to assume further duties as ordnance officer and first lieutenant for a cruiser that was far from ready for action.

When the ship arrived at Cherbourg, France, the aviators finally were able to serve a purpose relevant to their expertise: they were to disperse throughout the continent as aviation observers, another naval aviation first. Mustin, Towers, Bellinger, Herbster, and Smith immediately boarded their trains and went in search of intelligence.

War was raging in earnest on the western, southern, and eastern fronts, as well as at sea. As the German and French armies attacked and counterattacked in what became known as the Battles of the Frontiers, Mustin visited a number of French aircraft facilities; he met with famed aviator Louis Bleriot and toured his works, and he paid visits to Murane-Saulnier, Nieuport, and Salmson. He found to his disgust that the French were leagues ahead of the Americans—in particular the Curtiss operation—in everything from industrial infrastructure to equipment, aircraft, and support. France had been outspending the United States in aviation by a factor of sixty. By comparison, he reported to Bristol, U.S. planes were "a lot of junk."

He was still angry. Writing Corinne on 19 August from Cherbourg, he griped, "It is too discouraging, dearest,—if I thought that there had been any real need of our coming on this trip abroad, I would go through with it without grumbling. But it is now quite evident that our coming wasn't a real necessity and certainly not urgent enough to warrant smashing up our aero service. The Navy Department acted with its usual stupidity and exhibited the usual lack of preparedness for an emergency."

Soberly, he also conveyed his belief that a monumental carnage was about to befall Europe:

I am afraid it will be three or four weeks at least before I am home again and if it were not for the fact that anyone's personal affairs pale in comparison with the thoughts of terrible events over here, I wouldn't be able to stand it. In a few days we expect to hear news of a battle [The Ardennes] where there will be about one million Germans against the same number of French, Belgians & English combined. The slaughter will be fearful for it seems the Germans are not bothering to take prisoners so the French will certainly retaliate. There are lots of stories about atrocities of the German troops in Belgium that come from fairly reliable sources,—but we can't be sure because all the news we get is censored by the other side. I am afraid this is going to be the end of Germany. It is evident that their campaign has miscarried badly and that they are away behind their schedule of operations in France; in the meantime Russia mobilized in much less time than any one could expect and they will throw such an enormous army into North Germany that the Kaiser will have to draw off some of the troops from the French border. Also England is landing about a quarter of a million men, probably in Belgium. It is all very sad when one thinks of the tremendous number of men that are going to be killed and the suffering and poverty that is bound to follow. Then if Germany is wiped out there will probably be bickering over the spoils that will bring about war between Russia and England, and then they will all be at it again.

On 28 August, at Falmouth, the *North Carolina* received orders to Turkey. Great numbers of Americans were in the Near East and thought to be in desperate need of the ship's gold to fund their voyages home. The orders were "the last straw" for Mustin. The following day, he wrote Bristol a blistering letter detailing his view that through high-handed mismanagement his boss had allowed the Navy to shunt aviation and its aviators aside.

Now that the Navy had the Office of Naval Aeronautics, Mustin wanted Bristol to issue him clear orders that specified what his authority would be. He challenged him, writing that he intended to leave aviation duty unless "we can start work this autumn with a definite status both in military and financial matters." He was outraged because, although he had been commanding officer of both Pensacola and the training ships for seven months, he had been "shanghaied," and he insisted that it not happen again. To Mustin's mind, his boss was unfit for his responsibilities. "[F]or some reason that I can't explain I have not been able to convince you that my ideas . . . carry more weight than the ideas that you get from sources that are unsupported by practical flying knowledge." With this letter, he had virtually declared war against Bristol.

Mustin unloaded to Corinne in a second letter that same night.

After being treated the way I have been in this incident I certainly am not going to spend all my hours at work. It was a very rough letter that I wrote, and if he gets mad enough he may get me in trouble about it. However it was a personal letter in answer to a personal letter from him; besides, if I am threatened with a court martial I will notify him that I will give the whole business—including certain official correspondence—to the Press, which will show there has several times been a really criminal neglect of us in the Navy Department. In any case as the matter now stands, I will either get what I want in the way of a definite status for aviation and myself or I will be out of it altogether. And if they don't do what I want,—I will apply for retirement from the service. I have never been so angry about my treatment by the Navy Department, the whole business, to aviation as well as to me has been horribly unjust.

His bitterness did not abate. In a 2 September letter to Corinne, he wrote,

It is almost a month now since we sailed from Boston and apparently nothing has been done towards getting us back. I think it is now up to Captain Bristol to resign from aeronautics and let a real man take his job. Of course he is making all kinds of excuses but there can be none that are valid. It all in the end amounts to this: he let the Bureau of Nav. shanghai his officers; he also let the Division of Operations,—the office he is in—take away the aeronautic ship just at the time when we ought to be making every effort to get our pitiful little aviation equipment ready for possible service. My personal grievance in being superseded in command is nothing in comparison to the crime that has been committed in having all aviation work stopped.

Then he added, "No man who has the instincts of a gentleman would let an officer who serves in his department of the Navy be put in such a humiliating position."

On 20 September, the *North Carolina* was at the mouth of the Dardanelles. The U.S. ambassador came on board for consultations to determine where the ship would go. Mustin wrote that he had "gotten in such a rage over this business that I have felt on the verge of going crazy. But fortunately I can almost always sink my troubles in oblivion by working on some invention." This time, he was working on "drawings for an instrument that is a necessity on scouting flights at sea, and I have made up my mind that for the rest of this cruise abroad I will use my spare time and considerably more to making money. For the last two weeks I have done nothing beyond the bare necessities in the executive job, for my whole idea now is to make the Navy Department pay me in hard cash for their unjust treatment of aeronautics and the humiliation of my being deprived of my command."

The instrument, a modified sextant, was for "aeroplane scouting at sea which has developed in a surprising way into some new methods of air navigation. It is a new field and I already have enough material for a small book on a subject in which I will be a pioneer." (The following July he would report, after testing at Pensacola, that by incorporating a gyroscopically stabilized artificial horizon into a sextant an aircraft might be able to navigate at sea. Mustin later generated recommendations for the Navy's first aircraft instrument requirements that included the sextant.)

His work did not prevent him from ruminating on his battle with Bristol. On 28 September, he sent a cablegram to Daniels about his boss. He wrote to Corinne that the cable "shows up the whole damnable situation of Aeronautics. (It cost nearly a hundred dollars, but the Government pays for it.) I sent it because I believe Captain Bristol must surely be concealing or trying to cover up his mismanagement of our affairs. I have hopes that this telegram will bring things to a head, but in any case it will make an official record in the Department that will show in future years what a fearful handicap I have been working under."

On 25 October, the *North Carolina* was off Beirut in an effort to protect U.S. interests. Because he had succeeded as an observer in France, Mustin was not sure whether he would remain in Europe or come home. His uncertainty continued to 5 November, intensified by the prospect of action for which the ship was inadequately prepared. For three days, the ship stood ready on a signal from the president of the American College to land five hundred marines and bluejackets. Another plan, even more desperate, called for her to shell the city.

"Oh Dearest," he cried in a letter to Corinne, "will this affair ever end?" He continued,

> The ship is of course tied here hard and fast although we are worse than useless: my meager little landing force couldn't hold out very long if the Turks really wanted to come in and clean us out. Within an hour's ride on horse back they have a regiment of cavalry—all veterans—and at Damascus there are 20,000 troops officered by Germans. However I have picked a very strong position in the American College grounds and we could make a pretty good resistance if they don't use artillery and aeroplanes.
>
> The effect this affair has had on me is really very serious for I am afraid it has so embittered my spirit that I will never recover from it. Have I permanently lost faith in my country and all ambition to be a strong factor in the development of our Navy? If so my life is ruined, for no man can stand still; if he doesn't go ahead he will fall behind. In my opinion any man who has none but the selfish interests of himself and his family at heart is a moral degenerate, and a nation composed of a majority of such men is on the decline.

On 13 November, he wrote, "Will our boys want to go into the service, do you think? I would do everything in my power to prevent it; but a curious part about the Naval life is that in the course of time one forgets the hardships and suffering and remembers only the glories."

Mustin's impressment was almost at an end. His cablegram to Daniels might have had effect. On 2 December, Bradley Fiske got Mustin detached from the ship with orders to take passage on the *Vulcan* for the United States. He left two days later and after a stopover in England took passage on the liner *Finland* with three other officers from the section, arriving in New York on 28 December.

Once stateside, Mustin received orders for temporary duty at the Office of Naval Aeronautics to report his findings to Bristol. He would not have to deal with his Washington nemesis for long. In January 1915, new orders returned him to Pensacola where, after five months, he would finally retake charge of the Naval Aeronautics Station.

The Mustins returned to quarters on Admiralty Row, the line of the white painted wooden houses overlooking the palm-lined bay. For the family, it was a delightful time, when Lloyd and Henry could enjoy and observe their father in action ashore. The posting was austere, and Corinne found and kept a cow in the yard for fresh milk. On Saturday nights, she and Mustin frequently danced at the nearby San Carlos Hotel, where a palm court orchestra played in the large Spanish dining room.

That winter in Washington, the Navy underwent an organizational shake-up with the appointment of the first chief of naval operations. On 3 March, Daniels passed over twenty-six rear admirals and five captains to appoint William Shepard Benson to the new and controversial four-star office. It was widely assumed that Benson got the nod over many better qualified senior officers precisely because he would not be one to exert strong leadership. Unfortunately for Mustin and his fellow aviators, he was known to be unsympathetic to aviation.

In April, Mustin's title in Pensacola changed to commandant of the Naval Aeronautic Station. In the year's listing of aviators, his number was still three, based in part on his senior rank. In the end, his number would be eleven, in line with the Navy's ultimate decision to rank aviators in the order in which they had qualified. The title and temporary preferment did not bring any noticeable increase in clout, however. As yet having no new students to train, he dedicated some of his energies to overseeing the continued development of the shipboard catapult. On 16 April, fitted on a barge, Richardson's new cat launched the Curtiss AB-2 flying boat with Bellinger at the controls, the first of a number of test launches. On 8 May, Ens. Melvin Stoltz crashed his AH-9 hydro and died, the first casualty since Murray had plunged into the water in February the previous year.

Despite yet another tragic setback, Mustin persisted in preparing Pensacola and the aviation community for war. His detachment conducted antisubmarine patrols and spotted for battleship target practice and for mortar fire from coast artillery. He also had them exercise bombing techniques and, in the process, determined a requirement for a good bombsight, a version of which went into development a year later.

The Office of Naval Aeronautics got $1 million in 1915 funds. While still a paltry sum in the Navy's overall budget, it nonetheless was an increase. Although some of the appropriation went to a dirigible program, supported by Bristol but opposed by most aviators, the sudden infusion allowed Pensacola to return to the business of training new students. On 1 July, the first ten arrived.

In Washington, Benson's accession exacerbated the differences between Fiske and

Daniels. One bone of contention was the concept of a government aircraft facility at Philadelphia's League Island. Since 1912, Mustin had pushed for such an enterprise in his hometown. When he reported what he had learned about French facilities and industrial preparedness for war, the idea assumed added weight, especially for Daniels. Although a Progressive and a trust buster, the secretary saw a government-owned and -operated facility as a competitive tool for production of a product for which the government was the sole customer. Fiske, however, remained adamantly opposed.

Later in July, having crossed swords with Daniels one too many times, Fiske was out as operations aide. He had been rather stiff as an aviation advocate, but he nonetheless had been an advocate at the top, and his removal did not bode well. Fiske had been Bristol's protector, and now the latter was vulnerable to those who still were not convinced of aviation's operational promise. The ax finally fell on 12 October, when Benson issued a directive that returned aviation to the Material Division, effective on Bristol's departure.

Mustin was determined that progress in Pensacola would continue. On 13 July, two days early, Lt.(jg) Marc "Pete" Mitscher eagerly reported for training and promptly went aloft in the Curtiss AH-2, possibly with Mustin. Also in the class was Lt. (jg) George Murray, who had trained initially at Guantánamo in 1913. Both Mitscher and Murray would become fast friends of Mustin and later mentors to his boys.

Now boasting 58 officers, 431 enlisted, 33 seaplanes, and 3 dirigibles, Pensacola was coming of age. The aviators were attracting the interest even of Hollywood, which at one point came to film their exploits. The times were as wild as the men. Mitscher, Ellyson, Bellinger, Chevalier, Whiting, and Herbster were aviators who liked their drink and, according to one local Pensacola playwright, boasted that "the Mustins gave the best parties in town."

On duty, however, Mustin was a demanding commander. On 9 September, the *North Carolina* finally pulled into Pensacola to serve as station ship. Her arrival coincided with the completion of more than a year's development of Richardson's shipboard catapult. The cat went aboard for a series of launches involving dead loads, all witnessed by four-year-old Lloyd Mustin, who was already showing an interest in all things Navy.

Mustin was determined to be the one to make the first cat shot from a ship under way. Much was at stake. He had convinced Bristol that if aircraft were to go to sea with ships they would launch from either a platform on the fantail or a catapult on an aft turret. This test shot would go a long way toward proving the concept of a cat launch. The expectation was that it would be a major event. As such, it drew even the lukewarm Benson to Pensacola.

On 5 November, Mustin strapped himself into the AB-2, the plane Bellinger had been flying off the barge. On a nearby pier, Lloyd and his brother sat, legs dangling over the water, and watched the catapult shoot their father off the fantail of the *North Carolina* and into the history books.

Spectacular though the test was, Benson was unimpressed.

Mustin, also, had reservations. Although the cat launched the plane, he could see the design was mechanically defective and had it removed for modification. When the reworked catapult was reinstalled on the ship, it was found to interfere with the guns. The continuing problems dampened his enthusiasm for the system. It now was clear to him: Whatever the launching and recovery system, operating from battleships alone would condemn aviation to a support function. Mustin saw aviation as an offensive naval force in its own right. He saw planes carrying the battle to the enemy, large numbers of aircraft operating in tactical units. That vision called for a dedicated ship to carry them. As early as 1914, Mustin and Towers had talked about a "platform deck aviation ship."

The Navy was coming to accept the idea that planes would operate with the fleet. The issue for the next decade or so would be *how*. What kinds of aircraft would the Navy use, and how would ships launch and retrieve them? Chambers had regarded the high seas as a "universal aerodrome" and thus supported the seaplane. Both the line and the aviation communities, however, felt that he did not appreciate how seriously the launch and retrieval of seaplanes in tactical situations would restrict fleet operations.

At this point, the seaplane had application as a scout and possibly as a spotter, but the notion that it could be used as an offensive weapon still was premature. On the other hand, in 1912, Fiske had registered a patent for an air-launched torpedo to be carried by a seaplane, to defend the sea lines of communication to the Philippines. The seaplane would have to be land-based to operate in advance of the battleships, or the battleships would have to be fitted with a catapult to carry the plane. Because of this, Chambers was wedded to the cat and actively engaged in testing Richardson's early designs at the Washington Navy Yard.

In December 1914, Bristol took a more conservative position: Aircraft were useful *only* as spotters. He spurned the notion that planes could deliver any offensive punch. This initial shortsightedness was changed by the war, however, and he moved into Mustin and Towers's camp as an advocate of a so-called aircraft carrier. Daniels accepted that naval aviation was useful for offensive and defensive operations, but both he and Benson opposed any aircraft-carrier notions.

Mustin would not yet play a major role in this debate. Following the cat shot, Bristol kept him busy exploring the link between naval aviation and commercial aircraft production. He sent Mustin on a tour of the nation's production factories, which were rumored to be fulfilling foreign orders. Such was not the case with the Wrights, but Curtiss and others had produced aircraft for foreign customers. On the whole, however, Mustin determined that U.S. industrial capacity could support wartime production for the Navy.

Bristol also ordered him to begin training enlisteds, the first of whom reported in January 1916. Per instructions, Mustin had selected eight petty officers and two USMC sergeants. He was able to establish a temporary rating—machinist, aeronautics—for those on aviation duty, and he and Bristol then managed to work together to make the rating permanent.

Their good relations would not last long. On 6 January, another Pensacola reorganization detached Mustin as commandant, upon relief, and assigned him to temporary duty at the Aeronautic Station at Pensacola. In February, Bristol realized he had to leave Washington. He had antagonized too many and, without Fiske, was wholly vulnerable. To save his career, he asked to return to sea with the *North Carolina,* the aviation support ship. It would spell more trouble.

On 4 March, five days after Bristol submitted his request, Benson abolished the Office of Naval Aeronautics and the director title and assigned Bristol's old duties to Lt. (jg) Clarence K. Bronson. One of Mustin's students at Vera Cruz, Bronson was placed in the Material Division in the Office of Naval Operations, reporting to Capt. Josiah S. McKean, who was not an aviation advocate. Benson's reorganization gutted aviation and distributed its functions across the bureaus, but it was McKean who emerged as the administrative force with which Mustin and his fellow aviators would have to reckon.

Bristol got his orders to command *North Carolina* in time to skipper the ship for that spring's fleet exercises off Guantánamo. He arrived in Pensacola as commander of the Naval Air Service with supervisory responsibility for all aircraft and aircraft stations, in effect Mustin's relief. It was another slap.

Inevitably, Bristol and Mustin, two strong-willed officers already poles apart in temperament and policy, clashed. As Bristol prepared his ship for the fleet exercises, he was delayed by continuing problems with the catapult, and he found his aviators untrained in scouting. Once into the exercises, he complained that the planes and ship were not at the level of readiness he should expect. He further alleged that in his zeal for aviation

Mustin had ignored shipboard maintenance and had not adequately prepared the *North Carolina* for sea. Bristol was proceeding on the assumption that he would run naval air ashore and afloat.

While Mustin was getting increasingly snarled in his dealings with Bristol and the Navy Department, Corinne was wrestling with two active boys. Needing help with the cooking and housekeeping, she decided to invite to Pensacola her twenty-year-old cousin from Baltimore, Bessie Wallis Warfield. Born 19 June 1896, Wallis was the daughter of Alice Montague and two decades later would become the Duchess of Windsor.

Sometime in April, Corinne met Wallis at the Gregory Street train depot. At home, she set her up in the sunny guest room, and Wallis immediately turned to helping with the cooking and housekeeping as arranged. In the evenings after the boys went to bed, the Mustins would party. Years later, Mitscher would remember fondly sitting with Mustin on the Quarters Eye porch, where they all used to "get tight" with Wallis.

In May, Corinne felt it might be preferable to formalize her cousin's social introductions to the base. She invited three young aviators to lunch, one of whom was the dashing Earl Winfield Spencer. Win and Wallis immediately connected, and within a month, he proposed.

Mustin had little time to think of matchmaking. Bristol was criticizing his administration of the station continually, and when his "nagging became unbearable," Mustin asked for a board of investigation that he might "prove the Department has always neglected the station." Aboard the *North Carolina,* Bristol was claiming that equipment problems were preventing him from developing tactics. He blamed Mustin. In late May, Benson finally intervened and on 1 June put Bristol in charge of tactics development and aircraft afloat and Mustin in charge of Pensacola. The delineation removed Bristol from any responsibility for naval aviation ashore.

Mustin's problems worsened, however, when on 9 June a Wright pusher, a class of airplane aviators had long protested as being unsafe, crashed, killing Saufley and another aviator named Rockwell. Years later, Wallis, as the Duchess of Windsor, would remember Mustin brooding over his fights with Bristol and having to deal with the accidents and deaths. She wisely decided it was time to escape the Florida Panhandle heat and return to Baltimore to plan for an autumn wedding.

Later in the month, Mustin went to Washington to appear at General Board hearings on the future of naval aviation. Bristol's problems in tactical development must have carried weight because, among the board's observations in its 24 June report, it said the Navy had not paid enough attention to strategic and tactical possibilities of the air arm. The board concluded that "aeronautics does not offer a prospect of becoming the principal means of exercising compelling force against the enemy," and that naval aircraft had use only for scouting, patrolling, spotting, and controlling gunfire from ships. It further suggested the formation of standard two-plane air divisions—one to each battleship and two to each scouting ship—and of an additional three-plane coastal division for patrol.

The idea that naval aircraft did not have any tactical application as an offensive weapon, especially against battleships, provoked a forceful response from Mustin. Convinced that his adversary and the rest of the nonaviators who supposedly ran naval aviation in Washington were not sufficiently aggressive on its behalf, Mustin proved a very outspoken witness at the hearings.

Initially, Mustin had supported the use of light hydroplanes on catapults, but now he was arguing for heavier planes on carriers to attack enemy battleships. Realizing that the enemy would have planes competing for air superiority, he also argued for fighters to clear enemy aircraft from the skies over the battle zone. With his 1916 testimony, Mustin thus became the first senior aviator advocate of the aircraft carrier, which he now flatly supported over the catapult.

Mustin did not stop there. He argued that the Navy was wasting its effort with dirigibles, another of Bristol's pet schemes. He wanted to kill the program to free funding for a high-speed aircraft armed with machine guns and bombs and for a fast fighter to protect a class of bomber. Among his arguments for a fighter was the fact that modern aircraft, which he had seen as an observer in France, could fly above the effective range of the 5-inch antiaircraft gun, which he said was some six to ten thousand feet. In addition, the requirement for maneuverability meant that a fighter had to be a plane without pontoons—that is, a better performing land plane, a concept supported by Towers. Simply put, Mustin envisioned not one but three types of aircraft—a torpedo carrier, a spotter/scout, and his naval fighter—and a class of ship that could support them all.

He had finally tossed his gauntlet before the battleship admirals. His 1916 General Board testimony epitomized Mustin as a naval officer who approached the development of naval aviation, not as a scientist, engineer or administrator—although in a sense, he had a measure of all three—but as a tactician. At his core, Mustin was a warrior.

The General Board of 1916 recommended that the Navy spend $5 million on aviation over next three years.

Mustin's war with Bristol had become public, and the feisty maverick now appeared to have allies in Congress. He testified before the board on his support for a Naval Flying Service, with aviators as officers in the Navy but in a distinct arm akin to the Marine Corps. Earlier in the year, Representative Fred A. Britten had written Daniels suggesting that he put into his Fiscal Year 1917 Naval Appropriations Bill a provision for a Naval Flying Corps in which officers could rise in rank only to captain, unless they managed to have substantial sea duty. It is possible Mustin had been in contact with Britten, who was a close friend of Moffatt.

Mustin returned to Pensacola in time for the devastating 5 July hurricane. Driving 104-mile-per-hour winds and rising waters threatened the Mustins' home and surroundings, prompting the family to bring their milk cow into the dining room for safety. Even inside, water from the ten-foot storm surge rose to the height of her udders, so terrifying the animal that she never again gave milk. When the wind and water subsided after five days of lashings, Pensacola had lost eighteen souls and damage to the base was more than $1 million. Two more violent storms followed in October and January, finishing one of Pensacola's worst years for weather.

In Washington that August, naval aviation underwent yet another reorganization. McKean's bureaucracy continued to be unresponsive to the perspectives of the aviators and engineers.

Matters worsened steadily for Mustin. A letter signed by Daniels, but probably prepared by Benson, practically accused him of "responsibility for Rockwell's and Saufley's deaths by wrong flying instruction methods" and ordered him to reply. Asking for a court of inquiry, Mustin countered with his own accusation that "the real responsibility for those deaths" was "primarily the Navy Department, secondarily Bristol." As was becoming depressingly familiar for him, the Navy took no action.

He wrote Corinne months later, "After the selection board has met, I suddenly get those unfavorable reports of fitness of Bristol's and as I am advised to return them *immediately* by registered mail, special delivery I have no time to answer them in detail. . . . Result is I am condemned without trial and lose my commission as a Comdr.; Bristol's reports and Benson's 'concurring in part' are enough to queer me in a board of 9 Rear Admirals of whom there are only 2 I have ever served with."

Undaunted, Mustin pressed ahead with his causes. In October, he wrote that the Flying Corps must have an independent director of naval aeronautics who was "a qualified aviator." Supported by Benson, McKean argued the opposite case, stating that aviators must return to sea after they are too old to fly. Mustin now was serving on borrowed time.

At sea, Bristol and the *North Carolina* were ordered to the Caribbean on an exercise with destroyers—in reality, to observe allied operations. He remained at sea until 12 December, when he was relieved. Control of naval air at sea, without title, passed to Rear Adm. Albert Gleaves, the Atlantic Fleet destroyer commander who flew his flag on the armored cruiser *Seattle,* a ship with her own planes and an improved catapult. After the change of command, the *North Carolina* went to Portsmouth, where she subsequently got her own catapult upgrade.

On 8 November in Baltimore, Wallis and Win Spencer's wedding was held at the Montague family church, Christ Episcopal. In December, the couple returned to Pensacola to Number Six Admiralty Row, a few houses down from the Mustins. What should have been a happy time for the newlyweds turned stormy. Although a capable aviator, Spencer drank heavily. With his fellow prankster Chevy Chevalier, he danced on tabletops and caused ruckuses at the San Carlos.

Feeling the breath on his neck from continued Washington scrutiny, Mustin insisted the workplaces be dry. According to one Wallis biography, he had to wrestle with a number of aviators who sometimes enjoyed "bull shots," a cocktail of beef bouillon and vodka, before taking to the air. Spencer liked to tease him by keeping his office water stored in gin bottles, which an angry Mustin would discover during Saturday morning inspections.

For Mustin, as 1916 closed, he could point to just two achievements for naval aviation in which he had a hand. He had succeeded in getting a manufacturing capability for Pensacola and he had helped design uniforms and insignia for aviators. Naval aviation was in a nadir, and Mustin was in very bad odor with the brass. On 30 January 1917, he was detached home to await orders. The next day, the Navy revoked his designation as a naval aviator. In effect, he was fired. He was passed over for captain and ordered on 4 February to report as executive officer of the battleship *North Dakota*. It would be his time in Coventry.

At his change of command in Pensacola, five Curtiss planes were to do a flyover. Two nosed under on takeoff. One ditched after flying only a few minutes. A third piloted by his friend Pete Mitscher had to land on shore with a split propeller. In the end, only one plane managed to fly the farewell. It was an ignominious display that, in a perverse way, validated everything for which Mustin had fought and the Navy's leaders had chosen to ignore.

Chapter 9

Returning to the Game

In mid-winter 1917, the Mustin family left Pensacola and headed north for Philadelphia. Corinne and the boys joined Ida and Father Lloyd in Germantown, living at 233 Harvey Street, and on 18 February, Mustin reported to the *North Dakota*. A *Delaware*-class battleship, she no longer was a ship of the first line. She had been in reserve at the Philadelphia Navy Yard for some time, but as the United States drifted into war, she was returning to sea. Three days after Mustin reported, she passed into Tangier Sound in Maryland's Chesapeake Bay for several weeks of target practice, gunnery drills, and tactics. The Navy was training its officers and men in protected waters, mindful of Germany's submarine warfare.

In early April, as President Wilson prepared Congress and the American people for war, the *North Dakota* still was in the bay, conducting drills. She received notice by radio on 6 April that Congress had declared war, and for the rest of the year and throughout the hostilities, she would serve as a gunnery and engineering training ship, based alternately in Virginia's York River and New York. Notwithstanding two decades of trumpeting for a battleship navy second to none, in World War I most of the U.S. battleship fleet would operate in virtual backwaters. Having spent years wrestling with the gun club on behalf of aviation, the irony for Mustin was especially bitter.

In Washington, at the aviation desk in the Office of Operations, Towers had returned from Europe to succeed Bronson as the officer in charge of aeronautics. The Navy would not permit him to make too great an impact. In May, it would order Capt. Noble E. Irvin, another gun club appointee known not to be disposed to aviation, to take charge over Towers's head.

After a month at sea, Mustin again was despondent. Chafing under his line duties as executive officer, he wrote Corinne a disconsolate letter on 11 March:

> My heart is not in this kind of work and I feel that for the best interests of the service I should be back in aviation. . . . I would be mighty glad if you did see the Secretary. Here is the situation in a nutshell: Bristol and McKean and the Bureau of C & R and Steam Engineering (also to a certain extent Benson) realize they have made a dismal failure of naval aeronautics and they require a scapegoat; I am elected to the position and since my mental attainments are too well known in the Navy to be attacked successfully, they make reflections on my administrative and executive ability.
>
> The gist of Bristol's reports [is] that I am not fit for important independent duties. Yet my record before that ought to show that I have had an unusual amount of independent duty and have always "delivered the goods." . . .
>
> Instead of getting unfavorable reports as commandant of Pensacola if justice had been accorded me I would have had special commendation; if I had not had unusual administrative ability, executive ability, tact and extraordinary capacity for hard work that place would have died a natural death long ago. . . .
>
> As soon as my detachment from Pensacola is decided the Dept begins granting additional officers and the clerical force I had needed and been trying to get for years. Recommendations of mine about aviation equipment that have been pigeonholed from a year to two years begin to go through as soon as it is decided to "can" me.
>
> The treatment of me has discouraged and disgusted all the aviators (except perhaps Towers who has been abroad so long he knows nothing of the situation) who, I feel sure, are loyal to me and have confidence in me.

The bitter truth was that naval aviation was going to war without Mustin.

In London, William S. Sims, now a rear admiral, had command of U.S. naval forces in Europe. Into the war's third year, the Allied situation was desperate, particularly in Britain. The German submarine stranglehold had taken serious effect on the economy and morale, and Sims had immersed himself in finding a way to defeat the U-boat threat. One proposal, originated by Whiting with Sims's support, was a seaplane operation against German submarine pens on the North Sea coast. A ferryboat would carry the planes within striking distance of the facilities at Kiel, Cuxhaven, Wilhelmshaven, and Heligoland Island.

Sims's chief engineer, Hutchinson Cone, had command of U.S. naval aviation in Europe. He and Sims were eager to mount the operation with the British. Handling the liaison were four captains: N. C. Twining, Sims's chief of staff, F. H. Schofield, Dudley W. Knox, and H. C. Yarnell, plus two assistants, Capt. Luke McNamee and Col. R. H. Dunlap, USMC. By October, the Royal Navy was behind a second iteration of a strike plan that would have seaplanes launching from towed lighters. This version got approval from both governments, who agreed to divide the effort equally.

Mustin no doubt followed these developments. A decade before, Sims had been the star to follow and had enabled him to make his mark in ordnance and gunnery. So would it be again in 1917 with aviation.

All the elements were in place. Sims was in command in London. The Navy had in mind an operation that would use aviation offensively. The only thing required was for Mustin to apply his inventiveness and operational experience to supply the recipe.

As fortune would have it, Daniels sent a navy-wide radiogram appealing for war-winning ideas. On 19 August, Mustin responded with a novel but comprehensive operational concept to use aircraft in large tactical units to strike the pens. His initial plan had four objectives: "(1) Damage and disorganization of the shops and equipment at Emden and Wilhelmshaven by continuous bombing. (2) Torpedo attacks on German submarines and other ships of the enemy fleet inside the North Sea Bases. (3) Torpedo attack on the German fleet when at sea near the North Sea Bases. (4) Damage and disorganization of the works at Essen by continuous bombing."

Mustin considered the possibility that the strikes could be joint air operations, but in his view, the balance of air power on the Western Front was too even to allow the Army to divert any of its planes. The mission would require hundreds of aircraft, which meant the operation would have to be a naval one.

The main challenge was distance—the reason the Allies had not attempted air operations against the pens before. Mustin's solution was to use large numbers of bombers, each mounted on what he called a sea sled, a fast and powerful small craft. The concept, Lloyd later noted, actually had its genesis in Pensacola a year earlier, when his father began to contemplate alternatives to the catapult. While observing a prior version of the sled being used as a crash boat, he had pondered how and in what circumstances he might use its operational potential as an aircraft launching platform. He did not intend his sea sled concept to be an alternative to an aircraft carrier, however. It was merely a special-purpose supplement, for combat operations of a particular place and time. Using the sleds for a sustained attack on the pens could prove the offensive use of naval aviation as a tactical force.

The plan proposed by Whiting and the British had resolved the distance issue with the use of towed lighters, but their approach still required the seaplanes to launch from the water. Drawing on his experience at Vera Cruz, Mustin noted that seaplanes needed either smooth water or a catapult. They were poor climbers, and their motors were unreliable for a long flight. The sled obviated these problems. It could operate in rough water, and its shallow draft permitted it to take the plane inshore much closer to its target. As a bonus, when planing, the sled would draw only a couple of feet, so it could operate over German minefields. During the takeoff run, the combined thrust of the sled and plane's motors would enable the craft to quickly reach the speed for planing and lift-off. While acknowledging that the sleds could not retrieve returning aircraft after the mission, Mustin wrote that the craft could tow them.

The numbers were wildly ambitious. Mustin called for three types of plane/sled combinations: six hundred fighting/scouting units, a thousand bombing units that each could carry a 500-pound bomb, and twelve hundred torpedo/heavy bombing units, each with a Caproni bomber to carry a 2,000-pound bomb. Anticipating bombing and torpedo errors and attrition, he wanted a mass force capable of mounting continuous attacks.

Mustin's original idea was to have the auto industry build the sleds. The previous year, the automobile manufacturers had gotten into aviation through the efforts of Rear Adm. David W. Taylor, chief of the Naval Construction Corps. On 3 July, the Packard factory had delivered the first Liberty aeronautic motor to Taylor, thirty-five days after presenting original sketches. With the rising Navy demand for aircraft for the war, Taylor had recommended to a sympathetic Daniels the establishment of the Naval Aircraft Factory in Philadelphia. The facility was authorized in July, and in October manufacturing began on a flying boat, the F-5L, with final assembly the following April. Mustin wanted to capitalize on this effort. Altogether, he was confident that he could conduct the operation at a cost less than that being proposed for using ships and seaplanes.

For the first raid, work could begin on beaches—in advance of hangars and warehousing. Mustin could assemble units in England, and the sleds could cross the English Channel to Texel Island under their own power. An alternate plan was to use an English base at Yarmouth in the Yare River; however, from that location a strike on Essen would be impossible. Against the pens at that distance, destroyers would have to recover planes by towing; the German submarine threat prevented them from stopping to use their cranes. British submarines, however, could recover pilots. In conclusion, Mustin recommended that his plan be "kept under the control of the Navy," adding that he wanted to take part in "active operations."

Mustin's plan made its way to Benson, and by November, it was getting serious attention. On 1 November, Irvin wrote Cone in Paris. In his reply, Cone responded positively, requesting Mustin's services "because he is the senior man who knows the game of aviation." Irvin, in effect, refused. Cone continued to work on Benson directly, attempting to get Mustin posted to Sims's staff in London.

In December, Mustin's fate turned for the better. Benson and the British Admiralty endorsed his plan. On 22 December, he finally received his commission as a regular commander, backdated to 1 July. The final imprimatur came on 31 December with a directive from Towers. He wrote that the plan "seems to be feasible but more definite computations should be furnished. . . . In order to accomplish this I recommend that Commander Mustin be ordered to temporary duty in Operations, Aviation Section, and the Bureaus of Construction and Repair, and Steam Engineering be requested to complete and check the plans, cooperating with Commander Mustin in this work. This model can be undertaken from present general plans."

Thanks to his inventiveness and his friends, Mustin was back in the game.

Before Mustin's detachment from the *North Dakota,* an event occurred that over time would have a mortal effect. On 15 January 1918, the battleship was maneuvering with the fleet in a storm off Cape Hatteras. The gale was brutal, lashing the ships with raging winds and heavy seas. Mustin was on the bridge when a sudden swell struck his vessel and washed three sailors overboard. Two quickly were lost to the sea. The third, Fireman H. L. Legette, was visible but drowning in the bitterly cold waters.

Immediately, Mustin directed the maneuver of his ship toward Legette. Once in position, he raced to the quarterdeck, had a bow line attached to his waist and leapt overboard. Reaching the unconscious fireman, he supported him in the water with his legs until the men aboard ship were able to haul them alongside.

The seas reportedly "were tossing the vessel about like a cork and both men were in danger of being crushed against the ship's side or under a heavy gun." With one hand, Mustin held the line. With the other, he grasped Legette. His men struggled for some time to hoist the pair to the deck, while the swells repeatedly pounded Mustin against the side of the ship.

For his heroics, Mustin received the Treasury Department's Gold Life Saving Medal and a commendation from the Navy for his handling of the *North Dakota*. According to a fellow officer, Mustin made light of the incident, saying it was "in the line of duty." On the contrary, it was an unusually gallant act for the executive officer of a battleship. In a little more than two weeks, he would turn forty. For a man his age, the strain was immense. His health would never be the same.

Towers's December directive finally took effect on 14 February 1918, when at last Mustin was detached and ordered to the Bureau of Construction and Repair in Washington to begin working on his sea sled project. It was the perfect place to put the plan together. The bureau had responsibility for design and fabrication of airframes, flying boat hulls, and wings. He would be working directly with Admiral Taylor.

Mustin reported on 26 February, immediately applying himself to developing the material and organizing a series of air raids on Heligoland and the Northern German Submarine Base, planned for the spring of 1919. The Navy finally was putting some weight behind aviation. On 7 March, Daniels overrode Benson and ordered Irvin to be director of naval aviation, a title that had been on ice since Bristol's departure.

Mustin's project advanced rapidly. On 27 May, he and Taylor awarded the contract to design and build sea sleds to Murray & Tregurtha. Under Taylor's direction, Mustin and the firm developed the lines of the steel-framed hull.

For the seaplane, Mustin contracted with the Italian builder Caproni, with whom the United States already had cut a deal to get two hundred bombers for the Army. Hutchinson Cone, who had been relieved as commander of the U.S. Navy's air bases in France by Thomas Craven, and Sims planned for the Italians to deliver thirty planes in June, eighty in August, and twenty per month thereafter.

By the end of June, the British–American towed-lighter project was under way at a base at Killingholme, Ireland, with a U.S. detachment in command. In August, however, a German zeppelin monitored an exercise rehearsing the Heligoland attack, prompting the British to cancel that operation.

By autumn, Murray & Tregurtha delivered two of what were called Mustin Sea Sled

Airplane Carriers. The sleds were fifty-five feet long and were driven by four 450-horse-power marine engines. By this time, the project had moved to Hampton Roads, where Mustin worked with naval constructor Jerome Hunsaker to modify a Caproni Ca.5 bomber provided by the Army.

On 14 October, Mustin was temporarily appointed a captain from 21 September, and on the 26th, he accepted the appointment and executed the oath of office. Events continued to move his way.

In November, Mustin held his first sea sled trials with the Caproni. The sled was able to reach a speed of fifty-five miles per hour by itself and sixty miles per hour with the plane on board with its engines running to provide an extra boost. On 15 November, the unit tested unsuccessfully at Hampton Roads because of trouble with the plane's release mechanism. Mustin performed additional tests on 7 March 1919 with a land version of the Curtiss N-9 seaplane, piloted by Lt. (jg) F. M. Johnson, USNR. The following day, Johnson repeated the launch, this time with an observer on board.

Addressing the sea sled concept in a 1919 debrief before the General Board, Mustin said that in the end the authorities did not go for the Holland plan and were going to use bases in England. Flights would have commenced from the sleds some forty to sixty miles from Heligoland and returned to England. He was never able to launch the Caproni because of trouble with the releasing gear on the sled, he reported, but had no problems when using the smaller N-9. He quoted an autumn 1918 production study that claimed the manufacturers could have delivered three hundred boats, sufficient to start the bombing campaign in the spring.

The 11 November 1918 armistice closed the book on Mustin's operation, but the research community did not forget the sleds. In 1940, the Navy was looking "to obtain the best possible craft for motor torpedo boat purchases with the highest degree of efficiency in operation." A department report asserted the Mustin and Taylor's work "resulted in round bottom and V bottom boats and Sea Sleds not yet surpassed in the Navy. . . . It is believed that this speed achieved in 1918 exceeds that of any craft now in operation or under construction in the United States Navy." Naval architect George F. Crouch, who received $15,000 in 1939 from the Navy for a V-bottom design, said "the Sea Sled type of construction is superior to that of any V bottom boat in speed, riding qualities and weight carrying ability."

After the 1919 trials, Mustin's sea sleds returned to crash boat duty. For taking seaplanes to sea, the Navy would return to other mechanisms built on existing hulls.

Aviators and gunnery types continued to wrestle with attempts to mount launch platforms on gun turrets.

While in London, Sims had been impressed with the Royal Navy's progress in naval aviation with the fleet. Twenty-two British battleships had turret platforms. In December 1918, Sims had sparred with Benson, ever skeptical about aviation technology, over an idea to acquire from the British thirty-six wheeled aircraft to put on U.S. battleships. Much to Benson's displeasure, the aviators succeeded in mounting a platform on the battleship *Texas* and putting aboard a wheeled Sopwith Camel that made its first launch on 9 March 1919.

Another concept gaining credence was the aircraft carrier. On 2 August 1917, Royal Navy Squadron Commander E. H. Dunning had made the first wheeled landing on a carrier under way when he landed his Sopwith Pup on the *Furious*. It was another first that fueled Sims's and Mustin's view that the carrier would revolutionize warfare at sea. They had the support of the influential Atlantic Fleet commander in chief, Adm. Henry T. Mayo, who was by the end of the war very much an aviation proponent. Mayo believed strongly that an aircraft carrier could and should operate with battleships. As the 1919 General Board began to address aviation, Sims and Twining, now captain of the *Texas,* argued that the skies would be crucial to victory in any future battle at sea.

At the 1919 hearings, Benson said wheeled aircraft on carriers were "essentially undesirable" and that the ship type was good only for transport and service of seaplanes. Notwithstanding the British—and now the Japanese—carrier programs, his view reflected that of the bureaus. Given their expectation that postwar funding would be tight, they stood solidly behind battleship modernization, not carriers.

On 18 March, Mustin gave testimony before Admirals Fletcher and Albert G. Winterhalter on air policy for the future and the general subject of the policy that should govern the development of aircraft. Mustin reiterated his view, first expressed to the board in 1916, that the service should have three shipboard aircraft types—in order of importance, a scouting/spotting machine, a torpedo/bomber, and a fighter.

Mustin's key criterion for the fighter was the ability to climb fast and reach twenty thousand feet, to attack zeppelins. He thus wanted a land machine with air bags that would inflate to float the plane for retrieval. Pontoons, he argued, detracted from performance. At the time, Mustin was keen on the Loening monoplane that the Army was using. Grover Loening was a New York aeronautical engineer who had been with the Sturtevant Aeroplane Company, which had built and tested his design of a steel-framed, fabric-covered combat fighter in 1915. The drawback was that he had no factory and had constructed only two planes.

Mustin plugged for two types of shore-based aircraft: a seaplane and a land machine fitted with air bags. With respect to the Navy's plan for maritime patrol stations, he noted that bad weather, that is, heavy seas, would hinder seaplane operation, both in terms of takeoff and landing. Land bases were thus critical for Navy maritime patrol as a substitute for seaplanes in bad weather.

In terms of the festering interservice roles-and-missions debates over who controlled aviation and where, land-based naval air was an important counter to the Army, which was attempting to divide the air picture at the coastline. Mustin was doing everything he could to make the case for land machines in the Navy, concluding that the board could call all its aircraft types seaplanes "because they fly over the sea." Wheeled aircraft were the thin end of the wedge to get funding for the carrier.

Mustin said he agreed with the board's current specifications for the carrier, in that it endorsed wheeled aircraft. The board's position helped sway the decision on the *Jupiter,* one of the latest *Neptune*-class fleet colliers. Against the wishes of the battleship admirals, the Navy would convert the ship to its first aircraft carrier, the *Langley.*

In June, the General Board concluded in its report that "to enable the United States to meet on at least equal terms any possible enemy . . . fleet aviation must be developed to the fullest extent. Aircraft have become an essential arm of the fleet. A Naval air service must be established, capable of accompanying and operating with the fleet in all waters of the globe."

Aviation had turned the corner, and the Navy finally was moving toward Mustin's vision.

After his testimony, Mustin returned to Hampton Roads. On 27 March, he reported to the air station for additional duty as a member of the board that would develop Navy aviation policy. Headed by Capt. David F. Sellers and including Whiting, Bellinger, and Naval Constructor Yates, the group's activities were in step with the General Board's interest in the impact air power would have on the fleet.

In May, Mustin was assigned to represent the Navy in an interagency group studying aviation organization in Britain, France, and Italy. Appointed by Secretary of War Newton D. Baker and led by his assistant secretary, Benedict Crowell, the mission also included an Army colonel and lieutenant colonel as well as a number of industry and Department of Commerce officials. Its goal was to learn how the United States could keep its aircraft industry alive in peacetime and able to expand in national emergencies.

In August, the Crowell mission issued its report recommending establishment of a separate government department of aeronautics, with the Navy, Army, and Department of Commerce represented. Mustin had promised Daniels, who had his suspicions about Crowell's intent, that he would oppose any attempt at unification of the air services, but he was outvoted by the other representatives. As one account read, "Violating its precept, the mission favored a single national air force and placing technical functions in civilian hands."

Daniels and the Navy first had become sensitive to the unification issue that March, when Hunsaker arrived in Washington after a sojourn in Europe. Returning to the United States on the liner *Aquitania* with the controversial Brig. Gen. Billy Mitchell, Hunsaker got wind of the general's plan to establish an independent air service. A decorated combat airman, Mitchell was preparing to cross swords with both the Army's "ground-minded" infantry and artillery and the Navy's battleship admirals. His object was a united air force that would replace the Navy as the nation's "first line of defense."

Mustin had agreed to Crowell's report on condition that naval aviation remain with the Navy, that naval aviation personnel remain under the Navy with regard to operations and training, and that naval aviation equipment remain under control of the Navy. For some reason, he signed the report, upsetting Daniels and many others in the naval aviation community. In his own minority report, Mustin noted that aviators in Europe wanted only naval aviators to serve their fleets. Two congressional proposals, the New and Curry Bills, resulted, both providing that the aviator who was senior in commissioned service would assume the rank of major general and would head a single air service. Mustin was senior to his Army counterpart aviator by two weeks and thus would have gotten the post and a two-grade promotion; nevertheless, he opposed any united air force.

On 7 April, Capt. Thomas Craven had relieved Irvin as director of naval aviation. At last Mustin allies with clout were moving into senior positions. Buoyed by the General Board's support for the carrier concept, Mustin and Towers impressed on Craven the need to fund the *Jupiter* conversion. Craven responded by going over Benson's head to Daniels, getting funds into the fiscal year 1920 Navy budget for the Navy's first ship for "carrier-borne" aircraft and additional conversion funds for two seaplane tenders to support "water-borne" aircraft.

On 1 August, one month before retiring as chief of naval operations, a displeased Benson responded by removing Craven's title, reducing him to a section head in operations and reorganizing naval aviation yet again. Within weeks, Adm. Robert E. Coontz, considered more attuned to the aviators' cause, became the Navy's second chief. The aviators still faced entrenched opposition from McKean, now a rear admiral, who was still chief of the Navy's Material Division.

The General Board's support for a naval flying corps, together with intensifying outside pressure for unification from Mitchell and the Crowell report, eventually would pull the Navy together to create a Bureau of Aeronautics. By 1922, even officers most antagonistic toward aviation would agree on the need for such a bureau to protect naval aviation assets and the Navy itself from Mitchell's specious assaults.

Chapter 10

Aviation in the Pacific

As the United States entered the 1920s, the heart and soul of her fleet was the battle-ship. During World War I, however, the U.S. Navy had undergone a series of techno-logical revolutions—in aviation, submarines, and radio—that had forced on the sen-ior leadership a number of hard decisions in terms of technology, tactics, and organization.

Still at the helm, the battleship admirals resisted the development of aviation, jus-tifying their opposition in the context of the times. A postwar United States had returned to isolationism. The trauma and scale of the European conflict had moved national sentiment firmly toward pacifism that expressed itself in the drive for disar-mament and for reductions in the army and navy budgets.

Aviators were looking ahead to future wars. Unfortunately, they also had to accept the hard truth that naval aviation had not shown itself to be a decisive element in the war. The U.S. Navy had expanded the number of officers and men in aviation and deployed them to Europe on the ground, but aviators could point to no large integrated tactical action against land or sea targets, however many individual sorties they could boast.

Ironically, the battleship admirals likewise were at a loss for any decisive action to support their cause. During the war, U.S. battleships had served primarily as training assets in the western Atlantic. The only integrated actions the Navy could attempt to trumpet were its tactical use of submarines and of destroyers for antisubmarine warfare during convoy operations.

The battleship navy thus was on the defensive. Despite the lessons of the war, the gun club still regarded future naval warfare as a struggle between battleships for control of the sea. The aviators concluded otherwise. Given the tight budgets, the battleship admirals needed to husband funds; the aviators wanted more. It was a recipe for conflict.

Mustin personified these battles. Because of promotion requirements, he missed some of the seminal events in the march of naval aviation. His outspokenness meant that indignant superiors on his selection boards and those who oversaw his detailing to line assignments sought to punish him—or at least that was how it appeared to him.

As Archibald D. Turnbull and Clifford L. Lord characterized him in their history of early naval aviation, "Mustin, a foremost expert in gunnery long before he took to the air, never lost his vision of 16-inch turrets thundering at an enemy far beyond the skyline visible from the bridge above them." At the outset, then, he built his vision for naval aviation around putting ordnance on target. As he matured and gained seniority, he would complete that vision, not as a gunner but as a tactician. The next war, he could see, would be against Japan, and he wanted to be able to take the war to them—with naval aviation and carriers.

By 1919, the Navy was getting anxious over Japanese developments in the Pacific and had transferred a number of ships from the Atlantic. The United States realized after the Paris Peace Conference that it had a gap between its Far East policy and its ability to implement it. Specifically, the Open Door Policy in China clashed with what Japan regarded as its special interests on the Asian mainland. In a military sense, Japan's League of Nations–awarded mandate over the Marshall and Caroline Islands threatened U.S. sea lines of communication to the Philippines.

In June 1919, the Navy reestablished the Pacific Fleet and established the Fleet Air Detachment after determining that Japan was its greatest potential enemy. At the time, Adm. Hugh Rodman was Pacific Fleet commander in chief. Twining, now a rear admiral, was his chief of staff. Together, they represented a more pro-aviation inclination than had their predecessors.

On 1 October 1919, Mustin received orders to command the battleship *Wisconsin,* and he detached from the Bureau of Construction and Repair three days later. His new ship was in reserve, and she was to remain inactive at the Philadelphia Navy Yard until her decommissioning on 15 May 1920. Mustin also drew additional duty as a member of the American Aviation Mission, reporting on the Inter-Allied Aeronautical Convention, which the United States did not in fact ratify. An adjunct to the Paris Peace Conference, the convention arrived at forty-three articles that dealt with all technical, operational, and organizational aspects of civil aviation, in particular the principle of sovereignty of national airspace, and led to the creation of the International Commission for Air Navigation.

In all probability, Mustin fought the orders, for they were modified to allow him to return to the bureau on 22 October. On 20 November, he got new orders to San Diego to take command of the *Aroostook,* a mine layer newly converted to an aircraft tender. Having assisted Towers and Putty Read in their momentous transatlantic flight from Newfoundland to Portugal the year before, the *Aroostook* had been on the West Coast for only a month when the Navy formally established aviation as part of the Pacific Fleet. Mustin's assignment included command of the air detachment, which was divided into three divisions: land plane, ship plane, and seaplane.

He arrived in California in early December. It was to be a reunion with some of his closest colleagues. Towers had been in San Diego since October and would be his chief of staff. Since 8 November 1917, Win Spencer had been commanding officer of the naval air station at Coronado's North Island and in charge of training. Mustin requested and got Mitscher to join him on the *Aroostook*. Mitscher came dual-hatted as senior squadron commander and commander of the detachment of air forces at the fleet air base in San Diego.

In January 1920, Mustin went up the coast to March Field at Riverside to take the Army Air Service course in land flying and aerobatics. Corinne and the boys arrived in Coronado mid-month, setting up house at 800 A Avenue, very near the Spencers. Together, the Mustin, Towers, and Spencer households would host the aviation social set in Coronado. When not partying at home, the gang would descend on the Hotel Del Coronado just down the street, where the three couples would play bridge, bezique, and backgammon.

Corinne's coming was a particular relief to her cousin Wallis, who felt isolated by life in Coronado. In the early 1920s, the town was somewhat of a backwater for pennywise junior officers, and both Wallis and Lily Towers were champing at the bit for something more than a succession of aviator blowouts. Despite Prohibition, the Towerses were known for their strong martinis and wild parties.

International society did come to San Diego at least occasionally. On 7 April, Wallis's future husband, the Prince of Wales, paid a visit aboard the battle cruiser *Renown.* Mustin ordered a formation of flying boats to meet the ship, and invitations followed for Mustin, Towers, Mitscher, and others, along with their wives, to attend a swank mayoral ball that night at Hotel Del. The next day, the prince invited them to come aboard the *Renown* for a grand reception of some four hundred guests. The Spencers, however, did not attend either function. By this time, Win's drinking meant his appearance at such events was a risky proposition at best.

Among Mustin's initial objectives as commander of his air detachment was proving the contribution that aviation could make to gunnery. In the March 1919 Atlantic Fleet exercises, Twining's *Texas* had conducted a main battery exercise that proved not only the use of aircraft for spotting but also the need for command of the air. Twining also had validated Mustin's contention that pontoon planes were neither fast enough nor maneuverable enough to tackle wheeled fighters in aerial combat. In the Pacific, the Japanese would have plenty of land-based aircraft on their island chains.

In February 1920, the Pacific battleships converged on San Diego for four months of drills. Among them was the *Mississippi,* commanded by Capt. William Moffett. Although skeptical of aviation in 1913 when Towers had first tried to proselytize him at Guantánamo, Moffett had embraced and advocated aviation while commander of Great Lakes Naval Training Center, establishing its first aviation detachment. His *Mississippi* was the Navy's second ship, after the *Texas,* to have a launching ramp over one of her turrets.

Mustin drew Moffett to him, recognizing in the more senior captain his potential as the Navy's eventual standard-bearer for aviation. He spent long hours conveying to Moffett his view of aviation's future as an offensive component of the fleet.

First, Moffett needed to see for himself how effective aviation had become in spotting gunfire. In the early 1920s, ranges had reached over the horizon with "plunging fire" that relied on battleship-launched spotters. In late May, Mustin and Towers put Mitscher in the air with his F-5Ls, Curtiss JN "Jenny" observation/trainers, and Sopwith Camels to spot for the *Mississippi.* As a result, the *Mississippi* got the highest gunnery score of any ship in the Pacific Fleet, nearly equaling all the other battleships' scores combined. On 10 June, the planes used wireless Morse code to transmit to the gun boss ranges to twenty-two thousand yards. In Admiral Rodman's opinion, Mustin had proved his case for using aircraft as spotters. Naval gunfire had entered a new era.

In July, the Navy designated Mustin's command Air Force, Pacific Fleet. Over the summer, he and Towers reorganized the force into squadrons of fighters and patrol planes, with the idea of moving further beyond seaplane operations. Added to his detachment Mustin now had de Haviland DH-4 observation planes and the new Vought VE-7 trainers. He used this extended variety of land aircraft to train for carrier operations that would begin when the *Langley* entered the fleet in 1922. Mustin put Mitscher in charge of land training and built an 836-foot wooden platform, an area somewhat larger than the anticipated flight deck, on North Island.

Also in July, Mustin had three F-5Ls fly nonstop to San Francisco. During the nearly seven-hour passage north, the planes maintained radio communication to a distance of more than two hundred miles. It was the first of three such long-distance flights in preparation for a much longer exercise Mustin was planning for the late autumn. In an October demonstration, he had Towers, Spencer, and Charles P. Mason scout the fleet on its return from Hawaii. Despite very bad weather, the aviators made the intercept 165 miles off San Pedro.

Thanks to the extensive work of Mustin and others, the U.S. Navy finally had accepted aviation to the extent that it could support scouting and spotting. By 1921, planes and catapults were on all battleships in the Atlantic, and they soon would go on ten scout cruisers of the *Omaha* class.

With these and other exercises and efforts under his belt, Mustin also that month developed a tactical aviation manual. He still wanted to prove the feasibility of naval aircraft as a tactical striking force, and he also was eager to surpass the distance of the transatlantic NC flight the year before. His thought was to mount an operation similar to his sea sled plan in the Pacific, where the tactical need would be to support the defense of the Philippines or to attack Japanese units threatening the Panama Canal.

In addition to the famed transatlantic flight of Towers and Read, in 1919 flying boats on the East Coast had made a trip from Norfolk to Guantánamo, flying in hops from tender to tender. Mustin proposed to do the same; however, his Balboa flight would be three times the distance. A by-product of the flight would be the heretofore nonexistent aviation data on Pacific ports his crews could gather. In addition to a report on matériel, he would file a second on harbors.

For the trip south, Mustin got Rodman to provide support with seven ships: two tenders, two tankers, and three mine sweepers. Nine Atlantic F-5Ls supported by tenders would fly simultaneously from Hampton Roads to Colon, on the Caribbean side of Panama. On 29 December, low clouds threatened rain. Not a breath of wind rippled the water of San Diego Bay. At 8:00 A.M. Mustin led twelve F-5Ls and two of Towers's

NC flying boats into the air. Heavy with fuel and spare parts, the flying boats flew in pairs, careful to remain beneath any overcast at a constant five hundred to a thousand feet. Each had two pilots, a radioman, and two mechanics. Mustin flew in the "Number 9" with Lieutenant (jg) Spaulding.

They were on the first of what would be a 3,019-mile series of beach hopping flights, billed by *The Philadelphia Enquirer* as the "Longest and Most Hazardous Sea Flight in American History." This leg was a 325-mile run to Bartoleme Bay, a third of the way along the coast of Baja California. The next was the 257 miles to Magdalena Bay. There the planes rendezvoused with the *Aroostook,* aboard which Mustin and his crews spent New Year's Eve watching a film.

The third leg took them to the southernmost tip of Baja California. Ahead was the 350-mile stretch of open water to the Mexican mainland. Setting out on the crossing, Mustin underestimated the wind. Steering 25 degrees off course to the left caused him to miss the mine sweeper *Kingfisher,* the first of two guard ships on station along the planned route. On 3 January, he made Banderas Bay after what had compounded into a 445-mile run. The aviators found the harbor dangerously exposed and rocked continuously by swells that put considerable stress on the seaplanes. En route to Acapulco, however, conditions were calm, and Mustin reported seeing giant rays and turtles in the waters below and a great forest fire raging ashore to the east. Arriving, they were relieved to find the harbor sufficiently sheltered to allow the mechanics to work on the seaplane engines. At this point, Towers and his NC team had trouble with the engines on their supporting ship and were rendered nonoperational.

Still ahead was potentially the most perilous part of the flight: the passage into Oaxaca's Gulf of Tehuantepec to the harbor at Salina Cruz. The gulf had the reputation as the most treacherous water between Cape Horn and Alaska, with especially dangerous and unpredictable winds off Chipequa Bay. On 7 January, Mustin was flying with Spaulding in the "Number 9" when a violent gust slammed the nose and left wing upward. He pushed the wheel forward, twisting it hard left while booting a hard left rudder. Even with Spaulding adding his weight to the controls, the plane nevertheless hung in a stall. Another sudden gust knocked it into a dive. With the wheels clamped to their chests, the pair saw the air speed meter climb past seventy knots before they finally were able to lift the nose. The wind continued to buffet the plane as Mustin put it to sea.

The weather quickly worsened, the waters below turning an angry black, flecked by streaks of white. The wind shifted to the north-northwest. For the next hour, Mustin flew a nearly uncontrollable plane twenty miles to Chipequa Bay. Exhausted, he gave the controls to Spaulding and ordered his radioman to send a message to the others to land there. The radio, however, had gone dead.

Spaulding managed to put the plane on the water. Overhead, they saw the other NCs making their way through the turbulence en route to Salina Cruz, still unaware of Number 9's situation. After an hour, the crew attempted to resume their flight. Just as the plane was airborne, a violent gust knocked its starboard wing tip into the water, gashing its float. Mustin ordered his men to ride the port wing to keep the other clear of the water.

As Mustin and his crew secured themselves to the port wing, his mechanic jury-rigged a boatswain's chair from the starboard wing and pumped water from the float. A shark began to circle as he fastened a temporary patch over the gash. By the time he had finished the repair, it was too late to attempt a takeoff. The men had to spend the night on water, accompanied by more circling sharks. By morning, the weather had cleared, and the seaplane was able to cover the fifteen miles to Salina Cruz in half an hour. When Mustin arrived, he found the tempest had damaged a number of aircraft. Only four were able to get into the air the next day. The others remained behind for repairs, unable to continue the flight until early on 11 January.

The next leg was a grueling 485-mile stretch to El Salvador's La Union Harbor in the Gulf of Fonseca, where Mustin waited for all the planes to rendezvous. Then followed a comparatively easy hop to well-protected Punta Arenas, Costa Rica. On 14 January, the planes arrived in Bahia Honda, Panama, a 243-mile flight from Punta Arenas. The final leg was another 243-mile course to Balboa. They arrived over the canal on the fifteenth, having flown 3,019 miles in seventeen days. The planes averaged 51.6 flying hours for an average speed of 58.3 knots.

Mustin took his twelve planes across the isthmus to the naval air station at Coco Solo, where they remained for five weeks of overhauls. Each aircraft got a new engine.

For the return trip north, Mustin wanted to replace the slower mine sweepers with destroyers. Rodman gave him five. On 23 February, he led his flight into the air from Balboa to begin retracing their hops to San Diego. He revised the northward route to bypass Salina Cruz and Banderas Bay.

For the return flights, the weather was mercifully uneventful. The aviators had learned to avoid turbulent air by climbing to three thousand feet. During the northbound trek, his planes suffered fifteen forced landings, and one sank while being towed by a destroyer.

On the afternoon of 10 March, Mustin reached the final destroyer position as he approached the Coronado Islands southwest of Tijuana. Looking at his fuel gage, he saw he had just enough gas to reach San Diego, as long as the head wind he was bucking did not increase. Continuing northward, he observed a gradual lessening of white-caps on the water. The wind appeared to be dropping.

At 3:15 he passed inside the islands. Shortly thereafter, a formation of nine DH-4Bs arrived to meet him. Approaching the Tijuana shoreline, he could see to his right the historic marble Boundary Monument overlooking the Pacific—"a very welcome sight," he later reported. At 3:40, he "passed over the Strand and into San Diego Bay accompanied by one of the Fleet Air Force Voughts." Seventeen minutes later, he landed in the bay and taxied to the beach. Glancing at his fuel gage, he saw he had one gallon remaining.

NC "Number 5" had arrived fifteen minutes earlier, the first of the eleven planes that would make it to San Diego that day and the next. The northbound flight time totaled sixteen days, seven hours, and thirty-five minutes, the last plane landing with a time that bettered the southbound flight by twenty minutes.

Mustin's 6,076-mile flight demonstrated that the strategic range of flying boats enabled them to operate with the fleet. His Panama journey was 1,800 miles longer than the transatlantic trip. One newspaper account headlined Mustin and his aviators as "Columbuses of the air."

Chapter 11

BuAer and Henry Croskey's Legacy

As Mustin was in the air returning from Panama, Washington was in the midst of a changing of the guard with the arrival of Warren G. Harding's Republican administration and a new Congress. Among the issues that confronted the new president was the growing Army-vs.-Navy rancor generated by Billy Mitchell and his noisy campaign for a united air force. Looking for postwar economies, Harding entered office on 4 March 1921 supporting the unification idea.

General Mitchell had become assistant to the U.S. Army's chief of the Air Service in 1921 and was inundating political Washington and the press with his ideas on the primacy of air power. Part of his argument was economic—that it would be cheaper to defend the U.S. coastline with unified aviation than with a navy. His envisaged his new armed service as land based and possibly including Army aircraft carriers. Land-based aviation also could be an offensive force that could project power to Asia and Europe using northern air routes over the continental land bridges, as Read had demonstrated with his May 1919 transatlantic flight.

Mitchell's public relations blitz horrified even the battleship admirals. Many now felt that the Navy needed to institutionalize naval aviation as soon as possible to preempt any attempt to pry it from the service.

For a year, an influential memo from a naval reservist advocating a Bureau of Aeronautics had been circulating within the Navy Department. Daniels and Roosevelt had become supporters of the bureau idea, and Harding's new secretary of the navy, Edwin Denby, arrived to find Coontz and a number of other senior officers in full support. Change was afoot. In Congress, Rep. Fred C. Hicks, a staunch Navy ally on the House Naval Affairs Committee, had introduced a bill to establish a Bureau of Aeronautics.

The leadership in the Bureaus of Navigation, Ordnance, and Steam and Engineering, along with the General Board, opposed the concept. Oddly enough, so did Craven, who had been serving as director of naval aviation for more than a year. Many gave him little chance at the title of Bureau of Aeronautics chief, however, because of his support for carrier funding in the fiscal year 1920 budget. He also lost a number of his aviator supporters when he later opposed the idea of converting battle cruisers to carriers, purportedly on the ground that they would be too slow to operate with the fleet.

A contender who had substantial support was Mustin. A strong proponent of carrier conversion, Mustin was the only bona fide naval aviator who was a captain. He declined a number of attempts to put his name forward, however, believing that the battleship admirals, fearful of a Navy-wide coup, would fight any aviator as chief of the bureau. Another more personal reason could have been his recognition that his health was failing. Several times during his command of the Pacific Air Force, chest pains so debilitated him that Towers had to assume his responsibilities.

By 1921, aviation's champions were well established: Ellyson, Whiting, Towers, and Mitscher. But all were too junior to lead naval aviation at so critical a time. Sensing that aviation needed an advocate who had seniority and the confidence of both the aviation and line communities, Mustin pushed another name to the fore: Capt. William A. Moffett.

As early as 1919, Mustin had written to Daniels and even to Crowell in the War Department supporting Moffett as bureau chief. He prodded Moffett to take the job, urging him to get support from the prominent Republican industrialist William K. Wrigley, with whom he had worked closely while commanding Great Lakes. Moffett agreed, and before the Harding administration had completed its first month in office, Moffett relieved Craven as director of naval aviation.

As Moffett moved through Washington circles that spring, he could see that his office would have to rise to Billy Mitchell's lobbying challenge. His first act was to tap Lt. Cdr. Richard Byrd, a savvy young aviator and the Navy Department's liaison to

Congressman Hicks. A scion of Virginia's Byrd political family, he knew how to work Capitol Hill.

By April, the Navy had succeeded in reversing Harding's position on unification. On 12 April, he told Congress he supported a Bureau of Aeronautics and separate air arms for the services. The statement gave Hicks the green light to proceed with his bill. The aviators rejoiced, confident that the president's about-face had saved their aircraft carriers and kept the ships in the sea service.

Opposition within the Navy remained, notably from a new quarter: Rear Adm. Joseph Strauss, who in June became the Navy's budget officer, a newly designated billet. The political momentum, however, was with the aviators. Hicks's bill became law, and on 25 July, the U.S. Navy established its Bureau of Aeronautics at Main Navy on Washington's Constitution Avenue, with Moffett as its two-star chief.

Promising Mustin that he would bring him to Washington, Moffett selected him right away as his assistant chief. On 29 June, Mitscher relieved him in San Diego.

On 25 July, Mustin arrived at the bureau to assume his new duties. He joined a staff of high-caliber officers, all hand-picked by Moffett. Capt. Alfred W. Johnson was Moffett's deputy until December, when he took command of the Navy's first lighter-than-aircraft tender, the *Wright,* with additional duty as commander of the Atlantic Fleet's air squadrons. Moffett put aviators in charge throughout the bureau. Whiting headed Plans and the carrier program; Hunsaker, the Material Division; Bellinger, the Flight Division. Aviation also had a key ally in Capt. Harris L. Laning, head of the tactics department at the Naval War College, who had responsibility for the war games. Also on board were Ellyson and eventually Mitscher.

Among his duties, Mustin guided flight training. With Byrd handling Congress, much of his work was with civilian industrialists, for which he could draw on the business savvy gleaned from his family, his patent experience, lessons from the sea sled project, and his lifelong recognition that warriors could not ignore the industrial dimension of new programs. Still in its infancy, aviation did not yet have an industrial center. Mustin realized, therefore, that aircraft could be manufactured anywhere—specifically, in the West, where the Navy could create a new industrial base with its own congressional constituency, separate from the infrastructure that supported the battleship in the East.

Prior to reporting to the bureau, Mustin had joined Moffett to witness the last phase of a series of tests off the Virginia Capes. The Navy had organized exercises to get detailed data on the effect of aerial bombing on ships and to determine how compartmentation could improve damage control. Mitchell, however, had been able to finagle Army participation to prove something else: the obsolescence of the battle-ship and the primacy of air power.

On 21 June, Navy F-5Ls at eleven hundred feet dropped twelve bombs on the German *U-117,* a spoil of war, sinking the submarine in short order. Eight days later, after receiving an alert that the radio-controlled U.S. battleship *Iowa* was in a twenty-five thousand square mile area, Navy aircraft located the target ship in one hour and fifty-seven minutes and attacked her with inert dummy bombs.

It was then that Mitchell was able to get the Army into the act in tests against other German spoils. On 13 July, army bombers sank the destroyer *G-102.* On 18 July, Army and Navy aircraft dropped seventy-four bombs to sink the light cruiser *Frankfurt.* The next day, Moffett and Mustin went to Norfolk to witness the culmination of the demonstrations, a two-day attack on the battleship *Ostfriesland.*

On day one, Navy and Marine Corps planes dropped fifty-two bombs on the ship. On day two, Army bombers delivered eleven one 1,000- and 2,000-pound bombs. The general predictably portrayed the exercise as heralding the end of the battleship. The Navy countered that the ship had been anchored and was neither maneuvering nor defending herself. In other words, the *Ostfriesland* was a sitting duck.

In spite of Navy attempts to convey that the exercise only illustrated the need for air protection, Mitchell seemed to win that round in the public relations war. Within the Navy, however, the bombing tests actually helped the carrier advocates, who maintained that the way to defend battleships against aerial threats was with carrier-based fighters providing air superiority.

The Washington Naval Conference, organized by U.S. Secretary of State Charles Evans Hughes, was a diplomatic expression of disarmament fever in reaction to the horrors of World War I. Because the naval arms race was deemed a major cause of the conflict, the conference aimed to restrict naval spending and construction. Delegates began their deliberations in November 1921 and within a month signed the first of two political agreements that aspired to stabilize the Pacific. The Four Power Pact dissolved the Anglo-Japanese alliance, a U.S. foreign policy objective, and the Nine Power Pact affirmed the United States' Open Door and Chinese sovereignty. On 6 February 1922, the United States, Great Britain, Japan, France, and Italy signed the key military agreement, the Five Power Naval Disarmament Treaty.

Together these pacts might have been good for U.S. foreign policy, but naval officers deemed them a disaster for the Navy. In addition to placing limitations on battleship displacement and armament and establishing ratios for capital ships among the five naval powers, the Washington Treaty stipulated that the United States could not fortify any of its Pacific possessions west of Hawaii—for example, Luzon or Guam. Britain could not fortify its possessions east of Singapore. The Japanese, however, essentially were free to deploy land-based aviation to their Pacific islands—an obvious potential threat to U.S. naval forces operating in the region.

The treaty included some provisions limiting the size of carriers but did not place limits on aircraft development. Mustin participated with Moffett in some of the twelve meetings of the Committee on Aircraft held between 30 November and 30 December, and afterward, Moffett put him in charge of redrafting aviation war plans in line with the treaty. Nine days before its signing, Mustin had finally gotten his commission as a regular captain, effective from 1 January.

It was now clear to Mustin and others that the carrier would be the United States' only meaningful offensive and defensive capability in the western Pacific. In view of the treaty's limitations, Mustin and fellow bureau staffers Johnson and Whiting emphasized speed. With Whiting, Mustin took the lead in pushing for fast carriers, stressing also the need for aerial scouting and overhead protection.

Having considered the carrier as a strike weapon back in 1916, Mustin was the first to suggest that aircraft at sea could equal the striking power of a battleship. In his gunner's mind, both aircraft and battleships were platforms that delivered ordnance on target—merely the means to an end. The carrier was not equivalent to the battleship but rather part of an offensive naval system. It was carrier-supported naval aviation delivering ordnance that was analogous to other combatants.

In March 1922, Mustin forwarded his draft aviation policy to Moffett. The document had support from Rear Adm. William Veazie Pratt, who was on the General Board, and Capt. Frank Schofield, who had commanded the *Texas.* The plan called for two fighters and two observation planes for every battleship and cruiser. One plane of each type would go on every destroyer leader, first-class destroyer, and submarine of cruising size. Aircraft tenders would have four observation planes and twelve patrol planes. Carriers would deploy with thirty fighters, thirty observers, fifteen scouts, and fifteen torpedo planes, the latter being too heavy and dangerous to launch from a catapult on a battleship or small combatant.

To get funding for more carriers, Mustin first would have to get support from the General Board to convert two battle cruiser hulls slated for scrapping under the Washington Naval Treaty. On 1 July, Congress authorized funds to make them the

Navy's second and third carriers, the *Lexington* and *Saratoga*—a major achievement for Mustin and the aviation community—but money was tight and line officers argued that scarce funds should go to treaty cruisers.

Mustin testified at two General Board hearings, on 3 March and again on 7 November. The chairman was Rear Adm. W. L. Rodgers, a scholarly naval officer who had written extensively on gunnery. Sitting with him was Vice Adm. Henry Huse, who had commanded U.S. naval forces in Europe during the war, and Joseph Strauss, the Navy's new budget baron. All were foes of aviation.

Mustin wanted three carriers to follow the *Lexington* and *Saratoga,* to reach the limit of the naval arms treaty. He was looking for thirty-three-knot platforms that could take eighty-five planes. His concept was for carriers to operate in task force formations, not independently. He wanted to have carrier-based bombers that could strike Japan ten times farther inland than battleship guns. With Laning at his side to discuss aviation in terms of war game results, Mustin characterized the War College rules as "extremely conservative." He took issue with the notion that a patrol plane kill required a division or more of fighters, and he further noted that in favoring bombers and torpedo planes the rules restricted the carrier allowances of fighters to a number below what he, as an aviator, would recommend.

Rodgers challenged Mustin throughout, as did Capt. Luke McNamee, the director of naval intelligence, who took aim at how the aviator proposed to compose a naval force to attack Japan. Although he had served with Sims in Europe early in the war, McNamee had been Benson's protégé later in 1917 and had represented him in Paris during the 1919 treaty discussions. He was not, therefore, disposed to any arguments for aviation.

On 10 August, via a letter from Moffett to the secretary of the Navy, Mustin's 1922 memo went forward officially as a four-year plan. Moffett did not get approval, however. Revised and resubmitted as a five-year plan, the final document called for a thousand-aircraft building program for fighters, spotters, torpedo bombers, and supporting equipment such as catapults. The plan also included a request for five aircraft tenders.

The General Board approved only an 870-aircraft program and reduced Mustin's plan to one observer and two fighters for each of eighteen battleships, two observers for each of ten cruisers, one fighter per ship for eighteen destroyers, one observer for each of nine submarines, and a few of each type of aircraft for support ships.

In the end, the Navy budget did not grant even these recommendations. Implementation of the 1922 plan did not come for another four years. Following later recommendations by President Calvin Coolidge's Aircraft Board, Congress passed the Air

Commerce Act of 1926 that provided funds for long-range development of army and navy aviation.

For a time, naval aviation would have to make do with the *Langley*. In March 1922, the Navy commissioned the ship in Norfolk, with Whiting in command. On 17 October, Lt. Virgil C. Griffin made the first launch. Nine days later, Chevalier performed her first carrier landing. On 18 November, Whiting made the first catapult shot. In the spring of 1923, Mustin was able to get the *Langley* to operate in Fleet Problem 1, which tested the defenses of the Panama Canal. There, the carrier demonstrated takeoffs and landings; it was the first full use of aircraft with the fleet.

When he came to the Bureau of Aeronautics in 1921, Mustin had moved his family to Washington, at 3610 Macomb Street, N.W. Just after his March 1922 testimony to the General Board, the pains in his chest worsened, probably aggravated by the stress of the bureaucratic wrangling that persisted around naval aviation. On 31 March, as a precaution, he updated his will to include his third son, Gordon Sinclair, born in 1917.

In January 1923, Mustin's condition became so serious that he was admitted to the Washington Naval Hospital, where he remained on and off through the spring. He was diagnosed with an aortic aneurysm. Whether caused by the strain of the 1918 rescue, his smoking, or high blood pressure, the ballooning in the artery was rubbing against his ribs. From time to time, the pain was excruciating. On 17 May, while still in hospital, he made yet another will. By 10 July, his condition had not improved, and the department ordered him to the Newport Naval Hospital for treatment. The Washington Naval Hospital discharged him the following day. On 12 July, he arrived in Newport and was admitted.

Leaving the three boys at their Macomb Street home with the Mitschers, Corinne joined her husband in Newport, staying with the commander of the Naval Training Center, Capt. Frank Taylor Evans, and his wife. It was apparent that Mustin would not soon be able to resume his responsibilities at the bureau. On 30 July, the Navy relieved him as the assistant chief but kept him on duty at the bureau. On 23 August 1923, not yet fifty years old, Naval Aviator Number 11 died.

Several days later, Corinne received a letter from Marion, Massachusetts:

My dear Mrs. Mustin,

I have just learned of the death of your dear husband, and I want to assure you of my heartfelt sympathy. He was one of my best friends in the service. More than twenty years ago when the navy found out that it could not hit anything, he was one of the first to support the effort for reform. With entire unselfishness, he gave it the full measure of his tireless energy and scientific knowledge, and it was largely due to him that we made such rapid progress in the beginning. His invaluable qualities of vision and imagination enabled him to see the possibilities of progress and his enthusiasm inspired others to their best efforts; and during the long period when the airplane was an object of derision as a naval weapon, he clearly saw its enormous possibilities and sustained the movement for its development against opposition that would have discouraged a man of less character and devotion. He was the real brain and spirit of this development, and his death has deprived the navy of the services of a loyal, devoted and progressive spirit; and I can assure you that his many friends in the navy, of whom I am proud to be one, will share in your grief in this great loss.

Very sincerely yours Wm. S. Sims

Mustin's bold vision for naval aviation would not come to fruition until 1930, when the U.S. Navy finally exercised carrier operations around a complete tactical unit—a carrier group consisting of one carrier, four cruisers, and two destroyer squadrons. It was then that the service seriously began to define the requirements for the fast carrier and the offensive tactical development to go with it.

That September, Admiral Pratt became chief of naval operations, the first to embrace naval aviation. In February 1932, during the annual grand joint Army and Navy exercise, Rear Adm. Harry E. Yarnell cleverly employed the carriers *Lexington* and *Saratoga* to demonstrate conclusively the possibility of an air attack on Pearl Harbor. The exercise proved Mustin's theories, but still the Navy resisted any promulgation of far-reaching conclusions.

Contemplating air strikes of this magnitude, however, highlighted one truth: Navy gunners had a lot of work to do in the area of antiaircraft armament, fire control, and doctrine. That challenge would be for the gun bosses of another generation and another Mustin—Henry Croskey's son Lloyd Montague.

PART II
The Gun Boss

Chapter 12

Growing Up a Navy Junior

"All through [the] early years of my life, I had started off with some very self-reliant and strong-minded ancestors, and found myself exposed to a father who was indeed self-reliant and strong-minded and didn't mind getting into controversies over the things that he believed required attention."

So began retired Vice Adm. Lloyd Montague Mustin in 1973 as he sat for the first of a series of oral history interviews for the U.S. Naval Institute. Henry C. Mustin had "made a tremendous impression" on his eldest son. Said Lloyd of his father, "His accomplishments and his relationships with other people were continuously being brought to my consciousness."

Lloyd was born on Sunday, 30 July 1911, in the family quarters at the Philadelphia Navy Yard. Almost two years later, he was joined on 27 March by a brother, Henry Ashmead, whom their father would call "Ashmead."

Lloyd's first memories were his childhood days at Quarters A, their white-columned, two-story house at Pensacola where the family moved in early 1914. The boys had a favorite nanny, Rose, a local African-American woman, while all the family benefited from additional household help provided by Filipino stewards off the battleship *Mississippi,* the station ship.

Henry C. Mustin proved to be the loving and attentive father that he vowed he would be. He introduced Lloyd and his brother both to facets of his life in the Navy and to the activities at Pensacola. Often, he accompanied them to the planes, lifting them into the seats and placing their hands on the controls. The boys were ever in his thoughts. One night during the 1914 Vera Cruz deployment, he wrote Corinne longingly, "I am wondering how my adorable little family is getting on; about this time in the evening Lloyd is probably fighting to keep from going to bed." In a later letter, he cautioned, "Don't let Ashmead fall off the porch; now that he is walking I keep worrying about that un-railed porch."

Henry C. returned from Mexico to entertain his sons with the little details that might interest a child. One particular story that stuck with Lloyd was his father telling him how the ship dyed the sailors' white uniforms khaki by dipping them in coffee before sending them ashore with the Marines.

The following summer, Henry C. taught his soon-to-be four-year-old to swim. He also started teaching him hymns. The boys were very much a part of their parents' lives in Pensacola. Lloyd and his brother watched the repeated launchings of dummy loads to test catapult gear, and they were there when their father made his historic 1915 shot off the *North Carolina*. Although well known to all the aviators at the station, the boys found two particular friends in Marc Mitscher and George D. Murray, who arrived for training in January 1915.

In the spring of 1916, Lloyd developed an infatuation over Corinne's young house guest, his second cousin Wallis Warfield, who was a member of the Mustin household during two lengthy periods through the year. Wallis would remember him bedeviling her with his persistent interest in his train set. Years later, Lloyd admitted that he was very jealous when she finally left their house to marry Win Spencer, Aviator Number 20. The year offered plenty of distraction, however. Lloyd was a witness to all the activities on the base and was particularly thrilled by the action in the aftermath of an accident, with the comings and goings of the crash boats. At home, he was witness to all the politics surrounding the establishment of naval aviation. Lloyd remembered seeing his father poring over various designs for the aviator uniforms and insignia on the dining room table.

Early in 1917, Henry C. again went to sea. Corinne was carrying their third child, Gordon Sinclair. As the United States prepared to enter the war in Europe, Lloyd got "parked" at Gunston School on Maryland's Eastern Shore. Set in a rural area on the Corsica River, Gunston consisted of a large brown-shingle Victorian farmhouse and outbuildings and enrolled about thirty boys and girls. It was owned by Sam and Mary Middleton, who were related to Corinne's sister Kate through her husband, Charles Phillips Hill. Lloyd called them "Uncle Sam" and "Aunt Mary."

Lloyd remained at Gunston until the spring of 1919, when Corinne and the younger boys went to Wakefield to stay with her mother. Henry C. was by then working in Washington and periodically would descend with news of all that he and naval aviation were doing. Lloyd specifically remembered hearing from him about the 16–27 May 1919 transatlantic flight of several NC flying boats from Trepassey Bay, Newfoundland, via the Azores to Lisbon. From time to time, the family would travel to Philadelphia to visit the Mustin side of the family. Lloyd began reading very early and was taken with Father Lloyd's book collection, which included a number of editions of *Robinson Crusoe*.

In mid-January 1920, Corinne and the boys joined Henry C. in Coronado. There, they found much the same excitement as they had experienced in Pensacola, except that Lloyd now was older—going on nine years old—and could absorb much more. Henry C. would take him down to the ships and explain to him the fundamentals of ship-handling, on which he prided himself. The aviation activity also was intense at the time, and Lloyd remembered in particular the work on the F-5L twin float torpedo planes and the torpedo drop testing in Spanish Bight, the body of water that used to be between North Island and the rest of Coronado.

In October 1921, when Henry C. returned to Washington, Corinne again took the children to Wakefield, where Lloyd and Ashmead went to school at Flint Hill. That winter had a great deal of snow, which afforded ample opportunities for sledding and snowball fights. The following spring, the Mustins moved to the house at 3610 Macomb Street, N.W., and the brothers went to John Eaton Elementary School on Thirty-fourth Street, N.W.

In the summer of 1922, Lloyd was again at Wakefield, this time without his family. While he missed his brothers, he thoroughly enjoyed the pool and his first rifle, probably given to him for his eleventh birthday. Into the autumn, Henry C.'s health began to deteriorate. By January 1923, he was in the hospital, and Corinne was spending more and more time at his bedside. To help take care of the children, Pete and Frances Mitscher came to live in the house. In July, when the Navy transferred Henry C. to Newport for further treatment, Lloyd and Ashmead returned to the Eastern Shore for summer camp at Gunston. It would be the first of a succession of five camp summers and two more school years at Gunston for Lloyd.

One of the Middleton sons, Atherton, ran the camp, which consisted of tent living, hard by the Corsica River. The camp regime fostered self-reliance. The boys and girls trapped muskrats in the marshes and hunted rabbits and dove. They learned to raise tents, a skill Lloyd valued when he went ashore on Guadalcanal during World War II. "I was the only guy who knew how to do it." Every summer, they rebuilt the pier, always collapsed by the previous winter's ice. In addition to participating in various intramural athletics, they canoed, sailed, and one year even built a log cabin. Once Lloyd and his cohorts found an abandoned rowboat in need of repair. They rigged a mast and sail and nailed a metal Sunoco gas station sign to the bottom to use as a keel.

In late August, Henry C. Mustin died. Lloyd felt that his family had little money left. In December, when George Barnett retired from the Marine Corps as a major general, Lelia once again took Corinne under her wing, Lloyd recalled. He maintained that his aunt took his mother to Europe, but it may have been only that she paid for the trip. Early in 1924, Corinne did cross the Atlantic, but according to biographers of the Duchess of Windsor, it was with her cousin Wallis. The two began their five-month trip on the *President Garfield*. They spent a great deal of time in Paris, circulating among the naval staff and embassy set with foreign service officers, who might also have been naval intelligence liaison personnel. One biographer tantalizingly alleges that the women acted as intelligence couriers, a practice supposedly common among trusted Navy wives.

The strain on the two elder Mustin boys, bereft of both their father and mother, must have been intense. Lloyd recalled that he and Henry "fought like cats and dogs." During a basketball game, the two brothers found themselves on opposite teams. The competition became fierce, and Henry tried to grab the ball from him. The boys threw punches, but according to Lloyd, that was their last fight.

In September, Corinne was home and staying with another cousin, Claire Bayless, on Gunston Farm near Centreville to be near Lloyd and Henry. She brought with her a number of gifts, one of which was a sailboat for Lloyd. He christened it the *Osprey*. Before long, the other boys had made copies and the children were able to hold races.

By 1925, Henry C.'s younger brother, John Burton, felt it was time for Lloyd to leave the rural innocence of Gunston. A lieutenant colonel in the Philadelphia Troop and a World War I veteran, Burton had inherited the Stratford Knitting Mill and was now a prosperous businessman with a house in Rosemont on the Philadelphia Main Line. He arranged for his young nephew to go to St. Luke's in nearby Wayne. In the autumn of 1925, Lloyd entered as a tenth grader. Like his father, he proved to be an all-around athlete, playing football, tennis, and baseball. In one sport, swimming, he was outstanding.

Corinne remained on Gunston Farm. Not only was it close to Gunston School, where Henry still attended, but it also was a convenient ferry ride across the Chesapeake Bay to Annapolis. There, since June, George Murray, now a lieutenant commander, had been establishing an aeronautical course at the Naval Academy. His wife, Margaret, had died in 1920, and George had not remarried. He and Corinne began seeing each other, at times with the boys in tow.

Although Murray was two years younger than Corinne, a mutual and deep affection blossomed. Sometime in the autumn of 1925, they announced their engagement. One newspaper account read that Murray and Mustin "were devoted friends and one of the prettiest features of the romance is the fact that its ripening was fostered by the young naval officer's keen interest in the three sons of his old friend, whom Mrs. Mustin has been struggling to bring up." The notice referred to an "almost immediate marriage" with a ceremony planned to be held at Wakefield.

The boys responded to Murray's sincere interest in their welfare with devotion, especially Gordon. The youngest, he perhaps knew his stepfather most intimately, and years later he named his first son George Dominic Murray Mustin. Lloyd remembered Murray as a thoughtful and considerate man who was always "quietly enjoining" him to do just a little bit better in every endeavor, particularly in his academics.

Lloyd continued to prosper at St. Luke's. His interests extended to model airplanes and later guns, all carefully recorded and captioned in his photo albums along with candid portraits of his friends. He shot his first rabbit in 1926. Two years later, he proudly photographed his armory of five rifles and shotguns, a testament to an interest in small arms that would last a lifetime.

Henry C.'s impact would continue to be felt by Lloyd and his brothers. On 17 September 1926, they attended the dedication of Mustin Field at the Naval Aircraft Factory in Philadelphia's Navy Yard. It was a major event that drew 1,500 spectators, among them Assistant Secretary of the Navy Theodore Douglas Robinson, Brig. Gen. Douglas MacArthur, Rear Adm. William Moffett, and Philadelphia Mayor W. Freeland Kendrick, who had been a childhood friend of their father's. The dedication took place toward the end of the six-month Philadelphia Sesquicentennial Exhibition, whose copresident was John Wanamaker. Thirty foreign nations attended the Sesqui, and all the planes from the exhibition flew in formation with aircraft of the Army, Navy, and Marine Corps to honor Mustin.

With the airship *Los Angeles* circling above, Robinson opened the ceremonies and escorted the Mustin boys forward on the dais. "The youngsters stood manfully facing the throng," read one press account, before pulling a lanyard that released twelve carrier pigeons. The birds flew away to various Army posts around the country carrying messages to the Navy, War, Commerce, and Post Office Departments, as well as other aviation activities, announcing the opening of the field.

Then Mustin's most senior classmate, Capt. William L. Littlefield, commander of the yard, unveiled a monument with a plate reading, "This Tablet Erected By His Naval Academy Classmates." The ceremonies continued with a skywriting of "Mustin Field," a flyover that cascaded flowers onto the tablet, a bombing demonstration by three Martin bombers, and a series of stunts culminating in "bubble busting," where aircraft chased balloons until breaking them all.

After his father died, Lloyd evidently did not feel any compulsion to make the Navy a career, but this event might have been a turning point in his thinking.

After the dedication, the Littlefields, who had a son also at St. Luke's, began inviting Lloyd for weekends, and he often would find himself exploring the Navy Yard by himself. One favorite route was into the back basin, where the old ships of the reserve force were nested into what was called "Red Lead Row." Among them was Dewey's flagship from the Battle of Manila Bay. "And one day standing up on the bridge of the *Olympia* and looking down over the bow, something came to me in a flash," recalled Lloyd. "Then, right then and there, and I've remembered it ever since—I want to go to sea, I do want to be a naval officer. I want to go out and have a part in running these things, these ships that go to sea."

Corinne, George, and Burton thereupon began the process of helping him secure a presidential appointment to the Naval Academy. In no time, they had the assistance of the influential retired general, James A. Drain, a former commander of the American Legion. On 24 January 1927, Drain met with President Calvin Coolidge and mentioned Lloyd's name. That afternoon, he put his endorsement in writing. "He is splendidly developed physically. He takes part in all of the major athletic sports, and his scholastic report for the past current month showed him first in his class and third in the entire school," Drain wrote. Citing Henry C.'s distinguished career, he added, "This young man, Lloyd M. Mustin, has precisely the breed and characteristics to justify confidence in his worthiness to be an officer of our Navy. I hope you can see your way clear to appoint him."

Evidently, the White House acted promptly on the request. Seven days later, Secretary of the Navy Curtis D. Wilber granted Lloyd permission to take the competitive examination on the ground that he was qualified for a presidential appointment as a midshipman at large. There was a catch, however: At fifteen, Lloyd was too young to take the spring 1927 examination. On 3 February, the Navy Department ordered him to take the 1928 exam at the Philadelphia Post Office.

The Mustins continued to press for an exception, engaging Maj. M. Carter Hall of the law firm Carlin, Carlin & Hall to assist. Drain wrote Hall on 12 February that he had met with the president again that day and was able to discuss the Mustin matter. He had tried to get the president to appoint Lloyd without the 1928 competitive exam, but Coolidge would not make an exception. He did promise, however, that if Lloyd did not finish first in the exam then he would seriously consider appointing him, should Drain raise the issue again.

Sometime in the spring, the trustees of St. Luke's sold the school buildings and grounds to St. David's Country Club. Given the delay until 1928, the Mustins felt the best course was to put Lloyd into Washington's Columbian Preparatory School—known familiarly as Shadman's, after its founder. At the time, the school was dedicated to preparing boys for the competitive exams for both Annapolis and West Point. Because Lloyd did not have a high school diploma, he would have to take all the exams.

Now that he would be in Washington, he was reassigned to take the test at Temporary Building Number 1 at Eighteenth and D Streets, N.W., on 18 April 1928.

On 9 September 1927, Lloyd started at Shadman's, which he found "dreary." Unlike St. Luke's, the school offered no athletics. In October 1927, Corinne and George left for the West Coast, where George had duty as the aviation aide to the commander in chief of the Battle Fleet. Lloyd went to live with his Aunt Kate and Uncle Charles Hill. On weekends, he visited Lelia and George Barnett at Wakefield.

Lloyd applied himself furiously to his task, inspired by Murray, who always encouraged him to do better. His confidence was brimming. "If I was as good as I thought I was," he later said, "I wasn't going to let anybody else beat me." Knowing that his future depended on his making the presidential list's top twenty-five, on 18 April Lloyd began his three days of exams.

While the Murrays were in Washington for a brief visit, a 15 May letter from the Navy arrived for Corinne Murray. George opened it by accident. It read that Lloyd had passed with a 4.0 in physics and a 2.8 in English. Murray forwarded it to Lloyd, writing in the margin, "Great work! Your mark in Physics gives me a great thrill, because I know you only had one year. *Keep it up*—make the best marks you can—you owe it to *yourself.*"

When the Navy Department published the presidential list, Lloyd stood number five. The eldest son of Henry C. Mustin was on his way to Annapolis.

Chapter 13

The Academy Years

IT ISN'T LUCK, IT'S SKILL

On the morning of 14 June 1928, Lloyd Mustin took a bus from his Aunt Kate Hill's house, where he had stayed during his year of prepping at Shadman's, and headed to Washington. There, he rendezvoused with three other Shadman's boys ready to enter the U.S. Naval Academy, and together they rode the two-car Washington-Baltimore-Annapolis electric train to Annapolis. On the way, Lloyd and William C. F. Robards agreed to room with each other, an arrangement that would last all four years. Arriving mid-morning, the boys passed their physical exams, and that afternoon in Memorial Hall they were sworn in before Commo. Oliver Hazard Perry's battle flag, emblazoned with the immortal words, "Don't Give Up the Ship."

Lloyd and his Shadman's crew were among the first inducted in his class. In the 1920s, entering midshipmen still arrived throughout plebe summer, and by the beginning of the autumn term, the class of 1932 had grown to some 630 plebes. The Naval Academy now was regiment-sized, with four battalions.

At sixteen, Lloyd felt he lacked the maturity of many of his classmates. Some were approaching twenty-one and had been active-duty sailors. Others had transferred from other institutions and had a number of university-level courses under their belts. Nevertheless, he eagerly rose to the challenge. Thanks to his experiences at Gunston, he did well in all the water competitions, the cutter races, and especially sailing. He was very competitive in athletics and clearly was going to be a swimming star at the academy. As a plebe, he was able to beat a number of the varsity midshipmen.

Lloyd also wanted to play football, but moving daily from the pool to practice field was hard on his body—a serious charley horse completely hobbled him. Weighing only 143 pounds, he realized football was not going to work. He decided to concentrate on intercollegiate swimming, where he would compete against the best in the Northeast.

The summer allowed little time for relaxation, but the plebes had Sunday afternoons to roam the yard and mix with friends. Before Shadman's, Billy Robards had gone to Severn School, another academy prep school up the Severn River, and knew a number of the local girls. One Sunday, he and Lloyd were walking around the yard when they spied two young girls sitting on the grass below Stribling Walk. Robards knew one, a fourteen-year-old Navy junior named Emily Proctor Morton. She was with Elizabeth Brainard, daughter of the academy's executive officer, Cdr. Roland M. Brainard. Emily and Elizabeth, known as Dodo, seemed to know everybody and in turn were well known to the midshipmen in the yard. Lloyd felt assured that through his well-connected roommate and his attractive young friends he would not be short of a social life.

On 28 September, plebe summer came to an end, and the rest of the regiment returned to start the autumn term. Quickly finding himself well behind the curve in academics, Lloyd struggled to make his grades. His particular challenge was chemistry, a course he had not taken before. For a time, he was lost in the ranks—at least until the swimming season began on 16 February. The plebe swim team opener was against a big-city high school, Baltimore Polytechic. Lloyd scored impressive wins in the fifty-yard and hundred-yard freestyle and as a member of the relay team. He was now in the limelight.

On 8 June, Lloyd began his three-month youngster cruise. He drew duty on the *Arkansas,* the cruise flagship, an oil-burner that originally had been a coal-burning battleship. By way of training, he and the other youngsters spent one month with engineers and two months on deck. They stood watches and had station assignments, including gunnery battle stations. The 1929 practice squadron went to southern Europe and England, stopping in Barcelona, Naples, Gibraltar, and Weymouth. Lloyd was able to make trips to Rome and to London. By 15 August, they were in Hampton Roads for a five-day visit, during which time Lloyd and his fellow midshipmen swimmers swam against the Virginia Beach lifeguards. While in Norfolk, he made contact with his old St. Luke's School roommate, Pat Mason, whose father was stationed at Fort Monroe.

Pat teamed Lloyd with his sister Ellen. After several dates, the pair made plans for Lloyd to return for his upcoming September leave.

On 19 August, the squadron left for the Southern Drill Grounds off the Virginia Capes for a week of short-range battle practice. Lloyd's gunnery battle station was in Turret Number Six, the after turret of the 12-inch battery. He was a powder man, one of the loading crew who handled the powder bags and positioned them in the breech behind the shells. The target practice rated each turret essentially on hits per gun per minute. Lloyd's turret, led by first-class midshipmen from the class of 1930, performed so well that it received an *E* for efficiency, an unusual achievement for a midshipman turret.

Notwithstanding the difficulties of plebe year, Lloyd had applied himself and finished well. In a class of 528, he stood fiftieth in order of merit. Unlike his rambunctious father, he received only twenty-eight demerits.

On 27 September, he was back at the academy to start his youngster year. By the end of October, he had hit his stride academically, doing especially well in mechanical engineering and ordnance. Years later, he said he liked these courses because they "represented the rationalization and the orderly organization of the facts of the world, the physical facts, and why they were the way they were." Once he and his classmates got into professional subjects, Lloyd felt he had an advantage—he was, after all, a Navy junior. He had read about naval ordnance while staying with his aunt and uncle, the Hills, who had had two boys at the academy. His good conduct record, however, took a hit that term; his first youngster report card hammered him with seventy demerits.

Over the Christmas break, Lloyd headed again to Norfolk. He still was interested in developing his romance with Ellen, and he also would be able to spend time with his mother and George, who had returned to the East Coast that summer and were living just north of the city. George was executive officer of the aircraft tender *Wright* at the time, but over the holiday, he got word that he was going to London to serve as assistant naval attaché at the U.S. embassies in London, Paris, Berlin, and The Hague.

Lloyd returned to Annapolis ready to throw himself into the swimming season. The first meet was on 22 February against Dartmouth, and Lloyd broke the academy record in the 440-yard freestyle by 8.4 seconds. It was a good start to what would be a winning year for the Navy team.

That winter, Lloyd began to notice trouble with his eyes. In early March, he reported his condition to the academy doctors, who hospitalized him for testing and observation. On 4 March, he was diagnosed as having astigmatism with near-sightedness. The news was a disappointment; he had wanted to be an aviator like his father.

Following June Week 1930, Lloyd remained at the academy for his Aviation Summer, when he and his classmates would get an introduction to naval aviation and aircraft. He remembered clearly his delight at the opportunity to fire a Lewis machine gun while riding in the rear seat in one of the trainers. "If I could see it, I'd hit it," he said.

Lloyd had begun to spend time with the Academy's smart set, which revolved around Emily Morton and Jane Snyder, the commandant's daughter. The girls ran with a solid Navy junior crowd. Staying with Emily that summer was her good friend Clair King, the fourth of six daughters fathered by Ernest J. King of wartime five-star fame. At the time, King was captain of the carrier *Lexington*. Clair had been friends with Emily since his last tour at the Naval Academy earlier in the twenties. Sometime earlier in the year, Lloyd's relationship with Ellen Mason had atrophied. With the swirl of activity that Emily engendered around her in Annapolis, Norfolk could have been a million miles away.

Lloyd had continued to advance in his class standing, finishing his youngster year thirty-sixth in a class that had dwindled to 464. He earned 128 demerits. As one of the younger members, he had not yet shown much leadership. He only stood 3.25 in executive aptitude for the service; it was an unimpressive 318th in the class standing.

The autumn term that began on 26 September 1930 would focus on more professional subjects. Finding a real interest in navigation and seamanship, Lloyd advanced in his class standing with each successive report.

He continued to thrive as a swimmer, as well. The 1931 season was the academy's most successful to date. In a 1 March upset over Princeton, Lloyd was the high scorer, with wins in the 440- and 100-yard events. Victory had hinged on the outcome of the relay, however. When Lloyd dove into the pool to swim the relay's final lap, Princeton had the lead. Lloyd passed his opponent for the finish; the Navy won, thirty-eight to twenty-four.

Also swimming with the Navy team that year was a third classman and native Annapolitan, Thomas Howard Morton, Emily's brother. A popular hometown hero, he came with a lot of fan support. At virtually every home meet, his mother, his sister, and a bevy of Navy juniors would line the first row of the stands. As the season progressed, it was clear to Lloyd that Emily's eyes were not always on her brother.

When not surrounded by her cousins and friends that winter, Emily was on the arm of Lloyd's classmate, Robert L. Baker, to whom she would become engaged. Though a good-humored Southern gentleman, Baker was not a standout among midshipmen.

Lloyd, on the other hand, had become a veritable king, and "the Natatorium was his castle," wrote Robards in their *Lucky Bag*. "Early in his career, Lloyd realized the futility of attempting to elude the femmes, so he started meeting them half way (in the yard, at the Main Office, or out in town), and he slays 'em all with a glance and leaves them to languish."

Emily recognized a Neptune when she saw one, and even at sixteen she had an expert eye. During a succession of football seasons, she had routinely appeared in the photogravure sections of the Baltimore papers along with Jane Snyder and others, all bedecked in Navy colors. Her name had prominently appeared with other Navy juniors in the Annapolis society columns, replete with captioned photos, that featured events at such local hot spots as the Annapolis Roads Beach Club.

As winter passed to spring, Emily's engagement to Baker passed into history, and she and Lloyd became an item in no time. By the end of May, Lloyd was smitten. Leading into the June Week festivities, he took Emily to the Ring Dance. Within the oversized rendering of the class ring for 1932, Emily dipped Lloyd's ring and a miniature into the waters of the seven seas before they put them on each other's fingers. Lloyd and Emily were engaged.

It was an engagement between two Navy families with deep traditions of service. Emily Proctor Morton was a daughter of the Navy. Her father and Lloyd's had been a class apart at the academy and had served together several times. It was through her mother, Grace Howard Morton, however, that Emily's military and naval line was most far-reaching.

Emily was the granddaughter of Thomas Benton Howard, one of the modern U.S. Navy's first four-star admirals and a hydrographer, who came from a distinguished military line traceable through the Revolutionary War back to Europe and the MacKay clan of Scotland. His maternal grandfather was an army general of the War of 1812 and Mexican War fame, Aeneas MacKay. His father, Bushrod B. Howard, was a close friend of Ulysses S. Grant, with whom he served in the Mexican War.

In the first year of the Civil War, Bushrod served as captain of Company I of the Nineteenth Illinois Infantry. On 17 September 1861, he and his company were traveling by train to Washington to join the Army of the Potomac. As the cars were crossing the Beaver Creek Bridge of the Ohio and Mississippi Railroad, the structure collapsed. He and nineteen of his men were among those fatally injured.

Before Bushrod died, Grant made it to his side and promised to look after his two sons, Thomas Benton and Douglas Alexander. Later, as president, he saw that Douglas went to West Point. Thomas entered the Naval Academy with the class of 1873. On graduation, Grant presented him with his commissioning sword. In 1879, he married Anne Jacobs Claude, daughter of the Annapolis mayor.

The Howards had three sons, all of whom went to the Naval Academy: Douglas Legate Howard, Abram Claude Howard, and Bushrod Brush Howard. Their one daughter was Grace Laurens Howard, Emily's mother.

Grace was the belle of Annapolis in the early years of the century. During the 1902–1903 academic year, the midshipmen regarded the nineteen-year-old as "the most popular lady in the Academy" and chose her to ring out the old year and ring in new year on the old Japanese bell. She reigned among the mids and junior officers—until she met Lt. Cdr. James Proctor Morton of the class of 1895. In March 1911, he and Grace were married at Christ Episcopal Church in Norfolk.

On 1 March 1912, their first child, Thomas Howard, was born. On 7 August 1914, while Morton was at Naval Academy directing the Postgraduate School, their second child, Emily, was born.

Morton spent most of his life at sea, winning the Navy Cross in World War I and dying young in 1924. Emily and Tom had been raised by their mother and her parents in Annapolis at the Claude family home at 8 State Circle, now the Governor Calvert House Hotel. In addition to their Grandfather Howard, their uncle, Doug Howard, also a Navy Cross recipient, was a major influence on their young lives. Doug and Ruth Howard's two oldest children, Jim and Anne, were virtually the same ages as their first cousins, and the four spent their childhood more as siblings.

On 4 June, the class of 1931 graduated. Two days later, Lloyd had his seabag packed and ready to go for his first class cruise. This time, the practice squadron would steam exclusively with oil.

Kissing Emily good-bye at the pier on Santee Basin, Lloyd boarded the *Arkansas* motor launch and made way once again to the flagship riding at anchor at Annapolis Roads. Almost two weeks later, the squadron met its first adventure. On 14 June, the ships received an SOS from Sir Hubert Wilkins, the Australian explorer. Wilkins and his volunteer crew of submariners and scientists were nearby, in a surplus U.S. submarine he had named *Nautilus,* dead in the water. They had been en route to Norway with the eventual objective of diving beneath the Arctic ice for a submerged run to the North Pole. Lloyd was in the mast when the ships spotted the sub. The *Wyoming* took the *Nautilus* in tow for some 890 nautical miles, until relieved on the twenty-second by a tug.

On 21 June, the *Arkansas* arrived at Cherbourg, where she would remain until 1 July. On this cruise, Lloyd and his class spent their first month with the engineers. The second month in Europe, they would be on deck. Westbound during their final month, they would draw duty in the navigation department. While with the deck gang, Lloyd's station was as coxswain of the number two motor launch, which had a midshipman boat crew. It was a sizable craft rated at 190 passengers. Drawing on boyhood experience at Gunston, piloting yachts up the Corsica River, he had no doubts as to his performance.

The squadron arrived in Kiel on 5 July for a four-day call. During the well-publicized swimming competition between the *Arkansas* and the *Wyoming*, Lloyd was a standout in the relays. From Germany, the cruise went to Copenhagen. There, Corinne and a woman friend joined Lloyd, where he and several mids squired them "to places they probably wouldn't have been able to go if they were alone."

On 11 July, the squadron steamed to Oslo for three days, then to Edinburgh from the sixteenth to the twenty-eighth. Lloyd was able to get leave to join his mother in Glasgow. Corinne had driven north from London to tour with her son through the Lake Country and around Loch Lomond.

After sojourns in Cadiz and Tangier, the midshipmen returned to Hampton Roads on 13 August for three days of society. The Navy and the city fathers had planned their liberty to the minute. Landing at 4:30 P.M., the mids were assigned to cars, each driven by a young and eligible hostess. They would go to a private home for a mixer, and from there to one or more of the dances that would begin at 9:00 P.M. at the Norfolk Country Club, New Chamberlin Hotel, Princess Anne Country Club, or Cavalier Beach Club in Virginia Beach, where Lloyd and his gang eventually found themselves.

On 18 August, the squadron returned to sea for nine days of short-range battle practice, during which Lloyd was a gun captain of a five-inch broadside gun. Early in one exercise, around the third shot of the first set, a flustered powder man failed to get the powder bag fully into the chamber. When another mid on the gun crew closed the breach, he crushed the end of the bag, which spilled both black powder and loose smokeless powder into the breach that now could not close. Realizing that his gun would lose points for any delay between shots, Lloyd meticulously swept the surfaces clean, notwithstanding that the inadvertent mixture of black and smokeless powders could self-ignite. By chance, the practice observers happened to witness Lloyd's grace under pressure.

One of the observers immediately reported the incident to the academy, which led to a 26 August letter of commendation from the superintendent to the commandant praising Lloyd for his most creditable manner during training. The superintendent directed him to issue Lloyd formal congratulations when he returned from his September leave. As a result, the academy appointed Lloyd as Third Company commander.

Lloyd finished his second class year standing sixteenth in his class of 440. He had a mere thirty demerits. Significantly, in his professional subjects he was first in ordnance and gunnery with a 3.65 and third in engineering and aeronautics. It had been the year of his maturing. He now stood 92 in executive aptitude, a tremendous advance over his youngster standing.

On 29 August, Lloyd departed New York on the White Star Line's RMS *Majestic* with his brother Henry to visit Corinne in London. The Murrays were living at 18 Carlyle Square in trendy Chelsea. To Lloyd's delight, he found that also in town was his cousin Wallis, who had remarried in 1928 to an American shipping broker, Ernest Simpson. When he was ready to return stateside, Lloyd discovered that his return ship, the Cunard Line's RMS *Aquitania,* had a delayed departure. He realized he would miss the start of the term on 25 September, but the academy fortunately granted him further leave.

When Lloyd finally returned to Annapolis, he found that Emily, too, had had an active social life that summer. It had been her brother Tom's Aviation Summer, and she took the opportunity to do the town with a number of his classmates from the class of 1933—in particular, Draper L. Kauffman. According to legend, by that September, Emily had collected seven rings. Kauffman's was only the latest. The showdown was at a dance at Ogle Hall, now the academy's alumni house on College Avenue. When Lloyd confronted Emily, she removed his ring along with the six others in her purse and threw the lot at him. He then took issue with Kauffman, who was later known as the father of the Navy's underwater demolition teams and was the academy's forty-fourth superintendent. Lloyd reportedly "won the argument."

Evidently, he was able to repair the damage. As a firstie and a three striper, he could go on the town every day to ensure his fiancée's troth. Emily still lived with her mother on the second floor of 8 State Circle. Lloyd's routine was to "dog trot" to Emily's for a fifteen-minute visit after swimming practice and then return with another "dog trot" to the Yard.

The 1932 swimming season was stellar for the mids. Lloyd captained a strong team that returned with all but two from the previous year. A sprint star in 100- and 220-yard events, Lloyd finished high among the Eastern League's top ten. Another standout was second classman Raymond Webb Thompson Jr., who finished second in the league. One of the best collegiate swimmers of his day, Thompson held the fifty-yard national record. For the first time, Navy hosted the Intercollegiates, where Lloyd came in third in the fifty. Yale finished first in the Eastern League. Lloyd's Navy swimmers ranked second.

As the year moved into his final spring in the yard, Lloyd's thoughts turned to June Week, graduation, and commissioning. On 4 May, the class of '32 had its class supper. On Monday, 13 May, Lloyd and Emily were at the Hubbard Boat House for the N Dance, honoring the year's midshipman athletes. That afternoon, he had requested his four tickets for the graduation exercises. His guests would be Corinne, his Uncle Burton, his Aunt Lelia, and Emily. His one great disappointment was that his Third Company did not win the company competition. He took it hard. By now, he had come to regard himself as a winner. As Robards wrote in their *Lucky Bag,* "Lloyd will reach the top in anything he undertakes, for 'It isn't luck, it's skill.'"

Now twenty, Lloyd finished eleventh in his first class year and eighteenth for the four years in a class of 423. He had twenty-five demerits for the year. In executive aptitude, he stood thirty-fifth. Lloyd had achieved star grades of 3.4, which for a second year in a row had entitled him to wear a star on his collar.

Since his return from summer leave in the autumn of 1931, Lloyd had courted Emily with corsages of pink or red roses for every occasion. Dated 1 June, the year's bill from the Annapolis Flower Shop at 68 Maryland Avenue to Lloyd's room at 2323 Bancroft Hall was $15.50, including Emily's corsage for the graduation ceremonies the following day.

As Lloyd prepared for his graduation and commissioning, he received among many one letter that would serve as his personal charge:

Bureau of Aeronautics
1 June 1932

My dear Lloyd:

It is hard for me to tell you of the extreme pleasure I feel in seeing you about to graduate from the Academy and receive your commission as Ensign. The deep friendship and sincere admiration and respect that I had for your father make me feel overjoyed that the name of Mustin is again on the officer rolls of the Service.

I know you will love the life, and you can have no higher ambition to work for than living up to the splendid reputation that your father achieved.

With my very best wishes for your success and my congratulations on your completion of the course at the Academy, I am

Sincerely yours,

Wm A. Moffett

The post-commissioning festivities always included scores of marriages, but Lloyd and Emily would not be so blessed. Corinne and Grace Morton vetoed any such proposition. Lloyd was twenty; Emily, seventeen.

Lloyd took solace in the fact that all freshly minted ensigns received fifteen-day memberships to the Army and Navy Club in downtown Washington. For several nights, he and Emily joined other young couples at the club dances. Lloyd stayed variously with his aunts, while Emily camped with Dodo Brainard, whose father had returned east to the Navy Yard.

Meanwhile in Annapolis, the discussions over the couple's future continued. Doug Howard eventually convinced his sister that Lloyd would make a more than acceptable son-in-law. Grace relented, conceding her brother's point that a marriage would have to happen quickly: Lloyd was to report to his ship by the end of the month.

Word got to Lloyd and Emily, who celebrated among their friends at Arlington's Army-Navy Country Club, where all consumed significant amounts of bootleg booze. The next day, they returned to Annapolis to get a marriage license from the Anne Arundel County Courthouse. Someone said a minister in Glen Burnie could perform the ceremony. Emily left by car with her cousin, Jim Howard, who was also her brother Tom's classmate. Lloyd followed with a convoy of friends who had partied with them the night before. Years later, he recalled that the minister could not marry them because the license was from a different county. In fact, Glen Burnie is in the same county as Annapolis. Whatever the real reason, the wedding party returned to Annapolis and St. Anne's, the Claude family's church, where they had their ceremony on 8 June. Grace held a reception at the Claude family apartments, 8 State Circle.

The couple had time for a two-week honeymoon. They spent a few days in Baltimore, followed by several nights in Washington at the Hamilton Hotel, then a favorite of midshipmen. The newlyweds went dancing at Club Michel at 1 Thomas

Circle, Washington's glamorous nightclub that hosted "Skin Young [of Paul Whiteman's orchestra] and his New York revue." From there, they went to Lloyd's Uncle Burton's in Rosemont.

When they returned to Annapolis, it was to pack and prepare to board a westbound train that would take them across the continent and into a life together in the Navy that would span the next five decades.

Chapter 14

On the Asiatic Station

BY THE SLOP CHUTE ON THE OL' WHANGPOO

The U.S. Navy of 1932 that Lloyd entered as an ensign was a world-class navy absorbed in the Pacific. World War I had left Britain economically exhausted, with a Royal Navy that was no longer the preeminent battle line in the world. Italy and France were restricting themselves largely to their own regional naval rivalry in the Mediterranean. Germany's fleet had been seized. As a result, the world's only other naval power was Japan.

By the 1920s, Japan clearly had become an expansionist military power. After declaring war on Germany in 1915, the Japanese launched their first campaign on the Chinese mainland, overrunning the German naval base and territory on the Shantung Peninsula. In 1917, pursuant to a secret agreement to support British acquisition of Germany's islands south of the equator in return for support of Japanese occupation of those north, Tokyo captured and occupied the German Marianas, and Caroline and Marshall Islands. Looking ahead, the Japanese viewed the Americans as their main geostrategic adversary. As such, their 1918 war plan proposed to start any Pacific campaign by capturing Guam and Philippines.

Since the Battle of Tsushima in 1905, the U.S. Navy had regarded the Imperial Japanese Navy as its Pacific adversary, as well. In 1911, it formalized War Plan Orange, geared to the defense of the Philippines. In essence, it called for the Army to hold Manila Bay until the Navy could reinforce or recapture the islands. The 1921 version of the plan, however, acknowledged Japan's regional naval superiority. It anticipated that the Navy would have to wage an island-hopping campaign from Hawaii through the Marshall Islands to retake Guam and the Philippines if they fell to Japan.

Although many U.S. naval officers could see the inevitability of a conflict with Japan, their prescience ran counter to postwar public opinion in the United States. The spirit of disarmament was high, as were pacifism and isolationism. When Republican President Warren Harding's secretary of state, Charles Evans Hughes, addressed the Washington Naval Conference on 12 November 1921, he astounded delegates by volunteering that the United States would build no more battleships and scrap those already under construction.

The Navy had to face both the Japanese threat in the Pacific and limits on its ability to counter it. In late 1922, it abolished the Atlantic Fleet and consolidated on the West Coast its first-line battleships into the U.S. Fleet. With twelve battleships and the carriers *Lexington* and *Saratoga* when commissioned, the U.S. Fleet was a four-star command based in San Pedro and San Diego.

One of the Washington disarmament treaties had established how many battleships each of the naval powers could have. The result, in terms of ship construction, was that the 1922 General Board policy for the next decade was to construct a treaty fleet, that is, one without new battleships. Throughout the interwar years, the Navy adapted to the treaty limitations by introducing new systems for existing battleships, new construction cruisers and submarines, and expanded aviation capabilities.

Of course, money did not flow automatically to any treaty fleet. Harding's Republican successor, Calvin Coolidge, was a supporter of continued arms limitation to reduce federal outlays and lower taxes. Republican Herbert Hoover, who entered the White House in 1929, was a Quaker and very much a disciple of disarmament. His secretary of state, Henry L. Stimson, was decidedly anti-Navy, and his secretary of Navy, Charles Francis Adams, had no clout.

In sum, pacifism, fiscal conservatism, and isolationism negated any potential for real naval expansion. Then, the stock market crashed in October 1929, and the subsequent depression certainly meant no money for shipbuilding. The worsening economic conditions that followed forced even London and Tokyo to reduce naval expenditures.

By 1930, the naval powers realized that the world economic crisis, together with the gaming of the 1922 treaty provisions, required their revisiting the capital ship ratios. When on 9 January 1930 George Murray, Corinne, and Gordon departed from New York for London on the SS *George Washington,* with them on the passenger list were Secretary Stimson, Secretary Adams, the General Board's Rear Adm. Hilary Jones, Adm. William Pratt, then commander in chief of the U.S. Fleet, William Moffett, Ambassador Dwight Morrow, and Senator David A. Reed. All were en route to the first London Disarmament Conference that would convene on 21 January.

Although the 1930 London Naval Treaty was popular internationally, its revised ratio allowed Japan to build more cruisers, destroyers, and submarines. The revision indicated to the Japanese that the United States would not go to war to enforce its Open Door Policy. Under pressure from Britain, the treaty also allowed more 6-inch and 8-inch cruiser construction, as well as acknowledgment of the so-called pocket battleship as a heavy cruiser class. In the United States, the Navy got one carrier and fifteen cruisers, but those ships did not slip down the ways until later in the decade.

With the 1930 elections, U.S. naval expansion got a powerful congressional ally when Georgia Congressman Carl Vinson became chairman of the Naval Affairs Committee. Vinson wanted more cruisers, destroyers, and submarines allowed under the London Conference agreement. By degrees, the political forces were aligning that eventually would reinvigorate the Navy, but for the better part of the decade, the service would have to swim against the tide.

After his graduation, Lloyd had less than the traditional month of leave. The Great Depression had put tremendous stress on economy, and to keep his travel expenses in fiscal year 1932, he had to report before 30 June. He and Emily took a train cross-country to Long Beach, where he would meet the *Augusta,* one of the United States' six treaty cruisers. His commanding officer was Cdr. James O. Richardson, who had been the ship's captain since her commissioning in early 1931.

As was practice at the time, Lloyd and his classmates received probationary commissionings as ensigns. After two years of commissioned service and successful completion of written exams, they would receive full commissions.

A half-dozen or so of the class of 1932 reported to the *Augusta,* including Lloyd's roommate, Billy Robards. The cruiser carried about thirty-five officers, roughly half her wartime complement. Whereas many midshipmen of the time still sought battleship assignments, Lloyd felt that battleship duty for a probationary ensign was little more than another practice cruise. Battleships had junior officer messes that segregated them from real responsibilities. On the cruisers, the ensigns messed with the other officers, and their responsibilities were real. In addition, the treaty cruisers had new gunnery systems. Their 8-inch batteries were long-range (35,200 yards). Thus, they could engage battleships.

When he asked for the *Augusta,* the ship had been homeported in Norfolk as flagship of the East Coast's Scouting Force. Lloyd had selected her for her home port, expecting to remain within easy reach of the academy, where its 1932 Olympic team would train. Along with Navy swimmer Ray Thompson, he was slated to go. Both reductions in strength and strategic concerns prompted the Navy to shift the Scouting Force to the Pacific, disrupting these plans. Lloyd decided to set this dream aside, although in fact the 1932 Olympiad was in Los Angeles. Now that his ship was in the Pacific, any attempt to train with other academy Olympians would conflict with his regular duties and adversely affect his class standing.

On the West Coast, the destroyers were homeported in San Diego. The battleships, carriers, and cruisers were in San Pedro and Long Beach, both of which had deeper harbors. In Long Beach, Lloyd and Emily found a fully furnished efficiency for $37.50 a month.

At the time, the Navy rotated its new ensigns through the ship departments. Lloyd's first assignment was to the communications division, then part of navigation, the senior department on the ship. For Lloyd, it was a rude experience. He felt the academy had prepared him inadequately for communications, and he found the procedures laborious and costly in terms of man-hours. Fortunately, he was reassigned after a month to the auxiliary division of the engineering department, where he felt very well prepared. Unlike the high-performance systems of today's Navy, the *Augusta*'s engineering plant was conservatively designed and thus was reliable and thoroughly maintainable. In addition, it had ample redundancy, which would prove vital in combat should the ship sustain battle damage.

In August, the *Augusta* went into dry dock at Mare Island, across the bay from San Francisco. By September, she was in Long Beach for gunnery practice that would last until Christmas. Although ammunition was in short supply, the force engaged in short-range, antiaircraft, long-range, and night battle practice.

Sometime before Lloyd went to sea for the 1933 fleet problem, Emily found she was pregnant with their first child. In February, the *Augusta* deployed with the father-to-be for the tactical exercise that took place annually in Hawaiian waters. While ashore in

Pearl Harbor, Lloyd coached the Scouting Force swim team, exercising his swimmers in the naval base's outdoor pool. When his team finally competed against the Battle Force swimmers, it won handily.

In March, the *Augusta* returned to Long Beach. At 5:54 P.M. on the tenth, Lloyd was below, engaged in the now familiar routines of the engineering department. Suddenly, he heard a roaring sound and felt a trembling, as if "an anchor chain [were] running out." Sprinting to the forecastle, he found nothing unusual topside but noticed a fire ashore at one of the oil tanks. An earthquake had struck the mainland.

What became known as the Long Beach Earthquake measured 6.4 on the Richter Scale. Although several miles from the epicenter, Long Beach and Compton sustained major damage. The *Augusta* put together a landing force that included electricians and pipe fitters to repair fallen power lines and ruptured gas, water, and sewer mains.

When the quake hit, Emily had been at home entertaining visitors. She had gotten herself and her guests away from the house, but it was immediately evident that the dwelling no longer was habitable. Faced with extensive damage ashore and continuing aftershocks, Emily eventually joined other wives and families who had come aboard ship for a few days until she was able to find another apartment.

Later in the spring, orders came for the *Augusta* to relieve the *Houston,* the flagship of the Asiatic Fleet on the China Station. Her new home port would be in Manila, where units wintered and received their overhauls. The *Augusta's* schedule called for a mid-July overhaul at the Puget Sound Navy Yard, but work would not begin until August, after the Scouting Force was able to find another ship to which to transfer the flag. In June, Emily left Long Beach for Seattle and eventually Bremerton, where she gave birth to their first son on 31 August. They christened him Henry Croskey Mustin after Lloyd's father.

Entering her overhaul, the *Augusta* prepared for what all hands expected to be an experience of a lifetime. The vast majority of the crew, at least those who were single, were eager to deploy and accepted or volunteered for orders to remain with the ship. To all officers due shortly for rotation, however, the Navy issued other orders, to avoid having to pay transportation costs to and from the China Station for them and their reliefs. Hence, Lloyd and his fellow ensigns provided the officer continuity. "We knew where all the bodies were buried, and we knew everything on the ship," he noted, "and we felt pretty important."

Cdr. Royal Ingersoll soon relieved Richardson and remained commanding officer until 16 October. His relief was Cdr. Chester W. Nimitz, a superior naval officer who would take the *Augusta* to China and who would leave his stamp not only on the ship but also on her young ensigns, especially Lloyd Mustin.

Nimitz excelled in training junior officers for command. According to Lloyd, he insisted on giving them early "responsibility associated with authority and above all a very real accountability." Right away, he drew on his young officers' knowledge of the ship to discover where those bodies where buried and then to see that the yard performed the needed corrections to his high standards. It was one of Lloyd's great lessons in excellence.

"One thing [Nimitz] believed in very strongly was that the junior officers should handle the ship." Lloyd adopted this view that the captain should not preoccupy himself with conning the ship—more appropriately "ensign's work"—lest he be derelict in his responsibilities for the combat readiness of his ship. As a destroyer skipper, Lloyd insisted that every officer stand watch. He rotated them daily from the combat information center to the deck watch. As a destroyer squadron, destroyer flotilla, and amphibious commander, he would penalize his captains if they did not delegate and train their junior officers. Whatever the operation, if a junior officer happened to be on watch, Lloyd insisted that he deal with it, even if it were a demanding task such as refueling at sea. "When their division officers are up there running things, whether they like it or not," said Lloyd, "the men subconsciously recognize a feeling of respect, and it just spreads."

Yard work completed, the *Augusta* sailed for Shanghai on 20 October. As Corinne had done during the cruise of the Great White Fleet, Emily planned on following the fleet while on the China Station. When the time came, the Navy paid for a through ticket for the nineteen-year-old mother and her nearly two-month-old son on the Dollar Line's *President Cleveland.* A great boon for Navy dependents, a Dollar Line ticket allowed passengers to disembark anywhere en route and reembark later on another of the line's steamers. On that trip, Emily and her baby would make stops at Yokohama, Nagoya, and Kobe before disembarking at Shanghai to rendezvous with Lloyd in a world of exotic adventure.

Americans had been preaching and trading in China for decades. Most were living in the Yangtze basin and around the treaty ports. The Navy had been patrolling Chinese rivers since 1850s. The Boxer Treaty put a large Marine legation guard in Beijing and an Army regiment at Tientsin. In the early 1930s, the Asiatic Fleet on the China Station was one flagship cruiser, nineteen destroyers, twelve submarines, and nine Yangtze Patrol gunboats.

On 18 September 1931, at Mukden in Manchuria, the Japanese Kwantung Army fabricated a Chinese attack on the South Manchurian Railway, an operation in which Japan had substantial investment. Japan thereupon occupied part of Manchuria, China's key industrial province. Although Japan now threatened Washington's long-standing Open Door Policy, which was supposed to keep imperialism in check in China, President Hoover refused Chinese entreaties for some kind of assistance.

The Mukden incident ignited a nationalism in China that expressed itself in a boycott of Japanese goods. In January 1932, the boycott came to Shanghai, and a riot engulfed the city on the eighteenth. The Japanese army took action against the Nationalists in Chapei. Surprisingly, the Chinese held firm, despite a Japanese aerial bombardment. Although British and U.S. ships were on station during the crisis, Washington gave the Navy firm orders only to protect Americans. The crisis abated only when the Japanese withdrew in the late spring.

Japan, however, would now extend its sector to the north of the Anglo-American International Settlement in Shanghai. In Manchuria, the Kwantung Army continued to advance. In August, Japan announced in effect its own Monroe Doctrine for Asia and that autumn recognized its Manchurian puppet state, Manchukuo. In March 1933, Japan left the League of Nations.

Lloyd's three-week trip across the Pacific was a miserable succession of winter storms. On 9 November, the *Augusta* finally moored in the Whangpoo River off Shanghai's Japanese sector. As soon as he could, Lloyd caught a tender and traveled upriver to the liberty boat landing at the Bund, the international financial and commercial center for the city. There, he found Emily and little Henry waiting for him.

During their first ten-day stay in Shanghai, the Mustins parked at the nearby Palace Hotel, which Lloyd characterized as "a real old pukka sahib type of place." They confined their entertainment largely to touring the city by rickshaw. Money was tight. Lloyd's monthly pay was only $183—$125 base pay, $40 married quarters allowance, and $18 subsistence allowance. About the time he arrived on the China Station, FDR instituted a 15 percent pay cut, which dropped his monthly total to a meager $165.

On 14 November, Adm. Frank B. Upham transferred his flag from the *Houston* to the *Augusta*. Within a few days, the *Augusta* was under way for Manila by way of Amoy, her next port of call and a regular stop for the South China Patrol, and Hong Kong. In Amoy, Lloyd was for the first time the senior patrol officer. He had no problems; he attributed that fortunate fact to the Navy's professionalism at the time.

Emily and the other officers' wives followed on the Dollar Line, going straight to Hong Kong. She and Lloyd rendezvoused and remained a few days, socializing primarily with foreign service officers and the Royal Navy, with whom relations were very good. With its activities centered around Kowloon, the British Far Eastern Fleet, Lloyd remembered, was quite sizable: one or two carriers, a nine-ship destroyer flotilla, and a six-ship cruiser squadron.

When the *Augusta* finally arrived in Manila in December, the Mustins stayed at the Bay View Hotel near the Manila Army and Navy Club. Eventually, they moved to Archisa Street, where they shared an apartment with a classmate, Herb Coleman, and his wife. Lloyd remembered that they had no screens and that they had to sleep under mosquito nets. With no commissary or post exchange available, Emily would buy their food from street markets.

For Lloyd, this first Manila visit was very busy. The *Augusta* went right into her gunnery exercises, having both to complete the 1933 round and then to conduct her 1934 exercises before March, when she would return to China.

Nimitz took fleet athletics very seriously. Participation was mandatory, and practice was during normal working hours. Every team on the ship had an officer as coach as they prepared for competitions in such sports as swimming, tennis, basketball, baseball, whaleboat racing, and even rugby. The *Augusta*'s first year, Lloyd's swimming team won the fleet championship. His classmate Muddy Waters coached and played on the rugby team, which won that championship, although it was not a sport anyone aboard had played before. In 1935, the *Augusta* captured her first Iron Man trophy, the annual award to the top ship in fleet athletics.

Small-arms marksmanship was another area of emphasis. In Asia, trouble was never far away, Lloyd recalled; every day in China naval personnel somewhere were at the receiving end of angry lead. Banditry was everywhere, prompting the railroads to put soldiers on the trains for protection. Small-arms training therefore was mandatory. Each year, the officers and men fired for qualification, using the rifle range at Mackinaia on Subic Bay.

As a junior officer, Nimitz had spent time on gunboat duty on the Yangtze Patrol and had a great deal of experience in riverine warfare, and he made certain that all his officers had small-arms training to enable them to lead their men in landing parties. Each of the *Augusta*'s sixty marines in her landing party and 220 sailors in her landing force had to achieve the level of marksman. Training was in pistols, rifles, Thompson sub-machine guns, Browning automatic rifles, Lewis machine guns, three-inch landing guns, one-pounders, and mortars. As the result of this push, the *Augusta* won the small-arms competition.

Intelligence gathering was another responsibility. Looking ahead to the possibility of war with Japan, Admiral Upham had the ship steam around Philippine waters to gather information on ports and shelters, verify and correct hydrographic data against Navy charts, and research potential airfields. Upham and others realized that in the event of capture, the thousands of Philippine islands would be too much for the Japanese to keep under surveillance and that this kind of information would be key to U.S. recapture of the archipelago.

On 14 March 1934, the ship went north again to Hong Kong en route to Shanghai. Just before she left Manila, a small surveying ship, the *Fulton,* had an engine-room explosion in the pirate area of Bias Bay north of Hong Kong. All hands had to abandon ship. The *Augusta* went for survivors, arriving the next day in fog. After returning the survivors to Manila, she continued to Hong Kong.

In early April, the *Augusta* arrived in Shanghai. By this time, the Navy had instituted the exchange relief to cover the dollar's depression-driven loss of value, which allowed Lloyd and Emily to rent a one-room apartment in a pension named Miss England's at 18 Chelmscott Gardens in the Vietnamese-policed French Concession. They also could afford an amah for little Henry. Her name was Su Ling, and she was with them for their entire time on the China Station.

The Mustins' apartment quickly became the social headquarters for Lloyd's bachelor shipmates. Lloyd, Emily, and their friends would go dancing every evening at the Little Club, a nightclub on Bubbling Well Road, and the art deco French Club, known for its great ballroom and bamboo dance floor that would flex with the dancers. For tennis, swimming, and golf, it was the Shanghai Country Club. Lloyd and Emily danced and dined in the clubs as often as they could afford.

When Admiral Upham transferred his flag to the *Isabel,* a converted yacht, for a sixteen-hundred-mile, month-long trip up the Yangtze, duties on the *Augusta* were minimal. Liberty began at 1:00 P.M., at which time Nimitz would organize for his officers sight-seeing excursions and guest lectures on China.

That spring, Lloyd and his swim team excelled in various meets sponsored by Shanghai's Foreign YMCA. A 19 May *Shanghai Times* subhead read "Mustin's Remarkable Display against Local Talent," leading a report of an event the night before at which the *Augusta's* mermen beat the Foreign Y and Fourth U.S. Marine teams. Lloyd broke the pool record for the one hundred with a time of 57.2 seconds.

With Upham still up the Yangtze, the *Augusta* went north to Tsingtao, a charming port resort that had been German until overwhelmed by the Japanese during World War I. Lloyd, who by now had been assistant navigator for a year, did most of the navigating, with help from the quartermaster. The *Augusta's* Tsingtao charts were based on surveys from 1845. Nimitz, who always planned ahead, made him get Chinese charts, which he reproduced and forwarded to Washington.

At Tsingtao, they learned that Admiral Togo, hero of the Battle of Tsushima, had died. The *Augusta* immediately returned to Shanghai to collect Upham and head to Japan. They arrived on 4 June, finding the damage from the hugely destructive 1923 Great Kanto Earthquake still evident, especially in Yokohama. The following day was the funeral, a major international event attended by the British, French, Italians, and Dutch as well.

Lloyd and other officers were privileged to visit the home of Yukio Ozaki, the liberal aristocrat who was the father of parliamentary politics in Japan. A close acquaintance of Eddie Pierce, the ship's regional expert, Ozaki and his half-American wife lived in Zushi, south of Yokohama on Sagami Bay. Security was tight. Ozaki had been the target of nationalist fanatics. While in port, Lloyd remembered also enjoying the beer gardens and conversing with the attractive "sitee-talkie girls."

The visit to Japan also was, of course, a prized opportunity to gather intelligence on the capabilities of the Imperial Japanese Navy. The conclusions were sobering. "One thing was that it was big," said Lloyd, "and the other was that it was good." Their social contact with the Japanese officers was polite but not cordial. "There was a clear sense of world rivalry, well recognized," Lloyd remarked. "When your instinctive reaction is that you two are on an inevitable collision course, the social relationships are inclined to be a little stiff, and they were."

The 8-inch cruisers at Yokosuka were massive. Japan was not limiting either its 6- or 8-inch classes to the ten thousand tons mandated by the London Treaty, as was the United States. "But it was the strong impression of all of us who looked and thought about what we looked at that this was indeed a tough, professional navy with dangerous units in it, and operating in the area at the time was their naval aviation . . . which was just as good as ours" and frighteningly similar. In addition, the Japanese had flat-bottomed, specialized amphibious assault craft, a class of ship not in the U.S. fleet at the time. Japan clearly was applying resources to building an auxiliary force not covered by the treaty.

On 18 June, the *Augusta* arrived back in Tsingtao from Japan. While Lloyd had been away, Emily had stayed in Shanghai with Henry and Su Ling and then caught a coastal steamer to Tsingtao, where she found another pension. The Mustins would share a floor with two apartments. Across the hall was Lloyd's friend Courtney Shands, a lieutenant aviator, who also was on the China Station with his family.

On 1 July, the 1935 fleet competition year began. The *Augusta* would compete against destroyer and submarine divisions in athletics, and she would win virtually every competition. In gunnery competition, too, she outclassed all. Two of her three main turrets, Number One and Number Two, got *E*s in short-range battle practice. In addition, they excelled in night battle practice, antiaircraft practice, day-spotting, and long-range battle practice in which, using only the main battery at extreme range, they fired with full charge ammunition ten salvos per gun at high speed.

In this, her first full competitive season, the *Augusta* won the battle efficiency trophy. The ship prepared meticulously and did especially well in night battle practice, an eventuality Nimitz anticipated and trained for, in spite of the War College's decree that commanders should avoid night combat. For the antiaircraft practice, they went farther north to Chefu, where they would shoot at target sleeves towed by utility planes. They did not, however, practice shore bombardment.

In September, the *Augusta* continued northwesterly to Chinwangtao, a rail head for Beijing where the Great Wall descends to the sea. The city was a coal-loading port that served also as a seaport for Tientsin, Taku, and Harbin in Manchuria. Since the Boxer Rebellion, the U.S. Army had a unit at Tientsin and a rifle range at Chinwangtao. There, the *Augusta* could conduct small-arms training. Lloyd was the officer in charge of the rifle and pistol teams. At the range, the men lived in tents. Lloyd remembered one incident when an errant practice fusillade hit a village behind the rifle range, causing a protest but fortunately no casualties. Goodwill was restored when the legendary Lt. Louis "Chesty" Puller, the ship's Marine Guard commander, proffered an ample payoff to the village elders.

Farther inland, bandits recently had kidnapped an American missionary and his daughter, and Lloyd had not wanted Emily to come to the camp. One day, he returned to his tent and found Emily there with little Henry and Su Ling. She had booked passage on a coastal steamer along with Catherine Nimitz and two of her children. While in the camp Henry learned to walk, taking his first steps in their tent. Afterward, Emily stayed for a time on the old transport *Chaumont* that was in the harbor. At other times, she stayed at the Khiland Mining Association guest house.

While at Chinwangtao, Nimitz gave his officers leave to sightsee in Beijing. In late September, Emily, Henry, and Su Ling took a connecting train to Si Nan Foo Junction and boarded the Shanghai Express for Beijing. In Beijing, they stayed at the Grand Hotel, "right in the shadow of the Wall." Lloyd joined them shortly for some touring. The walls around Beijing still had pockmarks from bullets and shells from the Boxer Rebellion. They went to the Forbidden City. One day, they took a train to the Great Wall, finishing the last stage of the trip by donkey.

When they returned to Shanghai, the Mustins lived for a week on the rue Molière in the French Concession. The *Augusta* was set for a lengthy autumn cruise to Australia by way of Guam for the one hundredth anniversary of the founding of Melbourne and Australia. The night before their departure, Lloyd and his fellow officers held a great party at the French Club, where they enjoyed escargots and a lot of drink. On 5 October, they departed and immediately hit a typhoon off the Yangtze. Battened hatches meant all hands had to remain below. Lloyd remembered his gang having a tough time, what with hangovers and the smell of garlic breath that hung in the stale air of officers' country.

After a stop in Guam and a trip through the Solomons, the *Augusta* arrived in Sydney on 20 October. After anchoring, the ship put her aircraft into the water. Lloyd had additional duty as the catapult officer, in charge of the two powder catapults and their scouting seaplanes, housed amidships. He hitched a ride as a backseat passenger with Slim Quilter, one of the *Augusta* aviators, who proceeded to fly his plane under the Sydney Bridge. Evidently, it had been done only once before, and reporters descended on the ship afterward. One of the main events of the port visit was the Air Force Ball. As the ship had fewer aviators than invitations, Lloyd and others donned some borrowed wings and went.

On the twenty-ninth, the *Augusta* arrived in Melbourne, where she remained until 13 November. The city's centennial generated "unbelievable" hospitality. Daily, the ship had invitations to four different social functions. The wardroom uniform of the day was always full dress; in addition to the social schedule ashore, guests continually were coming aboard for receptions. Nimitz posted a roster of assignments each officer would have to cover. The dollar was down in the region, but fortunately, the State Department reimbursed officers for the difference, enabling them to cover their additional personal expenses..

The ship finally finished her seventy-three-day, fifteen-thousand-mile cruise on 22 December, arriving in Manila to find the families she had left in Shanghai greeting her at the pier. Liberty would have to wait, however. Admiral Upham, who had been aboard for the cruise, had scheduled an admiral's inspection as soon as they arrived in port. The *Augusta* sailors had everything spotless. In Shanghai, the Chinese electroplated chrome plate on everything in the turrets, and the men paid for the work from their own pockets. The bright work "wasn't just clean. It shone. It reflected the lights around it," said Lloyd. "That was just the way the sailors responded to the overall leadership in that ship, which was imparted by the captain, through the command pyramid of his officers, and, obviously, of course, from the officers through the men." Many of the sailors so loved the duty on the China Station that they would re-up, and Nimitz ensured that professional standards were the highest "from truck to keelson." As a result, the inspection awarded the *Augusta* with an outstanding.

The inspection behind them, the officers and men fully enjoyed their Christmas holiday. After three years together, the crew had no need to train. Every day, they had most of their work done by 8:30 A.M. The rest of the day was liberty. The ship went into her yearly overhaul at Cavite, followed by time at the Olongapo dry dock.

Lloyd, Emily, and little Henry were by themselves in Manila. Su Ling had gone with them to Tsingtao and had returned to Shanghai, but she had no interest in going to the Philippines. Their Manila accommodation was the annex to the Boulevard Apartments on Dewey Boulevard, President Taft's home while governor of the Philippines. Every day, Lloyd would walk to officers' landing in front of Army and Navy Club and would return from the ship in the afternoon. Often, he and Emily would stay at the club to swim, dine, and dance.

During the winter of 1935, the *Augusta* again visited the southern islands. Upham and Nimitz understood that the United States would not be able to hold Manila in the event of war with Japan. It was crucial to have data on other potential facilities in the region, and that year they gathered particular intelligence on Leyte.

On 15 March 1935, the *Augusta* left for Hong Kong. Emily followed to Shanghai on another steamer. Lloyd arrived on the thirty-first.

During this time, the Navy instituted a system for standardized damage control with fittings designations. The intent was to maximize a ship's material readiness for war. Under the new emphasis, Red Whiting was the *Augusta's* damage control officer. Lloyd prepared the damage control check-off lists in his division, gaining a deep appreciation for damage control that would be put into practice later at Guadalcanal.

In a 12 April 1935 ceremony on the Whangpoo River, Chester Nimitz left the *Augusta,* rowed in a whaleboat by twelve of his officers dressed in nineteenth-century uniforms, and Capt. Felix Gygax assumed command. Before leaving, Nimitz advised Lloyd and his fellow junior officers to request their next duty in new-construction destroyers. In his new position as the assistant chief of the Bureau of Navigation, the predecessor to the Bureau of Personnel, he could ensure that they got it.

In May, the *Augusta* went again to Japan, spending two weeks in Yokohama, Tokyo, and Kobe. She returned to China to steam up the Yangtze to Nanking until, on 4 June, she dropped anchor once again in Shanghai. On the twenty-seventh, the ship departed for Tsingtao for her summer exercises and gunnery practice, during which time Lloyd was able to serve as a short-range battle practice observer on the gunboat *Sacramento*.

That summer, Lloyd and Emily lived in the center of town in the Strand Hotel, overlooking the beach. The Strand was a summer resort for wealthy Chinese and the international set and offered separate cottages, some of which were shared. Lloyd and Emily teamed with the Shands, spending much of their free time on the beach watching the children play. There, little Henry learned to surf.

On 30 September, the *Augusta* returned to Shanghai. Hitching a ride on board was the Army's legendary China hand, Col. Joe Stilwell, who would stay with the ship during her southern swing to Siam, the independent kingdom that separated the British and French in Southeast Asia. On the fifth, Adm. Orin G. Murfin relieved Upham as fleet commander. Three days later, the ship sailed to Bangkok with Stilwell.

Bangkok was a very social port call that involved a number of receptions for the British and American communities, as well as for the Siamese royals. From there, the *Augusta* went to Singapore and British North Borneo. On 11 November, she arrived in Manila, where Lloyd reunited with Emily and little Henry. It would be their last winter in the Philippines. After the annual overhaul and dry-docking, the ship left in late February 1936 for her most extensive swing yet through the islands, not to return until 29 March.

After only two days in Manila, the *Augusta* headed for Hong Kong, arriving on 2 April. While she was in port, Lloyd was detached. The Mustins were going home. They stayed for ten days at the Peninsula Hotel, and on their last night in Hong Kong, they had their *despedida,* a traditional farewell party for people leaving the China Station, in the hotel dining room. They then rickshawed to the pier and, with a number of friends, boarded the *President Jackson.* The party continued in their cabin with more roistering, singing such favorite China Station ditties as "Meet Me by the Slop Chute on the Ol' Whangpoo." Leaving their friends at the pier, Lloyd and Emily departed that night.

As the *President Jackson* left harbor, Lloyd took one last look at his first ship, beautifully lit by lights around the bay. "It was the last time I saw her until the middle of World War II in the Boston Navy Yard. I went aboard her, had lunch with a classmate who was by then a gunnery officer, Len Fraser, and Len insisted that we go down below and see his chief fire controlman, whose name I can't recall, who had been an enlisted man, a fire controlman in that ship when I was an ensign there. He had been there ever since. He had never been on any other ship. He refused to accept a commission or a warrant because he wanted to stay in that ship, and he did."

Chapter 15

The Making of a Gun Boss

After their farewell festivities in Hong Kong, Lloyd and Emily left on the *President Jackson* for Shanghai. Family members had sent them money for gifts to bring home, and Lloyd, his head spinning from the night's revelries, hid it so carefully in their cabin that it took him two days to find it. With money finally again in hand, they cruised for bargains on the Nanking and Bubbling Well Roads. On their last night in Shanghai, they went to the French Club for dinner and finished the evening at the Little Club cabaret on Bubbling Well.

Their next ports of call were in Japan: Kobe, Nagoya, and Yokohama. In February 1936, some fourteen hundred ultranationalist junior officers and their supporters had attempted a military coup, but by April, when Lloyd and Emily were in country, tensions had subsided. Lloyd remembered seeing news of the coup in the press but felt no anxiety.

After a three-week passage, Lloyd, Emily, and Henry arrived stateside in Seattle. They crossed the continent by train to Annapolis, where they stayed with Emily's mother. Proudly, they introduced their nearly three-year-old son to Emily's many relatives, in particular her uncle, Doug Howard, after whom she promised she would name her next child. From there, they went to visit the Murrays in Pensacola, where George was director of flight training.

In part thanks to Nimitz, Lloyd, a lieutenant (junior grade) since 2 June 1935, got orders to the commissioning crew of a new-construction *Mahan*-class destroyer, the *Lamson,* to be her assistant gunnery officer. Having served as torpedo officer on the *Augusta* before the Navy removed her torpedoes, he also got additional duty as the *Lamson's* torpedo officer.

Returning from leave, Lloyd was at the Gun Factory in Washington for instruction in the new 5-inch/38-caliber gun that formed the destroyer's main battery. The yard had no actual gun, however, so he devoted most of his time to learning more about range-finding. Initially, he lived in Washington with his Aunt Kate and Uncle Charles Hill, returning to Annapolis for weekends with Emily and Henry. Later, he bought his first car, a 1936 Ford convertible, for $600 and began commuting. His next instruction was at the torpedo school at Goat Island in Newport. Emily and Henry joined him and remained until he went to Bath to report to his ship, whereupon they returned to Annapolis.

The *Lamson* launched on 17 June 1936, and Lloyd joined her shortly thereafter during builder's trials off Rockland, Maine. She was a fast ship—for five passes over a measured mile, she averaged a blistering 41.1 knots—and her new technologies gave the commissioning crew the opportunity to develop new operational concepts for destroyers.

In October, the ship commissioning was in Boston, where the fitting out would be performed. Emily and Henry joined Lloyd, and the family took an apartment in Cambridge. Early in the fitting out, word came that the *Flusser,* a sister ship to the *Lamson,* had seriously fractured during a storm on her shakedown cruise. Subsequent inspection of the *Lamson* revealed cracks at the corners to the hatches of the engine room and at the end of the after deckhouse. The shipyard had to replace the plates with higher alloy steel, extending the fitting-out period into February. "That was a major structural change, and it was an eye opener to me," said Lloyd. "Up to that time, I had always assumed that the people who designed our ships knew what they were doing. Forever after, I assumed that they didn't."

In February 1937, the modification was complete and the *Lamson* made way for Newport to load torpedoes. From there, she began her shakedown cruise to Brazil. "We ran to Bahia at 22 knots, and it's over four thousand miles," Lloyd remarked in the early 1970s. "These new destroyers can't do that. They don't have those legs." After Bahia, they went to Rio and Buenos Aires before returning via Barbados.

After shakedown and a brief overhaul in Norfolk, the ship was headed for the West

Coast. In early June, Emily waved goodbye at the Norfolk pier, and Lloyd again was under way. On 30 June, the ship arrived at her new home port, San Diego. On 2 July, word came that the famous aviation pioneer Amelia Earhart was lost in the Pacific. The *Lamson,* the carrier *Lexington,* and two other destroyers departed within days to join the search for her and her plane. For nearly a week, the *Lamson* covered an area the size of Texas with planes at half-mile intervals in a search pattern around the Howland and Baker Islands, to no avail.

Having just learned how to drive, Emily made her way with Henry to San Diego. She was in Coronado and already had found a tiny bungalow at 435 C Street when Lloyd returned at the end of the month.

Lloyd was not in port for long. Gunnery practice always ran from late summer to the end of December; the fleet and tactical exercises came after. On 2 August, however, he went to sea on a major fleet tactical exercise. Operating in the eastern Pacific, the *Lamson* would test her new capabilities, in particular to determine how her speed could be used to tactical advantage. "My clear recognition [was] that we were . . . working in fleet operational areas that were new to destroyers," recalled Lloyd, "and that we were doing so because we had capabilities that were new to destroyers." Indeed, the ship was among the first destroyers to have antiaircraft guns in the main battery, primitive sonar, and speed. Her early antisubmarine warfare equipment was inadequate to that problem, but nevertheless, the 1,500-tonners such as the *Lamson* were the prototypes for the World War II destroyers.

As an assistant gunnery officer and an aviator's son, Lloyd was drawn to the challenges of antiaircraft fire. Like his father, he was energized by competition, and the *Lamson* managed to finish first in antiaircraft practices. He believed strongly that units become combat ready owing to "the stimulating effects of a properly regulated competition in which the winner is determined by the one having the greatest skill in the particular competition."

Lloyd became communications officer in addition to his other duties when the ship's previous communications officer was detached. Although he had no real communications training, he had a good chief radioman, and at the end of the competition year, the *Lamson* won the communications excellence contest for the flotilla of ninety destroyers.

On shore, the Mustins entertained extensively. Amid a routine of weekend parties, one notable Sunday evening Andy Richards, a Navy junior and friend of the family, invited Hollywood star Errol Flynn to Lloyd and Emily's bungalow. He had been water skiing on San Diego Bay, where he had met and befriended Flynn. Many guests arrived, and with not enough food on hand, a very pregnant Emily sent Richards to buy watermelon from a local stand, the only venue doing business on a Sunday. The shortage of food combined with a plenitude of hard refreshment made for a bash, capped late in the evening by a game of sardines. In the darkened cottage, none of the players was able to find Flynn, who had used his creative and acrobatic abilities to hide on the mantelpiece. In the end, the damage was slight; the only dent was to Lloyd's wallet. Flynn left the Mustins with charges for a number of long-distance phone calls.

Lloyd capped his duty with the *Lamson* on 10 May, when at San Diego's Mercy Hospital Emily gave birth to their second child. True to her promise to her Uncle Doug, who had died in December 1936, Emily named the baby Douglas Howard Mustin. The child, however, was a girl. The following month, the Mustins left for the East Coast. Lloyd's orders were to Annapolis and the academy's Postgraduate School.

By 30 June, just before the end of the fiscal year, the family had arrived in Annapolis. They found a row house in Dreams Landing, a new development several miles up the Severn River from the academy. Most of the residents were Navy contemporaries, of which almost all were Postgraduate School students and their families. Courses would not start until 1 August, and July was a relaxed leave for Lloyd, after virtually six years of sea duty. The Mustins and their student friends enjoyed leisurely evenings of card games and dancing at the Navy's social epicenter in Annapolis, Carvel Hall, across the street from the academy's Gate Two.

Lloyd requested and got a place as one of twenty-five postgraduate students for the two-year course in ordnance engineering, ensuring his return to the fleet in a gunnery department. That summer, the Navy had announced a new subdivision in ordnance engineering for fire control, for which students would spend their second year at the Massachusetts Institute of Technology. Lloyd was one of the officers, nicknamed "The Four Horsemen"—the other three being Horacio "Rivets" Rivero and Ed Hooper of the class of 1931 and Corky Ward of Lloyd's class of 1932—who opted for that specialty. Given the apparent aircraft threat to surface ships, the Navy especially wanted that subdivision to develop a mechanism to permit antiaircraft guns to follow rapidly and accurately the orders from the fire control system.

During the first year, Lloyd and his fellow students took the basic postgraduate courses at the academy. One required course was on leadership, taught by Capt. William Fechtler, and Lloyd regarded it with impatient skepticism. "I didn't understand then, and frankly I don't understand now how it is possible to teach leadership," he fussed to Naval Institute oral historian Jack Mason in 1973. "Leadership can be learned all right, and it can be developed all right, but leadership really is a relationship among human beings wherein some kind of relative gradations of authority and also of responsibility are in effect." In his view, the key to leadership is the ability to motivate others.

Near the end of the first semester, Lloyd and Emily were in Newport News, Virginia, for the 8 December christening of the destroyer *Mustin,* named after Henry C. Built by Newport News Shipbuilding & Dry Dock, the *Mustin* was a 1,570-ton *Sims*-class destroyer with four 5-inch/38-caliber single mounts. Emily was her sponsor, and her maid of honor was her first cousin, Anne Howard. Representing the Mustin side were Lloyd's brother Henry and their cousin Josephine Mustin, his Uncle Burton's daughter.

Lloyd's first year at the Postgraduate School finished in June, coinciding with the arrival of Emily's brother, Tom, and his wife, Marni, in Dreams Landing. Tom was to begin his first year of the ordnance engineering course in the fall. Also living on the row were the McCains, John and Roberta and their children, Sandy and John, who would have his own distinguished career in the Navy and Senate, and Emily's cousin Anne and her new husband, Lloyd's classmate, Donald Irving Thomas. Marni remembered another succession of summer parties and dances that would continue late into the evenings at one or the other of the Dreams Landing townhouses, upsetting the more staid McCains, who tended to retire early.

On 1 July, Lloyd was promoted to lieutenant. He had brief Washington duty at the Bureau of Ordnance and the Gun Factory before returning to Annapolis for rest of the summer.

On 1 September, Germany launched its blitzkrieg on Poland. Two days later, Britain and France declared war on Germany. President Franklin D. Roosevelt reassured Americans that the United States would remain neutral, but on the sixth, he initiated the Neutrality Patrol, which shifted some of the fleet back to the Atlantic. The women of Annapolis soon turned to sewing and knitting Bundles for Britain, Anne Thomas recalled.

The Mustins at this point were headed for Cambridge for the fall semester. Lloyd, Rivero, Hooper, and Ward were enrolled as graduate students at MIT's Electrical Engineering Department, chaired by Dr. Harold Hazen. A pioneer in machine computation and automatic control, Hazen was known for his theory of servomechanisms, the mechanical means to amplify low-power command signals to control the motion of heavy equipment. This technology, the Four Horsemen thought, was key to enabling rapid and accurate antiaircraft fire control. Also a Naval Reserve officer, Hazen understood what his students were attempting and its import and fully supported their efforts. When they arrived, their course of study did not have a thesis requirement, and thus they were not eligible for master of science degrees. Lloyd and the others persuaded Hazen that their program should allow each to do a thesis and earn a degree, and he made it so.

Ward and Hooper paired to apply Hazen's theories to the design of a servomechanism for the 16-inch guns on the new fast battleship *North Carolina*. Well into the first semester, however, Lloyd and Rivero had not yet arrived at their own project.

At Christmastime, Lloyd returned his family to Annapolis and went duck hunting with his brother Henry, then a reporter with the *Washington Evening Star*. While sitting in his duck blind on the Eastern Shore, Lloyd pondered the mechanics involved in the way the hunters were leading their ducks as they sighted for a shot. Before the end of the day, he had an idea to design an antiaircraft fire control mechanism that would rely on two gyros to measure lateral and vertical movement, thus providing sight setting to lead a target. Lloyd had a thesis topic. Rivero refined Lloyd's idea by adding a provision for range-finding, and together they presented the proposal to Hazen, who accepted it.

Lloyd and Rivero's object was to propose a technology that could substantially improve the close-in antiaircraft gun defense of ships. The Navy had addressed the long-range problem somewhat successfully with the introduction of directors for a group of guns, but Lloyd and Rivero were more concerned with short-range fire control against dive-bombers.

Typically, dive-bombers would approach in formation at ten thousand feet, then dive to four thousand feet and release at three thousand feet. A short-range gun battery would have to open fire before a plane descended to four thousand feet. Assuming the plane was traveling downward at four hundred knots, Lloyd reckoned, the battery would have to open with a six-second sixty-shot burst when the plane was at eight thousand feet. If the plane were to drop its bomb at five thousand feet, the battery would have to open fire when it reached ten thousand feet.

For the close-in air battle, the dive-bombers already would have broken formation and would come at a ship individually. The close-in defense for ships operating as a tactical force required individual gun control, particularly when the target was attacking another ship. The close-in weapon was, of course, the machine gun; thus, any fire control device would have to be small and responsive.

Heretofore, the Navy had relied on two approaches: tracer fire and the ring sight, introduced for aerial combat in World War I. Both had limitations, but the Navy accepted them, assuming that a plane would attack down the barrel. The limitations compounded, however, when a plane was attacking another ship. Whatever the approach angle, Lloyd understood the absolute need to calculate how far to lead a target and thus compute the angle of deflection.

Central to Lloyd and Rivero's thesis was an antiaircraft fire control device whose primary solution was the use of gyroscopes to measure relative target motion, together with the use of any available means, including visual estimation, to measure range. Their approach permitted development of a device that had very fast solution times, had a control accuracy adequate for close-in defense, and was simple and compact in size, that is, less than one cubic foot. They called it a lead computer.

With this mechanism, once the gunner had the target in his sights, the sight automatically would offset the line of fire—the direction of the gun—from the line of sight, having computed the appropriate lead angle between the line of sight and the line of fire. The lead computer would simplify the gunner's task. It was different from the ring sight in that "the gunner would then have to make but one alignment, that of front and rear sights on the target, in order to have his gun correctly oriented to produce hits."

Lloyd and Rivero then addressed whether the device should be in the gun mount. Weighing vibration from gunfire and muzzle gases against relying on tracers from remote observation that could mean corrections even farther off target, they concluded that the heaviest and most powerful gun mounts would require a separately mounted control unit, or director. It would use a stereo-spotting glass to "observe the offsets of various small deviations for normal flight conditions of our projectile." If the aiming station were within ten to fifteen feet of the gun, they argued, parallax errors would be negligible. Until radar came on line, the device would use eye estimates to incorporate range. Finally, they wrote, the design would have to allow for mass production.

Their concepts were close to those embodied in the Mark 14 and 15 gun sights, and variants, developed by MIT's Dr. Charles Stark Draper, whose gyro and instrumentation courses had helped them develop their thesis. Draper was a consultant to the Sperry Gyroscope Company, which manufactured the Mark 14 sight for direct mounting on the 20-mm machine guns and the computing elements for the Mark 51 "handlebar" gun director. He did not suggest any gun control applications at that time, but he later acknowledged Lloyd and Rivero's contribution to the development of his own concepts.

Lloyd felt that their thesis's greatest contribution was that it allowed them to argue effectively in the Bureau of Ordinance for the merits of Draper's initial 1941 proposals. "His first relatively crude test device, demonstrated as a 20 mm machine gun sight in firings against a towed-sleeve air target at the Naval Proving Ground, Dahlgren, Va., was regarded by some BuOrd old-timers as radical," wrote Lloyd in 1971. "But it became the basis for the U.S. Navy decision to finance development and procurement of his equipment." Lloyd later would note that, while it was difficult to determine how many of Draper's Mark 14 and 15 gun sights the Navy had used during the war, "the numbers were in the tens of thousands, and may have been as high as 80,000. They exceeded by a factor possibly as much as 20 or more the number of antiaircraft fire control devices of any other design used aboard ship by the United States or any ally or enemy in World War II."

On 16 May 1940, Lloyd and Rivero submitted their thesis, "A Servo-Mechanism for a Rate Follow-Up System," to MIT's Department of Electrical Engineering. The title and text were deliberately uninformative. Until 1946, the Navy classified the thesis and proposal as confidential.

With the end of their second year of Postgraduate School, the Four Horsemen began a series of duty assignments at Bausch & Lomb in Rochester, the Naval Gun Factory, the Bureau of Ordnance, and Dahlgren Proving Ground in the Northern Neck of Virginia, and the Mustins found themselves once again at Dreams Landing. That summer, Emily discovered she was pregnant with their third child, Thomas Morton Mustin, who would arrive the following February.

At the Bureau of Ordnance, Lloyd and Corky Ward had four weeks of duty at the Fire Control Desk. During that time, they got an introduction to Special Project Number One: radar at the Naval Research Laboratory. The cutting-edge technology had enormous implications for fire control, giving angular coordinates and range to target. Their main assignment, however, was to update the old instruction books on battery alignment and produce a new one on ordnance alignment.

The weakness of antiair warfare was driven home for Lloyd and his fellow ordnance officers by the continuing German attacks on British ships. They realized that the Germans had no naval air force, but they also understood that the Japanese did—and that it had been engaged in real combat in China for years and was battle tested.

In the autumn, Lloyd went to Dahlgren to continue his work on antiaircraft guns. The Navy's new 5-inch guns were effective against bombers in formation at long range but much less so at short range against dive-bombers, especially dive-bombers attack-

ing another ship. In addition, the 5-inch guns on destroyers did not have the elevation or the fire control for use against aircraft. Dahlgren was looking at a number of
alternatives—the Oerlikon 20-mm, the Navy's Browning .50 caliber, the U.S. version
of the Swedish Bofors 40-mm, and the somewhat dubious British Pom Pom. Lloyd was
variously involved in testing them all.

Of particular interest to the Navy was one of its own designs: the 1.1-inch machine
gun it was developing at the Gun Factory for close-in air defense. The 1.1s "had a course
of fire, and they had clip loading. The clips would go in a hopper on top. Two clips
would go in there side by side. One fed into the gun, and when it was empty, it would
triple latch and swing over and the other clip would go in, and you could take the
one out and replace it so you could keep on firing." During testing, Lloyd found the
gun could not fire two clips (sixteen rounds) continuously at high and low elevations
and that it had a particular problem with cold weather.

Manufacturing also was a challenge. The design called for extremely fine tolerances,
and the order called for great secrecy. Across the country, a number of firms were to
manufacture gun parts, not knowing how they were to fit together, and ship them to
the Gun Factory, which would assemble the guns.

When Lloyd reported to the Bureau of Ordnance that the gun did not work, Capt.
William H. P. "Spike" Blandy, the bureau's special assistant for antiaircraft, told him
to make it work. Blandy gave Lloyd, a lieutenant, full authority as a Dahlgren project
officer and at the same time put him in charge of the production division at the Gun
Factory. Lloyd also had complete authority in the design division from which the blueprints came. In sum, he could change whatever was needed to correct the manufacture of the gun.

Finally, the moment came to try the gun's two prototypes. Until that time, the gun
would fire only three or four rounds and then stop. One of Lloyd's 1.1 prototypes
opened by firing all its stack of ammo. Surprised, the Dahlgren staff gathered around,
and by the end of testing, a crowd had formed. "The word," said Lloyd, "was, get that
into production." In the end, he became the "czar of design, production and inspection" of the 1.1 Mark 1, Mod 2.

Lloyd's last responsibility on the project was to visit the contractors who manufactured the gun pieces to introduce them to the design modifications that relaxed
the tolerances. They were relieved. Their processes could not deliver the tolerances that
the Gun Factory could, which was part of the problem. Unfortunately, in the fleet,
the 1.1 never lived up to its promise at the proving ground.

While Lloyd was busy at Dahlgren, two MIT students mounted a Draper lead computing gyro sight, based on Lloyd's thesis, on the 20-mm Oerlikon gun for a test and demonstration. The students used two Pioneer Turn Indicators, once again demonstrating the advantage of Lloyd and Rivero's approach over control with tracers, which tended to lead a gunner to fire behind a target. Present at the test with Rivero and Lloyd was Cdr. William "Deke" Parsons, of Manhattan Project fame, who was the experimental officer at Dahlgren. Parsons's support ultimately led to the production decision for Sperry Gyroscope Company's Mark 14 gun sight.

Draper's important addition to the Mustin-Rivero concept was the means for fluid viscous damping for the gyros. The sight was eventually used with 20-mm mounts, and as part of the Mark 51 director for 40-mm twin and quad mounts. As the thesis prescribed, the director was displaced far enough to be free of gun vibration and muzzle smoke but near enough to need no sophisticated parallax corrections. The Mark 52 had a radar for range; the Mark 63 used the Mark 15 gun sight with a radar for unseen targets.

"[The gun sight] certainly became a revolutionary factor in the entire capability of the Navy to survive at sea in the war in the Pacific under attack by a very skillful Japanese naval aviation," wrote Lloyd years later.

Lloyd's success both with Rivero on the lead computer and as project officer at Dahlgren reflected his competence as an operational naval officer and his tremendous technical ability. His work on gun sights harkened back to his father's work with Sims during his battleship days. Ironically, Lloyd was applying it against aviation. His work at MIT provided the fulcrum for his career. He would go to sea, go to war, as a gun boss.

Chapter 16

First Blood on the *Atlanta*

The war in Europe and support for Britain and her prime minister, Winston Churchill, assumed strategic priority for Roosevelt. Such also was the view of military leaders in Washington: Gen. George Marshall, the Army chief of staff, and Adm. Harold "Betty" Stark, the chief of naval operations. Naval leaders in the Pacific, however, did not agree. Adm. James O. Richardson, commander of the naval forces at Pearl Harbor, wanted a more aggressive stance in the region and particularly resented having to keep the fleet at Pearl as opposed to operating in the western Pacific. On 1 February 1941, FDR relieved Richardson with Adm. Husband Kimmel. Despite history's later judgment, Kimmel assumed command also wanting the United States to adopt a more offensive posture.

After the Japanese attack on Pearl, Roosevelt began reorganizing for the conduct of a world war. In 1942, he transformed the Joint Army-Navy Board into the Joint Chiefs of Staff. One of the key players and a leading Washington opponent of the Europe-first view was Adm. Ernest J. King, who became chief of naval operations in March 1942. While the U.S. leadership applied itself to the war in Europe, King fashioned for himself and the Navy a free hand in the Pacific.

The U.S. loss of Wake and Guam in December 1941 rendered impossible a central Pacific campaign against Japan. King's new Pacific commander, who had replaced the disgraced Kimmel, inherited a truncated naval force grappling with how to prosecute a war in that theater. That man was former *Augusta* skipper Chester W. Nimitz. Notwithstanding his sure hand at command, Nimitz had to proceed cautiously. His orders to his tactical commanders were to govern themselves "by the principle of calculated risk."

With few exceptions, the United States was fighting a defensive war for the first eight months of 1942. Despite the controversial U.S. losses in May in the Battle of the Coral Sea, the Navy stopped the Japanese offensive thrust toward Australia. Tactically, Coral Sea was a signal event, the first naval battle fought with naval aviation and in which opposing surface units never saw each other.

After three years ashore, Lloyd received orders to the light cruiser *Atlanta* as assistant gunnery officer. On 25 August 1941, leaving Emily and the children in Annapolis, he reported to the Federal Shipbuilding & Drydock Company in Kearny, New Jersey.

The *Atlanta* was the first of eight in her class and one of the first ships commissioned after Pearl Harbor. Her armament included 5-inch/38-caliber and 1.1-inch guns. Given his time in the *Lamson* and at Dahlgren, Lloyd knew both systems cold. At six thousand tons, the *Atlanta* was the smallest cruiser built since the Spanish-American War. "Nobody knew what to do with her," Lloyd remembered. "She was really just a big destroyer, but even those 5-inch guns could shoot ten miles."

The *Atlanta* launched on 6 September, christened by *Gone with the Wind* author Margaret Mitchell. Three months later, the United States was a nation at war, and publicity spoke of her late December commissioning at the Brooklyn Navy Yard as "An Xmas present for the Axis." Lloyd, however, was critical. "The 'delivery' was a farce," he wrote. "We were no more completed, from a satisfactory operating point of view, then about 95 percent, Gunnery, 80 percent."

On 8 February 1942 and under the command of Capt. Samuel P. Jenkins, the *Atlanta* left New York for her shakedown cruise in the Chesapeake Bay—thought to be a haven from German submarines—followed by antiship practice at Casco Bay, Maine. On 14 March, she returned to Brooklyn for final fitting out. To ensure that his department was fully stocked with spares, Lloyd went to Washington and "drank a little coffee with my friends in the Navy Yard," where they were assembling the bins with parts for ships under construction. "And with the connivance of the people there, I robbed those bins. I'd take one of the parts from this bin, one from that, one from another so that I didn't strip anybody. I was able to fill up a trailer, which they marked for the *Atlanta,* and it was shipped to us."

Thanks to Rivets Rivero, who still was in Washington, Lloyd was able to get two Mark 37 radar directors, gun laying radars for fire control that determined the range of aircraft. When the systems finally were installed on the ship, Lloyd trained his gunnery department by having them track subway cars as they crossed a nearby bridge over the East River.

As they prepared to deploy, Emily joined him in New York for a four-day visit. "Very swell for a goodbye," wrote Lloyd. On 5 April, the *Atlanta* departed for Pearl Harbor. Through the Panama Canal, they entered the Pacific with great unease and the feeling that the Japanese could be operating east of Oahu.

On the last leg of the trip, the *Atlanta* made a reconnoiter of Clipperton Island in the eastern Pacific. Clipperton was little more than a guano mine, but the Navy thought the Japanese could be using it as a staging area for fueling their submarines. On arrival, they found a large white schooner behaving strangely. The *Atlanta* dispatched a very nervous boarding party, but all they found was the schooner's cook vainly trying to control the ship as she dragged her anchor. The cook was on board the shark fisherman alone; the rest of the crew had gone ashore.

Satisfied that Clipperton and the schooner were secure, the *Atlanta* continued uneventfully to Pearl, arriving on 23 April. Lloyd angrily chronicled in his diary the still evident carnage of 7 December. On 6 May, he wrote, "1,500 bodies are believed to be still in the damaged battleships. On these, still blacked out nights, with nothing stirring except the faint voices of the guns' crews on watch, the ghosts of some of those dead men stir. And ask: Why?"

Events in the Pacific were moving quickly. Vice Adm. William F. Halsey's Task Force 16 that had launched the celebrated 18 April Doolittle raid on Tokyo had returned just a few hours before the *Atlanta*'s arrival. George Murray, Lloyd's stepfather, was captain of the carrier *Enterprise,* which had accompanied the bombers. On 8 May, the second day of the Battle of the Coral Sea, the *Atlanta* got orders to join Task Force 16, then fueling in the New Hebrides. On the tenth, she left Pearl as an escort for a convoy to Nouméa, New Caledonia.

It was not a leisurely run. After numerous general quarters alarms provoked by false submarine contacts, "everyone had had their fill," Lloyd wrote. "Everyone is somewhat keyed up. Naturally. The Japs outnumber us to beat hell in this ocean, and we're up against a tough Navy that doesn't keep its BB's [battleships] home. With no air scouts and tied down to these two beefboats, the [destroyer] *McCall*'s and our 5-inch guns seem pretty small potatoes, to what we can easily run into. And with every day we get nearer to where they are loaded for bear."

On 19 May, they finally rendezvoused with Halsey as he was returning to Pearl. On the twenty-third, Lloyd wrote, "New information concerns Jap offensive against Alaskan area. Perhaps we'll see some cold weather. Also a pending grab by them against Midway again." Thwarted in the Coral Sea, the Japanese indeed were planning to attack Midway, but the Navy had cracked their code and saw it coming. The force continued to exercise repelling air attacks, and, wrote Lloyd, "all hands getting steadily better."

In Pearl, Lloyd was present at a 27 May shipboard ceremony on the *Enterprise* when Nimitz presented Murray with the Navy Cross for his role in the Doolittle raid. "The admiral remembered me; we had a talk on old times in the *Augusta,* etc. Sortie is tomorrow, with trouble expected early."

After the ceremony, Lloyd and his stepfather went aboard the *Hornet* to see her skipper, their friend Capt. Pete Mitscher. Lloyd was able to listen as the two captains shared tactical insights. Knowing that within days they would meet the Japanese again at Midway, their focus was on improving evasive maneuvers to counter enemy naval aviation. Previously, ships had thought the best course in response to an air attack was to break formation and scatter, but Murray and Mitscher arrived at a plan to maneuver together and thus maximize the fire support from the whole force to defend any single ship. The pair's idea was to maintain the escort screen around the carrier and the original relative positions of the ships in the force. During the meeting, Rear Adm. Raymond A. Spruance stopped by Mitscher's cabin and was impressed enough by the approach to agree to try it. With Halsey hospitalized with shingles, Spruance would be the officer in tactical command of TF 16. The admiral was a disappointment to Lloyd, however, who was appalled by his apparent lack of confidence.

On 28 May, the U.S. carriers and their escorts went to sea. Thanks to the Navy's code breaking, they left five days before the Japanese were able to set their submarine cordon, thus ruining their plan to ambush the U.S. force as it moved westward.

In his diary, Lloyd fretted over the senior admirals' predisposition to use naval aviation as their sole striking force. Confident of and fully versed in his available ordnance and gunnery, he felt that cruisers and destroyers should be employed as well. "And all this while our BBs are in San Francisco, reportedly. I can't understand the school of strategy that for any reason could keep them there under the present circumstances."

The *Atlanta* was positioned a couple of hundred miles northwest of Midway as part of the screen for Mitscher's *Hornet.* The battle raged on 4 June, but she did not fire a shot. Lloyd remembered the ship's rebroadcast of a Japanese frequency where one enemy controller was giving a running commentary on the battle interspersed with pained cries from his pilots. One newspaper account reported Lloyd drawling into a microphone, "That Jap seems to be telling Tokyo that he's getting something and whatever he's getting he doesn't like one damn bit."

The senior commanders' lack of aggressiveness outraged Lloyd. On the fourth, he wrote, "To my agonized amazement, we run away *all night*—a course about 120, averaged, for several hundred miles total ground covered since plane recovery. I can't see why, with radars thick in our outfit, and everyone with 30 knots plus, that we have anything to fear in moving the other way to take favorable position for further action, especially since the Jap air strength now seems done for." The next day he lamented, "God, now it is easy to see why our BBs should be here. Instead of going in for a decision, we keep out of sight and pick with dive-bombers." On 6 June, he continued, "This super caution cannot be explained to me as anything but wastage of glorious opportunity. . . . God—a radar directed night torpedo attack by our DD's [destroyers] would polish off these cripples in jig time—not to mention what five 8-inch cruisers could do to their 'burning' carriers and cruisers. But instead, we stay 150 miles away." By the seventh, he was exasperated. "We are now withdrawing—did so all night—leaving the BB, CV [carrier], and several DD's *still afloat.* This to my mind can find no excuse in any book. . . . It could have been a Salamis; it was a bush league brush. All because of Commander Task Force 16's horrible failure to seek a decision with his cruisers and destroyers, all concentrated and intact, against scattered small groups of the enemy, badly hurt, each one of which would have been snuffed out with consummate ease."

In truth, prior to Midway, Nimitz had given cautious orders to Rear Adm. Frank Jack Fletcher, the *Yorktown* TF 17 commander, and Spruance. But to Lloyd's mind, U.S. units could have pursued and sunk the wounded cruiser *Mogami*. It was indicative of the defensive attitude in the Navy at that stage of the war that they did not. Later, he would observe that the senior officers of the 1930s might have been "thoroughly professional in the school of the ship . . . but they were not offensively combat minded."

He also was annoyed that no apparent tactical command came from Fletcher and TF 17. Lloyd's attitude was that the "relentless pursuit of any enemy weakness was essential to success." At Midway, the commanders were far from relentless. With the sinking of the *Yorktown,* Fletcher was out of the action; he handed the reins to Spruance. It frustrated Lloyd that Spruance did not provide some of his unengaged screens to help defend the most exposed carrier, the *Yorktown,* which sank before his eyes, as he watched from the *Atlanta.*

Midway generally has been regarded as a turning point in the Pacific, but Lloyd took a contrary view. It might have been a psychological turning point, he said, but afterward "the Japanese were still considerably stronger than we were in the Pacific."

After Midway, the *Atlanta* returned to Pearl on 13 June and went into dry dock. Afterward and in preparation for deployment to the South Pacific, she did a quick round of gunnery training that included surface, antiaircraft, and night firing, as well as shore bombardment. Lloyd remembered his battery's total destruction of the towed target during surface firing, assuring him that he had aligned his battery well.

On the fifteenth, Lloyd Mustin made lieutenant commander.

After the Battle of Midway, King pressed for the U.S. Navy to go on the offensive in the Pacific. By this time, Vice Adm. Robert L. Ghormley had arrived as commander of South Pacific Force, the echelon between Nimitz and Fletcher, who was now a vice admiral and would command Task Force 61, the invasion force that would strike the Solomon Islands.

U.S. Navy leaders had decided on an island strategy to recapture the Philippines that would begin with the seizure of a newly constructed Japanese airfield on Guadalcanal in the Eastern Solomons. Japan saw the site as its own stepping stone to Australia. In the minds of both combatants, Guadalcanal was key to an offensive thrust.

On 15 July, the *Atlanta* left Pearl for the South Pacific with TF 61 and its new commander, Rear Adm. Thomas C. Kinkaid. Lloyd was guessing incorrectly that they were attempting a "grab at Rabaul," a base above New Guinea in New Britain that the Japanese were constructing as their next step beyond Truk. On 30 July, he wrote, "My birthday today. As a present I am back on the OOD [officer of the deck] watch list. Ever since between Pearl Harbor and Midway, someplace, I'd been standing watch in gun control. Where I'd a hell of a sight rather be."

Lloyd now knew that TF 61's objective was Tulagi, to the north and across the sound from Guadalcanal. As part of Fletcher's TF 61 invasion force, the *Atlanta* was operating with the carriers, and Lloyd was critical of his commanders' management of the fuel logistics during their holding pattern. On 6 August, the day before the assault, he wrote, "Though it seems unbelievable, perhaps we are undiscovered still. Or perhaps the trap is waiting to be sprung."

Years later, his perceptions modified by time and age, Lloyd recalled, "The days that I remember in the South Pacific were bright sunshiny days with soft trade winds. Sometimes there was so little wind that it was tough to operate aircraft. You had to steam at high speed and use up a lot of fuel to operate aircraft and usually in a direction that you didn't want to go."

On 7 and 8 August, the Marines landed on Tulagi and Guadalcanal. On day one, Lloyd reported, "No air opposition." Nevertheless, Fletcher and Kinkaid withdrew their carriers and screens on the eighth. "What an 'offensive!'" he wrote the next day. "They're so god damn scared their lousy carriers will get hurt that the whole effective Pacific Fleet hauls ass at the mention of a few Jap planes."

Lloyd was unaware that just past midnight that morning the Battle of Savo Island had exploded and the U.S. Navy had lost three cruisers and suffered serious damage to several other ships. The Japanese employed a most effective night gunnery tactic: They used seaplanes to drop parachute flares behind the U.S. ships, thus illuminating their silhouettes for the gunners.

Lloyd continued to rail about command fumbling. On the eleventh, he wrote, "It is clear in my mind, from the Coral Sea, Midway, and Tulagi campaigns, that we have no high commanders capable of playing ball in the same league with many of the Japs. Maybe we'll buy our way out of this war eventually by bringing in such a force that no brains and skill can prevail. Until we do that, our prospects are zero." After finally hearing about the full extent of the Savo disaster, he wrote, "And the general idea that everything is to be done by aviation has blinded our jug-heads to the possibility of anyone's doing anything any other way, or the need for providing against it." The defeat also underlined for Lloyd the import of flashless powder in night fights.

The Japanese had concentrated their forces largely around their base at Truk and were continuing to develop Rabaul. Intelligence indicated that an assembled naval force now was steaming to recover Guadalcanal. Nimitz and Ghormley ordered Fletcher to move his three carrier task forces northeast to intercept.

At the Battle of the Eastern Solomons, northeast of Malaita, on 24 August, the *Atlanta* finally would see her first action. She accompanied Kinkaid's *Enterprise* task force, TF 16, which included the fast battleship *North Carolina,* the cruiser *Portland,* and four destroyers. Together with the *Saratoga's* TF 11, they comprised Fletcher's TF 61.

The three-carrier Japanese force approached from the northwest. The U.S. force turned and ran southeast to launch aircraft, an effective tactic because it forced the enemy planes to expend fuel. The thirty-knot speed, however, was more than the *North Carolina* could manage. She fell behind, making it difficult to provide maximum protection for the *Enterprise.*

A number of Japanese planes managed to penetrate the U.S. counterstrike. They could see the huge white wakes of the U.S. ships at speed. The Japanese dive-bombers, Lloyd emphasized, "were the deadliest things in the sky bar none. Germans, Italian, British, U.S., none compared."

It was his first real action and a baptism of fire. The *Atlanta* opened fire with a director-controlled barrage. "Everybody opened up, and the sky was just a solid sheet of tracers and shell bursts, impossible to tell your own," Lloyd remembered. All were full deflection shots, where they jammed solutions into the computers while the planes were in their dives.

"The guns were just roaring, but I don't remember hearing any guns. The bombs were bursting, but I don't remember hearing any bombs ever," he said. "You were too busy, just too busy. I never remember any sensation of fear, concern or anything else. I had a job to do and so did the others, and we were doing our darnedest to do our jobs."

Three bombs hit the *Enterprise*. She continued making way, with at least one hole in the flight deck. Repair parties welded on steel plates to cover the damage, thus enabling her to recover aircraft as she later struggled to withdraw.

Of the estimated seventy-five Japanese planes that participated in the attack, U.S. forces downed all but thirty. The *Atlanta,* said Lloyd, accounted for five kills, although the action report credited her with only one.

This battle proved to Lloyd what he had expected: radar gave U.S. commanders a tactical advantage. By late 1941, radar was on several destroyers and cruisers and four battleships, but most commanders had little understanding of how they could use it tactically. The radar of the time was the original CXAM, a low-frequency search radar with long range. The *North Carolina* had the CXAM and was able to ping Japanese planes at a range of one hundred miles at fifteen thousand feet. This operational intelligence enabled the U.S. carriers to launch their defenders to meet the enemy and attack well before they reached the task force.

On 25 August, the *Enterprise* went to Pearl, and the *Atlanta* joined the *Saratoga* TF 11. Four days later, George Murray, now a rear admiral in command of the *Hornet* Task Force 17, joined TF 61. "I knew he'd make Admiral when he was a Lieutenant Commander, Exec of the *Wright,* and have thought so all the more ever since," Lloyd proudly wrote of his stepfather. "Not only that, but I know I will too if I survive this war. Also, if I don't tramp on too many toes in the meantime with my bitter criticisms."

On the thirtieth, he wrote, "My little Henry's going to be nine tomorrow (or is it today??). Wonder when (and if) I'll ever see them all again. How I miss my little family."

The next day, while they were "leisurely steaming along at 13 knots" south of the Solomons, the *Saratoga* took a torpedo. "Things are now shaping up just as I've said: that is, the Nips, at their leisure and in their own good time, have assembled a force that can make it plenty sad for us around here." Later in the month, they struck again, sinking the carrier *Wasp* and damaging the *North Carolina,* which had to withdraw.

The *Atlanta* formed a screen with other escorts and accompanied the *Saratoga* to Nuku'alofa, Tongatapu. They remained there from 6 to 13 September for stores. The battleship *South Dakota* also was at Tongatapu and out of action, having run onto coral. Lloyd was annoyed at the ship, especially her executive officer, who refused to give them any needed spares, despite the fact that she had just arrived in the South Pacific.

The logistics pipeline to the South Pacific was not always the best. Thanks to his acquisition of a large number of gun spares during the ship's fitting out, however, Lloyd felt his department was in fairly good shape. He finally was able to acquire additional spares and 20-mm guns from the cruiser *New Orleans,* which was escorting the *Saratoga* to Pearl.

The *South Dakota* was the flagship of Rear Adm. Willis Augustus Lee Jr., commander of Battleship Division Six. Lloyd was a great admirer of Lee, one of the few senior commanders of the time who understood and appreciated the tactical significance of radar. When the fast battleship *Washington* arrived in mid-September, Lee transferred his flag.

On 21 September, the *Atlanta* left Nouméa to join Murray's TF 17 at sea, east of the New Hebrides and Espíritu Santo. On the twenty-fourth, Lloyd "got a message this morning from George saying he was glad to have two Mustins (meaning me and the destroyer) in his outfit." From 26 September to 6 October, he was again in Tongatapu, where on the thirtieth he read a press report with a quote from Halsey, leading him to infer that the admiral had returned to duty. "Best shot in the arm we've had in a long time."

By mid-October, Nimitz knew the situation around Guadalcanal was critical. He and King now regarded Ghormley as too cautious and opted on the fifteenth to replace him with Halsey.

On the sixteenth, the *Atlanta* transferred at sea to Lee's surface force, TF 64. She would join Rear Adm. Norman Scott's TF 64.1, something Lloyd felt should have happened in August, when they completed the landings on Tulagi and Guadalcanal.

On Guadalcanal, the Japanese were busy reinforcing their positions. Their ships made routine runs at night down the Slot, the body of water within the Solomons chain. Halsey wasted no time going on the offensive. On 25 October, his orders to Lee's TF 64 and the carrier TF 62 were, wrote Lloyd, simply "Strike."

For the next two days, Lee's force attempted to intercept what the Navy was calling the "Tokyo Express." He had no success, but Lloyd rejoiced. At last, they were on the offense.

On the twenty-sixth, TF 62—Kinkaid's *Enterprise* TF 16 and Murray's *Hornet* TF 17—did encounter the Japanese in the Battle of Santa Cruz. Halsey's orders again were to the point: "Attack, Repeat, Attack." In the battle, the *Hornet* was on the engaged side with the Japanese. The *Enterprise* was to the east. Kinkaid delayed Murray's launching of his planes, and both carriers received grievous damage. When the *Enterprise* withdrew east, Murray felt Kinkaid had abandoned him. The next day, the Japanese advanced their surface forces to sink the *Hornet,* which, Lloyd believed, was sinking anyway. Once again, he faulted a senior commander, Kinkaid, for failing to prosecute the battle and take it to the carriers, whose positions he knew.

On the twenty-eighth, Rear Adm. Daniel J. Callaghan arrived on the *San Francisco* to replace Scott, who transferred to the *Atlanta* and broke his flag as Task Group 64.2. With four destroyers, the *Atlanta* would continue the daily escorting of Rear Adm. Richmond Kelly Turner's amphibious force convoys to Guadalcanal from Espíritu Santo via the Sea Lark, three unmarked channels through dangerous reefs. Scott had them transit with small convoys at night, the ships dark. Japanese air attacks were routine, usually two a day in the early morning by land-based Betty bombers from Rabaul. Fortunately, the U.S. forces got advance warning from the Aussie coast watchers. Marine aviation at Henderson Field, planes from Fletcher's carriers, and some B-17s from Espíritu Santo ruled the day. By night, "the Japanese ruled the Pacific. It was a busy time and it was a Japanese lake as we all knew. We were outnumbered and outgunned and outsmarted, everything at first."

The Japanese reinforcements on Guadalcanal were endangering U.S. forces ashore. In addition, west of the Marine positions around Henderson Field, Japanese artillery had been cratering the airstrip. Maj. Gen. Alexander "Archie" Vandegrift, the First Marine Division Commander, wanted a naval bombardment.

On 30 October, the *Atlanta* broke routine and brought on board several Marine officers for an operation to bombard the coast from Londa eastward to the Marine lines. According to one report, "the Mighty A started firing at Point Cruz, just north of the place were the Matanikau River pours into the sea, and continued past Kokoumbona to Tassafaronga. Within 20 minutes the paint was burning off the guns, the fantail was covered with empty shell cases and the sailors had to break out the hoses to cool off the guns. Ammunition dumps erupted with tremendous roars. Great fires blazed in the trees and undergrowth. Beach installations flew to pieces in every direction. The Japs fled helter skelter out of the jungle right into the devastating fire from the machine guns on the ship." At Tassafaronga, she devastated the barges landing supplies from the Tokyo Express. For two hours, the *Atlanta* maintained continuous fire.

In early November, intelligence began to flow on another buildup of Japanese surface forces at Truk. Lee and Scott wanted to seize the initiative and start forcing the enemy to respond.

On the night of 10 November, Scott left two of his destroyers to defend Turner's transports and in the *Atlanta* led his other two destroyers on a sweep around Iron Bottom Sound. They failed to make any contact with the enemy.

The next day, they rejoined Turner's convoy and defended against two air attacks. The Japanese first hit them in the morning with twelve to fifteen carrier-based dive-bombers. An intense air defense downed about half. The planes scored no hits on the transports. At noon, twenty-eight land-based aircraft appeared at about twenty-eight thousand feet, too high for the U.S. guns. Lloyd remembered waiting for them to drop to a height where he had a fire control solution: With Scott, that was all he needed. He did not have to wait for an order to open fire. The planes descended, and the screen commenced firing as they passed overhead to attack Henderson Field. The *Atlanta* accounted for two kills. The second Japanese strike also had no effect, other than the nuisance caused by American shrapnel that fell on the runway.

That night Scott did another sweep. Again, they made no contacts.

Early in the morning of 12 November, TF 64.2 regrouped with Callaghan's TF 64.1 and, with Turner's amphibious force, reentered the sound. Although Scott was more experienced at handling ships in formation, Turner made Callaghan the officer in tactical command, based on seniority. It was a poor decision. Scott was a combat veteran; Callaghan was unbloodied.

At the landing beaches, Japanese artillery was active again in the morning. Around noon, twenty-five Japanese land-based planes approached low on the horizon and began a torpedo run. Turner quickly got his transports under way.

Lloyd was displeased with Turner and Callaghan. They had put the *Atlanta* on the wrong side of the screen. Her batteries thus could not fully engage the Japanese attack. In addition, they forwarded no doctrine to govern distribution of gunfire against this dispersion of aerial targets. Nevertheless, the antiaircraft fire from the other side of the screen thwarted the attack. As planes spilled into the *Atlanta*'s arc of fire, two went down. Another damaged plane hit the *San Francisco*. U.S. fighters counterattacked later, recalled Lloyd, leaving probably only three or four planes to escape. The Japanese failed to get any torpedo hits.

The three air attacks had depleted the enemy's available air resources. Lloyd reckoned that the Japanese had lost all but some one hundred carrier planes. Thus he later felt that the air threat was well compromised prior to the battle that night.

On the twelfth, Scott would conduct his third night of sweeps, this time under Callaghan, as commander of what Turner had designated as TG 67.4.

The Japanese planned to bombard Henderson Field for two nights as preamble to landing on 14 November. On learning of a superior Japanese force approaching, Turner withdrew the transports. After escorting them through the eastern channels, Callaghan returned through Lengo Channel to meet the enemy. In effect, Turner had left him with five cruisers and eight destroyers, less than half the size of the approaching fleet and vastly inferior in weight and armament.

As it happened, the Japanese force numbered two battleships, a light cruiser, and fourteen destroyers. Three of the destroyers stayed to the rear on picket duty, escorting the eight transports that carried some forty thousand soldiers who were to retake Guadalcanal. Based on their success in the night battle at Savo Island, the Japanese were confident that their optical equipment would offset the supposed U.S. radar advantage. For his part, Callaghan might have interpreted Scott's success at Cape Esperance as reason to believe he could handle night engagements.

Lloyd's attitude toward Callaghan forecasts the criticism of later observers. First, he failed to issue a battle plan. "All we knew was that we were a column of ships." Second was his decision to assume a column formation. Some historians have supposed that he went with a column because it worked for Scott at Cape Esperance. In any event, Callaghan's column was three miles long. His flagship was sixth, two miles to the rear.

Third, although Callaghan had SG microwave surface search radars in his force, he apparently did not appreciate the tactical advantage they could provide. The *O'Bannon, Portland, Helena,* and *Fletcher* had SG radar but were in the fourth, seventh, eighth, and thirteenth positions, respectively. Lloyd felt Callaghan at least should have selected as his flagship the *Helena,* but instead he chose to fly his flag on the *San Francisco,* as had Scott at Cape Esperance. Perhaps Callaghan, her former skipper, felt more comfortable on the *San Francisco.* Lloyd believed the decision reflected his distrust of radar. Much later, in a 1990 interview, he claimed the *San Francisco*'s less capable SC air search radar was turned off during the battle.

As the battle lines closed, Lloyd and his men had been at their battle stations for more than sixty-five hours. At about 12:30 A.M., he told his after battery that contact with the enemy was likely this time.

At 1:00 A.M., the *Fletcher,* the lead ship, passed Lunga Point abeam to port, distance one mile. The course was 280 degrees at twenty knots. At 1:23, the *Helena* reported contact with the enemy on her SG radar. On a course of 140 degrees at 1:25 at eighteen knots, the Japanese approached with bombardment projectiles loaded on their shell hoists.

Lloyd said the *Atlanta* detected surface targets with her SC radar at twenty-two thousand yards. Using that contact information, she put both gun directors to the port bow and both batteries on the radar contact with two separate targets closing fast. His after batteries were tracking a light cruiser, the *Nagara.* Lloyd said he could see her in the darkness at six thousand yards.

At 1:29, Callaghan ordered a course change to 310 degrees. Lloyd was not so much concerned that he had opted to remain in a cumbersome column; it was what he did after contact that was the problem. Intent on giving a course to allow his column to cross the Japanese T, Callaghan's order in fact put his force on a collision course to run between enemy ships. While the course denied the Japanese battleships a range advantage over the U.S. cruisers and destroyers, the U.S. column would be shooting both ways.

Lloyd felt that if Callaghan had been on a ship with the SG radar and its planned position indicator (PPI), he would have seen the tactical picture more clearly and ordered a hard turn north, something he should have done with news of the *Helena* contact. Unfortunately, his use of the TBS, the talk between ships, Lloyd continued, involved a laborious procedure using a so-called shackle code for tactical signals. It clogged the net and, among other things, perhaps contributed to the *Helena's* inability to convey fully what her scope was indicating.

At 1:37, Callaghan finally ordered a course due north, 000 degrees, apparently in an attempt to correct his mistake and to allow his force to open with torpedoes and then gunfire. However, as the lead ships of the column commenced the turn, they masked all the gun and torpedo batteries on those behind.

Suddenly at 1:41, the lead ship, the *Cushing,* went left to 310 degrees, either to unmask her torpedo batteries or to prevent collision with enemy or both. All four destroyers in the van executed a ships left maneuver that forced the *Atlanta* to rudder hard left. Lloyd's directors had been training on the *Nagara,* now 60 degrees on starboard bow and heading 110 degrees. He also was tracking with his binoculars, and he estimated that moonlit target was now at three thousand yards.

At 1:42, the Japanese discovered the U.S. force. The battleship *Hiei,* the Japanese flag-ship, began hastily switching from bombardment to armor-piercing ammunition. The destroyer division commander on the *Cushing* asked for permission to fire, which Lloyd later regarded as indicative of Callaghan's failure to emphasize command initiative. At 1:45, Callaghan responded with what was effectively a non-order, to "stand by to open fire." For almost twenty-two minutes Callaghan let slip the opportunity for his radar-equipped commanders to get the drop on the enemy.

At the same time, the *Hiei* and main Japanese body went left to 080 degrees. At 1:47, Callaghan desperately ordered his column to resume its 000 degrees course. As ships passed on both sides, over the phones Lloyd said, "This is the real thing. Get ready to shoot." He ordered searchlights to strike arcs. Just as the *Atlanta* was turning to the north, the *Hiei* put her searchlights on the port wing of her bridge. Additional illu-mination possibly came also from the destroyer *Akatsuki.* Hearing no command from the officer in tactical command, captain, or his gunnery officer, Lloyd ordered, "Action [to] port. Illuminating ship is target. Open fire." Both gun groups slewed from star-board to 300 degrees relative on port. His estimated range was two thousand yards. "As soon as the directors said on target," said Lloyd, "I ordered commence firing and we did," adding that the *Atlanta* did not counter-illuminate.

Lloyd's battery fired first on the illuminating ship, and the forward battery followed, preempting and contrary to Callaghan's 1:48 order, "Odd ships commence fire to star-board, even ships to port!" He claimed he never heard the order and gave his own, "knowing that we were in a melee and that orders from higher authority could not be expected. And they wouldn't be very genuine if they were given."

The *Atlanta* actually had opened fire at twelve hundred yards, "and that's murder." Lloyd remained convinced that the target was a destroyer. His after group shot ten to twelve rounds and was the first to fire, demonstrating its great reaction time. Lloyd's open-ing salvo was four hundred yards short. He could see the splashes caught in the beam of the searchlight. His spotter laddered their fire upward, and the battery began hitting.

Immediately, the *Atlanta* began receiving hits, probably, Lloyd thought, from a destroyer on their south flank. The ships were now at six hundred yards. The *Akatsuki* and possibly another destroyer passed across the *Atlanta's* bow heading north, cross-ing the line of fire. The forward turret group thereupon switched to starboard, train-ing on the destroyer and, after about a minute, sinking her—so Lloyd thought.

The other destroyers on the flank had fired torpedoes. Suddenly, the *Atlanta* was rocked by an enormous explosion as a torpedo struck the port side between the forward fire room and forward engine room. The blast knocked out power and threw Lloyd to his knees. A second torpedo struck the ship but failed to detonate, probably because it was fired from such close range that the exploder did not have time to arm.

Offensively, the *Atlanta* was out of the battle but not out of danger. She was drifting into the Japanese line of march. The melee intensified, as she sustained hit after hit from both sides. Caught between the enemy line and her own, she was now a target for the *San Francisco.* Not five minutes into the action, she received gunfire from port that demolished the bridge superstructure and most of the gun batteries. These hits to the forward superstructure killed Scott.

One account reckoned that they were from *Hiei*'s secondary battery. Lloyd, however, was sure they were from the *San Francisco,* which opened fire from two thousand yards abaft *Atlanta*'s port. He recognized smokeless powder in the two or three salvos fired, and the slow salvo fire typical of U.S. 8-inch gunnery. The next day while conducting the damage assessment, Lloyd found eight-inch holes where the armor-piercing shells went straight through the ship without detonating. He also found traces of green dye around the holes: Warships used dyes to color the splashes to distinguish their own shots from another's in gunnery practice; the *San Francisco* used green. Lloyd's damage report listed nineteen 8-inch hits.

As another U.S. ship mistakenly raked her with machine-gun fire, the *Atlanta* continued gliding to the right of the battle line and toward the Japanese ships to take still more fire. In all, she took forty-nine officially recorded hits of assorted caliber at ranges of six hundred to just under two thousand yards, not counting the raking fire from machine guns.

On the *San Francisco,* a Japanese plane crashed into the forward superstructure, killing or mortally wounding Callaghan, the captain, and the executive officer. For another hour, the combatants would trade their murderous fire, but for the *Atlanta* the vital matter at hand was damage control. All able hands turned to fire fighting, even using lengths of telephone cables as long lanyards to put buckets over the side to gather water.

At first light, Lloyd saw what appeared to be a Japanese ship to starboard. He joined crew members in a general rush to the torpedo tubes, the one remaining operational weapon. He had a number of volunteers but no rated torpedomen. One account cited a "cool-headed" Lloyd manning the station with a signalman striker, J. W. Harvey, the only survivor of the signal gang. Very soon, they were able to identify the ship as the *Portland.* In any event, the ships were too close for the torpedoes to arm. Three other U.S. ships, destroyers, were drifting and burning nearby. The *Portland* later encountered and sank one Japanese destroyer, the *Yudachi,* which, with no stern, was steaming in circles.

Casualties from the night's battle were in the water all around. Small craft maneuvered to rescue survivors. "I certainly do remember vividly that one of them came alongside, a big Mike boat from Guadalcanal," Lloyd recalled, "and in approaching *Atlanta* it had picked up several other people. As it came alongside where I was standing at the rail (the rail was not very far above the water at this point) here stood up in the boat a Japanese boatswain mate. He had his white uniform jumper on, and his boatswain insignia were unmistakable on it. He was gesturing that he wanted some rags. He was showing us that he wanted rags. He showed us that he had about six or eight men there who were wounded in various ways and all covered with oil. He was taking care of them. A couple of them were Japanese, and a couple of them were Americans. They were all immobile. They were perhaps unconscious. This one Japanese boatswain mate had taken it upon himself to take care of all those sailors."

The marines ashore sent boats to assist in the rescue. The final total was 172 killed and 79 wounded. When it was all over, the Navy would lose four destroyers in addition to the *Atlanta* and another cruiser, the *Juneau,* in which the five Sullivan brothers had perished.

On the *Atlanta,* Lloyd continued to occupy himself with damage assessment, making his way to the ship's Mark 44 Director. "We had Director Officers on those. The port forward one was completely blown right off the ship, including the Director Officer. That port forward 1.1 was hit, direct hit on the gun, which is what started the fire in its Clipping Room. But when we were cleaning up things around the ship, I found pieces of that Director Officer which I personally dropped over the side . . . just pieces."

The ship continued to drift toward Japanese waters off Guadalcanal, well to the west of the Marine positions. As a precaution, Lloyd issued small arms to the men. They attempted to anchor, but the shelf was too steep to catch. Fortunately, the Navy tug *Bobolink* arrived and towed them toward Lunga, where they finally were able to anchor.

The ship, however, was taking on water faster than they could pump it out.

The captain, who was wounded, and the executive officer were there. The gunnery officer became the damage control officer, because he was gone. The engineer officer was gone. The navigator was gone. So the assistant engineer officer took over as engineer officer, and I became the gunnery officer, and we three with the captain and the exec had a council of war and decided that we couldn't save her. Furthermore, we received information that the Japs were coming in that night again, which they did, a couple of big cruisers.

Captain Jenkins did not want to risk the lives of his remaining 450 men. At dusk, on Friday, 13 November, "we had to give up and let her go down. So we finished her off with scuttling charges and down she went."

As one of the *Atlanta*'s plank owners, Lloyd left a part of him with her. Years later, when asked if he knew where his father's commissioning sword was, he replied, "I know exactly where it is. It's in my sea chest, in my cabin, at the bottom of Iron Bottom Sound."

The *Atlanta* received a Presidential Unit Citation for the First Naval Battle of Guadalcanal, crediting her with sinking a destroyer and repeatedly hitting a cruiser, which later sank. The award read that the ship "gallantly remained in battle under aux- iliary power with one-third of her crew killed or missing, her engine room flooded and her topside a shambles." When she sank, said Lloyd, she was eleven months old, had steamed more than a hundred thousand miles, and had fired ten thousand rounds of 5- inch, "which is about fifty years of normal peacetime expenditure, and she'd been in five major engagements." Even with one or two torpedo hits, he proudly observed, she had stayed afloat for eighteen hours.

As for Lloyd, he got a scratch on his lip from flying shrapnel.

In his after action report, Lloyd paid great attention to the lessons learned in dam- age control and especially to the need for a casualty power system and redundancy, ter- minal points, and portable cabling. To that end, he wanted ships to have an emergency diesel aft and forward. The Japanese had used flashless powder; Lloyd wanted that, too, for night engagements. Heretofore, the U.S. Navy had not been receptive because flash- less powder produced smoke, but at night, smoke did not matter.

In a 3 June 1943 narrative, he recorded that the *Atlanta* received about fifty hits. He offered that with a sixteen-gun 5-inch battery, she was appropriately an antiaircraft ship, especially since cruisers generally were not doing bombardment. He recom- mended that a task force should have at least one such light antiaircraft cruiser with every carrier. From another perspective, the light cruiser also was better able than a destroyer to maintain speed and operate with carriers.

In the evening of 13 November, the landing craft carrying *Atlanta* survivors dropped its ramp on a Guadalcanal shore. Lloyd waded through the shallow surf to the beach. Leaning against a nearby tree was his former academy duty officer, now a captain, Bill Greenman, skipper of the cruiser *Astoria,* sunk at Savo. Finding himself ashore, he requested and got command of the naval bases on Guadalcanal and Tulagi and the naval units attached to the First Marine Division.

"I would like to have you here on my staff," Greenman told Lloyd. "Let me send a message down to Admiral Halsey's headquarters saying that you concur."

"No, sir, Captain, I don't want to be on this island," replied Lloyd. "I belong at sea."

"Well, I'm sending it anyway," Greenman stated, thus making Lloyd his operations and intelligence officer.

Back home in Annapolis, news of the battle and the U.S. losses were in the newspapers. No one had any word, however, on who had survived and who had not. On Sunday, Emily took their daughter, Doug, to Sunday school at the Naval Academy Chapel. As the four-year-old stepped from the car, the chapel bells began to play "Eternal Father." Doug turned to see her mother weeping at the wheel.

George Murray had gotten word to Washington that Lloyd had survived; however, the naval officer trying to telephone Dreams Landing could not get a response. Emily was not answering the phone. Murray instructed the officer to ask for Henry, who several days later took the call, relieving the grim suspense.

On their first night on Guadalcanal, Lloyd assembled his men. As he did as a camp counselor at Gunston, he instructed them how to pitch their tents. Their first meal in days consisted of foxhole rations that the marines kept in their trenches.

That night, the Japanese unleashed another furious shore bombardment, as the naval drama continued. Planes flying from Henderson Field were trying to sink the stricken battleship *Hiei.* In the end, the Japanese finally torpedoed her. The planes continued shuttling to attack other enemy units that were making what would be their last landing at Lunga. The next morning the Japanese were unloading four beached transports. The Marines borrowed some of Lloyd's surviving *Atlanta* gun crews to man a 5-inch naval gun that shelled and destroyed the nearest transport. On the fourteenth, Lee arrived with his surface force and put an end to the immediate naval threat, only after a three-day battleship slugfest. On the fifteenth, the officers and men from the *Atlanta* joined with marines to fight in an expected attack that fortunately never came.

Most *Atlanta* survivors shipped out on 21 November to Espíritu Santo and ultimately Nouméa before going home. The destroyer *Mustin* escorted them.

Lloyd, however, remained, serving almost four months for Greenman. "I moved the convoys and what not off and on the unloading area when they came and, supposedly, controlled the boats." He started with "quite a little fleet," with four PT boats, a couple of subchasers, and eventually three little New Zealand corvettes, plus some thirty to forty miscellaneous small craft. By the time he left, he had increased his force to some fourteen PT boats.

On 30 November during the Battle of Tassafaronga, Japanese destroyers tried to reinforce or resupply the island. One intelligence report said a submarine was in the area. Figuring the sub was going to Komimbo Bay, Lloyd sent his PT boats from Tulagi fifteen miles to the north across the bay; they circled and approached from the west. With two torpedoes, they sank her.

For Lloyd, life ashore was very different from the stressful duties at sea in a war zone that he had known for months on the *Atlanta*. At times, it was bizarre. The Sunday before Tassafaronga, he had gone aboard the beached and torpedoed transport *Alchiba,* whose captain had been the first commanding officer of the *Mustin*. Lloyd and the skipper were drinking coffee in his cabin immediately below the bridge. "So, we sat there while hold number two continued to burn and ammunition continued to explode and these machine gun bullets would burn and propel themselves out."

Lloyd also remembered an island concoction combining the Solomons' wild limes, the Marines' ice-making plants, and Navy torpedo alcohol. "You could squeeze the lime juice into the ice making tanks with torpedo alcohol, and what came out was really something. If it was a quiet evening, another fellow and I would hop in a jeep and run over and see how our friends in charge of the ice plant were making out. We'd sit down and have one glass of this stuff, and it was plenty. It was really strong. It would come out of there sort of like sherbet."

As operations officer, Lloyd always had a problem with boat discipline during the unloading. On one particular day, however, he noted that "boat discipline evaporated. It was a little bit lower than zero." A long line of boats was waiting at a ship that was carrying a load of beer for the Army. "[O]ther ships with more mundane things like bombs and 155-mm projectiles and machine gun ammunition and beans, canned pineapple and what not were just lying there with no boats available to receive cargo that would be dangling from their cargo booms by the nets full." Once loaded with beer, the boats were proceeding not to the landing area but to an area down the coast to unload.

"The long and short of it was that of the thirty thousand cases of beer, hardly five thousand reached the quartermaster dump and there was a considerable dismay and concern expressed at relatively low levels in the Army, but it never went up the line." Maj. Gen. Alexander M. Patch, USA, who relieved Vandegrift and the Marines in early December, was well aware that the sailors and marines had been on the island since August, "and none of them had seen a can of beer." Lloyd surmised that he "chose to ignore this burglary of his supplies," being "quite confident that he could get more" in due course, "and indeed he did."

"What I am really not at all able to explain," Lloyd wryly offered, "is that when that day was over and I went back to my tent, I had become accustomed to finding cases of canned fruit and other delicacies arranged for by my tent mate Jack Wolf, the Beach Commander, and even bottles of whiskey which were quite a rare item on the Island. Here in our tent sat at least a dozen cases of beer, just sitting there on the floor on the tent level, and obviously, Jack had arranged this, but I had no ready understanding of how, because I was pretty sure that the Army hadn't diverted any beer to us."

In late January, Lloyd finally got orders to report to the *Atlanta*'s sister ship *San Diego* in Nouméa.

"In February, the Japanese finally withdrew. It was the first time in Japanese history that they had been forced to give up territory that they had occupied. Thus the Japanese regarded Guadalcanal as the turning point of the war in the Pacific. They ran out of destroyers and cruisers."

On 9 February, after six months of costly and bloody attrition at sea and ashore, the United States finally secured Guadalcanal.

Chapter 17

At War, at Speed
with Pete and Ching

Sometime in late January or early February 1943, Lloyd finally left Guadalcanal, flying from Henderson Field on a Marine transport plane. The only seat was on one of the portable, collapsible gasoline fuel tanks carried in the cargo bay, but he was happy. He was off the beach and returning to sea.

The six-hundred-mile flight was to Espíritu Santo, a French island in the New Hebrides chiefly consisting of coconut plantations. In February 1943, it was the most advanced U.S. base in the South Pacific and was becoming more important every day as war matériel began arriving in abundance. The one drawback, Lloyd remembered, was the flies: They thrived on the rotting windfall coconuts.

With the few possessions he managed to take from the *Atlanta* and a pair of Marine-green trousers and field shoes he had gotten on Guadalcanal, Lloyd reported to the cruiser *San Diego,* a sister ship of the *Atlanta* and one of the escorts for the carrier *Enterprise.* Her commanding officer was Capt. "Blunderbuss Ben" Perry, an officer with a lot of gunnery experience. Perry was greatly disturbed that his gunnery department seemed so ineffective and brought Lloyd on board as his assistant gunnery officer to fix the problem.

Lloyd quickly discovered that the guns were badly out of alignment. The fix was easy: He first aligned the guns and then aligned the mounts to the directors. As he went, he trained the ship's gunners so they could do alignment themselves. Gradually, he saw a change in attitude from "'I don't know what's wrong' to 'I don't know what is wrong, but I am sure I can find it and fix it,'" he recalled. "I could just watch these people get a whole new feeling of confidence in their equipment and their ability to handle their equipment because of little things like this."

He also trained his department in antiaircraft fire, although he never got a chance to work with them in action. Lloyd's procedure called for the director pointer and trainer not to check fire when slewing the gun upward after following a dive, thus avoiding disrupting the rhythm of the loading crew. The 5-inch battery with the Mark 37 director system was said to require sixty seconds to arrive at a fire control solution on a surprise aircraft target. Later in the war, he would use the technique to get the time down to ten seconds and finally to six.

Lloyd was in and out of Espíritu Santo for the next six months. After the 30 January Battle of Rennell Island, it was quiet in the Solomons. The Japanese were withdrawing, and the United States was not yet ready to move up the island chain. In late March or early April, the *San Diego* was due at Devonport Drydock in Auckland, New Zealand, for a couple of weeks to repair underwater damage. There, it was blue-uniform weather, but Lloyd was still in what he had worn on Guadalcanal. He had to borrow a uniform from another officer and buy some black shoes from stores on a destroyer tender.

The New Zealanders showed the ship's crew uninterrupted hospitality. Unfortunately, the same could not be said of the U.S. Navy facilities. A USN hotel refused to serve the *San Diego* officers liquor, reserving its stock for the rear echelon based ashore. As Perry was senior to the local commanding officer, he immediately reversed that policy, said Lloyd.

The *San Diego* returned to sea, and Lloyd remained with her for a couple of operations. In June, he got orders for the States. He hopped by plane to Honolulu and then to San Francisco, where he tried for hours to get a line to Annapolis to tell Emily he was home. The military had priority for all long-distance calls, however, so he figured it would be easier to catch a commercial plane and just arrive on the family doorstep. He managed to jump on a United DC-3 to Washington's National Airport.

Once in Washington, Lloyd was able to hitch a ride to Annapolis and finally to Dreams Landing. It was about six o'clock in the evening when he walked in the door, his seabag over his shoulder. "The two older ones danced up and down and they were so glad, 'Daddy, Daddy,'" Lloyd recalled, "but the youngest, Tom . . . didn't know me at all. He had only been a year old when I had left, and he didn't remember me personally, but he knew my picture, and he heard his brother and sister call me daddy, so he knew that's who it was. He was very shy about this ostensible stranger he knew he was supposed to know, and this was daddy in the picture, so he stood on his head. This little round two-foot by two-foot fellow stood on his head."

The next day, Lloyd returned to Washington, expecting to get his specific orders. He discovered he had none. The Navy gave him a couple of weeks before ordering him to report to the Gun Factory's Gunnery Officers' Ordnance School to study gunnery installation for his next ship. Eager to return to the war, however, he persisted in asking for a ship.

In September 1943, he finally was able to report to the Cramp Shipyard in Philadelphia as gunnery officer for the commissioning crew of the *Miami,* a light cruiser with 6-inch guns. The ship was the shipyard's first ship construction since World War I. Cramp had been closed, and the yard was virtually derelict when work began. Trees were growing in shipbuilding ways and had to be felled before workers could lay the keel. Emily and the children soon joined him, taking an apartment at the Walnut Park Plaza. On 1 November, he made commander, to rank from the previous November.

With Lloyd was his former *Atlanta* shipmate Jack Wolf, who would be the assistant engineer. Lloyd and Wolf applied many lessons derived from their battle experience to the construction and made substantial contributions to the precommissioning effort. Lloyd was especially active in ensuring that the yard installed and leveled the gun mounts for proper alignment. Pleased with the cooperation from Cramp, Lloyd said it "produced a ship that never missed a mission; whereas none of her sister ships could make that same statement." Commissioning was on 28 December 1943.

Only about 10 percent of the eleven-hundred-odd *Miami* crew had combat experience. The gunnery department was by far the largest on the ship, and training kept Lloyd very busy. Many of the young sailors were uncomfortable in a turret. "A lot of these kids were really frightened at the prospect of firing a gun, and this is a pretty real thing to close up a bunch of youngsters inside of a steel box in which are the gleaming well-oiled breaches of three monsters."

Leadership in the ship was weak. The captain had not been to sea since 1939 and had come from a desk job on King's staff in Washington. The executive officer had lost a destroyer in the Pacific and in effect was being passed over for captain. The senior officers by and large had not been to sea with this kind of armament. Lloyd made it happen. As he had in the *San Diego,* he devoted a lot of time to working on gun alignment, and his seniors gave him a free hand to do it.

In the winter of 1943–44, the *Miami* took her shakedown cruise to Trinidad and the Gulf of Paria. When she returned to the East Coast to begin training, Lloyd worked his gun crews so much that they exhausted their ammunition allotment. The *Miami* finished her predeployment with a post-shakedown availability in Philadelphia to correct her remaining problems. When she was ready for sea, Lloyd had to hustle a resistant bureaucracy at Fort Mifflin to get the maximum amount of ammunition, on the assumption that the *Miami* was heading to action in the Pacific. He got an appropriate and full mix for armor piercing and antiaircraft, but as soon as he finished loading, the ship got word she might go to the Atlantic to support the coming European invasion. In Boston, he had to swap his ammunition for shore bombardment ammo. No sooner had they done so and set to sea when new orders came for the Pacific.

On 16 April 1944, the *Miami* joined two other light cruisers, the *Vincennes* and *Houston,* on a trip through the canal to San Diego and finally Pearl Harbor. The passage was tough for Lloyd, who had been diagnosed with malaria, probably contracted on Guadalcanal. By the time they got to Hawaii on 6 May, he was on the mend. In Pearl, they swapped ammo for the third time.

U.S. forces in the Pacific were on the offensive, made possible by the arrival of the new *Essex*-class fast carriers and the wider presence of and familiarity with radar and its integration into the new combat information center suites that now gave the Navy an edge in night engagements. Nimitz completed the campaigns for Kwajalein, Majuro, and Eniwetok in the Marshalls ahead of his timetable, and his forces now were getting ready for a June 1944 operation to seize the Marianas.

"The force in the Marianas campaign was unstoppable," said Lloyd. "The U.S. outnumbered the Japanese in every class of ship." By one reckoning, Nimitz now had fifteen carriers, seven battleships, twenty-one cruisers, and sixty-nine destroyers.

In early June, the *Miami* and her two fellow cruisers rendezvoused with the operating fleet at Majuro, where the senior aviator, Vice Adm. Pete Mitscher, and his fast carrier task force, TF 58, were preparing to conduct the air strikes against Saipan, Tinian, Rota, Guam, Pagan, and the Bonin Islands in support of the campaign. The three cruisers joined the *Essex* carrier Task Group 58.4 as escorts. Generally, they would assume gun defense positions within a few thousand yards of the carrier.

Lloyd would reenter the action right away. On 6 June, Mitscher's force departed to launch its first assault. On the eleventh, four days of carrier strikes commenced on the Marianas, followed by another three days of attacks on the Bonins. On 15 June, the invasion force began landings on Saipan. Aware that a large Japanese force was moving to counterattack, Mitscher sought permission from Admiral Spruance, commander of the Fifth Fleet, to move to meet it. Not willing to leave his invasion force exposed, Spruance refused.

On the nineteenth, in the Battle of the Philippine Sea, the Japanese launched four waves of carrier-based aircraft strikes at Spruance and Mitscher's forces. By one account, over the course of the two-day battle, U.S. planes and ships downed all but thirty-five of the 430 aircraft the enemy hurled against the invasion armada in what would become known as the "Great Marianas Turkey Shoot."

Task Force 58 was west of Saipan. The *Miami* and TG 58.4 were just behind Lee's battleship line and to the west of Mitscher's main carrier forces. On the engagement side of the battle, Lloyd's batteries saw a great deal of action. The ship "could shoot like nobody else around," he said. Less than a handful of planes got through the U.S. defenses. One dropped a bomb on the *South Dakota,* and another made a run on the carrier *Essex* and missed. Although considered the weakest of the carrier groups, TG 58.4 scored eighty-two kills.

After the battle, Mitscher sent his planes to strike the Japanese force. The operation was memorable for what the historians have regarded as Mitscher's daring decision to turn on his lights to guide his planes home to their ships. In Lloyd's view, however, the risk was minimal: The United States had practically destroyed both Japanese aviation and surface forces in the vicinity, and Mitscher knew where their surviving submarines were lurking.

The battle concluded, the *Miami* returned with TG 58.4 to support the Marianas invasion, where the action had shifted to Guam. Mitscher's chief of staff, Commo. Arleigh Burke, was continually impressing on Mitscher how best to use his surface assets. One result of that input, Lloyd believed, was the *Miami*'s 27 June assignment to bombard Rota and Guam. In that operation, her targets included a number of fuel tanks, leading Lloyd to conclude, "Of course, this was the first time I'd ever had any of this kind of target practice and it immediately emphasized a point that I kept in mind forever after. . . . Open the action against the down wind target so that the smoke from it will blow away and not obscure the remaining target."

After the Marianas campaign, at the end of June, Spruance exchanged command with Halsey. Fifth Fleet became the Third, and all the task force and group numbers changed in suit. Under Halsey, the action was relentless. The *Miami* and the *Essex* group continued to strike Rota for the first four days of July, before retiring to Eniwetok on the sixth. Eight days later, they returned to the Marianas. For most of the month, the *Miami* operated west of the island chain with the carriers, as they gave close air support to ground forces still struggling to subdue Japanese resistance.

The main threat was from Japanese night torpedo attacks using long-range, land-based Betty bombers, each of which carried two torpedoes as well as bombs. Later in the autumn of 1945, when operating with TF 58.3, Rear Adm. Frederic C. "Fritz" Sherman contrived a notably successful defense.

At night, Japanese Emilys would drop flares behind the U.S. force to silhouette the ships for the Betty torpedo planes. The U.S. forces used smoke to disrupt the attacks. Sherman would maximize his screen's maneuverability by steaming at a fast twenty-five knots and then turn into the attack at speed "and keep turning to expose his lethal broadside battery as the fish would go by. If the attack continued, he would continue his turn to expose another broadside." For the *Miami,* muzzle smoke did not obscure the sighting: The cruiser used radar fire control.

Victory in Guam came mid-month, and by mid-August, Nimitz would install his headquarters at a command center built on the heights overlooking the U.S. invasion beaches at Asan Bay.

The *Miami*'s next action came in Tinian, Palau, and Yap, and in early August, she supported raids on Iwo Jima and Haha Jima in the Bonins before steaming to Eniwetok for upkeep. On 7 September, she was with her carriers again, supporting strikes on Peleliu and Angaur in the Palaus, the next island chain leading to the Philippines.

At various times, the ship would join Lee and his fast battleship Task Force 34. A consummate surface warfare tactician, Lee would augment his battleship force with ships such as the *Miami* on loan from Mitscher, who was very supportive of his approach. Lee would exercise maneuver orders extensively to prepare for possible surface engagements. Each ship had operation plans, operation orders, and written doctrine with existing standard signals. Lee also emphasized gunnery and would have his units practice their fire into each others' wakes to focus the patterns onto imaginary targets.

Lloyd would adopt this technique for the *Miami* and practice it whenever he could. "Thanks to this endless drudgery that I had imposed on our people in the *Miami* and constantly working at it, we were able to keep our patterns down to about four hundred yards, and that was about as small as I could get 'em."

Lloyd linked this approach with continuous rapid fire. At a firing elevation for eighteen thousand yards, at which the guns could load and eject their empties, "you simply closed the firing key and kept them closed, and each gun fired the instant its breach closed on a new load. So you just got a continuous stream after the first couple of shots. The gun to gun variations in loading time meant that since every gun fired as quickly as it possibly could without waiting for its companions, pretty soon you were spraying a hose out there."

From 12 to 15 September, the *Miami* bombed targets in the Philippines. During these strikes, her scout planes on four occasions rescued U.S. pilots shot down in enemy waters. For the rest of the month, she continued to support strikes against the Palaus and the Philippines, returning to Saipan on the twenty-ninth for replenishment.

In October 1944, the *Miami* was operating from the western Carolines, east of the Philippines, where the Navy had a large fleet anchorage and base at Ulithi Atoll. Mid-month, she was off Okinawa for strikes that ran from the tenth through the fourteenth.

The tempo of the Pacific war was rising rapidly. "The combination of submarine warfare on the shipping lanes to Japan, the prospect of MacArthur's return to the Philippines and Mitscher's force operating freely through the south Pacific battered Japan towards the end of the war," observed Lloyd. "It was really a combination of every form of pressure that we were able to bring to bear against the enemy that finally brought him to his knees, and anybody who knows anything about what it takes to win a war has to know that you only win by the result of an accumulation of pressures upon the enemy, constraints upon him, progressive whittling away of his capability to do what he wants, and a progressive whittling away of his capability to interfere with your doing what you want."

During TF 38 staff meetings that Lloyd attended several months later on the *New Jersey* with Halsey and Lee, he would always call Mitscher "Pete." Lloyd gave the venerable aviator full credit for this phase of the prosecution of the war. "[I]t was Mitscher who developed the force and developed the capabilities, developed the procedures and techniques, and developed the confidence in the members of the force that they could not be stopped."

Mitscher was an aggressive commander and now had the air defense capabilities to allow him full rein. "Advance carriers basing out of Ulithi," said Lloyd, "moved in on the Philippines, generally in the central areas. Meaning that we operated generally to the West of the Island of Leyte. It was going to be in this area, of course, that the landing forces would go ashore."

On 18 October, the *Miami* was off Luzon supporting carrier strikes in advance of Philippine landings. "What was really demonstrated was our ability to establish local superiority, crushing superiority in small areas of our choosing at times of our choosing, conveyed to us by the mobility of the carriers, the basis from which our aircraft struck." Their targets were some three hundred Japanese airfields that "were all fixed."

On the twentieth, the Seventh Fleet landed General MacArthur at Palo on Leyte Gulf and moved south to guard the Surigao Strait that separated Leyte from the Surigao tip of Mindanao.

To defend the Philippines, Japan had assembled three naval forces in a last-ditch effort to crush the U.S. landing. A northern force approached north of Luzon to lure Halsey away from the action. A powerful center force was moving from the west through the Sibuyan Sea, intending to pass through the San Bernardino Strait and follow the island coast south toward Leyte. A less potent southern force was heading toward the Surigao Strait to trap and destroy the amphibious ships in the Leyte Gulf.

Beginning early on 24 October, in the first of four actions that became known as the Battle of Leyte Gulf, Mitscher's aviators located and repeatedly attacked the center force in the Sibuyan Sea. Despite the Navy's air superiority in the region, the air assault failed to stop the Japanese ships.

When the force apparently turned from its course, Halsey concluded it was withdrawing. That afternoon, he had received word that the northern force had arrived off Luzon, and he ordered his carriers off Samar to speed north to assist in an attack, opting to leave the San Bernardino Strait undefended. When his three carrier groups rendezvoused late in the evening, they steamed north, led by TF 34 and the *Miami*. The battle commenced mid-morning and raged until the evening. In the end, TF 38 had sunk four Japanese carriers and several supporting ships.

Not one hour into the fight, however, Halsey learned that the center force in fact had reversed course again and passed through the San Bernardino Strait during the night. Now, all that stood in its path to the vulnerable beachhead on Leyte Gulf was a small Seventh Fleet force of six escort carriers and its screen of three destroyers and four destroyer escorts.

As Lee was closing on the northern force, Halsey ordered TF 34 and the *Miami* south to assist the escort carriers. Later on the twenty-fourth, Lee's battleships, the *Miami*, and others went after the central force, speeding southward along the Luzon coast toward what promised to be two desperate battles.

Fortunately, farther south the main body of the Seventh Fleet had devastated the Japanese southern force attempting to push its way through the Surigao Strait and forced it to withdraw just after daybreak on 25 October.

Miraculously, but at cost, the escort carriers managed to stop the center force, prompting the Japanese to retreat through the strait. When TF 34 arrived in the night of 25 October, it was too late to block the enemy retreat. However, the *Miami* and two other light cruisers, the *Biloxi* and *Vincennes,* found a night radar contact off the entrance to the strait and turned to open fire.

The ships attacked in echelon formation. The *Miami* was farthest away with her gun elevation at 18 degrees. Hence, said Lloyd, "I ordered rapid salvo fire and the result was that we fired salvos of twelve shots and they were very readily distinguishable from the other two ships' salvos." Twelve shots would go out in a cluster, and he could see them land with the splashes. The other cruisers also went to rapid salvo fire with shots that landed "all over the ocean." Lloyd's rigorous emphasis on continuous fire bore fruit. Outshooting her sister ships, the *Miami* fired 960 rounds to sink a large Japanese destroyer, the *Nowaki.*

After the engagement, Lloyd's unit continued heading south along the Samar coast. Lee's TG 34.5 disjoined and returned to TF 38 for refueling the next day. From 1 to 3 November, TG 34.5 operated as a surface striking force and then withdrew to Ulithi.

During the battle off Samar, the escort carriers saw the first organized use of kamikazes. Lloyd urgently needed to retrain his crews to counter this new threat. His new doctrine governing close-in antiaircraft fire required that his men withhold fire from the ship's twenty 22-mm gun batteries until the planes were within a thousand yards. To help them estimate the range accurately, he pasted on the back of the gun shields airplane silhouettes of a size comparable to how the plane would appear at a thousand yards.

On 30 October, McCain relieved Mitscher in the normal rotation. For the next month, the tempo relaxed: McCain, in Lloyd's opinion, was not the fighting naval commander that Mitscher was. The force would retire to Ulithi until later in the month.

"I was pretty vulnerable to being plucked out of the *Miami* for shore duty in Washington, which I didn't want," said Lloyd about his downtime after the Battle of Leyte Gulf. While replenishing in Ulithi, he ran into his academy teammate, Ray Thompson, who was serving on Lee's staff on the *South Dakota.* Thompson was agonizing over his situation at home, with a wife who had taken ill. Lee felt he should return to her. Thompson was looking for someone to relieve him as gunnery officer and suggested Lloyd, who "jumped at this offer with great enthusiasm."

Lloyd soon got the orders to the staff of Commander, Battleship Squadron Two, as Lee's gunnery, radar, and combat information center officer. On 25 November, he reported while at sea. One of Lee's destroyers approached the *Miami,* which was under way and making twenty-seven knots. As both ships continued at speed, Lloyd transferred by high lines. In turn, the destroyer transferred him by lines to Lee's flagship in an equally fast exchange.

The Pacific Battleship Force totaled ten fast battleships, four of which could make thirty-three knots, with the other six capable of twenty-seven knots. Although Lloyd had not previously chosen to serve in battleships, he quickly came to appreciate that the tactics and procedures closely paralleled those of cruisers. As he matured in his new billet, he also came to view his gunnery-officer role as merely an upgrade—from gun boss of one ship to gun boss for a whole group.

"Ching Chong China" Lee had been at Vera Cruz in 1914 in command of the Second Company of the cruiser *New Hampshire*'s battalion: In other words, he was a warrior who had been in action ashore. "Admiral Lee was really one of the best of our wartime commanders in my opinion, of all kinds: aviators, non-aviators and submarine, and I think by all odds he must have been the best of the surface commanders." He was second in command of the Third Fleet and thus, if necessary, prepared to command and direct the operations of the fleet in the ongoing war. He also was commander of the heavy surface striking force, a task force organization that existed on paper even though the ships assigned to it were normally dispersed among the several task groups of the carrier striking force. In addition, he was commander of the surface components of the task group in which his flagship might be operating.

In tactical command of TF 38 was Pete Mitscher, and "it was pretty clear that Pete and Ching Lee had a very high level of mutual esteem" as near contemporaries. "[A] very warm and friendly person . . . perfectly willing to listen attentively to anybody, any subordinate," Lee enjoyed "absolute respect, almost awe," Lloyd remembered.

When Lloyd arrived on board, Lee's force was en route to Ulithi. They returned to the Philippines for the December carrier attacks on Luzon and Manila to support the landings on Mindoro. They encountered no surface engagements at that time. Although the Japanese were hugging the China coast, they suffered devastating attacks by U.S. submarines.

From 30 December 1944 through 26 January 1945, Lee's battleships supported the fast carriers, "going after targets of opportunity in the China Sea" and alternating from strikes on Formosa to more on Luzon, to Cape San Jacques and Cam Ranh Bay, Hong Kong and Hainan, and finally on Okinawa. On 17 February, the *South Dakota* supported the fast carriers in their strikes against the Tokyo area and then against Iwo Jima on the nineteenth and twentieth in support of the amphibious landings there. The battleship squadron conducted one more strike on Tokyo before returning to hit Okinawa again on 1 March 1945.

Lee then returned to Ulithi to rearm. His next foray was again to Japan, where from 15 to 28 March his force supported carrier strikes against Honshu and Hokkaido. On the eighteenth and nineteenth, planes struck targets in the Kobe, Kure, and Kyushu areas. On the twenty-third, the task group returned to hit Okinawa again, this time with the whole fast battleship squadron, in advance of the Kerama Retto amphibious landings scheduled for 1 April.

For Okinawa, each of Mitscher's task groups included two or three fast battleships, three or four cruisers and twenty-plus destroyers. His other battleship divisions, with older ships, he would use for close-in shore bombardment. Farther away were destroyers in other task groups. The intent was primarily air defense.

> The idea evolved rather at the last moment that we should conduct the bombardment along the Southern coast of Okinawa by fast battleships, and the result of this was that on the day this decision was conveyed to us, Admiral Lee broke off with the fast battleships, all of them and a small group of screening destroyers and also a small group of the fast mine sweepers, which were the somewhat older destroyers the 1600 tonners.
>
> We were due to commence the bombardment at daylight the following day, so the Marine and I, his name was MacArthur, Lieut. Col. MacArthur, and I, who were the recipients of this, stayed up all night up there in flag plot, plotting. First of all, plotting all of these targets onto a single gridded bombardment type chart, making sure that this target information was conveyed to all of the ships in the force, and then making up a bombardment plan which ship would attack which target with how much ammunition, in what sequence, all of the plethora of detail, and we were able to get this information out.

The following day, Lee's force bombarded the southeastern part of the island, and would do so again on 1 April as landings took place in Kerama Retto. "The principal purpose was as a feint and whether or to what extent it was successful, I don't recall ever hearing any competent judgment," said Lloyd in his oral history.

On 7 April, all fast carriers launched attacks against an enemy fleet off southwest Kyushu, sinking the super battleship *Yamato,* two cruisers, and four destroyers. On 19 April, the *South Dakota* again bombarded southeastern Okinawa in support of a major Army offensive.

Five days after the initial landings, they had to deal in earnest with the kamikaze attacks. Lee was a great believer in radar, but he found the search-radar coverage of the area above the task force inadequate. The main energy beam projected horizontally. When the Japanese adopted kamikaze tactics, said Lloyd, they found they could go to a fairly high altitude "in this cone of almost radar silence overhead" to begin their attack.

Trying to modify his radar's capabilities against the steep-diving kamikaze, Lee finally had his crew remount it, angling it 30 degrees above horizontal to provide some overhead coverage. He still had to contend, however, with the radar's lack of IFF (identification friend or foe) capability.

In the Philippines, Mitscher and Burke had found that single destroyer pickets were especially vulnerable to the kamikaze and began to operate them in tactical units instead. After TF 58 lost its first destroyer in Okinawa, Burke again had the destroyer pickets operate as divisions that would maneuver evasively by tactical order of the commodore. The attackers then had to face the fire of four destroyers instead of one. Because the Japanese aviators by this time were less skilled, Burke's tactic made it hard for them to arrive simultaneously on the target.

The Task Force 51 destroyers guarding the transports close-in, however, suffered losses on the order of one a day, said Lloyd. The tactical doctrine publications, on which many commanders almost blindly relied, were simply not reflecting the recent lessons from the war. "Pete Mitscher and Ching Lee spent a lot of time trying to convey the sense of what we were doing with our pickets and why and what it was doing for us, as compared to the frightful situation that just went on and on and on there around Okinawa with respect to the destroyer pickets. It was murder. One a day is a tough rate at which to be losing destroyers in a campaign that goes on for eighty days."

The operating tempo at Okinawa was extremely high. When it was all over, the TF 58 had been under way for eighty-two days. When the tempo finally decreased, the *South Dakota* headed for Guam for repairs to her rudder and propeller. En route on 6 May while she was rearming from the ammunition ship *Wrangell,* a tank of 16-inch high-capacity powder exploded, causing a fire and exploding four more tanks. The ship lost three men instantly, eight others died of injuries, and another twenty-four were wounded. The incident upset Lee, reinforcing his view that the Washington bureaus were not providing the fleet with the right kinds of weaponry for the task.

The accident underscored the real problem Lee had with the 5-inch VT influence-fuse ammunition that had come from the Bureau of Ordnance supposedly to deal with the kamikaze threat: It did not have a self-destruct capability. As a result, friendly fire incidents caused by spent antiaircraft shells were all too common. Lee complained bitterly to Washington.

Lloyd also observed Lee's response to another VT issue. The first antiaircraft VT ammo used a radio signal powered by dry cells to detonate the shell. After some time, however, a ship might have the uneasy task of replacing cells in unused stocks. As a consequence, the next iteration relied on a reserve battery with an electrolyte in a tiny capsule that would shatter when the gun fired and thus arm the shell. Inexplicably, given the serious kamikaze threat, the Bureau of Ordnance continued providing the fleet with fuses that could not arm at close range.

"The Bureau of Ordnance had increased the arming distance required for the flight of the projectile to something on the order of an average of about nine hundred or a thousand yards from what it had been, about three hundred yards," said Lloyd. "Of course, the point here was that a kamikaze attempting to crash on you and perfectly free to execute the most radical maneuvers as he came in was an almost impossible gun target until these last few hundred yards of his approach."

"Here, without any reference to the operating forces, the technical bureau back in Washington had just taken away from [our gunners] their chance to survive, to live, against this enemy threat."

Lee brought the problem to the bureau's attention and was ignored. His solution was to design an arming switch that activated centrifugally when the projectile fired and would remain armed as it slowed and then exploded—solving both the arming and the self-destruct problem. He then started copying his messages to Ernie King, thereby ensuring that the bureau "couldn't sweep it under the rug," said Lloyd. On Guam, Lee reinforced his case with Nimitz.

Headquarters at the time was busy planning the invasion of Japan. Lloyd's job was to work on a fast battleship bombardment plan to be used against some of the industrial facilities in the northern part of Japan that were beyond the reach of the B-29s flying from Guam.

The bombardment would occur on 14 July 1945, when the fast battleships shelled Honshu and the Kamaishi Steel Works. It was the first gunfire attack on the Japanese home islands by heavy warships, and damage was slight, much to Lloyd's annoyance. Because the task group commander had failed to account for the shorter range of bombardment ammunition, his first pass was out of range. He had to reverse his path and hence commenced firing upwind. The smoke thus obscured the targeting for the rest of the pass.

By this time, Lee would be in Washington—and not by choice. His briefings on Guam had not gone unnoticed by King, who ordered him stateside to organize what would eventually be known as the Operational Development Force that would test new weapons. When the *South Dakota* arrived in Leyte on 1 June, the orders had been waiting. Lee opted to take with him his flag lieutenant, operations officer, and Lloyd. The billet was right up Lloyd's alley. He would represent the fleet and shape research and development from the standpoint of the warriors.

The four departed Lee's flagship by PT boat, which landed them on Samar. From there, they flew to Guam, where once more they met with Nimitz. After three years of intense fighting, Lloyd was leaving the war in the Pacific. For his service in that theater, he would receive twelve campaign stars.

Corinne Montague Mustin Murray and George D. Murray, her second husband, on the occasion of their presentation to the Court of St. James in London. From January 1930 to May 1933, Murray served as the assistant naval attaché at the American embassies in London, Paris, Berlin, and The Hague.

Hank Mustin as a first class midshipman.

Hank and Lucy Holcomb at the 1954 Naval
Academy Ring Dance.

Hank, Lloyd, and Tom, 1967.

Hank and Tom in the Mekong Delta, Vietnam, 1967.

Tom, the Mekong Delta, Vietnam.

Hank and Lucy during the International Naval Review honoring the centenary of the Statue of Liberty, 4 July 1986, the Coast Guard's training ship *Eagle* is in the background.

Lucy Mustin and her sister-in-law Doug Mustin St. Denis at Lloyd and Emily's fiftieth wedding anniversary party in Coronado, 1982.

Hank and his second cousin Joe Howard in the Mekong Delta, May 1967.

Hank greeting President and Mrs. Ronald Reagan aboard the battleship *Iowa* during the Statue of Liberty centenary, July 1986.

Hank as Commander, Second Fleet, aboard his flagship *Mount Whitney,* while in command of a 1985 major fleet exercise in the Caribbean.

Hank and Lloyd, during Hank's change of command ceremony when he took command of the destroyer *Henry B. Wilson,* in San Diego, December 1968.

Henry C. Mustin's sons, 1944. From left to right, Henry Ashmead, Lloyd Montague, and Gordon Sinclair.

Lloyd, having pinned Tom's command at sea device during his change of command ceremony when he took command of the *Force,* 30 October 1970 in Pearl Harbor.

Lloyd Mustin swearing his grandson and namesake into the U.S. Navy, Hank at their side, 1981.

Hank and his three sons, Lloyd, Tom, and John, at his nephew Larry Baldauf's Coronado wedding, 1991.

The christening of the *Mustin* (DDG-89) in Pascagoula, Mississippi, on 15 December 2001. From left to right, Anne Howard Thomas, matron of honor (also maid of honor at the christening of the first *Mustin* [DD-413] on 8 December 1938), and sponsors Lucy Holcomb Mustin, Jean Phillips Mustin, and Douglas Mustin St. Denis.

Hank flanked by his sons, Lloyd Montague and John Burton, 1986.

Lloyd Montague Mustin as a first class midshipman.

Lloyd and his bride, Emily Morton Mustin, in Soo Chow, April 1934.

The surface effects of an underwater nuclear burst from an ASROC in the 11 May 1962 Swordfish test. In the foreground, the destroyer *Agerholm,* which fired the shot some four thousand yards to the detonation point at a depth of 850 feet.

Hank Mustin and his guitar, with his wife, Lucy, and Emily and Lloyd, sometime in the late 1950s.

Lloyd on shore patrol in a rickshaw in Tsingtao, September 1935.

Lloyd and Emily in Dreams Landing, Annapolis, in early 1942, just prior to his deployment to the war in the Pacific aboard the *Atlanta*.

Henry C. Mustin flying the Curtiss AB-2 from the Pensacola station ship, the battleship *North Carolina*, on 5 November 1915, the first catapult takeoff from a ship under way.

Lloyd, on right in baseball cap, aboard the *Miami,* her decks strewn with empty cartridge cases after bombardment of Japanese positions on Peleliu and Angaur in the Palaus, 7 September 1944.

Lloyd, Emily, and their children, Douglas, Tom, and Hank, at George Murray's Pensacola quarters, 1943, after Lloyd's first return from the wartime Pacific.

Henry C. Mustin (second from left) reporting to the Pacific Fleet commander in chief, c. 1920. The identity of the others is uncertain, but the admiral is probably Adm. Hugh Rodman and the aviators, John Towers and Charles Mason.

Emily Proctor Morton's engagement photograph, 1932.

Lloyd, as the commander of the destroyer tender *Piedmont,* with a Korean boy from Sacred Heart Kindergarten School, Chinhae, Korea, October 1954, during a port visit.

Lloyd and Emily with President and Mrs. Harry S. Truman at the Mustins' Key West quarters, Truman's former vacation White House, 1958.

Lloyd working in his cabin during one of the Dominic nuclear tests, 1962.

Lloyd on the bridge of the landing ship dock *Monticello,* his flagship during the 11 May 1962 Swordfish ASROC test.

Henry C. Mustin, Naval Aviator Number Eleven.

Corinne Montague as an ingenue.

Henry C. Mustin (holding ball), captain of his Naval Academy Class of 1896 champion football team.

Henry C. Mustin and his two elder sons, Henry Ashmead and Lloyd Montague.

The Mustin family assembled before the Mustin Beach Officers Club in Pensacola on the occasion of the induction of Henry C. Mustin into the Naval Aviation Hall of Fame.

Chapter 18

Coming to Terms with
the Postwar Missile Navy

In June 1945, Lloyd arrived in Washington with Willis Lee for a week's stop before heading north to Casco Bay, Maine, and Task Force 69, which in December 1947 would become the Operational Development Force (OpDevFor). They met with King and Burke. In preparation for the expected invasion of Japan, King wanted an operational commander like Lee to head a task force to test new ideas that would reduce casualties and increase weapon effectiveness. Arleigh Burke, now in Washington heading Fleet Readiness, would serve as Lee's liaison with the Navy Department.

In Okinawa, U.S. forces had encountered, in addition to kamikazes, piloted "Baka" rocket bombs and suicide boats. King and the Navy leadership realized that to defend their homeland the Japanese would use such weapons in a way that would maximize U.S. casualties. OpDevFor's principal goal, said Lloyd, was to improve fleet air defenses against the kamikazes.

On 2 July, Task Force 69 began operating from Casco Bay with two destroyers, two destroyer escorts, the former battleship *Wyoming,* now a gunnery training ship, and supporting drone control groups. Emily and the children joined Lloyd in Maine and found a cottage on Great Diamond Island, where TF 69 had offices ashore.

As gunnery, radar, and combat information center officer, Lloyd ran a demanding shop.

Many of the devices he tested proved to be failures. "The picture to me was clear. It was either 'this is good, let's get it, or this is no good, we can't afford to mess around with it.'"

One notable initiative on which he worked was the Mark 51 fire control director. Although it was designed as a handlebar director for use with antiaircraft machine guns, notably the 40-mm, the scientists felt it had application with the 5-inch gun against the kamikaze. Lloyd and Lee opposed the effort, believing that the Mark 51 system would not be sufficiently accurate with larger mounts. They also had serious objections after testing another radar device called a moving target indicator, supposed to discriminate moving targets from stationary background clutter. It not only failed to indicate moving targets but also failed to display significant non-moving objects—such as land.

When Lloyd nixed a third dubious device, an antiaircraft gun control, on the ground that it was difficult to maintain, Burke cautioned him against being "too cocky." He was getting a reputation as an operational type who set the development bar very high.

Lloyd relied on support for his positions from King's Operations Research Group (ORG) and its cadre of operations analysts that had enjoyed such success during the war in working solutions to the antisubmarine warfare problem in the Atlantic. In his early 1970s oral history, Lloyd noted, "The operations analyst knows what matters. He knows how to pick out what is pertinent and how to reject what is not with respect to whatever operation it is that he's engaged in, because he understands the operation. This was the key to the documented, enormous success in war on the part of ORG."

Lloyd got strong support from the ORG on the Mark 51 issue. As an alternative, he demonstrated that a Mark 37 director could direct accurate 5-inch fire onto a target in six seconds. The principal system on a destroyer, the Mark 37 was good for every requirement she would have to meet. "There was no better," he felt.

On 14 August, Lloyd was in Washington with Lee when word came that the war was over. He and his contemporaries partied at the Shoreham Hotel, where the liquor flowed freely. The next day, he had to travel to Casco Bay "with a hangover he thought he'd never live through." Overnight, the precise mission of TF 69 vanished, but the scientists who were driving technology developments remained.

In March 1946, the task force got a flagship, the amphibious command ship *Adirondack,* and moved south to operate from Norfolk. Lloyd got follow-on shore duty at the Bureau of Ordnance in the antiaircraft fire control section of the Research Division. He moved his family to Washington, temporarily into Corinne's empty house in Georgetown, and then to a house in Alexandria on Janney's Lane.

For the next two and a half years he was involved with transforming what had been Spike Blandy's wartime structure into an enduring peacetime organization. "By about 1946, we'd exploded the atom bomb," said Lloyd, "and such things as guided missiles were beginning to be a little bit more than a gleam in various people's eyes, and it was glibly stated that well, warfare with conventional aircraft, conventional bombs, and defenses by gunfire, and similar things, they're only memories anyway. We'll never have to concern ourselves with that again, so let's turn our attention to more interesting things. That is not the way it's turned out to be, of course."

Many naval officers were optimistic about the Navy's prospects for budgets and force structure. "This didn't include me," said Lloyd, "because it was easy for me to remember my father talking about exactly the same thing at the end of World War I."

Initially, Lloyd spent most of his time working on antiaircraft fire control. He remained a strong proponent of the proven Mark 37, which was capable not only of antiaircraft fire but also of antisurface-ship fire and shore bombardment. Skeptical of scientists eager to poach the taxpayer's dollar, he found himself at loggerheads with a bureau contractor, the Johns Hopkins University Applied Physics Lab, that was espousing the Mark 57 fire control director. The Mark 57 was a new iteration of the Mark 51 and in Lloyd's view still insufficient to direct 5-inch mounts. He worked to get rid of it and to introduce the Mark 67/68 to direct the heavy mounts.

The Applied Physics Lab (APL) typified for Lloyd the problem with the military-industrial complex. The Bureau of Ordnance had become heavily dependent on the lab, which had the contract for its Bumblebee Project to develop the Navy's first surface-to-air missile. In 1946–47, the lab was working on a ramjet—as opposed to a turbojet—engine designed to reach out sixty or seventy miles that eventually would power the Talos missile.

Control tests at Task Force 69 had demonstrated that the outer effective ranges for guns "were astonishingly short." Lloyd therefore saw no immediate justification for a gold-plated missile effort. "All you needed was something that was significantly longer in effective range than were the antiaircraft guns." His fire control section proposed to work with the bureau's missile section to adapt the radar for the Mark 37 director for an antiaircraft, guided-missile system that could go on board existing ships in the fleet.

The APL scientists, however, wanted a more ambitious radar and director and did not want to work with the Bureau of Ordnance on any approaches using existing systems—to the extent that the idea put APL director Lawrence Hafstad "in a rage." He threatened to drop the Bumblebee effort (Talos, Terrier, and Tartar) altogether if the bureau kept pursuing it. The issue went upstairs to the bureau's Research Division director, Ken Noble, who bought the APL case and dropped Lloyd's approach.

That and other decisions on Bumblebee would have a profound effect on the Navy and ship characteristics. When Lloyd was on the Atlantic destroyer force staff in 1950, he began hearing about the drawbacks of the Terrier. Because that missile had beam-riding guidance, it required a lot of shipboard space for radar tracking all the way to the target, meaning that the Navy had to remove other radar systems and ASW gear from destroyers to make room. His view was that the trade-off degraded other capabilities and made no operational sense.

"To carry the number of these missiles that the people decided they wanted and to carry this massive two channel fire-control system, all the reload missiles and the rapid reloading and so forth, we found ourselves with a system that really could only be put aboard cruiser-size ships."

The impact of missiles and their supporting systems on ships had been apparent to Lloyd from the beginning, and he was one of the few who thought the wholesale embrace of the technology was "an ill-advised policy." The missile proponents were saying, "Oh, the day of the gun is over, we're going to do it all with guided missiles from now on," he recalled. "That really was a pretty childishly immature approach, but quite a familiar one in my sort of cynical regard." He saw the handwriting on the wall as early as 1946, when some naval officers were smitten by what the scientists were offering and would yield to their arguments, fearing that any opponent would be labeled "an old stick-in-the-mud, a battleship sailor." It was "fashionable to be in favor of the missiles," said Lloyd.

This tendency had budgetary and force structure implications as well, "because to put all this gold-plating into everything we did afloat simply meant that the price of the individual ship began mounting out of sight." Industry and its allies in the Navy would promise to get the money from Congress, but "it never has worked that way," said Lloyd. "It never did. It meant that we just got fewer and fewer and, of course, as we got fewer and fewer, what we paid for what we got went up, so that diminished the returns even more drastically."

Lloyd made a case for gunnery that still has truth today for medium-distance engagements. "All the decision-making with target resolution, identification, and everything else capability stays back where the gun is. All that goes to the target is the projectile, and any time you have to continue delivering warheads on target over a long time, you had better interest yourself in this way of doing it, because it will give you the accuracy you need and it's the cheapest way."

Inevitably, his views on guns and missiles led him to get involved in the debates over ship characteristics. During the war, the Navy had established a Ship Characteristics Board composed of active duty officers, to supersede the old General Board. In Lloyd's view "the Ship Characteristics Board wasn't too effective, either, in perceiving and responding to tough compromises." The board operated mainly by a committee process based on majority vote, but ship characteristics, he felt, should have been the result of a long series of executive-level decisions.

One ship class to emerge during this time was the first postwar destroyer. Construction began on the first ship, the *Mitscher,* in 1949, after the design "just grew and grew and grew, as various people's ideas of new weapons and new anti-submarine weapons, and so on, were added, even though most of these new ideas were thoroughly untested and unproved and many of them never did prove out. Finally, the [*Mitscher*] grew so big in design that the hull was going to have to be built like a cruiser and thus would cease to be a destroyer hull."

Lloyd doggedly held to the belief that "destroyers were the kind we needed in quantity and that we had to keep them affordable." His view, however, did not prevail.

In October 1948, Lloyd was ready to return to sea. His orders were a delight: He was going to his first command, a destroyer, the *Keppler.* For the next two years, he would be in a position to implement all that he had learned as a commander, on a ship type he loved.

Chapter 19

First Command

A LOVE YOU COULD TASTE

The *Keppler* was a *Gearing*-class destroyer, the last class of destroyer built during the war. When Lloyd reported, she was with the Pacific Fleet and homeported in San Diego awaiting conversion to an antisubmarine escort destroyer. Lloyd now would have the opportunity to steep himself in antisubmarine warfare.

In 1948, the United States had reconciled itself to reversing postwar demobilization. The Cold War was under way, and tensions had risen steadily as the Soviet Union consolidated its grip on Eastern Europe. For the next four decades, war with the Soviet Union would remain the focus for U.S. and Western military planning and the determinant for postwar force structures.

The geopolitical standoff in Europe initially forced on the Navy responsibility for resupply across the Atlantic. As with the two world wars, the threat to that "Atlantic Bridge" was from the submarine. In the 1940s, the Soviets had virtually no capital ships, but they had submarines in abundance—some two hundred. Hence, the Navy's destroyer force would have to emphasize antisubmarine warfare, absent—for the moment—a credible threat at sea from the air.

When Lloyd arrived in San Diego to attend sonar school, he found that little had changed in ASW since his prewar tour on the *Lamson*. U.S. submarines relied on diesels to drive generators that powered the motors. In 1946, the United States began to convert about half its submarine force to Guppies—submarines with "greater underwater propulsive power." The problem was that the conversions required a snorkel to permit the boats to run submerged on their diesels and consequently made for easy radar detection. The sonar school suggested to Lloyd that the United States was somewhat behind in submarine technology and, by extension, antisubmarine warfare.

The state-of-the-art postwar submarine was the German Type XXI, a streamlined design with a high-capacity battery and electric-drive motors. The sub could reach bursts of speeds up to twenty knots. The Germans also had an electric torpedo that, unlike the steam version, did not emit a wake of bubbles.

The Type XXI had been designed for mass production at a rate of a score or more per month. A navy could build an extremely significant submarine force around the Type XXI in a relatively short period of time, if it had access to the technology. The Soviet Union had just that: It had captured eight Type XXIs and was "recruiting" the program's key German personnel, leading to dire conclusions in the Navy Department. Either the U.S. Navy had to find a tactical solution to countering the submarine threat, or it would have to resort to the strategic solution: attacks at source on the bases in the Kola Peninsula and Crimea in the European theater and on the Maritime Provinces (Vladivostok), the Kuriles, Sahaklin, and Kamchatka in the Pacific.

"You simply could not put a ship into a position for an effective depth charge attack against one of these things," said Lloyd, "unless the submarine made a mistake." Its underwater evasive speed gave the Type XXI the advantage. "It was futile to try to attack the submarine with one surface ship," said Lloyd. "Multi-ship attack was regarded as the only way to go." "Having once gained contact on a submarine, you should be prepared to hold on desperately, in order to be able to make an extended succession of attacks . . . to wear down the submarine's submerged endurance."

In January 1949, not long after he finished his sonar schooling, Lloyd took the *Keppler* to the San Francisco Hunters Point Naval Shipyard for full conversion to antisubmarine escort destroyer. The modifications were "half-baked," in Lloyd's view. The main conversion was the removal of the number two 5-inch gun mount and the substitution of a trainable Hedgehog, an ahead-thrown weapon that a ship could project while maintaining contact with the submarine. She also got a QDA sonar that was supposed to determine depth. Lloyd characterized the QDA as "a complete flop." It was an Americanized British device that even the best petty officers in the division could not maintain.

During the downtime at Hunters Point, Lloyd was sensitive to the morale of the crew. He decided to install an old slot machine in the after deckhouse. The yard workmen played the machine, and it generated enough money for the ship's recreation fund to finance three "super" parties. Unfortunately, his squadron commander was not entirely happy with the gimmick. When the machine finally went on the fritz, Lloyd removed it.

The *Keppler* remained at Hunters Point until May and on 9 June resumed operations on the West Coast. Although the fleet regarded her as one of the most modern destroyers afloat, it was unsure how to use her. In the end, the Pacific destroyer commander ordered her to San Diego's Underway Training Unit.

Once operating, Lloyd soon discovered that the previous commanding officer had not allowed his officers of the deck to conn the ship when they did maneuvers. Lloyd thereupon insisted that all six of his line officers would stand watch in rotation, one watch on deck and one watch in the combat information center, alternately, no matter what was going on—getting under way, coming into port, or refueling at sea. Morale immediately improved; his officers were "learning like mad, instead of drinking coffee in the wardroom."

It was Lloyd's opportunity to put into practice the command philosophy he had learned from Nimitz. "I had always been very much involved with the operating and seamanship aspects of going to sea. I was interested in it, and I loved it," he said. "I had lessons to teach to every officer in it, even though I had just come from shore duty. Because the lessons were the lessons of what, at the time, was sixteen years' commissioned service, which all but five of had been at sea, all over the world." His approach, he was sure, improved "the readiness of the ship to respond to any eventuality, foreseen and unforeseen, emergency or otherwise."

In Lloyd's view, the captain could not do his job properly if he permitted himself to be engaged by the endless details involved in conning the ship during an operation or exercise. He had to have officers whose capabilities in handling the ship he knew. "And unless and until he reaches that state of affairs," said Lloyd, "the ship is not as ready as it should be to do as good a job as it should do. Well, we got very quickly into that state of affairs in the *Keppler*." He had to relieve an officer of the deck only twice.

Lloyd did night ASW drills during which the subs would operate submerged with their running lights so the surface operators could better check the progress of their sonarmen skills. During that operating period, the *Keppler* received her second Battle Efficiency Pennant.

In October, the Navy reassigned the ship to the Atlantic Fleet, where the submarine threat was deemed to be. Knowing that he would be at sea for some time working the antisubmarine issues, Lloyd arranged with Emily for her and the children to stay in Coronado to finish the school year.

The *Keppler* left San Diego on 5 October 1949. On 20 October, she arrived in Norfolk and immediately commenced intensive ASW exercises along the Atlantic coast. During this time, the ship got an *E* largely for a shore bombardment exercise. She left Norfolk in mid-November for her new home port, Newport, Rhode Island, arriving on the twenty-seventh. She promptly returned to sea for additional antisubmarine hunter-killer operations.

During these fleet exercises, dubbed Operation Frostbite, Lloyd's ship carried Capt. Roy Hartwig's command pennant as Commander, Destroyer Flotilla Four. The exercises were conducted in the North Atlantic and Arctic, notably in the Davis Strait between Greenland and Baffin Island, away and secure from any Soviet poaching. Hartwig was the screen commander. Heavy weather proved to be a drawback to the surface forces. For one, the destroyers could not stand the impact of the heavy field ice. They also had to prevent the cooling water in the boat engines from freezing and exercise the guns regularly. After concluding the exercises, the *Keppler* toured through the Mediterranean.

The ship was operating in peak form. According to Lloyd, Hartwig later said "he had never seen a destroyer like the *Keppler* in all his career. She was the finest. And that's the way I felt about it, too. And I still do. She was beautifully built. I knew every inch of her from truck to keelson, as they say. . . . I just loved that ship, and I loved every moment of all this. I loved it so I could taste it."

In late January 1950, the *Keppler* returned to Newport. That winter, many of his Annapolis classmates came to town to attend the Naval War College, but Lloyd got orders to serve on the staff of the commander of the Atlantic Fleet destroyer force, Rear Adm. Slim Wooldridge, as antisubmarine warfare officer. Emphatic about the primitive state of ASW, Lloyd qualified his title, saying, "But I was no expert. I don't know if there were any experts."

In the spring, he fleeted up to readiness officer, adding gunnery, damage control, and engineering to his responsibilities. "The gunnery officer supposedly took care of seamanship, as well; that being sort of a deck function." Almost all the small staff was on the destroyer tender *Yosemite,* the flagship, and at sea, as was the rule in those days.

On 25 June, the Cold War went hot when North Korea invaded the south. Two days later, the Seventh Fleet deployed to Taiwanese waters in a show of force. It was clear that the Navy was going to play a major support role in the region and would require more ships than it had on hand. Postwar demobilization had reduced the Atlantic destroyer force to about sixty ships, and the Pacific accounted for only another thirty. Ships that had been mothballed were needed back in the active fleet.

Reactivating destroyers was a direct responsibility of Admiral Wooldridge, the type commander. It fell to Lloyd and his staff to deal with replacing many of the key items, such as rotted fire hoses and rubber gaskets and deteriorated aluminum radar antennas. Fortunately, they found the boilers and turbines still in superb condition. In the space of three or four months, the destroyer totals for the Atlantic Fleet went from 60 to 120 ships, creating a need to reactivate the naval reserves. "These people were extraordinarily well qualified," said Lloyd, "because they were primarily people who had just finished up World War II in 1945."

Wooldridge saw that he could use Lloyd's experience with the Bureau of Ordnance and the Ship Characteristics Board. As readiness officer, Lloyd became the Atlantic Fleet's "traveling man" on matters of design and the arrangement and layout of new ships. Much of his focus was on critical spaces: the air-defense station, the pilothouse, the open bridge, and the combat information center. Although his brief was for a destroyer type commander, he also addressed cruiser issues. Typically, his views were contrary to those espoused in Washington. In one notable victory, he recommended moving the Mark 56 fire-control director forward to a position not far abaft the number two stack to give full field of view and radar line of sight. The Bureau of Ships accepted the recommendation.

Lloyd also had a hand in the design and comment for the 3-inch .50 twin in an open mount for the *Dealey*-class ASW destroyer escort. "They were prepared 100 percent by operating line officers in the fleet, not by the staff engineer or the assistant chief of staff for material." His team pushed for and got a spray shield for the mount. The class also had abaft the number one mount a Weapon-A launcher. The ahead-thrown weapon had problems, however. Lloyd argued for building half the eight-ship class with the British Squid, another ahead-thrown weapon system with a heavier warhead that was a marginal improvement over the Hedgehog.

The real weakness of the *Dealey*-class was the decision to make the destroyer escort a single-engine, single-screw ship. "The cost in men and in dollars and in space, of the extra engine, is minor in relation to the cost of all these other very advanced things you're putting in these ships: new gun mounts, new antisubmarine weapons, new sonars, new electronics, new radio communications, capabilities far beyond what the World-War-II DEs [destroyer escorts] ever enjoyed. The cost in dollars is negligible," but a loss of power in submarine waters would make a ship "a dead duck." Lloyd was extremely bothered by this decision and where it led: "Not only was the *Dealey*-class built with a single screw, but every class of DE that we have built ever since then has been built with a single screw."

In 1951, Lloyd's senior on the *Augusta,* Rear Adm. Spike Fahrion, relieved Wooldridge. During Fahrion's time, Lloyd was able to do something to correct the vulnerability of the ships in Narragansett Bay to severe weather. Although the Navy had been operating from Newport since the turn of the century, it had no facilities to provide for alongside berthing for the fleet units. The anchorage was dangerous in severe weather, and the men had to take launches back and forth for their liberties. Lloyd felt it was time for a pier. With Fahrion's support, he went to the Bureau of Yards and Docks and after a tortuous authorization process got funds for construction of one then two piers. "The lesson to me there was that, by golly, if you have an idea that you think is good and you go after it, you can often get something done about it—often, not always."

In the winter of 1951, Fahrion took his destroyers to Key West to exercise an approach that OpDevFor had developed for multiship antisubmarine tactics. It actually involved only two ships, and, regardless of the range at which they detected a submarine, the destroyers had to be extremely close to the target to press a successful attack. Lloyd acknowledged the "ship-handling dangers—ships maneuvering at twenty-five knots, both of them inside a circle of perhaps a thousand yards' radius, and both of them focusing on the center of that circle, which was where the submarine was." The key was factoring the minute or so of time for the weapons to descend against the anticipated track of the submarine.

"Everybody joined up out in the assigned operating area, after dark, and ran through this tactic for hours. And they attacked him successfully and repeatedly—attack after attack. He was never able to break contact, they never lost him. There was always one ship in a good position to maintain sonar contact, regardless of what the other one was doing."

After the test, Lloyd wrote the instructions for the tactic. "I think we gave it the name of Operation Duet, a two-ship tactic," he said in 1974. "And it's our standard two-ship tactic today, as far as I know."

In January 1951, Lloyd made captain. While in Key West, he got orders to report to the Joint Chiefs of Staff to relieve Rivets Rivero in the Weapons System Evaluation Group. Rivero had suggested him as his replacement. The family was settled in their Newport house, and Lloyd tried to get the orders changed. He failed and had to report to Washington in August.

Despite his reservations about Pentagon duty, Lloyd approached the summer with joy. It was the summer that his eldest son, Hank, lifted his right hand in Bancroft Hall and took the oath to become a midshipman in the class in 1955. The Mustin tradition would continue into another generation.

Chapter 20

Early Exposure to Pentagon Politics

NOTHING BUT LOGIC

On 30 July 1951, Lloyd drove from Newport to Washington and reported for duty at the Pentagon—"no leave, no delay time, no travel time, no nothing." It was his fortieth birthday.

He arrived in Washington to find the city embroiled in the politics of national security. The year before, the Truman administration had issued its landmark National Security Council Document 68, committing national resources to a massive buildup of military strength to meet the communist threat. The United States was at war in Korea. The country was remobilizing. Gen. George C. Marshall, the new secretary of defense, was that summer in the throes of planning a two- to six-division increase to the Army's ground force commitment to NATO and Europe.

The mood in town was rancorous. In April, Truman had removed Gen. Douglas MacArthur from command of United Nations forces in Korea for threatening to expand the war into Communist China. His administration also was under attack from Republican Senator Joseph R. McCarthy, with his relentless accusations that the government harbored communists in the State Department and elsewhere.

When last in Washington in the late 1940s, Lloyd was absorbed in strictly technical Navy issues relating to ordnance and gunnery. The September 1947 establishment of the Department of Defense that merged the Departments of War and the Navy and created the U.S. Air Force did not directly affect him. He returned to sea before the USN and USAF went at each other's throats in earnest. The stakes were high: In question was which service was more relevant to a postwar strategic era and hence would have priority for taxpayer money.

The USAF needed a mission. Having pummeled Germany into submission and wrested capitulation from Japan by dropping atomic bombs on Hiroshima and Nagasaki, it had determined that it had one—strategic bombing. The National Security Act of 1947 and 1948 Key West Agreement so granted it.

Based on modifications to the Key West agreement, the Navy regained a stake in the strategic mission. The carrier admirals had been pursuing a supercarrier, the *United States,* big enough to deploy with bombers heavy enough to carry the obese atomic devices. The Air Force had proceeded with its own delivery program, the B-36 super-bomber. By 1949, this propeller-driven strategic bomber was on the verge of cancellation and would have died if not for the intervention of Secretary of Defense Louis A. Johnson. A former official at Convair, the B-36 contractor, Johnson chose to proceed with procurement and instead canceled the *United States,* five days into her construction. The admirals cried foul and "revolted."

The Navy's longtime congressional ally, Georgia Democrat Carl Vinson, chairman of the House Armed Services Committee, held investigations into the B-36 decision and hearings on the carrier cancellation to give the Navy a chance to express its position. To the embarrassment of the administration, the admirals did—in spades. As a result, the secretary of the navy fired his chief of naval operations, Louis E. Denfield, in November 1949. Johnson himself was replaced by George Marshall the following autumn.

The 1949 Soviet detonation of its first atomic bomb and the victory of the communists in China traumatized Truman's national security establishment. With the collapse of the British and French empires, the wise men of Washington saw themselves standing in the breach alone. In April 1950, Paul Nitze, director of the State Department's Policy Planning Staff, made the case to increase annual defense spending from 6 percent of national income in 1949 to 20 percent by 1954.

Large amounts of money were to go somewhere. Politics had failed the Navy in the B-36 flail, but the Korean War demonstrated its power projection capabilities while disproving the Air Force case that strategic bombing would win future wars. The interservice fight, thus, was still joined when Lloyd arrived to work for the Joint Chiefs of

Staff. He reported to an organization about which he knew very little: the military studies and liaison section of the Weapon Systems Evaluation Group.

It was not a Navy tour. For the first time, Lloyd was serving in a joint assignment. He would emerge with a profound understanding of the strategic and how it interrelated with the high-stakes politics of the Pentagon and the Joint Staff.

The idea for the Weapon System Evaluation Group (WSEG) originated with Dr. Vannevar Bush, MIT's renowned electrical engineer, cofounder of Raytheon, and Roosevelt's wartime scientific adviser. Bush had been impressed by Britain's use of operations analysis to improve ASW technologies and tactics and recommended to Truman that the Pentagon apply operations analysis to postwar problems. In essence, he saw the Cold War as analogous to the battle against the German submarine: Both were wars of attrition.

In December 1948, Secretary of Defense James V. Forrestal had chartered the WSEG under Lt. Gen. John E. Hull, USA, to provide unbiased technical analyses of weapon systems and programs for the Joint Chiefs. When Lloyd reported, the office had about thirty military officers and thirty civilians. "They composed what was called a study and analysis group. The military group was called a military studies and liaison group, and the civilian group was called the analysis and evaluation group. And the concept was that all of the actual analyses would be accomplished by the civilians, whereas the input information and the like would be put together by the people in uniform and handed over to the civilians."

The idea was to draw civilian analysts from various scientific disciplines and combine them with operationally experienced officers. The analysts took part in operations quite extensively. Gradually, they began to impose their own academic constructs on the operational data, and the WSEG moved from an operationally driven organization to one in which high-level scientific and industrial politics began to corrupt the analyses.

Given what was at stake for the Navy, Lloyd understood that his job on the WSEG included reporting to the Navy staff how the findings were playing with the other services in this tussle over strategic mission. During the B-36 hearings, the WSEG's supposedly impartial technical evaluation and decision to recommend the strategic bomber were critical to the go-ahead. The Navy recognized that the group's decisions had—then at least—the potential to carry weight.

As Lloyd set to work as a member of Rear Adm. A. B. Vosseller's team completing the strategic bombing study, the interservice politicking was "hot and heavy." Angered by the supercarrier cancellation, the Navy had pressured to have the WSEG analyze the effectiveness of strategic bombing of the Soviet Union. "Because, of course, the Navy was convinced that it couldn't possibly be helpful in winning a war," said Lloyd. "And it was a very expensive operation that was being foisted on the taxpayer by the Air Force." He felt the service had oversold the B-36. Given the trade-off between fuel and payload, it could not perform the strategic bombing mission, and fighter aircraft could intercept the bomber at forty thousand feet, as both the Air Force and Soviets knew. Yet, the Air Force kept selling the program.

In its analysis, the WSEG took the position that strategic warfare is essentially an attack on the economy of a country, and unless it defined the industrial structure of the Soviet economy, it could not really evaluate the effects. The issue was thus not just operational: The group now had to introduce intelligence estimates.

In one instance, the Air Force champions chose to accept, uncritically, the estimates on the volume of annual Soviet aircraft production. The WSEG questioned what factories supported the production, and it even identified one that was within sight of the U.S. embassy in Moscow. Lloyd maintained that nobody had asked the embassy to estimate production from that site. When someone finally did, the embassy reported that the factory was currently "in the bicycle-building business." The study uncovered "the weakness of that particular so-called intelligence estimate, arrived at entirely subjectively by those who wanted to argue that the Soviets had this huge air force, and bought off on by the remainder of the community whenever it came time to do a little horse trading to get some so-called agreed intelligence estimates."

The second phase of the study, on which Lloyd worked, also illustrated "some pretty frightening things" about the success rate of a strategic bombing operation. Under certain conditions postulated by the WSEG, as few as 25 percent of the B-36s would survive; of the 75 percent that did not, more than half would be lost inbound. Thus, nearly 40 percent of the B-36s would never reach their targets.

According to Lloyd, one attack profile called for the use of more than 100 atomic bombs, perhaps as many as 170. A second, intermediate weight of attack was on the order of 270. The highest level was just under 400 bombs, possibly 375. That knowledge led him to a then "extraordinarily closely held bit of information"—the extent and composition of the U.S. nuclear weapon stockpile. "It was in the order of three-hundred-plus weapons, less than four hundred, about four hundred," he said. "And the largest yield of these weapons was something like 130 kilotons, which, by standards of many years up to now, would be considered a relatively small nuclear warhead." The yields of the majority were actually in the several tens of kilotons range. As for the 130-kiloton bomb, it was "very dubiously regarded: it was thought to be unstable."

Hence, the numbers in the various attack profiles represented close to the maximum capability the country possessed at the time. Lloyd concluded that such a raid would provide "precious little effective capability." "But what it was going to do to Russia, to throw away these aircraft and these air crews' lives in what I would call an abortive attempt at strategic bombing, was not a part of that particular study." Lloyd offered his assurance that, despite its Navy origins, "the Air Force, even though they wouldn't admit it, found much food for thought in the strategic bombing study."

For its part, the USAF had requested an analysis comparing the effectiveness of nuclear and conventionally powered submarines. The WSEG was just finishing when Lloyd reported.

The Navy had come to the idea of using nuclear fission to provide propulsive power for submarines before the end of the war. In 1948, Capt. Hyman G. Rickover had taken charge of a group of scientists and engineers at the Naval Reactors Branch of the Atomic Energy Commission to develop the first nuclear propulsion plant. The Air Force hoped the findings of the WSEG study would embarrass the Navy at a time when it was lobbying for funds to build a nuclear submarine.

The Air Force saw the Navy nuclear program as an attempt to divert nuclear materials from strategic weapon production. Given the very limited nuclear weapon inventory of the time, Lloyd concluded that the Air Force had a point, but the case for the nuclear submarine was based convincingly on endurance. A World War II submarine managed at best a ninety-day mission, "pretty strongly enforced by the absolute basic of fuel." Because it had no requirement for oxygen for full power, a nuclear-powered sub could run submerged indefinitely.

In its findings, the WSEG expressed its preferences in ratios. Said Lloyd, "In the mission where the nuclear propulsion gave you the least advantage over conventional, the ratio was 5:1 in favor of the nuclear submarine and that mission was the conventional attack mission." With straight reconnaissance, the ratio was approximately twenty to one. Another operation was in the range of ten to twelve to one. Case closed.

The month Lloyd arrived in Washington, Congress funded the world's first nuclear submarine, the *Nautilus*. Construction began the following June, with launching in January 1954.

The Air Force also had pressed for the WSEG to analyze the Soviet submarine capability to interdict the U.S. wartime resupply of NATO via the Atlantic. This study had obvious programmatic implications for the Navy.

At the time, the media had been trumpeting the Soviet submarine threat. From the naval standpoint, the publicity was a two-edged sword. The Navy could build on the publicity to "bludgeon Congress" into appropriating more funds for air, surface, and subsurface antisubmarine warfare. On the other hand, the Air Force had been fueling the issue to the point that the Navy now feared Congress might force it to apply much more of its resources to antisubmarine warfare and leave the business of strategic bombing to its service rival. "So just exactly how to interpret this was always, in my mind at least, a question of choice not always wisely made within the Navy Department."

In this case, Lloyd thought that WSEG took a valid view of the Soviets' submarine capability. It dismissed the threat "almost out of hand." Intelligence indicated that the Soviets then had a submarine fleet of some 450 boats. Those with professional knowledge recognized, however, that "this was a very second-rate submarine outfit." The only new Soviet submarine design was the *Whiskey* class, which had very limited operating characteristics in terms of both surface and submerged speeds.

The Navy's operational plans called for blockading the Soviet submarines in the Baltic and Black Seas and to the east of the Kola Peninsula by mining the choke points in the Kattegat and Skaggerak, the Bosporus, and in the Arctic approaches, respectively. The WSEG study's quantitative factoring of the mining countermeasures yielded an "unexpected bonus . . . namely, how to calculate mining requirements." The group's staff included a Turkish scientist, Leon Alaoglu, who had developed the method of analyzing the mine-laying requirements that would produce a level of threat within a geographic area. The Navy later adopted Alaoglu's method, after the WSEG found application in a follow-on study that evaluated the Soviet aerial mining threat.

The latter study determined that, from bases in Europe, all the Soviets needed was two squadrons of aircraft—forty-eight planes—assigned to sea mining to create a level of threat equivalent to the loss of one ship a day in British ports alone. Taken together, the two studies pointed to the conclusion "that the submarine threat, to NATO operations in particular, was essentially minor, but the mine warfare threat was substantial."

Lloyd was fully engaged for half a year in another WSEG study, chaired by Jack Lathrop of the Boston research-and-development contractor Arthur D. Little, that looked at carriers and their ability to take the war to the Soviet Union. "Jack Lathrop had the bit in his teeth and was charging toward an answer that suited Jack Lathrop, and suited a few other people around there. But it was giving Abe Vosseller absolute fits. And it was giving the group of Navy people in uniform absolute fits, also."

Vosseller felt Lathrop had overestimated the effect of a Soviet air attack on a Navy carrier task force. "Jack Lathrop chose to credit these percentages of hits to Soviet aviation, which had never, in its history, attacked a combatant naval force at sea, let alone a U.S. naval combatant force at sea, which was organized and trained and indoctrinated to put up some fantastic defenses, as had been demonstrated historically." Vosseller asked Lloyd to check how Lathrop assembled his data.

Lloyd drew from his air defense experience in the Pacific to disprove the operational validity of the notional attack. He soon found that Lathrop had posited a stream raid, a single column of planes, a tactic never used for a torpedo attack, but had applied percentages from a Navy tactical doctrine publication that gave estimates for an attack by a formation of planes in a wide line abreast. "It's simply untenable to claim the percentage of torpedo hits that hopefully can be achieved by that geometry of the attack if you postulate some other geometry of attack, which indeed is just as diametrically opposite to that form as one could conceive. Whether or not it could ever be flown is another question." Lathrop had demonstrated his basic ignorance of the operational feasibility of his own construct.

"Well, I pointed out to Abe—here was the flaw in Lathrop's logic. And this just delighted him," said Lloyd. "I've often thought, in thinking back, that the fact that I saw that and pointed it out to Abe may have been, as much as anything else, the reason why I got selected to be a rear admiral a few years later. And it was nothing but logic, no science, no nothing."

The battle was yet to be won, however. Lathrop's assistant, Gordon Dewey—whom Lloyd considered a "charlatan"—took the view that U.S. radars were not as efficient as they were assumed to be in their ability to vector fighters for interception. Lloyd's argument against this assertion was based on his own air defense experience during the war, but Dewey was close to Al Robertson, the WSEG deputy director and another senior civilian, George Welsh. "Gordon was in the lodge, and he knew the password and the grip. What he said was not to be questioned in any way, unless you could uncover some logical defect that was too massive to ignore." Lloyd had to spend several months carefully massaging his numbers to a level of damage estimates that the Navy could accept but were "to the satisfaction of the scientists."

The second part of carrier study addressed what damage carrier task forces could do to the Soviets. Operating in the Med against various targets, the carrier force using propeller-driven Skyraiders could deliver something like 4,500 tons of air-to-ground ordnance in a typical two- or three-day strike cycle. At high speed, the carrier task force would close on a target area, unload at a maximum delivery rate, and then withdraw from enemy range to reload and replenish. Relying only on Army Air Corps wartime operational statistics that for one did not reflect the superior sustainment capabilities of a carrier, Lathrop and Dewey objected to the scenario. The review board, however, sustained Lloyd.

The study did uncover a vital fleet shortfall. Many naval auxiliaries had gone into mothballs, and only one ammunition ship was operating in the Atlantic Fleet. Hence, the carriers were good for only two days of operation. The finding was so persuasive that, even though it disrupted other elements of financial planning and programming, the Navy moved quickly to recommission its ammunition ships. "If nothing else came out of that particular study, at that time, that one thing alone was important."

Another project that kept Lloyd busy was a study on North American air defense. He was skeptical. The Soviet air bases closest to the continental United States were in northeastern Siberia, and the logistic support going into those bases was barely enough to keep alive a very small-sized garrison, let alone an extensive air strike capability. The USAF, however, was eager to get into strategic defense. Dewey, the radar consultant, and others "just lapped this up, because this was their life's blood," said Lloyd. "I was left with a desperate feeling that in order to preserve an enormous Air Force organization, air defense–fighter squadrons deployed all across the country, and radars deployed all across the country and all across Canada, and out on the two oceans, and the SAGE system automatic controls—the country was being asked to foot a $15 billion first-cost bill."

By 1954, Lloyd had had his fill of studies, analyses, and Pentagon politics: He wanted to *do* something. It was his time for a deep-draft command, perhaps an amphibious ship. In the spring, he had begun contacting the Bureau of Personnel for his next assignment. He was anxious to return to sea before the Navy forgot him.

Chapter 21

A Destroyerman at
Home in the Pacific

In the spring of 1954, Lloyd was hoping for a deep-draft command on the West Coast. He wanted to return with his family to their home in Coronado. Months later, when his orders came, they were to the destroyer tender *Piedmont,* homeported in San Diego. "I look back upon that news with a pretty clear recollection that I was a little disappointed," Lloyd recalled. He saw a tender as a support ship that performed her functions in port. He wanted an amphibious ship whose duty was more of an "operating job."

Lloyd and Emily left Washington in September with their youngest son, Tom. Hank was starting his first-class year as a midshipman, and Doug was in her senior year at Saint Agnes in Alexandria, Virginia, as one of the school's few boarders. In October, Lloyd joined the *Piedmont* in Yokosuka, Japan. She was alongside a pier and due to leave for Sasebo the following day for the change of command ceremony.

One of three ships in her class, the *Piedmont* was the flagship of the commander of the United Nations Blockading and Escort Force, CTF 95, at the time Rear Adm. B. Hall "Red" Hanlon. The ship had been active with the Seventh Fleet during the Korean War, with four war-zone tours, during which she provided tender services to U.S. destroyers as well as to ships from Canada, Colombia, New Zealand, South Korea, and

Thailand. The 27 July 1953 cease-fire agreement had ended the war, but U.S. naval presence in regional waters remained.

The ship was in Sasebo for a few weeks, servicing the destroyers assigned to her. Always mindful of the importance of small arms, Lloyd trained his sentries at a nearby Japanese army rifle range. As not a single officer or senior petty officer in the ship knew how to organize and conduct a firearms instruction or target practice on a firing range, Lloyd led the initial instruction himself. When the weather was good, they would shoot in the morning, picnic in the grass for lunch, and shoot again in the afternoon. They conducted their pistol training in an old warehouse. In time, the ship would win all the Pacific Destroyer Force small-arms proficiency honors.

At the end of October, the ship went to Korea. Confident of his ability to navigate those waters, Lloyd soon stopped using a pilot. As he had done with the *Keppler,* he insisted that his officers of the deck conn the ship, notwithstanding the fact that a tender presented more of a challenge than a destroyer.

The *Piedmont* had been on station for nine months when she was relieved in late autumn. To get his crew home in time to make their Christmas travel arrangements, Lloyd got permission to steam directly to San Diego without the usual stop at Hawaii. En route, they came across a Japanese trawler dead in the water with engine problems. Lloyd's mechanics had her running again in three hours, and the *Piedmont* was able to make San Diego the day before the recruiting commands went on leave. The appreciative crew beat the holiday rush for travel tickets.

After Christmas, the tender got orders to repair an Atlantic destroyer squadron just reassigned to the Pacific. According to Lloyd, the squadron was in terrible material condition. Not one ship made Panama without going dead in the water; the unit had to interrupt its transit of the canal for repairs. Each ship again went dead in the water on the route north to San Diego. When the squadron finally arrived, Lloyd found that all the ships had new crews—assigned in an effort to accommodate men who did not want to leave their home ports on the East Coast. "I thought it was relegating the ship and the welfare of the ship to a position secondary to that of various individuals, and I didn't think that was right and I still don't."

On one ship, Lloyd went below, into the machinery spaces, and "it was just frightening to be there. Steam hissing out of joints everywhere, and rust and streaks of rust running down the paintwork. And the lagging on the steam lines all half off, in terrible disrepair."

Sometime later, the commander of the Pacific cruiser-destroyer force shifted his flag to the *Piedmont*. As a consequence, the ship moored at the flagship buoys with major telephone and teletype connections. Considering the links vital to his job, "the flag was very reluctant to have us get under way," Lloyd noted. "Well, this didn't bother me in the least." Swinging on a buoy for the remainder of the competition year, however, did lower the ship's readiness scores in battle efficiency. Because of her tender availability work on the Atlantic destroyers, she excelled in repair, but she did not win that year's competition.

Lloyd made sure the *Piedmont* could provide unique tender services, and soon she was a favorite among the destroyer skippers. Thanks to his repair officer, they were able to find a source for the more saltwater-resistant copper-nickel piping that allowed them to replace galvanized fire-main piping. "We could even replace sonar domes. I don't know of any other tender that ever replaced a dome, but we did." He claimed his ship even modified the bridge of a destroyer.

The next year, Lloyd's first full year aboard, the ship won the battle efficiency competition. "Nobody was even close," largely because of the ship's repair factor. The *Piedmont* thereafter won for five years in a row, earning a gold battle efficiency *E*.

For the nine months the ship remained in San Diego, Lloyd was able to catch up on some family time. "It was just thoroughly pleasant being there in Coronado, fixing my own little house ashore, when I wasn't aboard ship fixing something."

In June 1955, Hank graduated from the Naval Academy and Doug graduated from St. Agnes. Hank had been engaged a year to Lucy Holcomb, one of Doug's classmates, and the three drove across country together in a new light blue 1955 Ford convertible that Hank had bought for his parents. For the next three weeks, the Mustin home was full. Lucy and the three Mustin children partied nonstop until Hank put Lucy on a plane to Washington and deployed on his first ship, a Pacific Fleet destroyer.

In August, the *Piedmont* returned to the Western Pacific. During one twenty-four-hour period of the crossing, Lloyd elected to run slightly faster than the prescribed speed to get ahead of the ship's scheduled position. He then stopped mid-ocean and held a series of drills. For the crew, it was a lifeboat drill. For the officers of the deck, it was ship-handling, trolling for a marker to perfect their skills at mooring to a buoy.

Of course, Lloyd had to emphasize gunnery as well. Almost any day that the *Piedmont* was under way, they were shooting guns. Lloyd realized that a lot of the crew were gun-shy. "And there's no way of getting over that except experiencing it." The ship had four 5-inch guns, and by that November, three of the mounts had *E*s painted on their turrets. That total, said Lloyd, was more than in all of the ninety destroyers in Cruiser-Destroyer Squadron Pacific. "It was about that time that I acquired the nickname 'Gunsmoke,'" he added.

By the autumn of 1955, the character of Western Pacific deployments had changed. With the end of the Korean War and the strategic nuclear focus of the Eisenhower administration, the carriers, with nuclear-capable bombers now on board, began to operate in single-carrier task groups off the coast of Asia, from Japan almost to the Philippines. The Seventh Fleet routinely deployed to positions near the carriers, and it shifted half of its support, including the *Piedmont*—repair ships, tankers, and store ships—from Sasebo to the Philippines.

When he arrived in Subic Bay in December, Lloyd found that he had new orders, to command a Pacific destroyer squadron. He was relieved later in the month in Manila. Not scheduled to take command until January, he caught an eastbound Pan American Stratoliner and took hops across the Pacific to Guam, then Wake, then Honolulu, and finally San Diego. He arrived at 850 B Avenue just in time for Christmas 1955.

Lloyd was the first in his class to get a major command afloat. After the holidays, he returned to Subic Bay to take command of Destroyer Squadron 13. On the day of his change of command, his division in the squadron, Destroyer Division 131 (DesDiv 131), was just arriving for an overhaul, alongside the *Piedmont*. His flagship was the short hull destroyer *Blue*. Once aboard with his pennant, Lloyd felt very at home.

At that time, the Western Pacific carrier force included five single-carrier task groups, typically one carrier with a cruiser and destroyer squadron escort. Each division had one radar picket destroyer with a height-finding radar, an enlarged combat information center, and other electronics such as the tactical air navigation beacon transponder that guided planes in their return to the carrier. Most of the time, however, Lloyd's first division operated independently of or in rotation duty with the second division, DesDiv 132.

Before Lloyd took command, the ships had been too busy to complete their gunnery exercises for the competition year. His first priority was to make good on that requirement. Said he of his commanders, "These young fellows got their introduction to me via scheduled gunnery practice on the day of our departure from Subic." After witnessing poor results from off-set shooting, Lloyd aligned DesDiv 131's gun batteries, which improved performance substantially.

After a stop in Singapore, the division went for two-week rotation duty to relieve DesDiv 132 on the Formosa patrol that guarded the strait between the Nationalists on

Taiwan and the Communists on mainland China. En route, he found that the ships had not been using their submarine radar direction finder, the BLR-1. Because the patrol had potential for submarine contact, he had his ships maneuver to allow each ship to calibrate the gear by relative bearing to account for magnetic interference from their masts and other electronic equipment on deck. Afterward, in a carrier antisubmarine exercise to the east of Taiwan, he tested the direction finders and found that two ships could use them to vector another destroyer to a spot where she could use sonar to keep a submarine submerged and unable to fire a shot.

Two destroyers at a time operated from Kaoshiung in southern Taiwan during the patrol. Lloyd felt that the national command guidance for rules of engagement was incomplete, and he emphasized to his captains their duty and right to self-defense, regardless of what was said in Washington.

The patrol passed without incident, and by February Lloyd was in Yokosuka. Also in port was Destroyer Squadron 15, under the command of his friend Capt. Lawrence Baldauf, the father of Doug's fiancé, Larry Baldauf. Larry was one of Hank's classmates and subsequently had gone to flight training at Pensacola, where he and Doug were to marry on 11 February. On the day of the ceremony, Lloyd and Larry Sr. gathered at the Yokosuka officers club to toast the marriage. The following month, Lloyd had to miss a second family wedding, Hank and Lucy's 3 March ceremony in Alexandria.

By the time Lloyd's divisions rejoined as a squadron to return to the West Coast for overhaul, he had concluded that their "combat readiness was just nonexistent, because it was not pushed." En route, he exercised extensively. When they hit the West Coast, he felt that his division at least was "four crackerjack ships. They were good and they knew it." There followed three months in San Francisco for overhaul and then refresher training off San Diego.

On 29 October 1956, just as they were preparing to deploy again to the Western Pacific, Israel attacked Egypt in an attempt to seize the Suez Canal, which Egypt had nationalized. The ensuing crisis included an exchange of superpower nuclear threats, initiated by the Soviets. DesDiv 132 went to sea to form a radar picket line from Alaska to Hawaii as an element of strategic defense against a possible attack on the United States. On 8 November, the crisis abated, and Lloyd's division got the go-ahead to proceed to Melbourne as planned.

Australian hospitality immediately swept Lloyd and his division into the 1956 Melbourne Olympics and a swirl of social activity that ran from the opening ceremonies on 22 November to the close on 8 December. Lloyd got an invitation to attend the swimming events in the royal box, where he sat behind Prince Philip, the Duke of Edinburgh.

By Christmas, Lloyd was at sea between Guam and Japan. Arriving in Yokosuka a couple of days later, he ran into a family friend, Lt. Gen. Freddie Smith, who had command of the Air Force Far East. His headquarters were in Nagoya, where Lloyd went to a "progressive party" on New Year's Eve and played golf the following day. When Lloyd arrived in Sasebo sometime later, Smith arranged to fly him to the Korean island of Cheju-Do, home to an Air Force radar station, to hunt pheasant and duck. "A number of the crew of this radar station were country boys who had grown up all their life hunting. And they acted as the guides for these hunting parties. They had built a lodge with non-appropriated funds. And all you had to do was make reservations at this lodge and arrive over there. And you'd have a lot of hunting. And we did."

Through the winter of 1957, Lloyd's squadron operated with the carrier *Bennington*, flagship of Rear Adm. A. P. "Putt" Storrs, commander of Carrier Division Five. Storrs had his carriers deployed much of the time in their nuclear strike positions against the Soviet Union and Communist China. "Putt ran realistic operations. We were so close to China that a great deal of what we would do, we'd do in radio silence; because we knew that they had a very extensive and efficient radio-intercept and direction-finding network."

While in Hong Kong, Lloyd got word that Rear Adm. Chester Wood, commander of the Pacific Cruiser-Destroyer Force, had selected him to be his chief of staff. When he arrived in Subic Bay with his squadron in early March, he was relieved. He headed home to San Diego "amidst the dire predictions of everybody, and a certain amount of fear and trepidation of my own." Wood had a reputation as being a "stiff-necked old son of a bitch."

Lloyd returned to the States with some available leave. He and Emily went north to visit Corinne, who still had her San Francisco apartment. George Murray had just died. Doug was living in nearby Mountain View and expecting her first child. No sooner did the Mustins arrive than Doug on 15 March gave birth to their first grandchild, a baby girl, whom she named Corinne. Doug remembered her father as "tender and wonderful" with the baby. Lloyd remembered little Corinne as "just so appealing that we couldn't resist whatever was supposed to be done."

In early April, Lloyd reported for duty on Wood's staff. The admiral had been Roosevelt's assistant naval aide early in the war, and Lloyd soon discovered that he was "just the most delightful person." Because the Pacific Fleet had fewer cruisers, his force included destroyers as well. Lloyd knew both the hardware and training shortfalls in the destroyer force from his time in the *Piedmont,* and Wood put him to work immediately on training.

One June day as he was meeting in his cabin with his staff, Lloyd got a phone call. He had been selected for rear admiral. It was a deep selection, and he would have to wait some time before a two-star billet would open. In the meantime, Wood took advantage of the nod to assign Lloyd to another staff duty as representative in Washington, on behalf of Wood and Pacific Fleet commander in chief Adm. Maurice E. "Germany" Curts, on the Ship Characteristics Board for new destroyers and frigates. For the better part of a year, Lloyd was transcontinental, traveling from Los Angeles on some of the last propeller-driven commercial coast-to-coast services.

In 1955, Arleigh Burke had become chief of naval operations and, under the influence of the Atlantic Fleet, had adopted ideas about destroyers that the Pacific Fleet did not support. Wood and Curts sent Lloyd to Washington to represent their view: The Navy needed destroyers in quantity. "And when you have these ships in these quantities, there have got to be certain features of economies of cost, and economies of operation and so on, reflected in them. . . . otherwise you can't have the numbers you need," said Lloyd.

Washington, however, was going in another direction with the support of Rear Adm. John C. Daniel, Wood's counterpart in the Atlantic Fleet. "At that stage of the game, DesLant was saying guns are obsolete; we don't want any more guns on our destroyers. We want missile-armed destroyers. That's the weapon of the future."

Lloyd and his Pacific Fleet superiors accepted that missiles had a place on destroyers, but they also believed that destroyers had to be numerous, affordable, and expendable. He argued against the "fancy gadgetry" of the Terrier missile program and its follow-ons that were known to be too large, too expensive, too complex, and with too much capability. He felt similarly about the antisubmarine rocket system, which did not need the extended ranges that required additional funding to achieve.

Lloyd lost the argument, and the Navy persisted with its ideas for gold-plated destroyers. Congress, however, looked at the cost figures and said no. As a result, for years "we did without."

The views of the Atlantic Fleet had an impact on training as well. The Atlantic Fleet had specialized its destroyer force in either antisubmarine warfare or air defense. Pacific Fleet destroyers had remained "general purpose." Before Lloyd arrived on Wood's staff, Washington had sent a frustrating directive ordering the Pacific Fleet to reduce its training requirements to a common standard. Wood had Lloyd tackle this issue, but they "lost that battle. And as a result, a long step downward or backward was made in the mandatory training requirements for the destroyers."

The crux of the issue was shore bombardment exercises. With only the controversial practice range at Culebra Island east of Puerto Rico, the Atlantic Fleet did not have the same opportunity to practice that the Pacific Fleet had, with its training area on San Clemente Island, convenient both to San Diego and Long Beach. When the Office of the Chief of Naval Operations put an end to the competitive exercise program and the schedule and requirement for scored, quantitatively evaluated, military functions for ships, it left Wood "in a mood of considerable disgust." It also hurt operationally. As Lloyd would note, in the latter stages of the Vietnam War, the Navy delivered a hundred thousand rounds a month in shore bombardment support, "considerably heavier than an average load we ever reached in World War II."

Lloyd felt the decision on exercises led to the Navy's acceptance of mediocrity. "They can't steam and they can't fight, and people know it," he offered in the early 1970s. It began at "that time, right there in '57 and '58, when the fleet abandoned its former standards of readiness."

In the early spring of 1958, Lloyd got his two stars and orders to command a destroyer flotilla in the Atlantic. In April, he left Wood's staff. With thirty days accumulated leave, he and Emily prepared for a relaxed drive across the continent to Newport. Once there, he would find his duties would have very little to do with destroyers—by order of the president.

Chapter 22

From Argus to Berlin

AN OPERATIONAL FLAG
OFFICER IN THE STRATEGIC REALM

Departing for Newport, Lloyd and Emily left Tom in Coronado with Emily's cousin Anne Thomas and her family. Their second son had just two months left in his senior year at Coronado High School. From there, it would be plebe summer at the Naval Academy.

Lloyd and Emily first drove north to San Francisco to visit Corinne and then continued leisurely eastward. In mid-May, they arrived in Newport and immediately moved into the house they had bought when last there in 1950–51. Lloyd remembered that New England was enjoying beautiful early summer weather.

The Atlantic destroyer force had three flotillas and was double the size of its Pacific counterpart. Lloyd's Destroyer Flotilla Two (DesFlot 2) specialized in antisubmarine warfare and convoy escort. DesFlot 4 addressed destroyer maintenance matters in Norfolk. DesFlot 6 worked primarily on air defense. Now a two-star, Lloyd looked forward to commanding his fifty-odd ships and introducing his own readiness concepts.

Reporting aboard the flagship of the Destroyer Force Atlantic Fleet, however, Lloyd found a different future waiting. "Here, Lloyd, you better read these," the chief of staff told him, handing him a set of messages. They were top secret, relating to the immediate conduct of at-sea atmospheric nuclear tests called Project Argus. A presidential order of 22 May instructed Lloyd to report in Washington to the chief of naval operations by a date that already was several days past.

The original order had gone to Rear Adm. Courtney Shands, Lloyd's aviator friend from their China Station days, but Shands had suffered a heart attack, so Lloyd got the nod. He later learned that Admiral Burke had said that they were the only two who could do the job. Shands had a lot of nuclear experience; Lloyd had none.

The July 1946 atomic weapons tests at Bikini had taken place while Lloyd was at the Bureau of Ordnance, but he had no part in them. During his WSEG days, he had taken the Albuquerque five-day introductory course and all along had been exposed to the policy-level issues associated with strategic bombing. He knew the rudiments of nuclear propulsion thanks to the *Nautilus* submarine program and, as Wood's chief of staff, had been exposed to the Regulus cruise missile carried aboard cruisers. Beyond these brushes with the nuclear field, Lloyd was a novice.

The Defense Department's Advanced Research Projects Agency had overall responsibility for Argus and provided most of the funding, but the Washington-based Armed Forces Special Weapons Project (AFSWP) would conduct the program. Under the law, the AFSWP acted for the Atomic Energy Commission (AEC) and was in charge of any military functions involving atomic material. Its director was Rear Adm. Butch Parker, and he was responsible for all interagency planning and coordination. The "nuclear weaponeer," Dr. Frank H. Shelton, was the chief scientific adviser.

The Navy would have operational command for the project, and Lloyd would command the special task force, TF 88, organized to plan and conduct Argus. He went right into it.

In essence, Argus would involve firing a rocket with a nuclear warhead that would detonate in the upper atmosphere. The object was to test a theory conceived by a Greek engineer, Nicholas C. Christofilos. Knowing that atoms and energy rays released in a nuclear detonation collide with atoms in the atmosphere to make a fireball, Christofilos theorized that a small nuclear detonation in the earth's magnetic radiation belt could release free electrons, electrically charged particles, that might be trapped in the earth's magnetic field. Within seconds, they could migrate around the earth and create a shell. Moving at close to the speed of light, this shell of relativistic electrons would be powerful enough to destroy physical objects such as incoming nuclear warheads.

Certain of the import to potential defense applications, Christofilos put his idea in the hands of the National Science Foundation. The idea then went to the president's scientific advisory group, chaired by Dr. George Kistiakowsky, a veteran of the

Manhattan Project. Kistiakowsky wasted no time recommending that the Argus tests be done and put the project before President Eisenhower. "We were still smarting a little bit from [the Soviet launch of Sputnik]," said Lloyd, "and this was conceived by some as regaining a little prestige in the world scientific community." Eisenhower made the decision to proceed in April, and in May Lloyd got his orders.

During this period, the United States and the Soviets both had made overtures for a moratorium on nuclear testing. Washington was keen to set 1 September as the deadline, hence the rush to conduct Argus and to complete ongoing nuclear testing at the Pacific Proving Ground and the atmospheric detonations. This would mean Argus would have to conduct and finish testing in something less than five months.

Argus, moreover, did not have a site. It could not piggyback on the existing test facilities at Eniwetok and Bikini. Neither was located at a conjugate point in the magnetic field, that is, where the lines of force came back to earth. Such points all were well above or below the equator.

The optimum trajectory of the rocket under consideration was some thirteen hundred miles. For safety's sake, the launch had to be that distance from land in any direction, which meant a shot from a Navy platform somewhere in the middle of the South Atlantic. In the end, Argus chose a conjugate point near Gough Island and Tristan da Cunha, even though a rocket still could reach South Africa or Argentina, even Chile or Antarctica, if the fuse failed.

During the planning period in June and July, Lloyd and Emily drove weekly between Washington and Newport. Lloyd would spend weekends in Newport doing the admin work associated with his flotilla command. They would return to D.C. on Sunday night so that he could continue the Argus planning for an August launch. At issue still were the kind of nuclear device to use and how to get it to required height.

Only the AEC had the authority to detonate nuclear warheads in peacetime. After some preliminary planning, Lloyd and Parker met with financier Lewis L. Strauss, chairman of the AEC, in his Georgetown office. Strauss asked only "if the test would go okay." They said, "'Yeah, we think so.' And he said, 'Well, okay.'" The project got the warheads released from AEC on the ground that the test was safe, "but it wasn't safe at all. . . . That thing could have gone off and come right down among the ships, if only one stage of the rocket fired. One stage firing would start the timing mechanism and if it came back down on your deck, that's where it was going to go off."

As a further indication of the import of Argus, the project got four Lockheed rocket engineers on loan from the Polaris missile program, the Navy's crash effort to develop its first underwater-launched intercontinental ballistic missile. Lockheed was developing a three-stage rocket, the X-17, for the Polaris program to test the reentry vehicle. The Argus rocket was an X-17A with a Genie W-25 air defense nuclear warhead and radar beacon for tracking. Sandia National Laboratories provided the fusing and firing of the weapons and was the custodian of the warheads until they were launched. The test called for two rocket launches. As a backup, Lloyd wanted a third and spent considerable effort to get components to assemble it.

On 15 or 16 June, he briefed Burke and identified their critical paths. At the conclusion, Burke asked what he thought were the chances of success. Lloyd replied, "'About 50-50.' He let it go at that. He didn't say why." A few years later, Burke said he had been "too damned cocky." Some analyst in the Operations Evaluation Group in the Navy Department evidently had told Burke before the briefing that the odds of success were very long. Ordered by the president, Burke had to proceed regardless and thus gave the go-ahead.

The Soviet Union had not done high-altitude nuclear tests, and the great secrecy surrounding Argus was vital to avoid any Soviet satellite monitoring or other observation. "The cover plan was essentially an operational matter," said Lloyd. "That was my baby." The Pentagon, Joint Chiefs, and Navy Department's abilities to do covert operations, he added, were "pretty primitive in that stage of the game."

Within his command, Lloyd issued his crews extreme-weather clothing and screened training films on arctic exploration as part of the deception. The main worry was their being tailed by Soviet trawlers, so he was careful to disguise the movements of the task force. The units would not completely rendezvous until they were in the South Atlantic. The converted seaplane tender *Norton Sound* would do the launches. Her original capability to bunker a million gallons of fuel for her seaplanes had been converted to hold water ballast when she became a test bed for rockets. Lloyd had the bunkers reconverted. The *Norton Sound* sailed from the West Coast, ostensibly for the Pacific Proving Ground. She would not refuel again until she got to the South Atlantic.

Lloyd and his flagship, the antisubmarine carrier *Tarawa*, and two destroyers and two destroyer escorts were ready to sail on 6 August. A serious tanker collision in the mouth of Narragansett Bay delayed them by a day. Once at sea, the units rendezvoused with two tankers, the *Neosho* and *Salamonie*, from Norfolk, and together they steamed east, using their planes to scout for any merchantmen to avoid. Mid-Atlantic they turned south and went into radio silence.

On the way south, the Navy rerouted radio traffic from the *Norton Sound* so it looked as if she were communicating to elements in the Pacific Fleet. The task force arrived on station about 25 August. Messages back to Washington were relayed via Asmara or Suez using a key link, the Chief of Naval Operations High Command net. Burke was nervous and wanted to monitor the test. Within the task force they used line-of-sight UHF, but that presented problems when communicating with the weather pickets a couple of hundred miles north and to the west. They resolved the problem by using high frequency radio, breaking radio silence for only the three days before the launch, when the weather picket destroyers to the west sent general weather reports to no particular addressees. They also would break radio silence for the launches, when, Lloyd argued, it would be too late for anyone to attempt any instrumented observations.

Lloyd remained on the *Tarawa*. In the final days before the first launch, the destroyers and destroyer escorts continued their searches. Fortunately, no contacts appeared. Fuel consumption was high, and the *Salamonie* soon exhausted her fuel supplies and left.

The instrumentation and equipment for tracking and observations were on board the *Norton Sound* and another tender, the *Albemarle,* deployed to the northern conjugate point. Aircraft flying from the Azores had instrumentation for making observations above the clouds. Instrumented rockets would launch from Wallops Island, Maryland, and from U.S. sites in North Africa. The task force also had its own aircraft.

For the launch, the *Norton Sound* would steam in the middle with the *Tarawa* and *Neosho,* with tracking radars to either side ten miles abeam and a destroyer with Zuni high-altitude sounding rockets. The tracking radars were World War II Army SCR-584 van-mounted radars modified by the Air Force for missile tracking—the first such application ever attempted. The radar crews practiced their tracking on the Zunis.

The X-17A rocket had no guidance and no self-destruct. The warhead had a seven-minute fuse, however, so if the rocket failed to launch, it probably would not detonate. Attaining the right trajectory still was a challenge. The X-17A was a fin-guided rocket and thus required some weather-cocking into any relative wind. The surface wind was strong. The task force attempted to minimize it by steaming downwind at eighteen to nineteen knots. On top of that, they had to account for pitch and roll.

The first shot was on 28 August. A National Science Foundation scientist on Argus, Bill Thaler, had linked the project with the Explorer satellite program, getting some instrumentation on the Explorer IV and V satellites that could record electrons in the magnetic field. The Explorer IV launched on 26 July and remained in orbit through the test and into the next year. The Explorer V, however, failed to orbit. Argus had to base its launch time on the single satellite. Explorer IV would travel over North America eastbound and then cut southward to the South Atlantic, passing overhead every ninety minutes.

The first Argus shot went about 6 degrees off the vertical. The Lockheed engineers had incorrectly calculated the weather cocking and the adjustment for pitch and roll. The shot lifted high above the clouds, where it suffered possibly a second stage but most likely a third stage ignition failure. It descended 250 miles from the task force and detonated at an altitude of some eighty to a hundred miles, far below what the project wanted. Flying below the cloud cover, the task force aircraft were unable to make observations. Although a relatively small detonation, the blast from the 20-ton warhead proved Christofilos's theory.

Two days later, the second shot was close to the vertical but had another third-stage ignition failure. The device detonated right above the task force at about 180 miles. This time, the aircraft flew above the clouds and were able to make observations.

Several days later, TF 88 attempted the third shot. It failed to get off the pad. The log read that it was a misfire, but Lloyd believed it was an electrical or mechanical circuit interruption external to the missile. He maintained that a solid propellant rocket would not misfire. "It fires, or it explodes, that's about the option I remember."

After considerable time finding and correcting the problem, the engineers got a launch that was almost perfect. Atmospheric conditions were a high haze. The device detonated at an altitude of four hundred miles. The burst was clearly visible on deck and ignited the aurora borealis.

The Argus tests proved Christofilos's theory, "but precious little information really was gathered compared to what we now know or ought to know." For some eighteen days thereafter, observers recorded the Argus effects at a very low level. In the end, however, the scientists concluded that the shield idea was not achievable.

The radiation safety provisions were routine. Lloyd had film badges on some personnel and ordered others surreptitiously placed in exposed positions. In the end, he maintained, no one was exposed to measurable radiation. Those aloft in the aircraft had slightly more exposure because they had a few miles less of air blanket, although the distances still were ample.

Sometime later, Lloyd learned that the *New York Times* had gotten information on the proposed test about the time he got the job. Thaler and some foundation colleagues had leaked it to reporter Hanson W. Baldwin. The government put intense pressure on Baldwin and the *Times* to sit on the story, and they did for almost a year.

Although Lloyd was not involved, the United States had planned a series of post-

Argus tests using a megaton weapon at an altitude of 100 to 150 nautical miles to try for a much stronger Argus effect. Work was suspended, however, with the testing moratorium. For his role in Argus, he received the Legion of Merit.

In October, Lloyd and elements of his task force returned to Newport, where he set to work on the routine business of his flotilla. For the next four months, he focused primarily on additional duty as commander of the newly formed Antisubmarine Defense Group Charlie, one of the Atlantic Fleet's three task groups in its hunter-killer task force. The two other groups each had an antisubmarine carrier, but Defense Group Charlie was composed only of destroyers, destroyer escorts, and three squadrons of P2V patrol aircraft.

Into the winter, Lloyd tested antisubmarine defense tactics with a notional eighty-ship convoy in a lengthy series of exercises off Newport against submarines from Groton, Connecticut. His escort unit was a division of destroyer escorts and one patrol plane, rotated continuously from a twelve-plane squadron, that would defend against a division of four submarines. In one part of the exercises, the convoy made five transits through the operating area. The antisubmarine force was able to counterattack nineteen of twenty submarine attacks successfully, frequently with a weapon dropped from the patrol plane. The conclusions were impressive. Antisubmarine warfare had advanced to a tactically credible capability.

In February 1959, Lloyd returned to command Task Force 88 in combined antisubmarine warfare training operations with the navies and air forces of a number of the Latin American countries, the predecessor to the annual UNITAS exercises. After the South Atlantic Force worked with South American navies on the Atlantic side, Lloyd took his force through the Panama Canal to exercise on the Pacific coast from Colombia to Chile.

In March, while Lloyd was in Chile, the *New York Times* broke the Argus story. The front-page headline on the nineteenth read, "U.S. ATOM BLASTS 300 MILES UP MAR RADAR, BLUR MISSILE PLAN; CALLED 'GREATEST EXPERIMENT.'" Lloyd's picture was on page sixteen. Baldwin reported that the test was "regarded by some of its leading participants as the greatest scientific experiment of all time." He noted that scientists were arguing to make findings public under the spirit of the International Geophysical Year. The impact of the story was immediate. While hosting a number of Chilean VIPs aboard his flagship, Lloyd had to switch from his expected briefing on antisubmarine warfare to brief Project Argus instead.

Years later, Scott Jones, a retired Navy commander, claimed that the Office of Naval Intelligence had penetrated the cover of the Argus operation after the conclusion of the tests. Lloyd's response to both the *Times* story and Jones's contention was characteristically pithy: Baldwin "did not have the part that mattered, which was the timing, and this CinCLantFlt counter intelligence operation penetrating after the fact, that couldn't have mattered less. What mattered was to penetrate it in time for the Soviets to get their satellite up there, which didn't happen."

The Soviets claimed to have read the Argus results. Lloyd maintained, however, that the United States never had any indication of intelligence-gathering activity on their part.

Shortly after returning from South America, Lloyd got orders to command the naval base at Key West, Florida, a dual-hatted billet that included command of the Key West Force. On 13 June, he began his duties.

For the first time in his career, Lloyd enjoyed a somewhat relaxed duty station. The Mustins' quarters was in fact a two-unit residence that President Harry Truman had once converted into his vacation White House. Because the base had no golf course, President Dwight D. Eisenhower had returned the quarters to the Navy, along with the White House furniture. Living in such splendor meant that Hank and Doug and their families could come for extended holiday visits, as duty would allow.

Despite Ike's rejection of the place, Washington had not forgotten it. The Pentagon and Navy Department used Key West as entertainment for junketing VIPs. Lloyd and Emily's guest book reads like a *Who's Who* for senior military and defense officials, both foreign and domestic. The principal draw was sport fishing, a hobby Lloyd quickly adopted. Key West had dedicated crews and a number of a crash boats rigged for deep-sea fishing.

Operations from Key West included training in aviation and antisubmarine warfare, including the testing of torpedoes, depth charges, and air laid mines, and development of buoyant ascent escape procedures. Lloyd essentially was punching his shore-based command ticket, for in less than a year he was ordered to Washington for another tour at the Office of the Chief of Naval Operations.

In May 1960, Lloyd reported for duty as the antisubmarine warfare readiness executive in the Office of the Chief of Naval Operations, where Arleigh Burke was in his fifth year as the Navy's top officer. Burke had created the billet several years earlier, so that

Lloyd's predecessor, Rear Adm. Red Yeager, would report directly to him. As antisubmarine warfare readiness executive, or Op-001, Lloyd would be on his personal staff.

Burke wanted Op-001 to focus on ASW readiness in the fleet, which Lloyd chose to interpret as readiness, as opposed to advocacy of new sonar or weapon design.

Bringing a destroyerman's point of view to the table, Lloyd worked closely with Burke on developing a Navy position on antisubmarine warfare in its dealings with Congress and industry. In his attempt to modernize the postwar Navy, Burke had been trying to balance the competing service needs. According to Lloyd, his first priority was to increase the number of carriers and aircraft. The Air Force, however, still was accusing the Navy of not having put sufficient resources toward ASW requirements. Lloyd believed his billet was a Burke ploy. "Op-001 was really only a figurehead. It was supposed to fend off the press and fend off the congressmen, and come up with glib answers as to how what we were doing was just right."

The issue that the Air Force and the military press continued to trumpet was what Lloyd regarded as the "phony" Soviet submarine threat of 1960. The Soviet sub force still was primarily the coastal *Whiskey*-class. And he was confident that the Navy could handle even the newer and better *Romeo* and *Sierra* classes with existing systems and doctrine.

Washington's systems focus also overlooked U.S. operational advantages. The U.S. Navy had extensive and successful World War II experience; the Soviets did not. Its antisubmarine warfare plan in the Atlantic included a forward ambush line of submarines at the choke points where the Soviets would emerge from their bases. A second line would extend across the Greenland-Iceland-U.K. Gap, supplemented by maritime patrol planes from Greenland that, with their periscope detection radars, would locate the submarines when they snorkeled. Offensively, the Navy would conduct surface hunter-killer operations. Convoy escorts would provide close-in defense, as the Charlie Group had demonstrated. Finally, the United States had its sound surveillance system sensor devices strung along the U.S. coast.

The mantra Lloyd and Burke repeated was that the Navy must have the ability to apportion scarce resources correctly. Hence, given the tight money situation, he opposed on principle any new ASW research and development programs.

As for torpedoes, Lloyd felt that the existing Mark-43 homing torpedo and older torpedoes could readily attack a *Whiskey*-class submarine. Ships equipped with the SQS-4 sonar indeed later proved able to handle *Romeo*-class submarines in the 1962 Missile Crisis. "We made contact with every one, held onto it to fuel exhaustion, and forced it to surface." The later and larger SQS-23, according to Lloyd, could cope very well with the Soviet nuclear submarines that were beginning to enter the fleet in the early 1960s.

"The way in which the clamor was always raised was that our equipment isn't good enough. And so the reaction of all of the half-informed was that we've got to put ever more money into research. And ASW, in the United States Navy, had become the happy hunting ground of the research organizations." In Lloyd's view, however, the issue was not research and development but procurement. "Quality-wise we were in very fine shape. We were completely on top of the problem. But quantity-wise, we were not. We had these good things developed, but we were not providing them to our operating forces in the necessary numbers."

In January 1961, a new Democratic administration swept into Washington under John F. Kennedy. The president had won by the narrowest of margins and could hardly claim a mandate for change, but with his "New Frontier," he acted as if he did. Bureaucratically, it was a far-reaching changing of the guard, felt most acutely in the management of national security.

Working with Burke, Lloyd witnessed one of the Navy and Pentagon's earliest policy-level frustrations with the Kennedy administration, the Bay of Pigs disaster. At 7:30 on the morning of 17 April, the day of the invasion, Lloyd was in the flag plot with Burke, who was "tearing his hair out and telephoning the White House." Late the night before, Kennedy and his senior national security officials had brought Burke into the Oval Office and told him the invasion was proceeding. Burke advised that to be successful, it would need U.S. air support, and he asked for permission to engage. To Burke's horror, Kennedy refused, because he did not want the United States "involved."

A CIA operation, the invasion did not include the Joint Chiefs of Staff in the planning or the military in the chain of command. Burke had learned of the operation through Gen. Lyman L. Lemnitzer, USA, chairman of the Joint Chiefs, who had been told to keep the information from his fellow chiefs. On his own initiative, Burke ordered the carrier *Essex* and her air group to leave Guantánamo and station nearby for possible assistance. Kennedy's refusal to release these Navy assets resulted in the slaughter of the invasion force, international embarrassment for the United States, and heartbreak for Burke.

His order to the *Essex* was particularly noteworthy: In 1958, the Defense Reorganization Act had removed the chief of naval operations and his fellow service chiefs from the operational chain of command. According to Lloyd, however, the unified commanders did not fully assume their statutory authority until after the Missile Crisis, and Burke's action proved it. He had issued an operational order, despite the law and despite a decision by the administration to run the operation through a chain of command led by the CIA.

In June 1961, not two months after the Bay of Pigs, the Soviets again tested Kennedy. At the Vienna Summit, Soviet Premier Nikita Khrushchev threatened to sign a separate peace treaty with East Germany, in effect ending guaranteed Western access to Berlin. East-West tensions escalated through the summer. On 17 August, after closing the border for four days, the Soviets began constructing the Berlin Wall in response to increasing emigration to the West.

National Security Council staffer Carl Kaysen, a Harvard economics professor, prepared a study on options for a limited nuclear first strike against Soviet military targets in response to any direct military action in Berlin. Lemnitzer rejected it. In mid-September, Gen. Maxwell D. Taylor, USA (ret.), Kennedy's special military adviser, would present another version of Kaysen's study, but the president and his secretary of defense, Robert S. McNamara, had problems with the military's strategic targeting plan on which it was based.

In principle, Kennedy wanted nonnuclear options. He was predisposed to a response from the sea and hoped it could counter any Soviet blockade of Berlin. According to Lloyd, Kennedy was considering his own naval blockade of the Soviet Union. To that end, the president put the question to McNamara, who in turn put it to Burke: If the United States were to conduct a war at sea against the Soviets, could the Navy handle the Soviet submarine threat?

Because antisubmarine warfare was the brief for Op-001, Lloyd gave the official Navy response through channels and ignited a firestorm. In short, his answer was "Yes, we could." This upset both the director of surface warfare and the Atlantic Fleet commander in chief, Adm. Robert L. Dennison, who were not so sure. Both called him on the carpet. Vice Chief of Naval Operations Adm. James S. Russell had to moderate what had become a very contentious internal Navy issue. He took Lloyd to Norfolk to meet with Dennison. In the meeting, among others, were Lloyd's friend Rivets Rivero, who was Dennison's deputy chief of staff and chief of staff for operations, and Joe Grenfell, commander of the Atlantic submarine force. Lloyd restated his case and responded to questions. "I swear I must have melted my collar umpteen times over," said Lloyd, "because I was the only person arguing that we could stand up to the Russians if the President wanted us to." The meeting ended inconclusively. Only Russell appeared to agree with him; the others did not voice any opinion. As the operational commander, Dennison would have given his response directly to Burke. Lloyd believed that in turn Burke took the discussion directly to Kennedy, bypassing McNamara.

"I think this question had been asked privately from Kennedy to Burke, and was probably answered privately, from Burke to Kennedy. But it must have leaked out, because the problem went away," Lloyd noted. By mid-October, Kennedy and Khrushchev would agree, via their "pen pal" correspondence, to work together to resolve the crisis peacefully.

In early August, when he relieved Burke as chief of naval operations, Adm. George W. Anderson Jr. abolished Op-001. He wanted the director of surface warfare once again to absorb antisubmarine warfare. Lloyd then became Op-32, director of ASW, with executive authority for air, surface, and subsurface antisubmarine warfare, an arrangement that particularly upset the submariners. The reorganization also gave him an orphan, mine warfare. For the rest of his time in the billet, Lloyd's job was routine.

The day Anderson assumed command, Lloyd got word that the Soviets had announced the boundaries of a danger area. For some two months, the Pentagon had been getting fragmentary but mounting intelligence that they were preparing to break the nuclear testing moratorium. On 31 August, Khrushchev announced the abrogation. The next day, the Soviet Union detonated what would be the first of some fifty-nine nuclear tests in 1961, followed by another seventy-nine in 1962.

The Soviets thus presented Kennedy with another crisis. On 15 September, the United States responded by renewing underground testing in Nevada with the first of forty-five tests under Operation Nougat. It took Kennedy until 19 October, however, to approve planning for a resumption of atmospheric tests. Not until November would he issue orders to form a joint task force to conduct them. Commanding the naval component would be the seasoned operational commander of Project Argus, Lloyd Mustin. The gun boss soon would be testing the most awesome ordnance ever devised.

Chapter 23

Operation Dominic

SHOOTING SWORDFISH IN A FISH DESERT

Into the autumn of 1961, the Soviets continued nuclear testing at their Arctic site on Novaya Zemlya. By one account, between 10 September and 4 November, they detonated twenty-four atmospheric shots. Many in the Atomic Energy Commission's nuclear labs felt strongly that this Soviet abrogation of the 1958 moratorium justified a U.S. renewal of atmospheric nuclear testing to close the so-called missile gap trumpeted by Kennedy during his presidential campaign.

On 21 September, however, the administration had circulated through high government circles a National Intelligence Estimate in part stating that the Soviet Union had only some ten to twenty-five intercontinental ballistic missile launchers and would not have the capability to increase those numbers in the near future. With Kennedy's approval, Deputy Secretary of Defense Roswell L. Gilpatric, exactly a month later, gave a speech that deflated any notion of his previously vaunted missile gap. He reassured his audience that the United States was not dangerously behind the Soviet Union in its nuclear capabilities but actually possessed a substantially larger nuclear arsenal.

On 23 October, the Soviets detonated the first of what would prove to be two of the largest atmospheric thermonuclear explosions ever. The second was eight days later. One of the tests was an airdrop of a fifty-plus-megaton device designed to produce an explosion approaching a hundred megatons. The Soviets claimed the shot released an energy equal to ten times the total number of bombs used in World War II—including the two atomic devices used on Japan. In view of the widespread contamination, Lloyd characterized these and other blasts at Novaya Zemlya as "some of the dirtiest shots in history."

The device was a bomb wholly impractical for use as a missile warhead and thus of dubious military value. Its purpose was political intimidation. Kennedy got the message. On 1 November, his administration decided to prepare for atmospheric tests in the Pacific.

The task to plan and conduct the Pacific atmospheric tests fell under the AEC and the Defense Atomic Support Agency, the successor agency to the Armed Forces Special Weapons Project. The Joint Chiefs of Staff exercised operational control. At their direction, Lt. Gen. Lyle Booth, USA, director of the Defense Atomic Support Agency, formed a task force, Joint Task Force 8, to do the testing, code named "Dominic." Booth gave command of JTF 8 to an Army engineer, Maj. Gen. Alfred Dodd Starbird, who had served as the AEC's director of military applications. His scientific deputy was William E. Ogle, of the Los Alamos Scientific Laboratory. Ogle had participated in every AEC atomic test since the Manhattan Project. The Air Force deputy task force commander was Brig. Gen. Jack Samuel, JTG 8.4.

As had been the case with Project Argus, the Dominic tests would be mid-ocean and thus would have heavy Navy involvement. When Vice Chief of Naval Operations Jim Russell looked for candidates to command the Navy task group to support the tests, he found "nobody wanted the job." He thus turned to Lloyd.

On 30 November, Lloyd reported to JTF 8 as the Navy's deputy task force commander and commander of the Navy task group. The joint task force already had begun its work in a vacated CIA building south of Washington's Independence Avenue and Potomac Park. "An extraordinarily congenial group of people assembled on November 25th and really started doing things to be ready by April 1st," the readiness-to-test date set by the administration.

Although he had agreed to initiate immediately the Nevada underground tests, Kennedy was reluctant to pursue atmospheric testing, and he insisted that the government keep Dominic secret. The Soviets certainly were not unaware of U.S. preparations. Kennedy, however, was extremely sensitive to public opinion, both at home and abroad. More directly, he presided over a divided administration that already was in disarray over the Bay of Pigs and the Berlin crisis.

Lloyd characterized Kennedy as "whipsawed" by his advisers. On one side were those who had insisted that he take advantage of the Soviet abrogation. This group included John A. McCone, his director of Central Intelligence, who had been AEC chairman from 1958 to 1960, and the chairman of the Joint Chiefs of Staff, General Lemnitzer. In the middle was Dr. Glenn T. Seaborg, the AEC chairman, who, despite being a Nobel prize winner in chemistry, was, to Lloyd's recollection, "so indecisive."

Seaborg's weak hand aside, the AEC labs argued successfully for three sets of test objectives. The first was a series of weapons development tests to determine whether the nuclear warheads already in the stockpile or under lab development worked. A second set sponsored by the services and the Department of Defense would be operational tests of complete weapon systems—for example, the Air Force Atlas intercontinental ballistic missile, the Navy Polaris submarine-launched ballistic missile and antisubmarine rocket (ASROC), and the Army Nike Hercules air defense missile. The third set would be a series of high-altitude weapon effects tests.

It was in this third set, said Lloyd, "where the real fumbling went on: What we were going to do and when, and where. And they changed every day before breakfast and again before dinner." A third group of various officials with nuclear arms control backgrounds began to pressure Kennedy to consider alternatives. In DoD, most of the resistance Lloyd encountered came from Harold Brown, the new director of Defense Research and Engineering. Brown had been the senior science adviser to the 1958–59 Geneva nuclear disarmament talks that had put the moratorium in place. In the White House, the pressure came from MIT's Jerome B. Wiesner, Kennedy's science adviser, who was instrumental in establishing the U.S. Arms Control and Disarmament Agency. Wiesner viewed testing as unnecessary: Scientists could replicate test results with calculations.

With so much contradictory input, Kennedy had trouble making any decision on the weapons effect portion of Dominic. "That test was really a comedy of Washington-level fumbling and indecisiveness and inability to make up your mind." Lloyd felt that the president had little confidence in his key people, a characteristic he shared with Defense Secretary McNamara. "I soon began to feel that one of the world's least decisive people was President Kennedy."

The administration also had made the decision not to do any more testing in the U.S. trust territories, namely, the Pacific Proving Ground in the Eniwetok and Bikini atolls and Kwajalein in the Marshall Islands. The earlier Bikini and Eniwetok barge and tower shots had been dirty and had contaminated the waters six hundred miles south of Honolulu. The decision not to use the PPG meant that Dominic would be a maritime operation; although the Navy would not be involved technically, the operational demands on its assets would be extensive. In the end, Lloyd had command of several task groups totaling eighty ships and twenty-two thousand men. The Air Force assigned two thousand men, most of whom were directly involved in the technical work of the tests. The Army had only some 750 on board. Although JTF-8 was an Army-led joint task force, the service was not an enthusiastic participant. Starbird's headquarters staff boasted only about twenty Army billets.

With no hope of using existing U.S. nuclear test sites, JTF 8 began to look at Johnston Atoll and Christmas Island. Johnston was sovereign U.S. territory 720 miles southwest of Oahu. Christmas Island was twelve hundred miles due south of Hawaii. Under a condominium, the United States and Britain exercised dual sovereignty over the island, where the British had conducted their own nuclear tests.

Contamination was an issue in the negotiations with the British. The Air Force proposed a solution: air drops of nuclear devices over the ocean to an altitude where the fireballs would not touch the surface. To make the drop, B-52s would fly from the Naval Air Station at Barbers Point in Oahu to a point in the middle of a danger area south of Christmas Island, where a barge would carry an instrumentation array.

Although British agreement was not immediate, JTG 8 began to plan around the air drops. The task force began establishing its operational headquarters on Ford Island in Pearl Harbor. During the actual testing, all senior commanders planned on shifting their flags to the carrier *Wasp*.

On 22 February, the British finally gave official permission for the United States to use Christmas, and JTF 8 made the decision to relocate all its headquarters functions to the island. On 2 March in a nationwide address, Kennedy announced he would resume testing unless the Soviets agreed to a test ban treaty. In late March, Lloyd and the senior Dominic leadership left Washington for the Pacific.

Given that the first tests would be air drops over the open ocean, one of Lloyd's initial challenges was to find a way to moor the instrumented barge that would serve as the target for the drop. The raft equipped with a strobe and radar beacon would provide a fail-safe guide to vector the B-52s to the drop zone. Lloyd put together a Navy team that in the end developed a deep-sea mooring procedure enabling them to moor in nine thousand feet off Christmas. The approach worked so well that they later were able to moor on the eighteen-thousand-foot shelf off Johnston Atoll, where they moved the operation for the last five air drops in the autumn.

The air drops would comprise the bulk of the Dominic testing, twenty-nine of the thirty-six detonations. Their intent was to evaluate the AEC labs' advanced designs from prior to and during the moratorium years. These warheads essentially had new yield-to-weight ratios. The drops also included other warheads already in the stockpile that had not been tested after the 1958 moratorium.

The Air Force was predominant in this set of tests. In addition to the B-52s, General Samuels had instrumented Air Force aircraft airborne during each test to fly through the mushroom cloud with mounted windsocks to collect particles. U-2 reconnaissance aircraft would fly from Hickam Air Force Base, Hawaii, to provide weather information.

According to Lloyd, JTF 8 did not get the final go-ahead to test until 20 April. Kennedy had planned to make the announcement on the twenty-first, saying that the Soviets had not agreed to stop their testing and that U.S. tests would resume the next day. But because 22 April was Easter, he delayed his announcement until the twenty-fourth. The first airdrop followed on the twenty-fifth, and Dominic was under way.

The first drop was five thousand feet above the water south of Christmas Island. Lloyd remembered that it came within seventy feet of the target. It was followed quickly by three more drops. Thereafter, the program would continue regularly until 11 July, for a total of twenty-four air drops at that drop zone.

After the United States had exploded four nuclear devices, Dominic was a secret no more. The 4 May issue of *Time* magazine put Bill Ogle on its cover. The caption was "U.S. NUCLEAR TESTING The Shot Heard Round the World." In a photograph on page twenty-one, Ogle shared the limelight with Lloyd, Starbird, and Samuels.

Although Lloyd was involved in preparations for the air drops, his primary attention was on planning and conducting the Navy's two operational tests, each of which had its own task group. The Polaris shot was TG 8.8; the ASROC, TG 8.9. He got the order in late February or early March to launch both a Polaris and an ASROC by May.

The initial problem was simply getting a Polaris submarine. In the winter of 1962, the Navy had only six commissioned Polaris boats and did not want to release any from the deployment cycle, especially given the tense international situation. Lloyd was able to get the sixth, the *Ethan Allen,* which was still in shakedown but had a perfect missile record, having fired seven Polaris missiles successfully.

Lloyd's TG 8.8 flagship for the Polaris test, code-named "Frigate Bird," was the *Norton Sound.* She had left Point Mugu, California, and joined with the *Yorktown* carrier task group, which had come from San Diego to provide security. The launch point was about a thousand miles east of Christmas Island.

The *Ethan Allen* was an East Coast submarine. To get to the rendezvous point, she had to make way from Charleston, South Carolina, through the Panama Canal. The transit would be impossible with the extended mast necessary to enable the task group to see where the submerged boat was for the launch, so, instead, Lloyd used helicopters to hover over the sub that would launch from a depth of one hundred feet. The helos could see her through the water, said Lloyd, "which was as clear as gin."

With Lloyd on board the *Norton Sound* was the Polaris pioneer Rear Adm. Levering Smith, director of the Navy's Special Projects Office. The operational responsibility for the Polaris launch was Lloyd's alone, however. Years later, he confided to Ogle his mental approach to the shot. "That was the only missile in the entire U.S. inventory that had ever been fired with a nuclear warhead. The ASROC was the only other nuclear weapon, other than conventional air drop bombs. Well, those two things were really my responsibility, and I was the one who was supposed to worry about them, but I just went blithely along telling myself that all would be okay because all these smart people are working on them, and it was supposed to work and so it would work."

On 6 May, Lloyd got permission to launch. In the control station with Smith by his side, he gave the order. The missile fired and lifted from the surface. Ominously, the track on the automatic plotting table looked "like a drunk snake going home." Lloyd and Smith rushed on deck and saw that the missile had emerged from the water and was rising normally. On the tracking table, however, "the higher the thing got the wider the swings became." They soon realized that the motion of the ship caused the track to move back and forth. "Nobody had thought to produce ground-stabilized coordinates to show on their plotting tables, a fairly easy solution."

Flight time was thirty minutes. The missile flew to within half a mile of the intended impact area and detonated a 125-kiloton warhead with a megaton of yield.

Flushed with success, but "in a state of near collapse" from lack of sleep, Lloyd transferred his flag from the *Norton Sound* to the *Yorktown*, which would reform with other ships as TG 8.9 for the ASROC test. As he was making way to his next rendezvous point, some six hundred miles to the west-southwest of San Diego, three more airdrops proceeded at Christmas Island. Lloyd transferred again to the landing ship dock *Monticello*, his flagship for the shot.

The AEC was very worried about contaminating the waters and the tuna production so close to San Diego. Christmas Island was not an option because of strong currents. However, according to a Scripps Institute expert, the area off San Diego was, surprisingly, a "fish desert" where the danger of generating radioactive fish was supposedly nil.

The ASROC test was called Swordfish. The intent was to determine the minimum safe range for a ship to fire the weapon. The rocket had a ten-thousand-yard range and would detonate at a depth of eight hundred feet. The Navy had said the minimum distance should be four thousand yards. To test the effects, the task group located an unmanned and instrumented destroyer, the *Bausell,* two thousand yards from the intended impact point.

On 11 May, the destroyer *Agerholm* fired the ASROC with a W-44 nuclear warhead on a fourteen-second, four-thousand-yard flight that splashed and detonated at 850 feet. The detonation was above a two-thousand-foot shelf, which allowed the task group also to determine the effects of a secondary shock wave reflected off the bottom. Scientists had theorized that the reflected wave could be greater than the surface shock wave. It was not.

Sensors registered the blast throughout the Pacific Basin. The reverberations disabled for half an hour the West Coast sound surveillance system that ran from Washington State to San Diego—the only one the United States had at the time. The only other casualty, according to Lloyd, was on a Navy tug that hit the hot pool, giving the whole crew a lifetime radiation dose.

The task group concluded that the Navy should revise its doctrine to permit ships to fire from a range as close as two thousand yards. Analysis of the shock waves provided some tactical conclusions, principally that the dual-capability ASROC presented a dilemma to an enemy submarine seeking to escape its effects. If the submarine assumed the rocket was loaded with a conventional torpedo, the best escape would be to dive. If she assumed it carried a nuclear warhead, the best escape would be to rise to a shallow depth. Making the wrong assumption would be fatal.

Swordfish was the only underwater test of the ASROC warhead and the United States' last underwater test. Said Lloyd, "The technical people stated the conclusion that that one test had given us more information on underwater nuclear detonations than all others previously conducted in the entire U.S. nuclear testing program."

The shot revealed a problem in the ASROC firing fuse that could have resulted in premature detonation just after launch. Lloyd immediately reported that finding to Washington. Also,

it proved something that people had known for a long time, which was that the ballistics in the computer that controlled the flight of that ASROC were wrong. The ASROC landed in the water five hundred yards away from where it should have landed, because of a ballistic error that had been recognized long ago, and nobody had gotten around to fixing. It was sort of like nobody having gotten around to fixing that potentially catastrophic ASROC nuclear fuse detail.

After reporting these findings, Lloyd speculated whether the Navy Department would address them. He got his answer six years later, as Defense Atomic Support Agency director. To his shock, it was in the negative.

After the ASROC test, Lloyd returned to San Diego and caught a C-135 to Christmas Island, where another fifteen air drops would continue into July. By this time, Starbird had shifted his flag to Johnston Atoll to ready the site for the first of the Thor missile launches for the high-altitude shots, code-named "Fishbowl." Lloyd's duties were to support the air drops and put together the Navy surveillance units that would police the danger area around Johnston.

In late May, McNamara called Lloyd and Ogle to Washington to give him and other senior defense officials a briefing on Dominic's progress. At one point during the visit, the pair met with the president in the Oval Office to stress the need for continued testing. Lloyd presented Kennedy with a selection of detonation photos that he had released to Dominic personnel for their private use. The president was aghast. Fearing leaks to the press, he ordered immediate classification and instructed Lloyd to collect all the photos he had disseminated. It was an instruction Lloyd chose to ignore.

Before he returned to the Pacific, he was able to get to Annapolis with Emily and Corinne to see Tom graduate from the Naval Academy. Like his brother before him, Tom had requested—and received—first duty on board a San Diego destroyer.

While Lloyd was stateside, Starbird began his high-altitude tests at Johnston Atoll. After considering the lift options, JTF 8 had decided to use Air Force Thor missiles for their supposed reliability. The Thors were to lift their payloads to six hundred miles and then begin descent. The warheads would detonate at up to 250 miles to evaluate the effect of high-yield explosions against ballistic missile reentry vehicles. The testers needed to know how vulnerable U.S. reentry vehicles would be to a Soviet detonation and how effective U.S. detonations would be against the Soviets. To get the data, in addition to the nuclear warhead, each missile would carry two dummy warheads as notional reentry vehicles that Lloyd's task group would retrieve from the sea.

Surveillance for the tests was not a great problem, as the United States had announced the danger area widely. The main issue was the fear of retinal burns. The blast would not present problems as long as the Navy ensured that unprotected fishermen remained over the horizon. No location on tiny Johnston Atoll afforded any safety in the event of an engine failure or other malfunction during the launch, so Marine Corps helicopters evacuated as many as 2,500 personnel before each shot to the offshore ships of the Navy task group.

To assist in tracking, the Navy provided its radar tracking ship *Range Tracker,* which had the facilities for calculating an instantaneous impact point for the missile. "We managed to rig up a remote display, from that into our command bunker on the island, so that we could keep track of where it would land if we had to detonate it."

Starbird attempted his first Thor shot, "Bluegill," on 3 June, while Lloyd was still stateside. The shot had problems prior to launch with the range safety radar. Five minutes into the flight, the *Range Tracker* failed. Unable to monitor the flight path, the range safety officer destroyed the missile ten minutes later, prior to detonation of the warhead.

When Lloyd returned, he arranged for another dish to serve as a backup for Starbird's next shot on 20 June. This attempt, dubbed "Starfish," suffered an engine failure, and Starbird had to destroy the Thor at eighty to ninety thousand feet. Lloyd said that even though the high explosive destroyed the warhead without producing a nuclear yield, the blast was visible in Honolulu, some eight hundred miles away.

On 9 July, Starbird launched "Starfish Prime." This shot was successful—with the minor exception that the blast released electrons into the magnetosphere and damaged satellites, one of which was British.

Following Starfish Prime, JTF 8 conducted two more air drops off Christmas Island, the last of which was on the eleventh.

On 25 July, Starbird tried to repeat his first test, calling it "Bluegill Prime." This attempt was particularly disastrous. The missile engine malfunctioned immediately after ignition, and the range safety officer fired the destruct system, destroying the missile while on the launch pad. The blast demolished the launch complex and spread plutonium contamination throughout. The accident delayed high-altitude testing for almost three full months as the joint task force struggled with complete site reconstruction. Starbird and his advisers had to reconsider alternatives to the Thor, whose reliability now was in question.

By September, Kennedy was wrestling with the upcoming Mercury 8 flight, which would bring astronaut Wally Schirra into the Pacific for his landing. NASA officials were worried that new high-altitude shots would increase radiation levels to the point of endangering his life. Indeed, Air Force satellite sensors later confirmed that radiation from the July test was still present in the upper atmosphere. On 3 October, Schirra took his flight, landing safely northeast of Midway Island.

On 15 October, Starbird attempted a third Bluegill high-altitude Thor shot called "Bluegill Double Prime." This one suffered a booster failure. When the missile veered out of control and began tumbling, range safety had it destroyed by remote control, 156 seconds after launch. Directly overhead, radioactive debris showered Johnston but fortunately caused no casualties.

The same day, halfway around the world, Kennedy saw the first reconnaissance photos of the Soviet missiles in Cuba. Despite the escalating Soviet–U.S. tensions, the Dominic missile launches continued. On 20 October, Starbird fired the "Checkmate" test, this time using a Strypi test rocket. The United States was not blinking. Neither were the Soviets. On 22 and 28 October and 1 November, they launched three missiles from Kapustin Yar on the Volga River, each detonating a high-altitude nuclear explosion.

On 26 October, JTF 8 launched another Thor, "Bluegill Triple Prime." The nighttime detonation, approximately nineteen miles south-southwest of Johnston, was at thirty-one miles, low enough for a fireball that glowed for thirty minutes and was visible in Hawaii. That day, McNamara called Starbird to Washington to head his Defense Communications Agency, at the time a shell organization. As Starbird's only two-star deputy, Lloyd relieved him for the last two air drops and two high-altitude tests.

Still on Christmas Island, Lloyd was closing operations there and completing the transfer to Johnston Atoll. On 1 November, a final Thor shot, "Kingfish," launched, according to Lloyd, with a two-and-a-half-megaton bomb from the warhead stockpile. This shot went to sixty miles. "The whole sky overhead at Johnston Island was brightly illuminated by the auroral effects, not the flash of the detonation. That was 1,200 miles away." Lloyd could see it from his position on Christmas Island. "It lighted the whole sky over my head, with a complete unbroken sheet of yellow light. And this was that same effect that we'd been trying to determine the existence of in the Argus tests. It was really there." He was referring to the electromagnetic pulse that, among other things, opened garage doors in Honolulu.

Lloyd's Navy task group had the job of retrieving the eighteen dummy warheads that were to determine the effects of electromagnetic pulse on reentry vehicles. It recovered all but one, which had broken into pieces.

On 2 November, Lloyd's designation as Commander, Joint Task Force 8, became official. He would conduct the one remaining Dominic test: the Nike Hercules shot.

On 4 November, Lloyd took the shot, code-named "Tightrope." It was a success and the last ever U.S. atmospheric test.

The Dominic high-altitude tests had proved conclusively the need to harden warheads. As a countermeasure, the Nike Zeus program would pursue a warhead that would detonate with a high X-ray emission to destroy incoming reentry vehicles above the atmosphere.

In the wake of the Cuban missile crisis, it was obvious that the United States and the Soviet Union would arrive at some kind of limitation treaty for nuclear testing. As a result, the Defense Atomic Support Agency's activity shifted to a readiness-to-test program. Into 1963, Lloyd wrote much of the operation plans for a 1964 readiness program, with a detailed set of orders. For example, his weather annex described the number of stations and their names and who was going to man them.

On 5 August 1963, the United States and the Soviet Union signed the Atmospheric Test Ban Treaty, putting a halt to any further atmospheric and underwater testing. Lloyd felt very strongly that the Soviets had gotten all the data they needed from their extensive 1961–62 testing and thus were more than happy to sign, knowing that the United States had the short stick in a number of areas. Future data would have to come from underground testing, which was not as useful as atmospheric tests.

Lloyd was especially troubled by the lack of good data on electromagnetic pulse effects and how that would affect development of countermeasures. Recalling in the 1970s the Kingfish test, he noted, "You're dealing with the kind of force such that one existing warhead, of the kind we have, and of the kind that we know the Soviets have, could be detonated at altitude above roughly the center of this country, and it would probably totally and permanently disable every telephone switchboard in the country. . . . And things can be done about that, but nobody's doing them."

Under the readiness-to-test concept, Lloyd became heavily involved in upgrades to Johnston. The immediate need was to increase its size and capacity. This involved dredging the channel, lengthening the airstrip, and building facilities for 3,500. Even with the treaty, Washington wanted the atoll to be in a condition to resume testing on thirty days' notice.

"It's just not the sort of thing that you think of a seagoing, Navy admiral as ever having anything to do with. And yet, frankly, it was fun while it lasted. I was having a wonderful time," Lloyd recalled. Given the absence of organized recreation, he found occasion to swim in the lagoon—until he discovered the sharks. The only other option was deep-sea fishing, a pastime he had learned to love at Key West and which he gladly renewed.

Lloyd was getting restless, however, in his position as JTF 8. He had been in the Pacific since November 1961 and felt he was "not working for the Navy." Worried about promotion to three stars, he began to lean on Chief of Naval Operations Adm. David L. McDonald for a fleet command. McDonald, however, needed to fill the Joint Staff's J-3 billet, director of operations, and he wanted to nominate Lloyd. Lloyd did not react favorably. J-3 not only would be his sixth two-star billet, but it also would be his fourth joint duty assignment, the kiss of death for a ranking naval officer. McDonald, however, persisted, and in the end was "so darn persuasive."

On the morning of 28 May, Lloyd transferred his flag from JTF 8 to the Pentagon, where he reported for duty as J-3. McDonald had a method. Operations were afoot halfway around the world, and the Navy needed a forceful voice on the Joint Staff. Lloyd was about to step into the vortex of Vietnam.

Chapter 24

J-3 and Vietnam

WRESTLING A FINE ITALIAN HAND

Well past midnight on Saturday, 6 June 1964, the phone rang next to Lloyd and Emily's bed at their Alexandria, Virginia, home. The Pentagon's National Military Command Center was calling to alert Lloyd that the United States had lost a Navy RF-8 reconnaissance plane over Laos, the first shoot-down of a U.S. aircraft in Southeast Asia. A week earlier, Lloyd had relieved Army Maj. Gen. Finn Unger as the Joint Staff's director of operations, J-3.

The downed aviator from the carrier *Kitty Hawk* required a rescue mission that Lloyd learned was now under way with Navy and Air Force assets and helicopters from Air America, the CIA operation in Laos. The command center was unable to patch into the call either Lloyd's immediate superior, the director of the Joint Staff, Lt. Gen. David A. Burchinal, USAF, or Defense Secretary McNamara. Both were en route from a conference in Honolulu with senior military and diplomatic officials in the Pacific.

When the center finally managed to reach Cyrus Vance, the deputy secretary, Lloyd gave him a situation report. Vance inexplicably told Lloyd to recall the rescue aircraft. Horrified, Lloyd asked the command center to keep trying to contact Burchinal, who he recognized was in a better position to get Vance to rescind his order.

Burchinal did eventually get the word and put Vance straight, but by that time, it was too late. The secretary of defense had been informed of the incident and had similarly instructed Adm. Harry D. Felt, commander in chief of the Pacific Command, not to issue a rescue order. McNamara told the incredulous admiral that he was acting on the recommendation of the Department of State.

The communist Pathet Lao captured the aviator, Lt. Charles F. Klusmann. In late August, he managed to escape.

"That was an abrupt introduction to my new responsibilities," Lloyd noted. "Things were pretty hot and heavy out in Southeast Asia, and unfortunately for the lives of young Americans, the fine Italian hand of McNamara was stirring the pot on everything."

This incident typified the cultural gulf that divided the military and civilian leadership in Washington. On the one side was the military, which sought to win a war against a defined enemy, North Vietnam, in a manner that best served the men who were doing the fighting. On the other was a civilian leadership that saw the conflict in the context of the mutual threats among nuclear powers, including China, and thus put priority on a negotiated settlement.

For three years, Lloyd as J-3 would be the Joint Chiefs' action officer responsible for the vast majority of Southeast Asia issues and the key Joint Staff player in the high-level Washington politics surrounding the war. He was present for every Joint Chiefs meeting on Southeast Asia, except when the chiefs debated in closed session. He also attended any discussion of recommendations going to McNamara or President Lyndon B. Johnson, many of which he wrote.

His focus would be on the conduct of air operations in North Vietnam, in particular, targeting and weapon selection. Adm. Ulysses S. Grant Sharp, who relieved Felt in late June, was similarly focused and regarded Lloyd, a fellow Navy man, as perhaps his greatest ally in Washington: "Not one single thing moved from this country to Southeast Asia except in response of orders originated in J-3 and signed by me in person." In crises, J-3 is the sharp end of the Joint Staff, and by temperament, Lloyd was a warrior willing to use the spear. To his relief, J-3 became a three-star billet in August. At last, he advanced to vice admiral.

The civilian leadership, concerned over the diplomatic sensitivities surrounding the fiction of Laotian neutrality, did not want the United States engaged in armed reconnaissance. The issue resolved within days with a compromise: The United States would conduct armed *escort* of reconnaissance in Laos and South Vietnam. Under the rules of engagement, the escorts could only return fire and could not attack targets of opportunity found during the reconnaissance.

Problems then arose over weapon authorization. Inevitably, the administration locked horns with the chiefs over one particular weapon—napalm.

Leading the civilians in Washington who argued for the prohibition of napalm was the new assistant secretary of defense for international security affairs, John T. McNaughton. His worry was the effect the use of napalm would have on domestic and world opinion, reflecting the Johnson administration's priority to manage communications as they related to Southeast Asia and the prosecution of the war.

In dueling with McNaughton, Lloyd was focused on the purely military—the commanders' responsibility to and for their troops in the field and sailors at sea. On behalf of commander in chief, Pacific, and representing the Joint Chiefs, he argued that rescue of downed reconnaissance pilots required flak suppression weapons to keep the enemy at bay. In dense jungle, the best flak suppressor was napalm. By the end of the year, Lloyd and the chiefs managed to get authority for the operational commanders to use napalm in armed reconnaissance over Laos.

On 2 August, Lloyd received another late-night phone call. North Vietnamese patrol boats had attacked the radar picket destroyer *Maddox* in the Gulf of Tonkin. The *Maddox* returned fire. Neither ship nor boats inflicted damage in the exchange, but naval aircraft from the carrier *Ticonderoga* sank one boat and damaged two others.

Lloyd arrived at the Pentagon at three in the morning. Following deliberations, orders went to the *Maddox* to resume her patrol and to another destroyer, the *Turner Joy,* to accompany her. The following night, the two destroyers thought they once again were under attack, although it is probable they responded to false radar contacts. This second incident prompted McNamara to respond. Despite his blistering criticism of the secretary generally, Lloyd credited McNamara as the driver behind the 4 August U.S. reprisals.

At the time, U.S. offensive military assets in the region were somewhat limited. With its planes in Thailand or in South Vietnam well south of the North Vietnamese border, the Air Force had no nearby strike capability. The *Ticonderoga* was the Navy's only carrier on station. The Joint Chiefs of Staff fortunately had been working on a plan to cover such contingencies: the "99 Targets Study" (later revised to 94). Two days before the attacks, Lloyd maintained, the chiefs had presented it to McNamara, who had objected to the amount of ordnance the plan would require if fully implemented. Nevertheless, Lloyd tasked his project officer, Col. Bob Jones, USA, to tailor the plan for an appropriate and immediate reprisal. Fortuitously, the PT boat base where the attack had originated and a nearby fuel depot at Vinh were on the list. Lloyd got approval to hit both and, acting for the chiefs, transmitted the strike order to Sharp. In the reprisal, the U.S. lost two planes, one flown by Lt. Everett Alvarez, the first U.S. prisoner of war.

The strikes had little military effect on the North Vietnamese and did nothing to induce them to abandon their support for the Viet Cong or negotiate any agreements. Although the administration was drifting toward some kind of bombing policy against the North, it was not there yet. Throughout the autumn presidential campaign, Johnson presented himself to voters as the candidate of restraint.

On 1 November, two days before Americans went to the polls, the Viet Cong conducted a mortar raid on the Bien Hoa air base, headquarters of the South Vietnamese Air Force and a base for U.S. adviser operations. The attack killed four U.S. airmen, wounded more than seventy, destroyed five B-57 aircraft, and damaged another fifteen. Although the Joint Chiefs immediately recommended strong reprisals, Johnson opted not to retaliate. Not only was the president mindful of the possible effect on the election, but McNamara and his civilian advisers were worried that retaliation would risk Chinese intervention. At the end of 1964, China was still the primary, albeit modest, armorer to the North. The Soviet Union would not commit to greater military assistance until the very end of the year, after it was clear that the United States was becoming ensnared.

Whether Johnson realized it or not, he was at a defining point for the United States in Vietnam. A president with an ambitious domestic agenda but little expertise in foreign affairs, he chose to create a National Security Council working group, chaired by Bill Bundy and staffed with some of the "best and the brightest," to review courses of action. Known as the Joint Planning Group, Bundy's team began meeting at the State Department on the morning of 3 November. Lloyd was the sole representative of Gen. Earle D. "Bus" Wheeler, USA, chairman of the Joint Chiefs of Staff. Representing McNamara was John McNaughton.

The assignment thrust Lloyd into the convoluted world of the State Department, which immediately struck him as schizophrenic and fickle. He found Secretary of State Dean Rusk eminently practical, but his under secretary, George Ball, was very much the dove. Lloyd's caustic view was that Ball was more concerned with world opinion and "given to bend to Communist objectives." When Rusk was in town, he ran the show; when not, the department echoed Ball's approach, designed less to win a war than to communicate détente.

In his opening day project outline, Bundy divided the work of the group into seven tasks, reserving for himself and McNaughton the job of writing a brief paper discussing three broad policy options. Lloyd's task was to analyze for Wheeler the different options vis-à-vis U.S. objectives and interests and propose specific actions. The Policy Planning Council representative would take Lloyd's work and "examine the political impacts of the most violent option first." From the outset, the Bundy group was disinclined to take the war to the enemy. By accident or design, the staff support would reinforce Bundy and McNaughton's predisposition to soft options.

The group's first job was to examine U.S. objectives and interests in South Vietnam, and it produced the most heated debates. At the time, the basic U.S. Vietnam policy was the securing of "an independent, non-Communist South Vietnam." In an early draft statement, Bundy presented two fallback positions that would have abandoned the South in spite of that objective. One would draw a new line for communist containment in Thailand. The second would conduct perfunctory military operations until Washington could negotiate a compromise settlement for South Vietnam. Lloyd countered immediately with "forceful objections" that evidently had effect. As a result, the panel "rejected [the fallback alternatives] before they were fully explored."

Following this exchange, representatives from the CIA, Defense Intelligence Agency, and the State Department Intelligence and Research reported on their assessment of the effectiveness of bombing the North. Essentially, the group questioned whether such a campaign would reduce the level of North Vietnamese support to the Viet Cong or break their will. In passing, it suggested that Hanoi could interpret LBJ's landslide election as affording Washington the flexibility to abandon South Vietnam. Again, Lloyd rose to challenge the view as too "negative." "If this means that Hanoi thinks we are now in position to accept worldwide humiliation with respect to our formerly stated objectives in Vietnam, this is another reason why it is desirable that we take early measures to disabuse their thinking." Lloyd then represented the Joint Chiefs' adherence to the domino theory, later writing in a memo to Bundy that it was "the most realistic estimate for Cambodia and Thailand, probably Burma, possibly Malaysia."

Regarding the intelligence assessment on influencing enemy will, Lloyd said the proper concern was capabilities. "The actual U.S. requirement with respect to [North Vietnam] is reduction of the *rate of delivery* of support to the VC, to levels below their minimum necessary sustaining level. . . . In the present unstable situation something far less than total destruction may be all that is required to accomplish the above." As for whether immediate and decisive U.S. reprisals would escalate the conflict, the intelligence panel itself, he noted, had accepted that North Vietnam and China did not want direct conflict with the United States and that China would not intervene beyond providing antiaircraft artillery, jets, and naval patrol craft.

In his 10 November memo to Bundy, Lloyd took him to task for a number of assertions in his draft on the objectives in South Vietnam and the stakes in Southeast Asia. Bundy had written that a guarantee to South Vietnam would require the United States to defeat North Vietnam and probably China in a major conflict. Restating his position, Lloyd offered, "Our first objective is to cause [North Vietnam] to terminate support of the [Southeast Asia] insurgencies. . . . To achieve this objective does not necessarily require that we 'defeat North Vietnam,' and it almost certainly does not require that we defeat Communist China. Hence our commitment to [South Vietnam] does not involve a high probability, let alone 'high risks,' of a major conflict in Southeast Asia." Bundy feared escalation to an almost inevitable "Korean-scale ground action and possibly even the use of nuclear weapons at some point." Lloyd said the risk would be more for the Chinese. "If China chooses to go to war against us she has to contemplate their possible use, just as anyone does—this is more of the 'risk' to *them*."

Lloyd summarized Bundy's position, saying that his draft understated the gravity of the possible loss of South Vietnam and overstated the potential risks of preventing that loss. Bundy had asked if honoring the commitment to the South was worth those risks. Lloyd responded, "Here again is emphasis on 'risk' and 'loss' to us, as though the harder we try the more we stand to risk and to lose. On the contrary, a resolute course of action in lieu of half measures, resolutely carried out instead of dallying and delaying, offers the best hope for minimizing *risks, costs,* and *losses* in achieving our objectives."

McNaughton and Bundy formulated three options. Option A proposed to "continue present policies" with current military operations and prompt reprisals for future Bien Hoas. Option B would continue current military operations with a systematic program of progressively heavier military pressures, quickly identified as the Joint Chiefs of Staff option. Option C would continue current military operations with milder military pressures and a declared U.S. willingness to negotiate. It was the approach that McNaughton and Bundy had favored from the outset—gradualism.

On the twenty-first, Bundy presented options to the National Security Council principals, who were, after review, stymied. After several days of debate, they finally agreed to recommend a two-phase program linking options A and C. For thirty days, the United States would increase military pressures on the North before moving to a campaign of air strikes to induce Hanoi to negotiate.

On 1 December, the two-phase plan went to Johnson, who approved phase one and deferred authorization for phase two. He wanted one last chance to stabilize the South before escalation. "Before Wheeler saddles up, try anything," McNaughton recorded Johnson as saying.

The fateful decision by committee led to a presidential non-decision already overtaken by events. On 15 October, a hard-line leadership had ousted Soviet Premier Nikita Khrushchev and the following month decided to provide military aid to the North Vietnamese. In December, the first North Vietnamese regiment entered South Vietnam.

Observed Lloyd years later, "The tragedy of it all was that when the shooting started over there we had within our hand all it took to bring the hostilities to a successful conclusion. This was the view that the Joint Chiefs of Staff strived to enunciate to the President."

On Christmas Eve 1964, the Viet Cong bombed the most visible symbol of U.S. military presence in Saigon, the Brinks Hotel bachelor officers quarters. The attack killed two U.S. personnel and wounded sixty-four other Americans and forty-three Vietnamese. Four days later, the Joint Chiefs of Staff recommended an air attack on the North in reprisal. President Johnson once again said no. For the second time in two months, the enemy had attacked and killed uniformed Americans, and their commander in chief would not respond.

Several service chiefs now considered resigning. Chairman Wheeler, however, was able to change their minds. According to Lloyd, they quickly came to the conclusion that the gesture would have been futile. McNamara controlled Pentagon press relations, and the public still was buying the line that he was putting the military straight. The chiefs feared ridicule, not just from McNamara but also from the State Department and the White House.

Johnson's first priority apparently was to support efforts to stabilize the politics of the South, but the military situation was worsening. Through the month, the political leadership in Saigon continued to squabble.

Lloyd and the Joint Staff were growing more impatient. On 29 January 1965, Wheeler wrote to McNamara to note the military's readiness for any future reprisals, voicing the imperative that they be timely. Lloyd and many other senior military were angered that U.S. servicemen in country had become hostage to a civilian leadership that was stuck in a reactive mode and allowing the initiative to pass to a purposeful enemy.

On 1 February, the Viet Cong proclaimed a Tet truce, honoring the Vietnamese new year. Six days later, VC sappers mortared the Marine advisers' barracks at Pleiku and the nearby helicopter base at Camp Holloway in the Central Highlands, killing eight men and wounding more than one hundred. On the eighth, Navy carriers launched raids tagged Operation Flaming Dart, the first overt U.S. attacks since the Tonkin Gulf reprisals. One plane and one aviator were lost. On the tenth, the Viet Cong struck a U.S. enlisted barracks at Qui Nhon. Twenty-three Americans died. The next day, Air Force and Navy planes conducted a second reprisal, in which three planes and one pilot were lost.

Despite his professed desire to protect against pilot losses, McNamara had loaded both reprisals with restrictions, principally the prohibition on napalm as a flak suppressor. In Lloyd's view, these constraints contributed directly to the losses. As with the attacks that followed the Gulf of Tonkin incident, he regarded both "graduated" reprisals as essentially futile.

On the day after the Pleiku attack, Lloyd and his J-3 staff had developed a plan for an eight-week bombing program against basing areas along the North's main artery to the demilitarized zone and other logistic support targets south of the nineteenth parallel. Primarily air strikes followed by armed reconnaissance, the plan also included renewed South Vietnamese raids by sea against the North and U.S. Navy intelligence-gathering patrols and naval bombardments, as well as cross-border incursions.

On 11 February, the chiefs presented the plan to McNamara. Two days later, the president approved Rolling Thunder, what would be a continuing air campaign against North Vietnam. It was not, however, the eight-week plan, but a tentative series of ad hoc strikes. For the rest of the month, the chiefs lobbied and failed to get political agreement on a "bank of targets" that would allow field commanders to time the raids according to their own operational conditions.

On 2 March, the Air Force launched the first Rolling Thunder strikes, losing four planes, three to antiaircraft fire. A flustered McNamara, unhappy with the meager military damage from the strikes, asked J-3 to do an analysis of the losses. After his staff reviewed data from six previous air operations, Lloyd reported on the tenth. Among his recommendations, he asked for napalm authorization, "optimum ordnance not yet available in the theater," and flexibility for the operational commander to time and select his strikes. Presidential approval for the use of napalm against targets in the North came that day, with first use in raids five days later.

Lloyd's second recommendation reflected his concern over shortfalls in the ordnance inventory. The cost-conscious McNamara was loath to increase production, said Lloyd, not wanting to finish any conflict with large stockpiles. Instead, his policy was to expend NATO war reserve munitions without replacement. The "optimum ordnance" to which Lloyd referred was such munitions as the Air Force M117 750-pound drag bomb, for several years not in production, and the Navy Mark 81 and 82, a program still in production but which McNamara refused to accelerate. It was not until April 1966 that Lloyd was able to get him to list the M117 and the Mark 80 series as critical munitions of the highest national priority for use in South Vietnam. He would not so designate the Mark 84 Mod 1 until January 1967. Lloyd also pressed for VT influence fuses for above-ground detonation and the Navy's long-delay fuses—optimal for use with munitions for interdicting transportation systems—both of which also were in short supply. McNamara refused to move on those requests as well.

Through February, the North Vietnamese Army continued to win major victories, and on 5 March, the United States put troops into Vietnam in a combat role, ostensibly for perimeter defense at air bases. On the twenty-first, the commander in chief, Pacific, presented the chiefs with a twelve-week plan to attack "more logical" targets to cut the North's lines of communication. Also frustrated by the conduct of Rolling Thunder, Sharp was disturbed by the selection of militarily insignificant targets and delays between strikes.

Still hopeful that he could improve target selection, Lloyd drafted a bombing campaign against lines of communication based on Sharp's plan, which focused on the rail system south of the twentieth parallel. Phase one also would hit radars and degrade what was now a North Vietnamese MiG intercept capability. Phase two would launch attacks north of the parallel and include strikes on the rail and highway routes to China, followed by raids on the port facilities and aerial mining. On 27 March, the Joint Chiefs presented the plan to McNamara.

Johnson and his defense secretary refused to approve any multi-week Rolling Thunder program. Said commentary in *The New York Times* edition of the *Pentagon Papers,* "They clearly preferred to retain continual personal control over attack concepts and individual target selection." Both target and ordnance selection now took place at Tuesday luncheons at the White House attended by the president and his senior civilian advisers. Prior to the summer of 1967, no military representative was present at those gatherings.

Notwithstanding opposition from Sharp, Lloyd and the Joint Staff, the chiefs, and the director of central intelligence, the civilian leadership appeared by April to be abandoning the bombing campaign. Inexplicably, they decided not to attack the North's ground control intercept radar system.

The secretary of defense forged an agreement among his disparate civilian national security team to "plateau" the tempo of the air strikes. The military objective for the bombing would not be destruction of the North's target complex but interdiction. On 21 April, he recommended to the president ground actions in the South, with no intensified air campaigns against North Vietnamese industrial targets, power plants, petroleum, oil, and lubricant (POL) complexes, or Hanoi-Haiphong.

Apparently, McNamara had gotten the chairman's buy-in. According to Director of Central Intelligence John A. McCone, Wheeler stated that

> the JCS unanimously supported the April 21st paper. He said it was necessary to deploy the additional men and to make preparations for still more men. He made no comment on the tempo of the bombing. He made no appeal for authority to bomb industrial targets, POL, power stations, etc. He expressed no concern over the idea that bombing would be carried on over a long period of time and, indeed, the operation itself would go on for a protracted period. He stated there was a need for more air power in South Vietnam because their air power was getting used up.
>
> His position was diametrically opposite from that taken by Admiral Mustin, Director of Planning [sic] for the Joint Chiefs, in his briefing to me ten days ago. In that briefing the Admiral said that we were using less than 5 percent of our air power and he strongly advocated bombing the targets which are excluded above.

Such disconnects occurred, said Lloyd, because Johnson would tell the chiefs "often only orally" that they had to frame their recommendations within his set of limitations.

Lloyd's attention for the next few weeks shifted to the Caribbean. In late April, the United States had to evacuate Americans from the Dominican Republic and intervene to restore order. Lloyd managed the military aspects of the intervention for the Joint Chiefs, a task that engaged him until mid-May.

McNamara's position momentarily hardened. His 1 July draft presidential memorandum called for mining and destruction of rail and road bridges and MiG airfields and surface-to-air missile (SAM) sites. The following day, a delighted Joint Chiefs endorsed the memorandum. A still cautious Johnson, however, reacted negatively. On the twentieth, McNamara submitted a revised memo that reemphasized interdiction within Vietnam while allowing for mining only in cases justifying severe reprisal.

Johnson, however, was pursuing another attempt to induce negotiations. On Christmas Eve 1965, he announced a thirty-seven-day bombing pause.

During the pause, the North Vietnamese restored and improved much of their damaged infrastructure and sent more troops and supplies southward. Photo evidence revealed that POL stores now were going into dispersed underground storage.

Admiral Sharp and Lloyd were convinced that the only way to get the North to negotiate would be to destroy its capability to provide logistic support to the Viet Cong. Still arguing for strategic bombing, Sharp pushed for an ambitious campaign to cut the lines of communication to China, attack the POL complexes, and mine the harbors, severing external support to North Vietnam. In an 18 January memo, the chiefs reiterated his plan to strike target systems, with the additional request for attacks on airfields and SAM sites. Possibly authored by Lloyd or his vice director, Air Force Maj. Gen. John B. McPherson, the memo said that far from discouraging Chinese intervention, restraint encouraged it.

Sharp and Lloyd had been arguing for an air operation to strike the two rail connections into China. One was a narrow gauge, single-track railroad, running from Hanoi northwest to Kunming. It was, Lloyd said, a rail line to nowhere, but years of U.S. reluctance to attack it gave the Chinese time to connect it to the rest of their rail system. The other railroad went from Hanoi to the northeast some sixty miles to the border and connected to the Chinese lines to Nanning and Canton. It also had been a single line, but as the war progressed, the North Vietnamese made it a double track.

In its inventory, the United States had the ordnance to deny replenishment by rail. An influence fuse bomb could land and detonate only in response to a passing target, as if it were a mine. Equipped with the Navy's delay fuse, such a bomb was appropriate for use around any transportation line, rail or road. Hence, the railroads were easily interdictable, but the civilian leadership placed such restrictions on bombing that it was almost impossible.

In addition to a campaign against the rail connections, Sharp repeatedly asked for permission to mine North Vietnamese harbors. As his Washington advocate, Lloyd argued what he considered a straightforward case. North Vietnam had only three deepwater ports: Haiphong, Hon Gai, and Cam Pha. They were "classic minable harbors," said Lloyd. "They had long approaches through shallow waters, and they had to dredge these narrow channels constantly to keep them open to ocean going shipping. Of course, a dredged channel is no wider than it needs to be to let the ships go through. All we had to do was mine those channels, and all of that sea going traffic would have ended, and the war would have ended not long after that."

The Navy had a full aerial mining capability, and the level of effort would have been minimal. "The operation to mine those three harbors to where not one ship could come in or go out could be accomplished by the aircraft from one aircraft carrier, one strike." Sharp's operational plans required only sixteen aircraft flying from carriers that had the ordnance already on board.

Lloyd noted that the sowing operation would have been in the offshore shallow channels beyond the range of antiaircraft batteries. It would have entailed small risk to those flying the missions and no risk to Vietnamese civilians. "They would be dropping them way away from land, and if any one of them blew up, no civilians would be harmed, nor any churches, pagodas, nor anything else. It would be all out there in the water, but no ships could go by."

McNamara and his civilian officials were "wringing their hands" over the possibility that mining would incite Chinese intervention, as had MacArthur's assault at the Yalu River border between China and Korea during the Korean War. Lloyd, however, objected to the parallel. In his view, the Chinese had a national interest in Korea, a country adjacent to Manchuria, their vital industrial province. North Vietnam, on the other hand, was on a distant and relatively undeveloped frontier. In addition, China was in no position to involve itself directly in a war with the United States over Vietnam. Later in the decade, Mao's Cultural Revolution not only would have a catastrophic effect on Chinese production but also would generate social anarchy.

McNamara had allies in the State Department who likewise opposed mining. The department would cite the need to honor the traditional U.S. stance on freedom of seas. For Lloyd, their position ceased to be tenable once U.S. servicemen started getting killed in combat. He would speak often of the outrage and frustration the aviators and carrier sailors on Yankee Station felt with every passing Soviet freighter, whose sailors would turn from sunning themselves to wave from the tops of the crates stacked tightly on the decks. Each crate was stuffed with SAMs, destined to be used against U.S. aircraft and personnel.

The critical issue of POL supply, Lloyd felt, also could be linked to mining. The North had no petroleum of its own. It started the war, said he, with fewer than ten coal-burning electric power generating stations and only one hydroelectric generating plant. Once they were destroyed, the North Vietnamese would have to depend on small isolated diesel plants for electricity. The semiportable diesel generators, as well as the petroleum to run them, entered the country by ship. The railroads and the trucks that carried food and ammunition ran on POL. As with much of the munitions, the trucks entered the country on ships.

In a 1 March memo, the chiefs reiterated the need for bombing. Sharp credited Lloyd and McPherson with getting him operational flexibility to conduct Rolling Thunder 49 in a way that allowed air strikes over almost all of North Vietnam. On 10 March, the chiefs urged POL attacks and mining to prevent resupply. On 26 March, the United States mined estuaries.

McNamara finally agreed to bomb POL sites. In April, the Joint Chiefs sent another memo requesting interdiction strikes, based on the military's knowledge that the Vietnamese were dispersing oil throughout the country in drums, using barges. McNamara supported that request as well. That month, however, Johnson gave approval only to plan strikes.

On 10 May, Sharp again asked to hit the North's POL. Finally Johnson relented, and on 22 June, the order came to bomb POL targets in Hanoi and Haiphong. Supplies to the Viet Cong stubbornly continued, however. Given the restrictions on how the planes were to attack the Hanoi and Haiphong port facilities, Lloyd and Sharp found that the North could maintain its resupply effort with dispersed supplies and modified import procedures. The Soviets supplied POL in fifty-five-gallon drums that the North Vietnamese off-loaded onto barges. As protection against further bomb damage, North Vietnam ensured that Soviet ships remained in port almost continuously. In sum, the POL campaign came a year too late.

McNamara was now thoroughly disenchanted with the bombing. The POL campaign would be the last major escalation of the air war that he would recommend. By September, he had shifted to emphasizing defense of the South and pacification.

In January 1966, an arms control advocate and McNaughton colleague from Harvard, Roger D. Fisher, had proposed a barrier along the north-to-south infiltration route in South Vietnam, essentially a line of sensors to trigger dormant munitions and signal for air attacks. McNaughton forwarded the proposal to McNamara, and the idea began circulating. It found its way to Sharp, Lloyd, and the chiefs, who were more than skeptical.

A group working under the auspices of the Institute for Defense Analyses and headed by Harvard's George B. Kistiakowsky worked through July and August to study the barrier and other technical aspects of the war. On 29 August, it submitted four inter-related reports. Together, they stated that the bombing had no effect on the POL resupply—if anything, more supplies were coming from the Soviet Union and China—and recommended the barrier.

On 3 September, McNamara asked the chiefs to look at the concept. The next day, at his behest, Rolling Thunder redirected its focus from attacks on POL to interdiction. On the eighth, Wheeler agreed to appoint Dodd Starbird to head Joint Task Force 728, the organization that would conduct the research and development on the barrier.

Lloyd said McNamara put this proposal, now called the McNamara Line, to the president some time in September. When the Office of the Secretary of Defense asked the Joint Chiefs of Staff for comment, Lloyd was in the hospital for a minor operation. As a consequence, the proposal went to J-5, Plans and Policy, who handled the response and gave the concept a qualified up-check, noting, nevertheless, a chain of technical problems that would require expensive solutions.

Problem number one, said Lloyd, was in the requirement for a line-of-sight radio to receive signals from the sensors. The radio would have to be on a Navy aircraft on station twenty-four hours a day—and that would cover only one portion of the line. The operation would require maritime patrol aircraft to fly from airfields, necessitating building more of them in country, a line item not in the construction plan. Logistic support would require another seaport. With the sensors in open country, in or near enemy-controlled territory, dedicated ground forces would have to protect them. To attack the enemy, once sensed, would require an area-type munition such as the CBU-24 cluster bomb. To produce enough CBU-24s to be effective would require an output from ten factories that did not exist. By the time the attack aircraft arrived on the scene, the target would have moved.

Despite all these objections, McNamara told them to proceed anyway. Notwithstanding his reluctance to heat munition production lines, the CBU bomb series was now his pet weapon. In January 1967, he made the CBU-24/29 the highest national priority.

As envisaged, the McNamara Line never happened. "Despite all sorts of special priorities and gimmicks the whole thing fell apart like the dinosaurs from its own monstrosity."

In May 1967, the president finally acceded to the military's persistent requests and agreed to hit the Hanoi power plant. McNamara and McNaughton were now out of step with the course of the air war. On 19 May, the day U.S. planes attacked the Hanoi plant, McNamara sent a draft presidential memorandum to Johnson announcing that he and McNaughton were departing from the U.S. commitment to support an independent, noncommunist South Vietnam. If the South did not help itself, they asserted, Washington did not have to continue the commitment. McNamara also restated his recommendation to reduce the bombing.

Advising McNamara not to forward his 19 May memo to the president, Wheeler rebutted by maintaining the commitment to South Vietnam and proposing expanded attacks on airfields, ports, and sea lines of communication, as well as mining. In his response, the chairman included another of Lloyd's Joint Staff studies stating that a partial or complete bombing pause would be an "aerial Dien Bien Phu."

The Joint Chiefs of Staff essentially were in revolt against their secretary of defense. The following day, McNamara ordered a new review of bombing options, and in four days the chiefs produced three memos: one that endorsed Westmoreland's recent request for an additional two hundred thousand ground troops; a second that proposed more bombing; and a third that advocated mining.

It was Lloyd's parting shot as J-3. On 25 May, he was relieved. He left behind a McNamara increasingly isolated in the administration. On 19 July, his key aide, John McNaughton, died tragically with his family in a plane crash. In late November, Johnson announced that his disillusioned defense secretary would leave his administration to become director of the World Bank. Rolling Thunder would continue in fits and starts for another year. Far from achieving its goals, the air campaign proceeded against what Lloyd came to regard as the most effective air defense system ever that contributed to the loss of more than nine hundred U.S. Air Force and Navy planes.

Reflecting on his time as J-3, Lloyd remembered how Wheeler would return from the White House late in the evening and ask him to come into his office where the chairman "would unburden himself."

"It was really the most frustrating piece of history you could ever go through," Lloyd bitterly recalled.

Here was the president who had been highly touted for his alleged ability as the greatest compromiser in the Congress, and his ability to get a compromise out of the North Vietnamese was something less than zero. They weren't going to compromise. There was no reason for them to compromise. Every day of the year, we were demonstrating to them that they could get exactly what they wanted, because we weren't doing anything to persuade them that that wasn't going to be successful. The longer Bus Wheeler went on describing what the president had to say, the more did it become apparent to me that the president had no realization that what was missing was leadership. But the person to provide it was himself, and he wasn't providing any of it at all. . . . The president didn't want the country to get behind the war. He wanted peace as usual, and business as usual at home. So a few thousand more American boys die in Southeast Asia; we'll send a nice telegram to their mothers and fathers. It was sickening to me to think about it. It was disgraceful.

Chapter 25

Career's End and Retirement

NEVER BETTER

Lloyd left the Pentagon in May 1967, putting the unfinished business of the Vietnam War behind him. After three years in a joint billet, he was eager to return to the Navy and hoped to be assigned to command of a fleet. He had three years in grade and for years had been one of the most senior in his class, but now, several of his classmates had passed him and had already acquired their fourth stars.

The action was in the Pacific, where the aviator admirals were getting the fleets, but Lloyd went to the Atlantic and another three-star billet as commander of its fleet amphibious force. It was a disappointment. His battles in Washington on behalf of Oley Sharp had made him few friends in the administration, and the posting was not merely the luck of the draw. The war was leaving its mark on both careers and families, and the Mustins were no exception.

In April 1964, Lloyd's brother-in-law, Tom Morton, then a rear admiral, had abruptly resigned his commission. As Sharp's war gaming assistant, Tom had crossed swords with Secretary of Defense McNamara and in particular with one of his whiz kids, Alain Enthoven, the assistant secretary of defense for systems analysis. After almost three years of battling against McNamara's service policies, he began to voice his growing frustrations to his fellow senior officers, privately noting how McNamara "was destroying the Navy."

In an attempt to save what had been a fast-track career, Vice Adm. William R. Smedberg, the chief of naval personnel, offered Tom the post of chief negotiator at Panmunjom in the Korean demilitarized zone. The job would have placed him far from Washington but still in line for a fleet command, and Lloyd tried to persuade him to take it, but Tom refused. To his mind, resignation was now a matter of personal honor.

After his separation, Tom came to see the civilian leadership, by virtue of its dubious policies, stumbling into an unwinnable land war in Asia. For Lloyd, the honorable course of action was for senior officers to remain in the service, prevail in the Washington policy debates, and thereby win the war. The views of these two men were by no means academic. Three family members had been or were about to be in-country, in combat. Lloyd's two sons, Hank and Tom, had consecutive service in river patrol boats. Their cousin, Joe Howard, flew helicopter support with the Seawolves. At virtually every family gathering, Lloyd and Tom would air their frustrations at each other.

Lloyd's son-in-law, Lt. Cdr. Larry Baldauf, also was outraged at the handling of the Vietnam War, but his protestations took a much more public form. In the autumn of 1965, disgusted with McNamara and the administration's conduct of the air war, Larry had tendered his resignation from the Navy, although his service commitment would not expire until June 1966. He had not drawn Vietnam duty himself, but a number of his friends already had either died in the enemy skies or were languishing in the Hanoi Hilton as prisoners of war. "Angry and idealistic," he believed the intelligentsia in Washington were "deliberately trying to lose the war."

When the Navy refused his request to resign his commission, Larry filed a lawsuit against Secretary of the Navy Paul Nitze in November. In the autumn of 1966, he lost his suit. His response was to "turn in" his wings and begin a letter-writing campaign to senior commanders, including Vice Adm. John J. Hyland, Seventh Fleet commander, and Adm. Roy L. Johnson, commander in chief, Pacific Fleet. At the same time, he published an article in *Aviation Week* saying that the CNO was attempting to solve the Navy's growing pilot retention problem by pressuring the civilian airlines not to recruit or hire naval aviators. In the spring of 1967, the Navy court-martialed Larry under Article 88 of the Uniform Code of Military Justice, alleging that he used contemptuous language against the president. In the end, the service dropped charges, issued a letter of reprimand, and in June granted him an honorable discharge.

Larry returned to Coronado. With the assistance of the John Birch Society, he went on a year-long nationwide speaking tour that included television appearances on such provocative fare as *The Joe Pyne Show*. In July 1968, he published a paperback, *Bah Bah*

Blue Sheep, that accused a number of senior naval officers of being "yes men" and injudiciously—and moreover inaccurately—cited Lloyd by name.

In mid-July 1967, Lloyd's eldest son Hank arrived in Honolulu and reported for duty as Oley Sharp's flag lieutenant on the Pacific Fleet staff. There, he learned what might have been the most compelling reason for his father's failure to get his fourth star: Admiral Sharp revealed his belief that Larry's actions weighed heavily in the selection board deliberations and ultimately sank Lloyd's chances for promotion.

However bitter the fruit of his Joint Staff labors, Lloyd was never one to dwell on a setback. In the summer of 1967, he and Emily moved to their quarters at the amphibious base in Little Creek, Virginia, and he turned to his new duties as commander, Amphibious Forces, Atlantic.

His force consisted of two amphibious groups: one deployed in the Mediterranean; the other, in the Caribbean. In early June, many of his units in the Med went on alert for possible operations in connection with the Arab-Israeli Six Day War. For Lloyd, however, the command would prove to be a year of routine care-taking.

Most of his effort went to administering his command from his headquarters in Little Creek or aboard the amphibious force flagship *Taconic.* Elements of his stateside force conducted various exercises and made port visits along the Atlantic and Gulf coasts and into the Caribbean. In the Med, his ships maintained what had become a routine postwar presence.

Years later, Lloyd remembered this tour more for the opportunity it provided to travel with Emily. Together they toured Europe; Lloyd attended a series of meetings with senior naval and military commanders in London and Brussels, where he met with the Supreme Allied Commander, Europe, Gen. Lyman Lemnitzer, USA. The second half of their swing was through the Mediterranean and took them to Heraklion in Crete and Naples.

Lloyd's dream of commanding a fleet would not become a reality. Indeed, according to his son Tom, he had wanted either to relieve Sharp, who retired in the summer of 1968, or to get the billet of commander, naval forces, Vietnam, that went instead to Elmo R. "Bud" Zumwalt. In July of that summer, against his wishes, he returned to joint duty and "the nuclear business" as director of the Defense Atomic Support Agency. Lloyd and Emily moved their household to quarters at the Washington Navy Yard.

Once installed at DASA, Lloyd was disappointed to find that his staff was made up largely of scientists pursuing weapons effects tasks and others charged with seeing to nuclear weapons logistics. He felt they were "completely non-oriented to anything operational. They were all nuclear types really." Immediately, he set to correcting this shortcoming, writing directives and policy documents that he hoped would form a record that he or his successors could later use.

Part of Lloyd's job was to evaluate and monitor the safety of nuclear weapon systems. DASA was addressing nuclear safety issues in the wake of several spectacular accidents, the latest of which had happened on 21 January 1968, when a Strategic Air Command B-52 crashed seven miles off-shore on sea ice in Baffin Bay near the Thule air and radar base in Greenland. The shock from the crash detonated the conventional high explosives in the aircraft's bombs and scattered radioactive debris over a twenty-acre site. The incident precipitated a crisis between the United States and Denmark that still reverberates today, as the Danes debate their participation in any ballistic missile defense scheme. Immediately after the mishap, the Office of the Secretary of Defense suspended routine Strategic Air Command bomber patrols with nuclear weapons.

As part of the decontamination of the crash site, the agency had to remove 237 tons of radioactive ice and debris. The United States lost four bombs, of which it was able to retrieve only three, in spite of an extensive underwater search by submarine. The cleanup continued until August and thus into Lloyd's watch.

Another of his duties was to advise the services and the Joint Chiefs of Staff of any technical problems or issues regarding their nuclear weapons that came to his notice. In one case, his experts discovered a technical feature of the B-52 bombing system that appeared to make it vulnerable to an unintended release of an armed bomb. DASA recommended some corrections to the Air Force, although Lloyd was never sure whether the service acted on it.

Early in the Nixon administration, Assistant Secretary of Defense for Atomic Energy Dr. Carl Walske formed a blue ribbon defense panel to review nuclear safety issues. Walske had been very unpopular with chief atomic scientists Bill Ogle and Norris Bradbury, both of whom worked at what was then called the Los Alamos Scientific Laboratory, one of the Atomic Energy Commission's major labs. The panel's report was coauthored by J. Fred Buzhardt, the Pentagon's general counsel. "Of course lawyers have the inept conviction that they know everything about everything and they're the best qualified people to run anything," said Lloyd. Buzhardt, he said, produced "the most arrant subjective nonsense you ever heard."

Walske wanted to take business from DASA and put it under his office as Chairman of the Military Liaison Committee. The blue ribbon panel recommended a civilian under the secretary of defense for operations. "What a fiasco," Lloyd said, "typical of their shallow perceptions."

During Lloyd's tenure as director, DASA was the executive agency for DoD participation in the cleanup of Bikini Atoll. It provided most of the men and equipment under Joint Task Force 8, which was supported by an Atomic Energy Commission contractor. The cleanup was completed on 27 October 1968, and in 1969, on 2 May, Lloyd gave Defense Secretary Melvin Laird a status report. Years later, he related how the remediation plan included replanting coconut palms to help the island economy. Unfortunately, all that the palms produced was "radioactive coconuts," evidence that the atoll would stubbornly remain uninhabitable.

Operationally attuned, as DASA director, Lloyd sought to involve himself in the entire range of nuclear weaponry, including delivery systems, as well as in the determination of U.S. nuclear posture. He thus advised the Joint Chiefs of Staff on the strategic nuclear attack plans against the Soviet Union and purposed to brief the CinCs himself—rather than sending an action officer—to help them determine their nuclear weapon requirements. "But the OSD subordinates still played their familiar game," he said, "and the [DoD] requests to the AEC reflected assorted political ideologies, not military judgments." In particular, John Foster, the director of defense research and engineering in the Office of the Secretary of Defense, who had a background in nuclear weapons, opted to make the decisions on nuclear weapon kinds and quantities without attention to CinC or the Joint Chiefs' recommendations.

Lloyd's DASA responsibilities did not include coordinating the design of weapon systems, and the Nixon administration and Laird, he claimed, refused to let the military act on some very attractive proposals. For example, the CinCs and the JCS wanted a warhead that could destroy Soviet missile silos. In the interest of détente, administration officials insisted that such a warhead would be destabilizing.

Once again, he was butting heads with what he saw as the Washington arms control cabal that was beholden to the 1963 Limited Test Ban Treaty. It "was supposed to be a great step toward doing something about nuclear weapons," said Lloyd, "but all it did was multiply by an enormous factor the cost of developing each new weapon which went right on anyway, because we had to keep up with the Russians."

The year before the treaty, he maintained, the United States had a stockpile of thirty thousand nuclear weapons that were immensely superior to the Soviets', and the Atomic Energy Commission had some twelve reactors to sustain them. When he arrived as DASA, the number of warheads was in decline. By 1968, "the stable of stumble bums

McNamara had assembled at the Defense Department had reduced the stockpile to 10,000 warheads, sustained by one or two reactors [somewhat of an overstatement]. The SIOP [Single Integrated Operation Plan] planners could identify more strategic targets, alone, than that, not to mention the needs for tactical weapons. This was systematic dismantling, unilateral disarmament, started by the Kennedy/Johnson Administration, and not reversed by their successors."

During his time, DASA was continuing underground nuclear testing at the Nevada Test Site and at the Cannikin nuclear test site under the seabed of the North Pacific at the Aleutian island of Amchitka. In 1969, the agency conducted forty-five underground shots in Nevada and one in Alaska. In 1971, Lloyd's final year as director, the totals were twenty-three and one. The one Cannikin test was to verify nuclear warhead performance for the Spartan missile interceptor. Conducted on 6 November, three months after Lloyd retired, it detonated a five-megaton warhead and resulted in one of the largest subsurface nuclear blasts ever.

In 1969, the DASA staff briefed the Scientific Advisory Group on Effects (SAGE) on the results of survivability testing of U.S. systems should they be exposed to nuclear attack. Particular worries were the durability of the Minuteman II guidance system against radiation, the hardiness of missile reentry vehicle, and the vulnerability of silo design and electronic systems to an electromagnetic pulse.

Operational effects such as an electromagnetic pulse disruption of buried communication links had intrigued Lloyd ever since the 1962 Kingfish test. He thus had DASA examine Soviet nuclear testing, including some of their earlier tests. In one series, the Soviets had launched missile warheads from one of their standard missile sites, along with additional warheads and devices, toward their impact site in Siberia. They would detonate nuclear warheads at varying distances from the test warheads, using extensive instrumentation to determine what happened. "How much blackout effect occurred over what region around the detonation? Were ground-based radars blanked out against follow-on warheads, for example? That's another one of these high-altitude effects."

Their tests gave the Soviets important data on the size and degree of the nuclear blackout effect around detonations in and above the atmosphere. One finding of operational significance was that ground-based radars attempting to detect and target another warhead would be unable to see through a large and very highly dynamic blackout region, moving at many miles a second.

Under Lloyd, DASA continually improved the U.S. capability to monitor these Soviet tests. Under the Limited Test Ban Treaty, it was a violation if, as the result of a test, radioactive material could be shown to have drifted across a border. While DASA's monitors readily captured evidence of Soviet violations, the United States made no charges. Defense scientists were grateful to get any material that drifted across the Pacific and analyzed it to determine what the Soviets were doing.

One such analysis confirmed that the Soviets had completed an extraordinarily sophisticated electromagnetic pulse test. Lloyd now had every indication that their data provided "them with minute details of information that are important to both sides of the question of nuclear missile offense and defense." Equally significant, he knew that the quality of U.S. data was not as good. As a result of their 1961 and 1962 atmospheric nuclear test programs, he concluded, the Soviets were years ahead in scientific and technical information on the nuclear blackout effect. It was, said Lloyd, "a bitter pill for the U.S. scientific community to have to swallow."

"And if you recognize that state of affairs," he later added, "then you find it easy to recognize why it was that [the Soviets] were so gracefully willing to let us join with them in a treaty which would deny ourselves the opportunity to accomplish the kind of test that they'd [already] accomplished."

Lloyd's career was heading to a close. Approaching his sixties but still in superb physical condition, he swam every day in the Pentagon Officers Athletic Association pool. One afternoon in the spring of 1971, he was in the middle of his laps, trailing at a cautious distance a swimmer in a parallel lane. As the pair approached the side of the pool, the man ahead made a careless turn. Flinging himself at an angle, he collided with Lloyd, poking a finger straight into his eye and rupturing the left eyeball.

The injury was most serious. Lloyd was in hospital for some time as doctors tried to restore sight to his eye. Their efforts failed. He would have to retire. A forty-three-year naval career was at an end, officially on 1 August.

Though the Mustins remained in the Washington area, buying a home in Alexandria, Virginia, Lloyd chose not to join the ranks of defense consultants. Instead, he became active in the National Rifle Association, of which he had been a life member since 1938. The winner of numerous NRA rifle and pistol awards, he served two terms as NRA president, from 1977 to 1979, during which time membership doubled to two million. Well into the mid-1980s, he worked for the organization as a volunteer emeritus and later was a member of the U.S. Olympic Committee for shooting sports, taking part in decisions to bring the 1984 Olympics to Los Angeles.

After a lifetime of long separations, Lloyd vowed that in his retirement Emily would go everywhere with him. They were frequent travelers, most often shuttling to San Diego to be with family and classmates for any occasion. Perhaps his favorite activity was deep-sea fishing. With his classmate and first-cousin-by-marriage, Don Thomas, he would go on excursions from such resorts as Cabo San Lucas at the southernmost tip of Baja California.

In the summer of 1988, Emily underwent an apparently successful operation to remove a brain tumor. She returned home, and Lloyd and the children, especially Doug, bravely attempted a variety of therapies to help her regain her faculties. Their efforts were for naught. The tumor had metastasized, and Emily died on 1 April 1989. The funeral service was at the Naval Academy Chapel, after which Lloyd laid his bride to rest in the family plot on Hospital Point, several stones from her brother, mother, grandparents, and other relatives.

Though he carried his loss with grace, Lloyd was bereft. His brother Henry observed, "He has always been a winner, but this was a fight he lost." Lloyd chose to remain in his Alexandria home, and for several years, his regular companions were the housekeepers who cooked and cleaned for him and his much-adored cat, Kate. Family events and holidays would bring him to Coronado, and when a small bungalow became available across the park from his daughter Doug, she and her brothers finally persuaded him to move there in July 1996. His grandchildren and great-grandchildren would visit daily to swim in his pool or a play in the park across the street. Said Doug, "There was not a child this man did not enjoy."

In 1998, Lloyd suffered a stroke that left him virtually bedridden. Between family visits, he would pass the time watching World War II documentaries on the History Channel. Doug recalled a favorite phrase of her father's on hearing the excited voices of his young descendants playing in his pool just outside his bedroom window: "'The peals of delight from those happy little people.' This lasted until the final days of his life, when a visit from any of his eleven great-grandchildren never failed to lift his spirits." The children's cards and artwork adorned the walls all around him.

As Lloyd's condition failed, his San Diego extended family moved their traditional Friday night feast, called "Family Night," to his bungalow. A dozen or more relatives and friends would gather in his living room for food and drinks. In groups of three or four, they would cycle to his bedside, where he would be happily sipping Black Label Jack Daniels through a straw. His particular joy was to sing along with them the many Naval Academy fight songs and in particular his favorite ditty from the China Station, "Meet Me by the Slop Chute on the Ol' Whang Poo."

On 21 January 1999, complications from another stroke finally took his life. The family held a memorial service at the North Island Chapel. They then returned him to Annapolis for a funeral service at the Naval Academy Chapel, after which he was buried with full military honors, at last to reunite with his beloved Emily.

"My grandfather was perhaps the most brilliant man I have ever met," said Lt. Cdr. John Burton Mustin, Naval Academy Class of 1990, "though the least inclined to bring that to my attention. His even-keeled nature and academic and professional achievements defined him as a man, and though his innovative and heroic naval exploits are well documented in the history books, he was simply a loving, supportive doting grandfather to my siblings and me."

Lloyd was an ordnance man whose experience encompassed the entire range of weaponry, from pistols to nukes. He was a naval professional par excellence, but as a man he touched lives not through the quantity of his moments, but through their quality.

"Later I asked my mom," said Doug at the 2001 christening of the *Mustin,* "'How did you stand it, Mom? He was away so much. He missed so many things, Christmases, births, graduations, weddings. You had to handle it alone.' Her answer to me was, 'I could stand it because I knew that when your father was standing on the bridge of a destroyer, there was not a happier man alive in this world.'"

For those who came to visit him in his last months and asked, "How's it going?" Lloyd's reply was always the same. "Never better."

PART III
The Surface Warriors

Chapter 26

Hank Mustin

CHILDHOOD AND USNA—
GROOMING FOR THE A TEAM

Of her eldest son, Henry Croskey Mustin, Emily would often say that he "was born with his feet planted firmly on the ground." In the late 1940s, while attending St. Stephen's School in Alexandria, Virginia, he would acquire the name Hank, as if to reinforce a rootedness, despite his many moves as a Navy junior.

Hank's earliest memories are of Annapolis in 1938 and the succeeding summers filled with swimming, sailing, fishing, crabbing, and family gatherings with his extended Howard and Claude family that numbered in the scores, many with a connection to the Navy and the academy. His closest companion was his first cousin once removed, Joseph Bowyer Howard, Anne Thomas's younger brother. Although a generation ahead of him, Joe was only six years older, virtually an older brother. A gifted athlete, Joe distinguished himself in lacrosse at Severn School and later at the Naval Academy, where he graduated in the class of 1950.

The Mustins spent the war in Annapolis. In the autumn of 1945, Hank started seventh grade. Within a few months, the family moved to Norfolk, where the school system operated on a split-year scheme. Not understanding the system, when the school official asked whether her son was in seven low or seven high, Emily replied, "Of course, he's in seven high," and Hank skipped half a grade.

The Mustins remained in Norfolk only until the spring of 1946, when Lloyd got duty with the Bureau of Ordnance. Upon the move to Alexandria, where the school system did not have split years, Emily registered Hank at St. Stephen's and was adamant that he would not repeat seventh grade. She succeeded in getting him into the last quarter of the eighth. In the end, Hank skipped a full year of his schooling.

Originally an Episcopal elementary school, St. Stephen's was at the time progressively adding high school grade levels. When Hank finished eighth grade, the school added ninth grade. The next year, it offered tenth. As a tenth grader, Hank was captain of the football and baseball teams. The high scorer on the basketball team and the player with the highest batting average on the baseball team, he won both teams' cups as outstanding player, as well as the cup for the school's outstanding athlete.

In the late summer of 1948, the family went to Coronado when Lloyd got command of his first ship. At fifteen, Hank was coming of age, and his successes back East transferred easily to his junior year at Coronado High School. During the football season, he began a friendship with another athlete, Jim Voit, an accomplished guitarist with a folk trio that played at all the high school and youth events in town. In the tradition of his musical grandfather, Hank decided to learn guitar, and Voit taught him.

When Voit and his trio graduated, Hank formed his own country western–folk group to replace them. In no time, they became a fixture within Coronado's teenage Navy circles. Nick Reynolds, the younger brother of one of Hank's friends, often would pester the group to let him join. Their response, said Hank, was always, "Get lost, kid; you're too young." Undeterred, Nick later would join two other folk guitarists and form his own group, known later to the world as the Kingston Trio.

For a year, Hank washed cars and cut grass to get the money to buy his first guitar. One of his regular customers was Frances Mitscher. Widow of the wartime hero Adm. Pete Mitscher, she was close to Hank's grandmother, Corinne, who with her husband, retired Adm. George Murray, frequently would come to North Island to visit the Mustins and their friends. The Murrays would host grand cocktail parties at the air station's flag cabin, and Hank often would find himself in the presence of such naval notables as Halsey and Nimitz. "The events of the war were fresh in these guys' minds," he recalled. "They would be talking over what now are the famous battles of World War II, and they'd be saying, 'Well, so-and-so was a nervous Nellie and a son of a bitch, and abandoned his ship too early.' They talked the way we do about guys that are the giants of history. All of that stuff had a great influence on me."

As a youngster, Hank loved to listen to every word, said Emily. It was all Navy, and he thrived on it. The Mustins entertained often, and the guests, Hank noted, were "the outstanding people from the Naval Academy." He respected and admired his father and his friends. "[T]here was never really any doubt in my mind from the earliest time I remember, I wanted to be in the Navy and be like my dad and follow in his footsteps." Lloyd "never said, 'You should go to the Naval Academy,'" said Hank, "but . . . in a thousand unwritten ways, I can see now, he set the stage."

In 1949, the summer between his junior and senior year at Coronado High, he went to sea with his father on his destroyer, the *Keppler*. Onboard for an overnight run to San Francisco for a Fleet Week, Hank took his guitar and entertained the officers in his father's in-port cabin. Later he went below and jammed with the sailors. The boy was a hit. That autumn, he played football and during the winter season captained the swimming team. In the spring of 1950, he graduated.

Not yet seventeen, he was too young for the Naval Academy, but neither Lloyd or Emily wanted him to do a year in a West Coast university, fearing the effect on his resolve. Lloyd expected Washington duty soon, and Emily preferred that he attend a "gentleman's school." The family decision was for him to enter the University of Virginia. Joining the freshman class that autumn, he entered Navy ROTC and pledged Sigma Alpha Epsilon. Following his father's athletic tradition, he also was on the swim team.

Hank's determination to attend the Naval Academy was unshakable. He took the entrance exam at the Charlottesville, Virginia, recruiting headquarters and then traveled to Annapolis to take the physical. After emerging from the eye exam, he joined the line for the next test, but he was despondent; he knew he had just failed the vision test.

The Mustins found a well-known Washington eye doctor whose claim to fame was a remedial vision program for his young patients. They would "look at a lot of colored lights and rotating things" and thus train themselves to pass the exam. "I think really what he did," Hank confided, "was teach you how to read the blurs." In his second effort, he passed the eye exam by the skin of his teeth.

Hank had competed for a presidential appointment, reserved for sons of military officers. At the time, the academy also had a program essentially for athletes, a Public Law 586 appointment from the secretary of the navy. The admissions office determined that he should enter via that route to release a slot on the presidential appointments for a non-athlete. Hank was finally set to be a midshipman.

On 2 July 1951, a third-generation Mustin walked into the Yard to report. By the time the entire class of 1955 reported later in the summer, its number had swelled to 1,094.

Two months short of his eighteenth birthday, Hank was, like his father, among the youngest in his class.

By 1946, the academy had grown to brigade size, and the competition for places on the sports teams was very keen. Some five hundred plebes submitted their names for plebe football. Although very much an athlete, Hank could see he would not make the cut. Reluctantly concluding that the swim team also would be beyond his reach, he turned to intramural sports, where he starred on the brigade champion swimming and water polo teams.

During plebe summer, he made what would be a lifelong friendship with a fellow athlete who was a college transfer from Stanford, Hugh Larimer Webster. A football player and another Navy junior, Webby remembered that they immediately "clicked." He was amazed at Hank's Navy savvy, which equaled, if not bettered, his own. Hank seemed to know many of the academy's senior officers and their histories—from Ike Kidd, the superintendent's flag secretary, to Joe Taussig, a third-generation Navy hero of Pearl Harbor.

Hank's roommate was a quiet New Yorker, Donald Charles Shelton. Webby roomed with John Anthony Adams, a Marquette transfer from Wisconsin. Though a good friend to them all, Shelton spent what time he had with his steady. Hence, Mustin, Webster, and Adams became an inseparable trio during their four years at the academy and remained close throughout their lives.

At the end of plebe year, their class had dropped to 914. Hank stood 581st. His best performance was in English, history, and government, where he was 94th. In conduct, however, he was 724th.

Hank was not a student, said Webby. He remembered routinely finding Hank catnapping on his light blue academy bedspread, known as the Blue Dragon. Wrote Shelton of his roommate in the *Lucky Bag,* "With the advent of Plebe year academics, a four year, tooth and nail struggle with the Skinny Department ensued. However, Hank was determined; he managed to tear himself away from his beloved Blue Dragon long enough to acquire the dope to emerge triumphant into a Navy career."

Hank did not regard himself as a very good midshipman and regretted his Naval Academy performance throughout his career. He had enormous respect for the institution, the professional subjects, and the history and the traditions of the service, but he felt many of the academy routines had nothing to do with the Navy. "I thought a lot of it was kind of Mickey Mouse," he said. "When I went on cruise, I was always in the highest aptitude marks in leadership, but when we came back to the Academy I just didn't like a lot of that unrealistic stuff."

The officer with the most profound influence on him was John G. Drew, his battalion commander, of the class of 1942. "He was as close to John Wayne as you can get." Another was Lt. Dave Bagley, a company officer who later became commander of U.S. naval forces in Europe. Also highly admired was the commandant, Capt. R. T. S. Keith.

"These guys had been at the Naval Academy together and were separated by two full grades in the officer structure of the instructors. The senior guys were combat veterans, and they had a whole different sense of what was important than the junior guys, who had never made it into the War. So the senior guys wanted midshipmen to be leaders, do well in athletics and pay attention to yourself."

Lieutenants filled most of the faculty positions, affecting adversely the academy's accreditation. More seriously for the midshipmen, they tended to focus on the "Mickey Mouse" stuff. As a consequence, Hank and most of his career-minded classmates revered the senior officers and held the junior officers in considerably lower regard.

The academy class of 1952 would graduate only 783 of the 1,042 who entered as plebes. The high attrition rates, running in the mid–20 percent range during the Korean War and just after, were the result of a policy that allowed midshipmen to resign until the start of their second class year. Many would enter from the Marine Corps, Army, or Navy and then immediately resign or purposefully fail their academics. Having prior service, they were not required to register for the draft. "So a large number of the people who were in there were glorified draft dodgers," said Hank. With the Korean cease-fire of 27 July 1953, more mids quit, married, or "deliberately bilged out."

Hank got his first crack at "the Navy's more realistic stuff" with Task Group 86.1 during the 1952 midshipmen's practice cruise to Europe. In the 1950s, the cruises did not go into the Mediterranean but instead went to northern Europe, followed by exercises and drills in the Guantánamo operating area. Hank and his fellow third classmen would serve as seamen on the cruise, and the first classmen would lead the sections. TG 86.1 included the most modern battleships, the *Missouri* and *Wisconsin*. Hank's assignment was to the *Meredith,* one of the destroyers that accompanied the *Missouri*. On 7 June, the cruise departed Annapolis Roads for Norfolk, where they took aboard NROTC midshipmen before going to sea the next day.

On 5 September, Hank and his class returned as third classmen. By now, he was wearing glasses and was somewhat fearful of the impact his vision might have on his future career. The Navy offered no eyesight waivers for either submarines or aviation; thus he never considered either of those two communities. "How am I going to keep my eyes good enough to get an unrestricted line commission?" he asked himself. "I concentrated on not having to go to the Supply Corps."

For the summer of 1953, the class divided into four battalions and went for two weeks of joint amphibious training with the West Point Class of 1955 at Little Creek, Virginia. Leave ran from 20 June to 20 July, after which the class returned for a three-week aircraft carrier cruise to Halifax, Nova Scotia, on the *Bennington* and *Valley Forge*. Flight indoctrination followed in Annapolis, during which time Hank enjoyed flying the pontooned N3N biplanes, nicknamed the Yellow Perils. Then followed another ten days of aviation orientation at the Naval Air Test Center at Patuxent River and additional instruction in the Philadelphia area that included hands-on training in fire fighting.

On the first day of Christmas leave, he took Johnny Adams to Alexandria, where they could unwind for several hours at the Mustin home before Johnny had to leave for Milwaukee. Adams remembered arriving at the Mustins' to find Hank's fifteen-year-old sister, Doug, playing a board game on the living room carpet with one of her school friends, Lucy Holcomb. Later in the holiday, Lucy's brother Russ got four tickets to a Harlem Globetrotters game and proposed that he and Hank double date. "I'll tell you what," said Holcomb, "if you can't get a date, I'll take your sister, and you take mine." After going to that Globetrotters game, Hank never dated anyone else.

Lucy's father, Russ Sr., was a colonel in the Army Reserve, an ordnance engineer from a well-to-do St. Louis family. Kay, her mother, was an elegant and soft-spoken Tennessean. Said Lucy, her mother was "ahead of her time because she had graduated from college." With a major in math and a minor in chemistry, she got a job as a lab technician in St. Louis, where she met and married Russ. When war came, Russ drew duty in the Pentagon, and the family moved to Alexandria.

In the late summer of 1951, just prior to her entry into ninth grade, Lucy met Doug Mustin poolside at the Army–Navy Country Club in Arlington. The girls immediately became fast friends. Through the winter and into the spring, Lucy and Doug would drive to Annapolis for basketball games, movies, and Saturday night hops and Sunday afternoon tea dances. For five dollars a night, they could stay at a "drag house," a boarding house for the midshipmen's girlfriends, usually run by a spinster or Navy widow. Their favorite was conveniently situated at the end of Hanover Street along the academy wall beside Gate Three. As Hank and Lucy deepened their relationship, Doug became the companion to a number of midshipmen, including Webby and a tennis star named Larry Baldauf, whom she would marry in 1956.

For the many June Week events at end of his second class year, Hank had Lucy on his arm. Half a year into their relationship, it was clear to both that they had found a partner for life. Hank proposed at the Hanover Street drag house, and at the Ring Dance of 1954, they became engaged.

On 5 June, Hank reported to the *Missouri* for his first class practice cruise, designated TG 40.1. First stop was Norfolk. Steaming from Hampton Roads on 7 June was memorable as the only time the four *Iowa*-class battleships—the *Iowa, New Jersey, Wisconsin,* and *Missouri*—ever operated together. Only the latter two ships continued eastbound, however. On this cruise, Hank was a "big wheel in the midshipman organization." He was the engineer officer. As with his other classmates, it was his time to supervise the third class at sea.

On 19 June, TG 40.1 arrived in Lisbon; the ships then were in Cherbourg from 3 to 10 July. Hank, Johnny, and Webby took the train to Paris, where they visited a Mustin family friend who was the naval attaché. While sightseeing, Hank bought a cheap guitar, and Adams remembered his strumming and singing in the Left Bank cafés as fans spotted them rounds of drinks. The entrepreneurial trio also financed themselves through cigarette sales. Able to buy a carton of American cigarettes for seventy cents from the ship store, they would hawk them to the French by the pack at a markup.

On 3 September, Hank and his classmates returned to Annapolis for their first class year. Into the autumn, Lucy and Doug were regular fixtures for the football weekends and other social events. On Sunday mornings, Hank, Webby, and the two girls would fulfill the midshipman chapel requirement at St. Anne's in the center of town. There, they would select a back pew, to allow the two mids to prop themselves against the girls' shoulders to steal some sorely needed sleep.

A two-striper platoon commander during the winter months, Hank graduated 503d of 742 and for first class year stood 447th. After several years of a 20-odd percent attrition rate, his class lost 32.6 percent, the highest rate since 1949. Many who remained, however, had distinguished careers. "I think we had seventeen flag and general officers out of the class," said Hank, "a really distinguished bunch of guys."

In the 1950s, the glamorous officer of the line was called a destroyer sailor—what Hank wanted to be. Service selection "was very different then, than it is now," he noted. "Then you went and drew your service selection preference out of a hat. It was a lottery. So if you wanted to be in one of the ships or homeports where there were too many candidates, you could have been out of luck."

Hank wanted a modern destroyer and Coronado as his home port. On service selection night, he drew a number high enough to let him pick a San Diego-based *Gearing*-class radar picket destroyer by name—the *Duncan*. He went into June Week a very happy man.

Lloyd was on another western Pacific deployment and unable to attend the graduation festivities, but he had sent Hank money to purchase a new family car with his midshipman discount. Hank bought his parents a baby blue 1955 Ford convertible. One afternoon immediately prior to June Week, he and Webby lowered the top of the new car and drove from Annapolis to view the house in suburban Bay Ridge where the Webster family would stay for the week. Tempting fate, the pair stopped on the way for a six-pack of beer.

Once in the community, Hank slowed the car as they scanned the street for the correct address. A crew-cut resident recognized Webby and stopped the pair. He happened to be a Marine captain who was one of the academy's company officers. According to Webby, the marine first hailed at the very moment Hank had "a can in his teeth." Thanks in part to the strenuous efforts of his uncle, Tom Morton, then a captain with Washington duty who lived with his family outside of Annapolis on Crab Creek, Hank was charged only with a Class A offense. His punishment was confinement to his room for the duration of June Week, with the requirement to report every half hour to the duty officer. The parties took place at the Mortons and elsewhere without him.

It was an unfortunate end to his academy career, markedly different than his father's but one very much in the spirit of his grandfather, whose record as a cadet was similarly checkered. Looking west, Hank was eager to enter the real Navy, where performance was not measured by grades or adherence to arbitrary regulation. He had set his course to be a bold leader of men who was prepared to sail into harm's way. Indeed, he had purposed to be an officer of the line, the classic breed of naval officer who, halfway through his career, would come to be known as surface warrior.

Chapter 27

The Young Destroyerman
in the Cavalry

Following the academy and St. Agnes commencement ceremonies, Hank, Doug, and Lucy drove the Mustin's convertible across country to Coronado. Lloyd, Emily, and Tom had returned to the family's house at 850 B Avenue the previous autumn, when Lloyd got his deep draft command in the Pacific. In late June, the three graduates arrived to enjoy a two-month leave filled with parties, swimming, and surfing before Hank was to deploy.

The trip was Lucy's first foray west of the Mississippi. The summer would serve as her introduction to Navy life ashore during the mid-1950s. Doug was heading west to attend college in San Diego. Quickly reentering the social whirl of Coronado, she reconnected with one of her academy companions, Larry Baldauf. Larry was set to go to Pensacola for aviation training, but as the summer progressed, he and Doug began to date steadily. Early 1956 would see two back-to-back Mustin weddings.

As the deployment date approached, a number of freshly minted ensigns began to descend on Coronado. Webby had drawn duty on the *Brown,* a destroyer in Hank's division. Before they left Annapolis, he had arranged with Hank to send his cruise box to 850 B, where they agreed to rendezvous on 1 August, the day they were to report to their ships.

Preparing for his departure, Hank put Lucy on a plane to Washington. During his deployment, she would remain with her parents in Alexandria and attend Washington's Holton Arms, then a junior college. On 1 August, he reported aboard the *Duncan* and then promptly returned home to await his classmate's arrival. Leaving it to the very last to report, Webby drove across country nonstop for thirty-six hours. When he arrived at 850 B, Hank piled him, along with Doug and Larry, into the family car and made way for a cocktail party hosted by his cousins, Anne and Don Thomas. Joined by a number of junior officers and Coronado High School friends, the gathering lasted until dawn.

Later that morning and somewhat the worse for the wear, Hank and Webby went aboard their ships. As the *Duncan* made her way through San Diego Harbor, Hank and the other two new ensigns were on the bridge with the captain. Word came that several small craft were maneuvering hazardously around the ship. "I went out to the wing of the bridge," recalled Hank, "and here's this gang of guys and girls in bikinis that I'd been partying with the night before, saying, 'See you in six months, Hank.' So, this was a source of great embarrassment to me. I was hoping the captain didn't hear who they were talking to, but he did." The craft also buzzed the *Brown,* prompting in Webby the same bemused discomfort. So began their first Western Pacific tour.

"In my view, at that time, the guys who sought adventure wanted to go on the Pacific," said Hank. Unlike the Atlantic Fleet, the Pacific Navy was self-contained, accustomed to operating at long distances at the discretion of the Pacific Fleet commander. "They used to say that the people in the Pacific fight the wars, and the people in the Atlantic talk about them."

"The fact that Coronado ships were in the Pacific Fleet was icing on the cake. I wanted to be in a destroyer in Coronado. I knew Lucy would like it, and my dad was out there as a destroyer tender commander."

The Korean War had been over for two years. The front-line mission of the Pacific Fleet was now patrolling the Taiwan Strait and protecting Nationalist China. Webby and Hank had only one goal—to be destroyer skippers. "The destroyers were the glamour element of the surface navy," said Hank. "If you were a destroyer sailor, you were the cavalry."

In those days, each destroyer division had four destroyers: one long-hull radar picket destroyer, a straight stick, long-hull destroyer, and two *Fletcher*-class 445s. Two divisions made a squadron. Pacific destroyers primarily were serving as escorts, screening the carrier battle groups in the strike force, Task Force 77.

Hank was fortunate to be in the *Duncan,* the division's radar picket destroyer (DDR). Before the Fleet Rehabilitation and Modernization Program, which added substantial antisubmarine warfare capability to World War II destroyers, a DDR was a coveted ship, and the *Duncan* had one of the earliest three-dimensional radars, the SPS-8. "But we could never get the thing to work. So we never really had height information." It was before missiles, and the DDRs were attempting only to track aircraft, then still propeller-driven planes with huge radar signatures.

A day after his departure, Hank had his first meeting with the *Duncan*'s captain, Cdr. Ed Conrad, to get his assignment. Asked what department he would prefer, Hank said gunnery. Conrad's other two new ensigns were from Purdue and Princeton, two famous engineering schools, but they were forestry and history majors, respectively. "I know what you took at the Naval Academy, because I took the same course," Conrad told his third new ensign, "so you're going to be an engineer." Hank thereupon became the fifth officer in the engineering department.

Among his other duties was watch standing, which on the *Duncan* came with surprises that revealed the lax state of morale in some quarters of the Navy of the mid-fifties. One night, a week into his first Pacific crossing, the ship was steaming in close formation, and Hank was on the bridge during the mid-watch. The officer of the deck turned to him and said, "Okay, kid, you've got it." With that, he eased himself into the captain's chair and went to sleep. Hank was conning the ship. Shortly thereafter, he had to give his first rudder command. He turned to the helm and to his horror saw no helmsman and no helm. Several seconds later, the sailor bounded into the pilot house with the wheel. Unbeknownst to Hank, the bridge watch played a game in which the helmsman would unscrew the helm from its mounting and run from his station onto the starboard wing of the bridge, around the pilothouse past the signalman's station aft, and enter from the port wing back to his station. His object was to return in time to reattach the helm and answer orders before the officer of the deck tried to maneuver the ship. "Needless to say," said Hank, "that game was soon ended."

Following two weeks of exercises in Hawaiian waters, the *Duncan* arrived in Yokosuka on 30 August. While in Japan, those officers on the *Duncan* whose service obligation ended with the Korean War went home. The ship went from twenty-two officers to eleven. Hank found himself now the second officer in the engineering department.

In the early autumn, while operating off Korea, the *Duncan*'s old movie projectors got beyond repair. When the ship put into Sasebo, Conrad ordered Hank to catch a plane to Subic and get a working projector from his father, who was commanding the tender *Piedmont*. The mission was a success. Coincidentally, Webby had become the movie officer aboard the *Brown*. Under way, he and Hank would swap John Wayne films by high line. The pair even arranged to splice newsreel footage from the Navy's 1955 Sugar Bowl victory onto one reel, to the delight of every academy grad. Hank was developing a reputation as the junior officer who could "make it so."

Liberty afforded other opportunities to build friendships. The postwar Pacific was an American lake where the dollar was strong. "I was richer when I was an ensign in WestPac than I've ever been in my life," said Hank in his interview with Dave Winkler of the Naval Historical Foundation. "A steak dinner was a dollar and a half."

On 29 October, the *Duncan* arrived at Subic Bay, where she would remain through Christmas. Because berthing facilities still were relatively limited, the division anchored, and liberty boats shuttled the officers and men to and from shore. On the Marine Corps birthday, Hank caught a launch ashore to the officers club at Main Navy to celebrate with his Marine classmate Phil Monahan. Sometime after midnight, the revelers returned to the landing and found no launch. Hank was unwilling to wait for the next one and decided to swim the five hundred yards to his ship. The following night, it was his turn for the duty. While he and the crew were watching a movie on the fantail, several sailors fished with chains baited with steaks. Suddenly a chain began to rattle against the side of the ship, and the men wrestled a large shark onto the deck. "So that ended the swimming," Hank observed dryly. "The Lord looks out for fools and drunks."

On 5 February 1956, the ship returned to San Diego, but the pace of work did not abate. Hank and his fellow officers each had the duty every third day. "You'd go to sea Monday and come in Friday, you'd have the duty either Friday, Saturday, or Sunday, and then back to sea again. Really it was a tough time, for morale and everything else," said Hank. "I don't think the Navy leadership would enforce such schedules these days, if they were to keep any sort of retention rates."

At the end of the month, the *Duncan* went to San Francisco for overhaul at the Mare Island shipyard. In March, Hank got leave to go to Alexandria, where he and Lucy married. They returned quickly to the West Coast, making their first home in a Quonset hut, so Hank could resume his duties during the overhaul. While at Mare Island, the *Duncan*'s antiair defense 40-mm mounts were replaced with 3-inch guns that could fire the new 3-inch round with the VT influence fuse.

On 4 June, the ship returned to San Diego and continued training with a new captain, Cdr. Pete Smith, a popular surface officer. Conrad, though a masterful ship-handler, had been reluctant to let his officers handle the ship. On the other hand, Smith believed that a great part of a skipper's job was to train his officers in seamanship and ship-handling. Hank benefited from Smith's insistence that he become expert in all facets of ship-handling, from piloting to close quarter station keeping and refueling at sea.

Arriving on board that June, fresh from Stanford NROTC, was Jim Toole. He first encountered Hank "dirty from head to toe with soot and had soaked through his wash khaki shirt and trousers." Toole introduced himself, and Hank squinted, smiled, and thrust forward a greasy hand, saying, "Welcome aboard. Good to see you." When Toole asked what he had been doing, Hank "chuckled and said that he had been doing a periodic boiler inspection that was required to ensure the tubes were all correctly intact after so many steaming hours, and that the soot was to be cleaned out. . . . Hank was a hands-on, get-down-with-the-troops officer," said Toole. "He was a professional who knew his stuff and expected you to learn your stuff soonest."

When Hank had the duty, Toole learned ship-handling very quickly. "The standard distance between ships was only five hundred yards, which is very close when operating at night and darkened ship at stationing speed of twenty-five knots," he recalled. "I stood bridge watches with Hank, and he was a task-master at running drills with his junior officer on the Signal Book and the Maneuvering Book, so that all who stood watch with Hank became very confident on maneuvering and ship-handling characteristics of the *Duncan.*"

In the meantime, Hank also was continuing to learn. While in San Diego, the chief engineer left, leaving him as department head. He came to rely heavily on a Chief Blazewski, a thirty-two-year veteran who "had a row of hash marks that were running up his arm." He took Hank under his wing, training him to ensure that they could run the department without too much meddling from above. Blazewski's style illustrated how the chiefs could hold a ship together, Hank observed. "You had this wardroom all of a sudden losing all of the experienced officers with very junior replacements, like me. And this sort of half-mutinous gang of draftees and other guys who couldn't wait to get out. It was a difficult time, and the chiefs made it all work."

Hank wanted to command a ship. Although a mere lieutenant (junior grade) as of the previous December, he got an important endorsement from Pete Smith, and in May 1958 the Bureau of Personnel gave him command of a mine hunter, the *Bunting,* homeported in Mayport, Florida. Five years junior to the officer he relieved, Hank became the young skipper of a crew of thirty and an expectant father as well. His first son, Lloyd Montague Mustin II, would arrive in February 1959.

Assigned to the harbor defense unit, the *Bunting* was alone among three carriers and a fleet tug. Her mission was to identify and plot all minelike objects in the Mayport Channel and approaches to maintain an accurate plot that, in the event of war and a Soviet mining of the channel, would enable ships to distinguish real mines from false positives.

The task had its challenges. Objects moved with the current. Merchant ships continually added heavy trash to the bottom. In no time, Hank realized that the mission was essentially a "make-work operation." He thus appreciated the need to build morale. Every time the carriers would deploy, the air station band would play, making for a ceremonious occasion, to the delight of both crew and dependents. He asked that the band extend the same courtesy to the *Bunting* whenever it deployed to Norfolk, and he got it. When the *Bunting* returned to her berth along the south wall, he would have his sea detail on deck to render honors to any carrier tied alongside the north wall. The relatively tiny *Bunting,* however, would steam past the much larger ship unseen, below the sight of the officer of the deck, and thus the carrier would never return honors. Hank's annoyance led him one day to pay a call on the executive officer of the carrier *Saratoga,* then the flagship of Rear Adm. George Anderson. After hearing his complaint, the good-natured executive officer assured him that the carrier would rectify the oversight. The next time the *Bunting* rendered the *Saratoga* honors, "all six of our sea detail came to attention and hand saluted, and six hundred guys returned it," said Hank. "My guys loved this."

During his final month in command, Hank took his father, by this time a rear admiral, on a day's operation. He borrowed a two-star flag from a signalman on the *Saratoga* for the day. When they returned that afternoon, Hank did not render honors to the carrier, knowing that Admiral Anderson was not on board and that Lloyd, on the diminutive *Bunting,* was senior. The *Saratoga's* executive officer happened to be sitting in the captain's chair on the bridge and noticed the *Bunting's* apparent lapse. "We finally got that wise-ass kid," Hank later heard that the officer had gleefully remarked. "He didn't render honors." The *Saratoga* signaled, "Why didn't you render honors when you came by?" Receiving Hank's reply, he jumped from his chair. "Son of a bitch! He's got his father on board." Putting his binoculars to his eyes, he saw Lloyd's borrowed two-star flag, so big it could not furl. In no time, the *Saratoga* sounded honors, to the delight of the Lloyd, Hank, and the *Bunting* crew.

Hank ensured that his ship excelled in the performance of her duties. During one Norfolk deployment, the *Bunting* found a World War II mine in Hampton Roads, a feat that greatly impressed the district commandant. On another occasion, while mid-ocean during a major storm, they had used a makeshift search plan to locate a sunken tanker. In every one of the mine force exercises during Hank's command, the ship received commendation.

Aware that he had placed himself in a relative backwater, Hank had been contemplating his next professional move. "My whole career was a series of battles with detailers about where I was going to go, what I was going to do; all of which I won, and a lot of which I got advice from my dad on." Lloyd acknowledged the fun Hank was having and the leadership experience he was gaining, but he advised that at some point Hank would need a technical education with an advanced degree. It was preferable to get that degree before he got too senior, when he should be a department head on a major combatant or an executive officer screening for a major command. The *Bunting* tour qualified as Hank's second sea tour, meaning that he was slated for a shore posting. "I had gotten some offers to be a flag lieutenant someplace and my dad said, 'You don't want to do that. You want to stay away from being a flag lieutenant until you're persuaded that the guy you're a flag lieutenant for will be a force in the Navy.'" He recommended that Hank go to the Postgraduate School, which had moved in 1952 to Monterey, California. Hank applied and was accepted.

In July 1959, just after arriving in Monterey, Hank made lieutenant and began his two-year postgraduate course. He had a real interest in ordnance and gunnery, but he lacked shipboard ordnance experience and thus could not get into the ordnance engineering curriculum. With an eye to the future, he took electrical engineering instead. "I had this idea that in terms of what the Navy was going to do in my career, the advances would be more in the area of electronics and electricity than they would in the area of propulsion, or any other area."

It was a prescient move. With the onset of the missile era, ordnance and electrical engineering were of the same piece, and Hank's two years at school coincided with the transition from vacuum tubes to transistors. He could be certain that his knowledge of the new technologies would have practical application once he returned to sea.

Already, Hank was maturing in his profession. While at school, he deepened a predisposition shared with his father to approach problems technically. He viewed naval officers as engineers, contrary to the growing trend in some quarters to see them as managers. To his mind, engineering was the basis of their knowledge. The tools of the trade were engineering-related, and mastery of those tools was vital, particularly when an officer was at sea.

In November 1960, Lucy gave birth to their second son, Thomas Russell. As it had been for Lloyd in Annapolis, the Mustins' time at the Postgraduate School was an enjoyable time of family and reunion. Larry and Doug Baldauf were in Monterey with their young children, as was Hugh Webster, who enjoyed both the occasional babysitting duties and the frequent parties when Hank and Doug would entertain with their guitars. In June 1961, Hank received his bachelor of science in electrical engineering.

Wanting to remain with the Pacific Fleet, Hank had asked for West Coast orders to one of the Navy's new guided-missile destroyers. Lloyd had advised that if offered a new-construction destroyer anywhere, he should take it. As it happened, he received East Coast orders to serve as chief engineer on the commissioning crew for the *Lawrence*. The missile destroyer was completing construction at the New York Shipbuilding Co. in Camden, New Jersey.

Until this point, Lucy had seen the Navy only from the "garden spots" of Coronado and Monterey. Camden was to be quite a change. In late June, Hank and Lucy, pregnant with their third child, Katherine Elizabeth, packed the boys into the car for another drive across the continent. En route, they heard on the car radio that the Navy was outraged at New York Shipbuilding's shoddy workmanship on the carrier *Kitty Hawk,* delivered in April. An admiral had gone public and threatened litigation. Knowing that the shipyard was financially unstable, Hank arrived prepared for the worst, anticipating a strained relationship at best.

As was customary, the Navy had assigned members of its first team to the commissioning crew. The ship was full of experience, particularly in the department heads and the technical ratings. Hank soon found he had to deal with a 1,200-pound-per-square-inch engineering plant that was, in his view, a "disaster." For six months, he battled the yard daily. "There were indications coming back that there were engineering problems, but the focus was on the missile system, the Tartar system, because it was the gee-whiz part of the ship."

Foremost among these problems was the inability to maintain the equipment at sea. The Navy's ship designers claimed that the boilers' automatic combustion controls eliminated the need to man a number of stations, in particular, around the feed pumps. As a result, the pumps and spaces had no ventilation and became too hot to touch. Routine maintenance at sea proved impossible, so his men had to maintain the plant during the weekends while the ship was in port. With the rest of the crew on liberty, the inequity made for a serious morale issue. The 1,200-pound plant was "one of the greatest mistakes that the Navy ever made," said Hank; by the early 1970s, its problems had infected the whole class of destroyers, leading the Navy to establish the Propulsion Examining Board (PEB).

Just before Christmas, the yard delivered the *Lawrence,* which was commissioned on 6 January of the new year, with Cdr. Thomas W. Walsh in command. She joined the Atlantic Fleet and the Navy's first all-missile destroyer squadron commanded by one of Hank's heroes, Capt. Ike Kidd. Her home port was Norfolk, and in the spring of 1962, Lucy and the children moved to Virginia Beach and the first house the Mustins would own.

During the Cuban missile crisis that autumn, the ship got orders to get under way. Although they understood that the orders had to do with Soviet missiles entering Cuba, Hank and the ship's company were not to tell their families where they were going, how long they would be at sea, or why.

The morning of 22 October, Hank left the ship and returned to his family for a few minutes to collect some clothes. "I'm leaving," he told Lucy. Fearing the possibility of a Soviet nuclear strike against the capital, he added, "I don't know how long I'll be gone, but I can tell you one thing. For Pete's sake, don't go to Washington while I'm gone." As soon as his ship cleared the harbor, however, Lucy packed the children into the car and went to her parents' home in Alexandria, as was her routine while Hank was at sea.

That evening, President John F. Kennedy went on national television to announce a quarantine of Cuba. The operation order had read that the *Lawrence* would participate in a blockade, but a second order came as she was leaving Hampton Roads, telling them to strike "blockade"—under international law, an act of war—and insert "quarantine." The *Lawrence* was en route to make the first interception of a Soviet ship. Halfway to her intercept point, an order came to change her destination. The destroyer *Joseph P. Kennedy Jr.* would conduct the first interception.

Glory thus snatched, the *Lawrence* remained at sea for eighty days, steaming in circles with the nuclear carrier *Enterprise* and other ships. At the operational level, the crisis devolved for Hank and the engineering department into a major test, one that they passed. Fortunately, Capt. Brian McCauley, the destroyer division commander, had been a chief engineer and recognized the challenge. Hank believed that McCauley's concurrent fitness report helped him get early selection for lieutenant commander.

Early in the quarantine operation, the Navy had begun to make plans to invade Cuba, but as Hank discovered later, Commandant of the Marine Corps Gen. David M. Shoup determined that, despite the eight carriers involved in the operation, the Navy did not have enough firepower to support an amphibious assault. That force had no guns larger than 5-inch. Recognizing the lack of fire support, Shoup soon became very vocal in his objection to continued construction of the new *Leahy*-class guided missile destroyer leader. It had no gun except a 3-inch saluting battery amidship. Eventually, the Navy put a 5-inch gun on the fantail on the final seven. "What were we going to do?" Hank observed derisively. "Shoot at these people while we were running away?"

When the *Lawrence* returned to Norfolk, the ship's first weapons officer left. Tom Walsh asked Hank to relieve him. "I became the first guy who was both the chief engineer and the weapons officer for one of these ships." Right away, he went to a thirteen-week fire control officer's school at Dam Neck, Virginia. Having just completed postgraduate school, he was on top of his game. "When they put the circuit diagrams on the board, I could solve them before the prof could walk through them, because I had recently acquired this electrical engineering degree."

During the course, the head of the short-staffed school asked Hank and four other junior officers to help him write a new naval warfare publication called "Fleet Air Defense," which became Naval Warfare Publication 32. With only six months on the *Lawrence* as chief engineer, Hank had been nonetheless standing watches on the bridge and in the combat information center. He thus had an understanding of all the tactical options for missile employment. The publication remained "90 percent the same" into the mid-1980s, when as Second Fleet commander, Hank challenged his staff and students to "get this publication out of the Stone Ages and bring it up to date." The 1962 effort by Hank and his fellow junior officers predated the introduction of the Navy Tactical Data System (NTDS) in the *King,* a *Coontz*-class guided-missile destroyer leader, and addressed defense against aircraft as opposed to missiles.

In mid-winter 1963, he returned to the *Lawrence* and deployed to the Med with the first nuclear-powered surface combatant, the *Bainbridge,* then classed as a guided missile frigate. Lucy joined him in Europe for three weeks, following the fleet with some other wives to Naples and France. Workwise, the *Lawrence* had no major casualties and some successful missile shots.

Once stateside, Hank got orders ashore. His relief, Lt. Greg Streeter, came to be a lifelong friend. Just previously, Cdr. Worth Bagley had relieved Walsh as the skipper, thus beginning a second deep friendship dating from the *Lawrence* that Hank regarded as "one of the defining professional relationships" of his career. Hank preferred orders to remain at sea, possibly to command a destroyer escort, and with Bagley's support, he presented his request personally to the Bureau of Personnel. His detailer lectured him on the importance of the shore establishment. "He treated me like an idiot," Hank said. Disgusted, he went to see his placement officer, Capt. Al MacLane. While he was in MacLane's office, word came that the executive officer of a new-construction guided missile destroyer, the *Conyngham,* had had a nervous breakdown. Although Hank was still a lieutenant, MacLane got him the job, with orders to report immediately to New York Shipbuilding.

The executive officers of new-construction guided missile destroyers were all lieutenant commanders with at least five years' seniority on Hank. On the other hand, he had served both as chief engineer and weapons officer on the commissioning crew of the second ship in the class. He knew the ships extremely well; he was well versed in the dealings with New York Shipbuilding, and he had gained invaluable experience with the missile navy, as MacLane had appreciated. "Al had gone way out on a limb by sending this very junior officer to such a job," said Hank. "I was the only lieutenant ever to be XO of a new-construction DDG."

He had knowledge that he could pass around the wardroom, and he did. After a lot of hard work, the ship "set all kinds of records, had the best InSurv [Inspection and Survey] that anybody had ever had, won all the *Es* as we did in the *Lawrence:* everything we did, we did superbly."

His skipper was Cdr. Paul Smith, a Navy SEAL, who did not have much experience as a ship handler. "Basically I was running the ship, as the exec," said Hank, "mainly because I was the only one who had any operational experience on the ship in any of the departments and was thoroughly checked out, while the captain was a real destroyer rookie."

Solid-state components had entered the fleet during construction of the *Conyngham,* so maintenance of the weapon systems was not the great challenge it had been on the

Lawrence. With the arrival of the *King* and the early version of the NTDS, Hank and his fellow officers were able to focus more on tactical development that incorporated the new capabilities.

By the early 1960s, with the introduction of missiles, the idea of antiair warfare was to launch a guided weapon that could make a kill in a single shot. The anticipated targets now were missiles instead of airplanes. The new threat required further refinements to antiair warfare tactics.

When the Navy came to appreciate that missiles presented increasingly long-range engagement issues, antiair warfare became an aviation as well as a surface Navy issue. Only aircraft could engage enemy aircraft beyond the surface to air missile range. The idea was to "shoot at the archer and not the arrow." One very real risk in a crowded sky was in shooting down friendly planes. Both the surface and aviation unions now had a stake in tactical development.

At the time, the Navy leadership came primarily from the aviation community. It believed that aviation could prevent Soviet aircraft from getting within two to three hundred miles of a battle group to shoot a missile. The debate over whether manned aircraft or missiles would best perform the intercepts devolved into a fight between unions over who would get the funds to structure the force.

Hank thus found himself involved in the genesis of fleet air defense against missiles, the tactical threat that would absorb the rest of his career and the next two decades of Navy development. After wrestling with these missile-navy issues, a tremendous number of ship captains and department heads, notably weapons department heads, would rise to flag officer rank into the 1970s.

In the 1960s, however, the Navy was paying scant attention to antisurface tactics, naval gunfire support, and gunnery in general. In July 1964, halfway through his tour, Hank made lieutenant commander a year early. Remembering Shoup's point that the surface Navy could not support an amphibious invasion of Cuba, he thought the *Conyngham* ought to spend a lot of time on gunfire support. The computers in the *Conyngham,* one of the last of the *Charles F. Adams* class, Hank knew, were digital and worked on Cartesian coordinates. The procedure "was borderline unworkable," he said. "The fire support doctrine had guys cranking north-south-east-west dials trying to get a vector at 45 degrees, so I invented a whole new procedure in which you used north-south-east-west coordinates instead of polar coordinates." To avoid the hand cranking, he had his department use a Cartesian plotting board that cut time by 70 percent and

increased accuracy. Wholly counter to the type commander's existing doctrine, his solution, despite record scores, earned the ship penalties during the force competitions at
Guantánamo for not following procedure. He persisted and eventually got approval for
his new gunfire support procedure, which was used throughout the destroyer force and
later employed extensively for naval gunfire support in Vietnam. For this work, he got
the Navy Achievement Medal, at the time rarely awarded.

The *Conyngham* spent many weeks at sea performing acceptance tests for the new
missile systems. Hank recalled that during her first year in commission the ship had
only thirteen days in Norfolk before she deployed to the Med. The destroyer conducted
a series of missile firings with the French navy and performed well, setting a record for
seven straight successful shots. She issued a press release touting her success—a move
that upset the Atlantic Fleet commander, who regarded the feat as a rather mean
achievement. "He didn't want it public how bad things were."

Hank's virtually uninterrupted sea duty made for a very tough time for Lucy,
who, left with three young children, was at her wits' end. He made certain that
she was able to join him on the Med deployment. Together, they had two weeks
in Paris, plus time in Naples and Barcelona. When they returned, it appeared that
the United States was slowly escalating into war. Hank, however, had orders to
the Naval War College.

Echoing Lloyd's sentiments, Hank regarded the War College as a gentleman's club.
"Unlike the Army where it was 'no war college, no general's stars,' the Navy would only
send officers that it could spare for a year. [The college] didn't task you or really require
a lot of commitment," he said. The course did require him to write a number of professional papers, one of which was on air defense and caught the attention of the college's president, Vice Adm. John T. "Chick" Hayward. Writing his thesis on the Yalta
Conference, Hank would finish the program as a distinguished graduate.

While at Newport, Hank decided to broaden his horizons to the larger questions
of politico-military affairs. Concurrently, he took George Washington University's
extension course for a master's degree in international affairs. The commitment was
intense and required him to study nights and weekends.

Also enrolled in the university's extension program were a number of students,
mostly aviators, who had returned from Vietnam combat. "I could see the similarities
between the way these newly blooded contemporaries of mine approached life and the
way the combat veterans of World War II had approached theirs when I had been a

midshipman at the Naval Academy." Intrigued, Hank chose Vietnam as his thesis topic. Steeping himself in the country's history, he was influenced by Bernard Fall's 1961 classic, *Street without Joy: The Bloody Road to Dien Bien Phu,* the account of the French army's eight-year war in Indochina.

A war was indeed under way. Not surprisingly, Hank felt its calling. Even before finishing his degree program, he was already plotting a course that would take him into the brown water of the Mekong Delta.

Chapter 28

Brown-Water Operations in Vietnam

TERRY AND THE PIRATES

In the spring of 1966, nearing the end of his program at the Naval War College, Hank came to Washington to the Bureau of Personnel to request his next assignment. While in town, he discussed his future with his dad. "At the end of every war, the Navy and all the services divide themselves up into those who fought and those who didn't. If you didn't fight," offered Lloyd, "it doesn't matter what the reason was, you're not going to stay competitive. So, go on over there and fight."

Thus advised, Hank went to the bureau the following day and requested Vietnam duty. The response was not encouraging. "We're not sending any Naval Academy graduates over there," said his detailer. "That's for a bunch of [limited duty officers] and ex-enlisted men." Apparently, the Navy Department's interest in the war stopped at the high-water mark.

Hank persisted, but his detailer was unmoved. He offered Hank a job as an aide in the Office of the Chief of Naval Operations, an offer he declined. Returning to the War College, he later received orders as flag secretary for the commander of naval forces in Vietnam. The Bureau of Personnel gave him just ten days to get to Saigon.

Lucy decided she would return to Coronado, where most of their family and friends were, while Hank was overseas. Wasting no time, they loaded the children and a few suitcases into the car for another drive cross country. They rented a house four blocks from Doug and Larry. Their furniture and effects would take thirty days to cross the country, and by the time they arrived, Hank was gone. On 7 July, attempting to make light of a deeply emotional parting, he left her the words, "So long, kid. I'll see you when I've won the war." For the rest of his life, he would hold in his mind the image of his "beautiful, young, pregnant wife standing in an empty living room, surrounded by three tiny children."

Hank crossed the Pacific "very unhappy." Ordinarily, he would have gone first to the river patrol boat school in Coronado, but his orders had him going straight to Vietnam. He chose to believe that the Navy had an urgent need for him, that he was replacing someone killed in the line of duty. "I got over there, and the guy I'm relieving meets me at the airport, at Tan Son Nhut, in whites," Hank recalled. "This was not my idea of Terry and the Pirates."

His assignment was to Saigon, to the staff of Rear Adm. Norvell G. Ward, a World War II submarine hero. Hank settled into a room in a hotel in Cholon, Saigon's Chinese section. From the outset, he made Ward's life "miserable." "Every day I went in and said, 'I got to get out to the field and get a job.'"

Two weeks after Hank's arrival in Vietnam, his cousin Joe Howard suddenly appeared. Joe was in Saigon for two and a half weeks of helicopter training with the Army, en route to the Mekong Delta to command a Seawolf squadron. During training, his sixteen-man squadron lived in a waterfront building, a few blocks away. Every day, the Army would shuttle them from Saigon north to Binh Long to train. His first day of training, Joe went on a combat mission. When the Army finally provided him with eight armed UH-1B Iroquois helicopters for his squadron, he left for the Delta and a base near Can Tho, on the Bassac River, the southernmost estuary of the Mekong.

In the summer of 1966, when the two cousins arrived in Vietnam, the United States abandoned its bombing campaign against North Vietnam's petroleum, oil, and lubricants. Disenchanted with its results, McNamara shifted to a more defensive strategy that stressed pacification in the South and interdiction of supplies to the Viet Cong.

In 1965, the Navy had begun Market Time, a coastal maritime interdiction campaign. In May 1966, the new emphasis prompted Operation Game Warden, to augment the river patrol boat force in the Mekong Delta to disrupt and hopefully sever the cross-river supply lines in the Viet Cong's regional stronghold south of Saigon. A key component of Game Warden was its air support element. To that end, in August,

Joe and his air crews from the Navy's Helicopter Support Squadron 1 replaced the Army personnel who had been operating in the Delta.

Left behind in Saigon, Hank was now even more eager to get into the real in-country action. He was frustrated to find himself merely a "Saigon commando." As for Ward, he was a naval two-star in a largely three-star army organization. He did not even have a seat in the senior officers' mess. "The Army had more generals in-country than they had in Europe in World War II," Hank maintained.

After four months of pestering Ward for a transfer, Hank finally got orders to be the chief staff officer for Cdr. Jim Cronander, the commanding officer of the Delta's River Patrol Group, TG 116.1. Arriving in Can Tho in November, Hank was the second senior naval officer south of Saigon.

Joe Howard, now ensconced as commander of the Seawolves squadron, was in Hank's operational chain of command. Right away, he took Hank on helicopter missions to familiarize him with "all the different spots to get an idea how to get his orders written." "He'd take a map and put all this stuff on it," said Joe. "The maps were pretty good."

When Hank began writing their operations, he continued to fly with Joe. Sometimes he would go on board one of the river patrol boats, an unusual practice for a staff officer. "There was wisdom in this," said Hank. "It allowed me to get a handle on what I needed to know." Often the pair would coordinate an operation and develop tactics. "For the [river patrol boats], it was really a reaction-type thing," Joe observed. "We really didn't know what we were going to get into, but we did develop our tactics to think of where we'd support them from. We'd know that if they went certain places, they were going to get fire. So, we'd ask them to wait till we were in a certain position, and as soon as they got fire, we'd come in."

With Joe frequently short on crews, Hank went on missions as a helicopter door gunner. Manning one of the flex guns, he flew on some eighty missions and, thanks to his cousin, got an air medal.

Market Time had dramatically reduced enemy infiltration by sea to the point where Viet Cong resupply depended primarily on the Ho Chi Minh Trail, which snaked through the remote jungles along the western length of Vietnam. To get those supplies to the Viet Cong and North Vietnamese Army forces in the Delta required the enemy to cross the rivers.

Riverine patrols had just gotten started with the arrival of the first Mark I river patrol boats. With a crew of four sailors, a Pathfinder surface radar, and two radios, the Mark I usually had two twin-mounted .50-caliber machine guns forward and M-60 machine guns or a grenade launcher amidships. Aft was another .50-cal. Its main weaknesses were its flimsy fiberglass hull and its water-jet engines that habitually were fouled by weeds. Hank often found himself over the side, among the water snakes and other denizens of the river, wrestling by hand the marine life clogging an intake.

Riverine patrols were for the young. At thirty-one, Hank was comparatively old. The heat and humidity were burdensome, and the lengthy patrols were a formidable test of endurance. A typical patrol was two boats operating for twelve hours, from dusk to dawn. The end of the patrol was the most risky. The Viet Cong knew the crews were tired, and if the night action had been heavy, the boats returned with little ammunition. Always, Hank had his boats vary their patterns.

The River Division 53 commander was Lt. Cdr. Jim Toole, his shipmate from the *Duncan*. In country since late April, Toole initially had a river section of ten boats that operated from Vung Tau, up the coast, across Ganh Rai Bay. In late June, the section moved to the My Tho River, the northernmost estuary of the Mekong, and in late July, another group of ten boats arrived to operate out of Vinh Long, on the Co Chien. In August, a third group of ten joined them at My Tho. "It was in October," said Toole, "that I personally took ten boats to operate in the flooded Plain of Reeds at the Parrots Peak of Cambodia until the flood waters receded." In that 27 September to 17 October upriver foray, Toole's raiders had no indication of an international boundary and passed into Cambodia to engage the enemy in a major firefight.

Toole had proved to be an aggressive commander, despite a policy emanating from Saigon that did not afford him much support. Headquarters instructions to TG 116.1, for example, said the patrol boats were to operate only in the center of the river, a procedure Hank immediately saw would not work for interdiction. The Viet Cong simply waited until the boats had passed to make their crossings. The Saigon policy also did nothing to encourage interaction with the local populace, thus ensuring that the Navy would not gather intelligence. When Hank moved to involve the unit in civic action programs, the intelligence began to flow.

With better intelligence, Hank was able to develop tactics for operations that would take the river patrol boats beyond the Bassac. Toole was operating primarily along the Ham Luong River, the estuary between the My Tho and Co Chien and an area controlled by the Viet Cong. In early January 1967, Hank accompanied him for prolonged reconnaissance that confirmed what would be required to wrest control from the enemy. Mid-month, he moved the amphibious landing support ship *Harnett County*, with twenty-eight additional patrol boats, to Dong Tam at the top of the Ham Luong, where it met the Mekong and My Tho for a coordinated assault against the Viet Cong stronghold known as the Thanh Phu secret zone. Toole now had tactical command of fifty-eight boats and was responsible for the continuous patrolling of that section of the Mekong River into the My Tho. "That required twenty-four hours, seven days a week, ten-hour patrols every day by each crew," said Toole. What made the task possible was the addition of the landing ship and the support Hank received from Joe and his helicopter detachment, now at Vinh Long. Until their arrival, Toole had gotten "zero support." Placing the detachment in Vinh Long provided the ten boats with immediate response overhead that could "catch the enemy in the act, or nearly so," he said. He credited Hank with driving the cooperation and innovative ideas.

These aggressive operations increased the risks, especially in the very narrow canals of the lower Bassac, where the range of tide was more than ten feet and the Viet Cong were becoming very active. If a boat got stuck at low tide, it remained there surrounded by dense jungle until the water rose.

On one patrol that Hank had chosen to accompany, a battalion-sized Viet Cong unit ambushed his boat in one such canal on the lower Bassac. The incoming rounds began to rip his boat apart. Not having a code book, he used plain language to report their position and call for an artillery strike. On his return to base, a communications security officer blasted him for revealing his position to the enemy. "I don't understand what more I could have revealed," Hank noted, "except to spot their incoming rounds, 'cause they were well aware of where I was at the time."

That close call on the lower Bassac made Hank "a different person." "I certainly had a different appreciation for what I thought was important and what wasn't important. And I, for the first time, started to see how all of these organizational matters make a big difference." This understanding of the operational impact of command relationships he would later apply most effectively as a three-star NATO commander executing the Maritime Strategy of the 1980s.

Hank made TG 116.1 far more aggressive with the addition of helicopter gunships and operations with SEALs. In February, two platoons from SEAL Team Two arrived in Can Tho. Working in sweeps that included Army special forces, Hank learned a lot about ground tactics, helicopter support, and amphibious operations. His hands-on approach gave him an appreciation of the strengths and weaknesses of operational intelligence. "I used to go out on the river, sometimes at night, on a captured sampan with a coolie hat on and a night vision scope to see what was going on," he recalled.

"One of the dangerous parts of that operation was coming back to the base, calling the sentries and saying, 'I'm coming in.' They'd still shoot at us."

Before he left the Delta, Hank was keen to see the brown-water Navy get the awards it deserved. After he and others drew the Navy Department's attention to the river patrol boats' work in Game Warden, TG 116.1 became a highly decorated unit, receiving the Navy's first Presidential Unit Citation of the war. Long after leaving Vietnam, Hank continued to push for the medals. Notably, he successfully routed the submission for Toole's Legion of Merit, not normally awarded to lieutenant commanders. Said Toole, "I would never have received it, if Hank had not pursued it and submitted it a couple years later after everyone forgot what I had done." Hank did the same for Toole's award submissions for Boatswain's Mate James Elliott Williams. After considerable effort, Williams received a number of medals, including the Silver Star, Navy Cross, and Congressional Medal of Honor, making him one of the most decorated sailors in Navy history.

Lucy had given birth to their fourth child, John Burton Mustin, in January. Due for leave, Hank arranged to rendezvous with her in Honolulu in March, thinking it would be their one opportunity to visit the islands. Some two weeks after he returned to Vietnam, informal word came that he was going to the staff of Commander, Cruiser-Destroyer Force, Pacific, in San Diego, but the Navy in fact had other plans. Lloyd and Emily had heard from their friend Rear Adm. Maurice F. Weisner, at the time the number two officer in the Bureau of Personnel, that their eldest son was going to Adm. Ulysses S. Grant Sharp's staff in Honolulu.

In May 1967, Hank returned home to California. Seasoned by combat, he had changed, but so had his country. San Francisco was preparing for the youth invasion that would become known as the "Summer of Love," and the national debate on Vietnam was becoming increasingly acrimonious. Indeed, during one of his first visits to his sister, Hank ran headlong into the controversy.

Larry Bauldauf already had begun making a stir before Hank had gone to Vietnam. Hank was not sympathetic to his brother-in-law's going public in a manner that was embarrassing to Lloyd, still director of operations on the Joint Staff. When Hank visited Doug on the day of his return, he found Larry's close friend, Tom Harkin, an NROTC aviator (and future Democratic senator from Iowa), already there. Harkin had turned profoundly antiwar and was as vocal in his opinions as was Larry, although their positions were poles apart. It was not long before Hank and Harkin began discussing the war and found themselves in violent disagreement. Having just left the war zone, Hank was angered to hear such negative sentiments from a uniformed officer, and he demanded Harkin step outside. Doug recalled that once in the backyard, he grabbed Harkin by the collar and thrust him against the side of the house. "I had never seen my brother like that before and have never seen him like that since."

For Hank, the war was unfinished business. Before he commenced his duties in Honolulu, the Bureau of Personnel sent him on a two-month speaking tour to military installations and Navy and Army ROTC units, complete with slides and war stories. He hit colleges and military centers all across the country. Notwithstanding all the media attention going to the antiwar activists, Hank encountered gung-ho midshipmen and cadets, most of whom were on their way to the war.

While in Washington, he visited with Emily and Lloyd, who was just leaving the Joint Staff. Skeptical of the orders to be Sharp's flag lieutenant, Hank asked his father's advice. "Go," Lloyd replied. "You'll learn more there than you could learn anywhere else in the Navy." Hank's assignment would expose him to senior wartime decision making and give him another perspective on the conduct of the war.

Sharp was a consummate operator, at sea and in Washington. A 1927 Naval Academy graduate, he had commanded a destroyer in World War II and received a Silver Star, and had served as commander, Destroyer Force, Pacific; commander, First Fleet; and commander in chief, Pacific Fleet. He already had worked with others in the Mustin family. Hank's uncle, Rear Adm. Tom Morton, had worked for him when he was the Navy's director of operations in 1962–63, and he certainly had valued Lloyd's work on his behalf in Washington. Hank would come to regard him as "one of the finest gentlemen that I've ever had the great fortune to be associated with, and who is one of the major influences on my career." In turn, Sharp would credit him as an "outstanding aide and adviser and good friend." In his detaching fitness report, he stated that Hank was "the best aide I've ever had."

In July, Hank arrived in Honolulu for the 17 July conference attended by President Lyndon Johnson and other senior military and civilian officials. He was the only naval officer on Sharp's personal staff who had brown-water service in the war. Recognizing he was a seagoing warrior indisposed to horse-holding for an admiral, Sharp told him to tolerate the job's downside in order to gain from its benefits. "Some people treat their flag lieutenant as a social aide to set up cocktail parties and meet people at the door," said Hank. "I had to do that, but he said that was more of a penalty, something I had to do in order to participate in the operation at his level. We'd go to meetings with the CIA guys, and I'd walk up with him to the door, and they'd say, 'Hey, only the Admiral.' And he'd say, 'No, he's with me.' I saw him argue things out with Westmoreland and McNamara and people like that." Regarding the experience as a gift, Hank witnessed the exercise of wartime operational control amid myriad political issues and interservice rivalry.

By the end of the month, Sharp's staff was readying their boss for a trip to Washington to testify before the Senate Armed Services Preparedness Subcommittee. Chaired by Mississippi Democrat John C. Stennis, the panel was preparing for a lengthy series of hearings on the conduct of the air war over Vietnam. The mounting accusations from Air Force pilots and naval aviators that McNamara and the administration were denying them targets had prompted a congressional review of the bombing policy.

By now, the administration recognized that Sharp was no longer a team player. For three years, he had consistently proposed expanding the bombing campaign over the North, to the point that he had antagonized the president. Adm. Thomas H. Moorer, at the time just tapped as chief of naval operations, remembered Johnson contemptuously and routinely referring to the Sharp as *That Man*. "'What is *That Man* saying now?' he would always ask," recalled Moorer.

Fearing Sharp's testimony would generate a public relations disaster, McNamara only then started approving the requested targets for Rolling Thunder 57. He anticipated that lawmakers would ask their star witness whether the Pentagon was denying him targets, and he instructed the admiral to say the requests had been approved.

One step ahead of McNamara, Capt. Rembrandt C. Robinson, Sharp's executive assistant—according to Hank, "a walking Joint Staff encyclopedia"—called the office of Democratic Senator W. Stuart Symington, a sympathetic panel member and air power proponent. "If you ask that question," he suggested to a senior staffer, "ask the next question, 'When were those targets approved?'"

The Stennis hearings opened on 9 August with Sharp the first witness. When asked the anticipated question, he responded as per McNamara's instruction. The follow-on came with a senator's question as to how long the target requests had been pending, Sharp said "as much as eighteen months," Hank recalled.

For two solid weeks, the top military brass criticized McNamara's policy of gradualism. On the twenty-fifth, the secretary of defense appeared as the final witness. He vainly attempted to defend his limited objectives approach. Six days later, the subcommittee released its highly critical report, sealing McNamara's fate. Johnson could see his top defense official had lost the confidence of virtually all of his military leaders, and in November, McNamara announced that he would be leaving government.

After the hearings, Hank returned to the Pacific Command routine. On 23 January 1968, while he was with Sharp in the Philippines, word came that North Korea had seized a Navy intelligence collection ship *Pueblo* in international waters off Wonsan. The Koreans had killed one crewman and captured eighty-two. It was not immediately clear whether the action was a prelude to some larger operation. Tensions on the peninsula were high. Two days before, North Korean commandos had attempted to assassinate South Korean President Park Chung Hee.

Within hours, Vice Adm. William F. Bringle, Seventh Fleet commander, and Adm. John J. Hyland, the Pacific Fleet commander, had worked the options and begun to position a naval force for any possible military response. Sharp wanted to take military action. Knowing that the North Koreans had taken the *Pueblo* into Wonsan, he ordered photo reconnaissance to determine her exact location.

By the following day, however, it was clear that Washington was electing to resolve the crisis through diplomacy. The priority was the return of the crew. Midday, Sharp ordered Hyland and Bringle to make no show of force. Nevertheless, Sharp was worried by the North's air power advantage over the South, and for the next two weeks he continued to move significant naval and air assets into the region.

Sharp submitted to Washington a conventional weapons strike plan and also readied his forces for various nuclear options. According to Hank, Washington chose instead a diplomatic solution, for fear of a Chinese response to any concerted military action against North Korea. With thousands of South Korean troops deployed to Vietnam and U.S. forces spread thinly throughout the world, another large-scale conflict on the ground in Asia would have been a risky proposition. As it happened, the United States was not able to secure the crew's release until December.

Just a week into the *Pueblo* crisis, after Sharp and his staff had returned to Hawaii, Vietnam exploded with the Tet Offensive. On the night of 31 January, Viet Cong and North Vietnamese troops assaulted more than a hundred cities and towns in the South and blew into the U.S. embassy compound in Saigon. Westmoreland stubbornly insisted that the offensive had failed. Sharp and his staff initially supported Westmoreland's assessment. By early March, however, Hank had arrived at the opposite conclusion. Sharp and Westmoreland "just didn't understand the extent of the anti-war sentiments in the United States," said Hank. "So that what in fact was a humiliating military defeat for the North Vietnamese ended up to be a diplomatic victory of the highest order." It was now clear that the North would win the battle of national wills off the battlefield. "[A]s far as I'm concerned," Hank noted, "the war in Vietnam was over with Tet."

His staff duties gave him further insight into the disconnected and at times competing command relationships and their adverse impact on the conduct of the war. Under Sharp, Hyland, the Pacific Fleet commander, directed the naval air campaign in Laos, Cambodia, and North Vietnam, and the commander of the Seventh Air Force in Vietnam and the Thirteenth Air Force, then based at Clark AFB in the Philippines, commanded the Air Force part of that operation. Westmoreland had responsibility for the ground war and, via his own three-star Air Force component commander of the Seventh Air Force, the air war in South Vietnam. Gen. William W. Momeyer wore both Air Force hats. Sharp was supposed to be Westmoreland's superior, but in practice, Westmoreland reported directly to Washington.

By this time, the administration chose to emphasize ground operations and pacification in the South as opposed to Sharp's air war in the North. In actual fact, Westmoreland was waging a campaign to become his own commander in chief for Southeast Asia. Sharp did not object, said Hank, as long as Westmoreland did not take any forces from Pacific Command. "And that's where the argument died."

The Supreme Allied Commander, Europe and the other commanders in chief were focused on the threat from the Soviet Union and China. They and Sharp did not want to chop forces from Europe or Korea to support Westmoreland. America's military was already stretched thin. According to Hank, the Navy had applied two-thirds of its assets directly or indirectly to the war effort.

Beyond the Vietnam war, the Navy still had to fulfill its larger deterrence mission, which required continual planning. Sharp ran war games to exercise the SIOP plan. The Navy's role in the SIOP was with its carriers, which would participate in a nuclear strike plan. The SIOP would go through continual modifications whose impacts would be on the location of the carrier launch points and as such required regular exercising.

In the spring of 1969, during one such exercise, a major typhoon, Jean by name, came through the western Pacific on 11 April and thoroughly disrupted the operation. The first draft of the report read that the typhoon prevented the carriers in the exercise from reaching their launch points, meaning that the Navy could not execute its SIOP responsibilities.

The draft exercise report, written by the Air Force operations deputy on Sharp's staff, had budget implications for Washington that the ever-astute Rem Robinson could see. In the context of the historical battle between the Air Force and the Navy over budgeting for strategic bombers and carrier-based aviation, the hidden message was "to correct the problem, buy more airplanes." Hank witnessed Robinson and the Air

Force deputy negotiate new language. Reminding him that the B-52s in Guam and Clark had to return to the States, Robinson asked him either to include that fact in the report as well or not mention either. In the end, they settled on a bland revision that said that bad weather affected both.

On 31 July, Sharp retired. Succeeding him was Adm. John Sidney McCain. Hank remained with McCain for several months, but his way of doing business did not mesh with the incoming commander's new guidelines. "I became pretty quickly identified with everything McCain didn't like," Hank said. Fortunately, Sharp had made it possible for him to advance to a destroyer command. "So I got out of there one jump ahead of the sheriff."

Chapter 29

On the Gun Line

DESTROYER COMMAND

In December 1968, in part thanks to Sharp's support, Hank got command of the *Henry B. Wilson,* a *Charles F. Adams*–class guided missile destroyer homeported in San Diego. The ship had returned recently from a western Pacific deployment that included time on the gun line off Vietnam as part of Operation Sea Dragon. In October, the Navy had canceled Sea Dragon in line with administration policy that restricted offensive operations against the North. Naval gunfire support would continue south of the demilitarized zone, and the *Henry B. Wilson* was to return to the war zone as soon as she was materially ready. This prospect suited Hank just fine.

Delivered to the Navy in 1960, the *Henry B. Wilson* had been "run hard" for eight years, and her engineering problems were evident. During her predeployment work-up, she had three superheater tube failures. Hank had firsthand knowledge as to the design flaws in the engineering plant, having run both the engineering and weapons departments on two other *Charles F. Adams*–class destroyers, and he wrote the type commander that all four superheaters required replacement. Against a fair amount of bureaucratic resistance, he got the ship ordered to Long Beach, where the yard made the swap.

Hank had taken command of a ship blessed with experienced officers and crew, but he was her first skipper with in-country experience in Vietnam. Their mission was naval gunfire support, and knowing lives ashore were at stake, he was prepared to drive his ship and crew hard. The gun battery consisted of two 5-inch/54 Mark 42 Mod 7 mounts—in Hank's opinion, a type of gun overdesigned and underengineered. The occasionally intense workload off Vietnam had put many 5-inch/54s out of action.

"On any given day, I later learned, half of the mounts were down for one reason or another," said Hank, "often for spare parts that were weeks and months in arriving in theater." Having two batteries, he was able to "cannibalize" one mount to keep the other firing. The experience persuaded him that all destroyers should have two guns in order to ensure that one would always be ready in combat.

Hank brought a war-fighting focus to his command. Enhancing his effect was the fact that Capt. Frank W. "Hank" Corley, his destroyer division commander, and his staff would be on board. The *Henry B. Wilson* would deploy as flagship of a phantom division. In reality a commodore of a division of just one, Corley nevertheless brought clout to the ship far beyond Hank's rank. The two men built a close and trusting relationship during the deployment, with Corley exercising particular care not to intrude on Hank's command of his ship.

The *Henry B. Wilson* left for the western Pacific in December with the carrier *Ranger*. Racing to relieve a carrier on Yankee Station, the *Ranger* steamed the two thousand miles from Midway to Yokosuka at twenty-seven knots. To stay with her, the *Henry B. Wilson* had run on all four boilers; according to Hank, his type commander told him that it was the first time a DDG had ever attempted such a feat. She burned fuel at a phenomenal rate and had to do high-speed, extremely close-quarter refueling in a following sea every other day.

One night in the middle of the run, Hank got a call from his chief engineer. He was preparing to secure the forward Number 1A boiler. The seams had ruptured on both the starboard and the port sides, and gas was leaking into the space. Hank went below and could see fire through the cracks. The overly cautious engineer wanted to "wrap" the boiler. Hank overruled him. "There's a war going on. We've got to get there," he stated flatly. "We'll fix it when we get to Japan."

When Hank and his senior chief boilerman, Teddy Ross, decided to use jacks and shoring timber to close the boiler, the chief engineer announced he was refusing to accept responsibility for the fix, in effect challenging Hank's command. Hank relieved him on the spot. When the *Henry B. Wilson* made it to Japan, Hank put the chief engineer ashore and notified the bureau that he had relieved him for cause and had a qualified relief on board. Taking a week to make the repairs "with Devcon and pop rivets," Hank then made way for Yankee Station.

The episode was a defining moment for the cruise. It was now clear to the ship's company that their captain would settle for nothing less than a commitment to combat readiness. "If we have problems, we're going to fix them," said Hank of his approach to command. "We're going to carry out our orders and our mission." The *Henry B. Wilson* was now an integrated extension of her commander's will.

En route to Yankee Station, the *Henry B. Wilson* hit a submerged object and damaged one of her two screws. While at Subic Bay for a replacement, she received word that the *Hoel,* another destroyer on the gun line, had an in-bore explosion as a result of a faulty cartridge. The Navy suspended all 5-inch firing in the Seventh Fleet until it could replace the ammunition with new lots. Hank realized that it could be months before replacement ammunition would arrive from the States. Simply stated, he would fail to meet his commitment.

Grabbing his weapons officer, Lt. Conrad C. Lautenbacher Jr., now undersecretary of commerce for oceans and atmosphere and administrator of the National Oceanic and Atmosphere Administration, he commandeered a jeep and drove in blinding rain to Subic's ammo depot. After crawling through acres of ammunition, they found twelve hundred cartridges from earlier lots. Hank arranged to swap the ammo with the defective lot on the *Henry B. Wilson.* After completing the transfer, he reported his readiness to deploy to Rear Adm. Doug Plate, his type commander, and Rear Adm. Worth Bagley, the western Pacific cruiser-destroyer commander. At that stage, the *Henry B. Wilson* was the only destroyer in the Seventh Fleet that had approved ammo. Bagley thus gave them the go-ahead to proceed to the gun line. Once again, Hank was operating in Vietnamese waters.

The *Henry B. Wilson's* mission while on the gun line was to support U.S. and South Vietnamese units operating ashore. The threat of counterfire was remote but a threat nonetheless. The enemy shore batteries had a superior range. For the destroyers to get within range of their targets, eighteen thousand yards, they had to close on the shoreline and navigate in shallow waters with dated charts, many of which were based on hydrographic surveys taken in 1898 or 1900. Often, the ships operated just a mile or two off the coast.

"[W]hen you're at sea, if you are given a mission and lives depend on it," said Hank, "you can find a way to do it. It's just a matter of doing it. And it's also a matter of knowing your stuff and being prepared to take some risks."

One operation was particularly memorable. While at anchor in Da Nang, the *Henry B. Wilson* got word that fifty miles to the south two North Vietnamese regiments had trapped a South Vietnamese regiment alongside the Cua Viet River. Hank got his ship under way in the middle of the night. Running on all four boilers at flank speed, they raced down the coast through the darkness, navigating by the 1898 charts.

At first light, they arrived off the action. To bring both mounts to bear on the enemy positions, Hank had to put the ship closer to shore, where the charted depth was less than the draft of the ship. Somehow they would have to thread their way over the shelf. To that end, he ordered Lautenbacher to get in his captain's gig to lead the ship to a spot from whence to open fire. Lautenbacher took soundings with a lead line and with a hand-held radio transmitted instructions to the helm until Hank passed the order to drop anchor.

The current and tide at the mouth of the river were strong and positioned the ship such that Hank could not bring both mounts to bear on the enemy positions as planned. Having to orient the ship athwart the current, Hank used what the Asiatic Fleet called a wind moor. Paying a line through the Number 6 chock, his deck gang bent it onto the anchor chain and then winched it until the ship was 90 degrees to the current and tide.

"We did this, in violation of all existing regulations," Hank noted. At the time the Navy prohibited gunfire support ships from anchoring, lest they become easy targets for enemy gunners ashore. When Corley appeared on the bridge and saw that the ship's guns were trained 270 degrees relative and bearing up the river, he said, "Great work." Ashore, a U.S. spotter called the shots. "Normally, it would take four or five rounds with corrections given in tens of yards to get rounds on target. In this case, the spotter's first correction was 'Left ten feet. Fire for effect.' We emptied the gun mounts by noon, twelve hundred rounds," said Hank. "We decimated these two North Vietnamese regiments, just a slaughter. We had no ammo on board at the end." For this action, Hank received the Vietnamese Cross of Gallantry.

Almost immediately, Bagley ordered the *Henry B. Wilson* to relieve a destroyer performing the radar identification duty on Yankee Station in the northern part of the Tonkin Gulf. Since 1966, the positive identification radar advisory zone (PIRAZ) had relied on a lone cruiser or destroyer to locate and track all planes over the eastern regions of North Vietnam and the gulf. The ship also would vector carrier-based aircraft to and from their targets and warn them of approaching MiGs. Destroyers equipped for PIRAZ duty carried Tactical Air Navigation (TACAN), a beacon that would determine the relative bearing and slant range distance of an aircraft.

En route, Hank discovered that the *Henry B. Wilson*'s TACAN was down as a result of a malfunctioning coil, with no spare on board and a lead time for replacement of over a month. Fortuitously, Hank had his Postgraduate School textbooks on board and was able to make the necessary calculations to jury-rig his own coil. Using parts on board the ship, he immersed a thick copper wire coil in a GI can full of oil.

"I was still the picture of confidence, till the time came to turn this thing on," said Hank. "And then I was conscious of the three to six megavolts that I was playing with, but I wasn't going to show any concern to the troops. So I hooked it all up. Then I got a long broom and I backed out the door and leaned in with the broom handle and flicked the thing on. The TACAN started humming; it worked perfectly. That GI can with that coil in it stayed there for the rest of the deployment."

Typical of the western Pacific destroyers, the *Henry B. Wilson* would return primarily to Subic Bay for her availability. In addition to her gun-line duties, she drew assignments to patrol the Taiwan Strait, escort carriers on Yankee Station, and exercise the single integrated operational plan. Nevertheless, it was her gun-line duties that were the most intense. "During that cruise we fired about eight thousand rounds, which was about eight years' worth of peacetime firing," said Hank. "The liners came out of the guns, the paint blistered off."

The *Henry B. Wilson* left the western Pacific for San Diego in March 1970 and later received the Meritorious Unit Commendation. Hank was able to point with pride to the fact that she never missed a commitment, but he regarded his most important legacy as "the knowledge and the attitudes of the people that have worked for you. Because after a while all the rounds you've fired and all the boilers you've fixed are just footprints in the sands of time. It's how you pass on attitudes that lead to winning that's important."

Hank wanted each of his officers to be a better captain than he. He insisted that his watch officers perform all the functions on the bridge. He gave them broad latitude to make mistakes, confident that they could make no mistake he could not fix.

"My experience in destroyers is that a captain who is a good ship handler, and who lets his officers handle the ship, can overcome a hell of a lot of sins and shortcomings in a lot of other areas. Because the way the ship is handled permeates the engineers, the boatswain's mates, all the people in the deck force, and it's the face that the ship presents to the outside world. And that's what the officers talk about in the wardroom."

His antisubmarine warfare officer, Lt. Tom Kenneally, was just one example. "He was the probably the best ship handler that I've been associated with, even better than I was;

there wasn't any question." Kenneally was especially proficient at maneuvering the ship during a replenishment at sea, where he could put the ship alongside an oiler at flank speed and back down full. "If there's anything I'm proud of in my career it's the young officers who have been associated with me who have risen to flag rank, including the present [chief of naval operations], Vern Clark, who worked for me twice."

In April, Nixon had announced Vice Adm. Elmo R. Zumwalt's nomination as chief of naval operations. On 14 July, the first of his famous Z-grams, policy directives to reshape the Navy, began to hit the fleet. Exciting change was afoot, and Hank wanted to join the team. Lloyd had told him once not to go to the Pentagon too early in his career or he would serve as merely a palace guard. "If you go there, and you're junior to the grade of commander, you're going to end up being the guy who goes around at 1630 every day and checks the wastebaskets to see there's no classified material in them." This time, however, Lloyd agreed that Hank had the sufficient seniority to make the tour a success. Unfortunately, the Bureau of Personnel had prepared to assign him to the Naval Ship Systems Command, the predecessor of the Naval Sea Systems Command. Hank was outraged. He told his father he would tell them he would resign if they forced that on him. Lloyd calmly replied, "You never want to make an offer like that, because they'll take you up on it. Find a way out, and if not, go to BuShips [sic]."

Hank returned to Coronado to find that Ike Kidd was to be commander, First Fleet. In August, the admiral arranged for him to come to his fleet, then homeported in San Diego. Two days before his change of command on the *Henry B. Wilson*, Hank got a phone call from Worth Bagley, who was on his first day of serving with Zumwalt. Bagley offered him a post in planning and programming, and Hank jumped on it. He immediately contacted his detailer, who was by this time impatient with the paperwork he was generating. The Bureau of Personnel canceled his orders to the First Fleet but refused to issue new orders in time for Hank's change of command.

"Where shall I say I'm going?" Hank asked his detailer.

"Fake it," the detailer barked, as the line went dead.

At his *Henry B. Wilson* ceremony, when it came time to read his orders, Hank simply stated with a wry grin, "Here are my BuPers orders. I'm under oral orders to proceed to the staff of the Chief of Naval Operations."

Chapter 30

First Duty at OpNav

A POLECAT AT A BEACH PARTY

As the 1970s began, both naval officers and outside observers recognized that the Navy needed a shake-up. Among the many forward thinkers was Secretary of the Navy John Chafee, who felt that after nine years of aviators as chiefs of naval operations, the service would benefit from a changing of the guard. Foremost, Chafee wanted a non-aviator who was young. In Elmo "Bud" Zumwalt, he found one.

At a 1 July 1970 ceremony at the Naval Academy, Zumwalt relieved Tom Moorer, who advanced to become chairman of the Joint Chiefs of Staff. At forty-nine, Zumwalt was the youngest four-star admiral and chief of naval operations ever. He had risen to the top position over the heads of thirty-three more senior admirals, including Lloyd Mustin, who, nevertheless, was a strong supporter.

A 1942 Savo Island veteran, Zumwalt had come to know the Washington game during his time as one of McNamara's systems analysts for the Navy and as an executive assistant to Secretary of the Navy Paul Nitze. Brilliant, but unimpressed by the education he received at the Naval Academy, he had a lifelong interest in the larger Soviet-American strategic questions.

International political theorists of his day observing the titanic U.S.–Soviet struggle generally felt that the United States was the status quo player and the Soviet Union was the expansionist. Immediately following World War II, the wise men of U.S. policy dismissed any notion of "rolling back" the Soviet advance into Eastern Europe and by 1947 had settled into a geostrategy first expressed as "containment" and later as "détente," the chosen course of Nixon's national security adviser and later secretary of state, Henry Kissinger.

Zumwalt did not wholly agree with détente. The Kissinger view held that the West was "on the wane" and that the Soviet empire would be the world power of the twenty-first century. According to Zumwalt, Secretary Kissinger had charged himself with presiding "over the smooth transition into inferiority." A decade ahead of the geostrategy of the Reagan era, Zumwalt was not satisfied with maintaining a status quo with the Soviets. He was hostile to the proposition that the U.S. foreign policy establishment would deed them the world. Bud Zumwalt wanted to win the Cold War.

In 1970, very few Americans were aware of the rise of Soviet sea power. Adm. Sergei Gorshkov was completing the Soviet Navy's transition from a coastal defense force, primarily of submarines, to a blue-water fleet that would project Soviet power worldwide. Zumwalt, however, saw that the Soviet Navy soon would be in a position to challenge U.S. naval power projection—most specifically, support of NATO in the Atlantic and on the alliance's flanks. In stunning congressional testimony in March 1971, he would state his belief that the Soviet Navy had the capability to defeat the U.S. Navy in any fleet-on-fleet duel.

The linchpin of the NATO strategy for the nonnuclear, conventional defense of Europe was resupply via the "Atlantic bridge." If the Navy could not decisively win the battle of the Atlantic, the whole NATO strategic rationale would be undercut and a nuclear exchange inevitable. Heavily committed in Vietnam, the Navy had no forces available to increase its presence in the Atlantic and the Mediterranean. Moreover, its cruisers and destroyers in the Pacific had spent the previous decade bombarding the Vietnamese ashore and supporting air strikes on the North. As for power projection, the Navy was essentially unopposed. It had not trained with simulated fleet-on-fleet tactics against an opposing blue-water fleet, because no one then considered the Soviet Navy to be anything more than a coastal defense force.

In a real sense, the Soviet Union had succeeded in miring the United States in Southeast Asia, while it moved to shift the global correlation of forces in its favor. Zumwalt knew the United States had to disengage from the war—soon.

On his return from Vietnam, Zumwalt had initiated a review of the Navy, based on this geostrategic understanding. The resulting initiative, called Project 60, aimed to redirect the Navy from an emphasis on power projection to sea control. His logic was powerful: If the Navy had to move from point A to point B, it had to have sea control to do it, and if power projection required it to be at point B, then without sea control it would have no power projection.

Whereas the postwar era's great power projection programs involved carriers and submarines, Zumwalt's sea control navy essentially would be the submarine force and a conventionally powered surface fleet. To support sealift across the Atlantic bridge, the fleet would add new classes of sea control ships optimized for antisubmarine, antiair, and antisurface warfare. Zumwalt called his approach the "high-low mix," high being the expensive, high-capability platforms and low being cheaper and expendable sea control ships.

His program would have to compete for funding with carrier aviation, the heart of postwar naval force structure, programs, and personnel, not to mention the industrial base. Project 60 was predictably popular among the destroyer Navy, but the aviators, the nuclear Navy, and the high-end shipbuilding, aircraft, and electronics industry were outraged. Zumwalt was preaching heresy, and his initiative was guaranteed to be divisive.

Energetic in pursuit of his vision, Zumwalt sought equally energetic officers to be his subordinates. His key pick was Rear Adm. Worth Bagley to be the Navy's planning and programming boss. Bagley, whom Zumwalt called a "brainy destroyerman," also had worked as an executive assistant to Nitze. A second key selection was another tin-can sailor, Capt. Stansfield Turner, later President Carter's director of central intelligence, who had been Chafee's executive assistant. In the months before Zumwalt's change of command, Bagley and Turner led his Project 60 review.

In August, Bagley established himself officially as the director of Project 60, which put him in charge of program development. Hank arrived later in the month, and Bagley immediately assigned him to be his special assistant and project officer for the initiative. Hank also reported to Capt. James H. Doyle, who was in the budgeting branch under Bagley. "My association with Bagley and Doyle," he said, "was extraordinarily rewarding, both personally and professionally."

For the next three years, Hank would serve as the sharp end of their spear in the bitter internal struggles over the direction of the Navy. "The problem in a nutshell was that power projection was the private purview . . . of naval aviation. Everything that you did to emphasize sea control had to come out of the hide of naval aviation."

To finance Project 60's sea control force, Zumwalt wanted to cut the Navy in half. During his years, the active force went from 769 to 512 ships. What he failed to realize, said Hank, was that the Washington bureaucracy would "gleefully" accept his force structure cuts but would decline to return the savings.

The Navy had not seen such a chief of naval operations since Arleigh Burke, and Zumwalt pursued his objectives in a similar manner, often bypassing the chain of command, infuriating many admirals who were senior to him in years of service. Convinced of the rightness of his approach, Zumwalt did not "sugar-coat the pills." His first move under Project 60 was to cancel all the World War II *Essex*-class carriers, thereby reducing the Navy's total carrier force from twenty-six to a stated requirement for fifteen. He then transferred the antisubmarine warfare responsibility to the attack carriers and reconfigured a number of aircraft complements into dual-purpose wings that included an antisubmarine capability. He also cut fixed-wing aircraft programs. He then proposed a so-called sea control ship, a small carrier having neither catapults nor arresting gear, that would rely on vertical aircraft and helicopters.

The aviators were apoplectic. Since 1945, said Hank, they had taken the attitude that "the main battery of every combatant should be resident on the flight deck of the carrier." Suggesting otherwise was the development of the cruise missile, particularly the antiship variants already in the Soviet Navy, that demanded the U.S. Navy to disperse firepower across a number of surface combatants instead of concentrating it on the decks of fifteen carriers.

The aviation community argued that A-6 Intruder attack aircraft could counter the Soviet surface fleet antiship missile shooters; thus, the Navy did not need its own antiship missile, the Harpoon, enthusiastically promoted by Zumwalt. As head of the joint plans section in Jim Doyle's planning branch, Hank first cited the twenty-seven-carrier requirement in the Joint System Objective Plan, the force structure bible, and then noted that the Navy only had fifteen. He then asked rhetorically how the service could fill the firepower gap without buying more carriers and more planes. Dispersing offensive firepower via the Harpoon was one of the answers that had the added bonus of trumping the Soviet efforts to counter fifteen U.S. carrier targets.

The debates over sea control versus power projection were brutally contentious. In an effort to mediate the battles among the surface, aviation, and undersea communities, Zumwalt established the Chief of Naval Operations' Executive Board, which consisted of himself, his vice chief, and selected three-star admirals. The board had a secretariat of two: Capt. Bob Monroe and Hank. Together, the pair published the agenda, wrote the issues for each meeting, and reported the minutes and decisions. "Of course, whoever's got the pencil has got enormous power," said Hank, "and Bob Monroe was the single smartest person I ever worked for."

Although Zumwalt was opposed on cost grounds to the *Los Angeles*–class attack submarine, he supported the program and temporarily worked a compromise with the nuclear Navy's baron, Adm. Hyman G. Rickover. He finally locked horns with Rickover over his decision to cancel expensive nuclear-powered surface ships and study the idea of conventionally powered carriers. According to Bagley, Zumwalt could support Rickover's nuclear-powered destroyer but not in the numbers the aging admiral was suggesting, nor at the expense of other surface modernization. The CNO, thus, favored the *Spruance*-class DDG, a concept that had originated with McNamara.

Originally conceived as a single-purpose antisubmarine warfare destroyer, the *Spruance* was supposed to work in tandem with the single-purpose DXG antiair warfare ship. The antiair destroyer was also to have the Typhon weapon system, an expensive Aegis predecessor, but the Typhon never made the grade. Both the system and the DXG were canceled. In 1968, funds went to the *Spruance,* leaving the Navy with no comparable ship for air defense and a severe force-structure void in the destroyer force.

In an effort to save his nuclear-powered destroyer, Rickover went over Zumwalt's head to John Warner, who had succeeded Chafee as Secretary of the Navy in May 1972. Labeled by his own staff as a "tower of Jell-O," Warner was very much in the aviators' corner and no friend to Zumwalt and the surface navy. In July 1973, however, Zumwalt found renewed favor in Secretary of Defense James Schlesinger, who was able to get President Richard Nixon to say that it was not in the interest of the country for the *Spruance* to be nuclear powered. It was a defeat for Rickover and the end of any continued authorization of nuclear-powered surface combatants.

Zumwalt and Bagley felt that the Navy had to disperse offensive power through platforms other than the carrier. To add capability to battle group operations, they wanted submarines with the Navy Tactical Data System, Harpoon, and Tomahawk cruise missiles that could integrate into the strike forces when required. In the 1970s, however, the Navy lacked the technology to implement their ideas. The executive board thus carried the debate to all the issues associated with long-range targeting and the inadequacies of sonars.

By virtue of his role on the board's secretariat, Hank often was in the crossfire. At one meeting, submariners and surface line officers considered whether Harpoon should go on the *Los Angeles*. As the submariners already had funding for the long-range Mark 48 torpedo, Hank took the position that the submarine had no requirement for the weapon. He also noted the problems of targeting an antiship missile with a periscope distance to the horizon of about four miles; he asked why the Navy should procure a weapon for submarines that they could not target.

After the meeting, the two-star admiral responsible for the submarine Harpoon program put his arm around Hank's shoulder and asked, "What was your name again?" Hank replied, "Mustin."

"Are you up for captain?"

"No sir."

"Well, you will be some day."

Intense CEB discussions involving the Aegis weapon system also pitted destroyer sailors against aviators. Designed initially for a larger nuclear-powered cruiser, subsequently canceled because of cost considerations, the Aegis needed an expensive redesign to fit it into the smaller *Spruance* hull. Air defense dollars would have to pay for it—funds that the aviators wanted spent on their air superiority fighter, the F-14 Tomcat, named after Vice Adm. Tom Connolly.

At one of the early board meetings on the characteristics of the *Spruance*, Connolly had taken issue with the idea that the carrier air wing would have to provide a defensive umbrella over the ship. "I just have one question here. Who's escorting who?" asked Connolly. "Is the carrier escorting the *Spruance*, or is the *Spruance* escorting the carrier?" "Everybody had a chuckle," observed Hank dryly. "Not a bad question."

At the end of the day, among the programs begun or accelerated during Hank's time on the executive board were the *Spruance*-class destroyer, the Aegis cruiser, the *Nimitz*-class carrier, *Los Angeles*–class submarine, and the Trident nuclear-powered ballistic missile submarine. The aviators got their F-14, and surface ships got the Aegis weapon system, the Tomahawk, the Harpoon, the SLQ-32 electronic warfare combat system, the Phalanx close-in weapons system, the lightweight, automated Mark 45 5-inch/54 mount, and towed antisubmarine warfare arrays.

Zumwalt was pleased with Hank's key supportive role in these efforts. Halfway through this tour, the admiral wrote him a fitness report that said he was the best commander in the Navy. "So naturally I was selected for captain, almost three years early, which was unheard of at the time. It caused a lot of ill will in a lot of places."

Hank often was cast in the role of point man. When Zumwalt read reports that Seventh Fleet ships were exhausting their ammunition, he ordered him to take a month-long tour of the Western Pacific to determine the severity of any material deficiencies. Hank visited forty ships and their captains, most of whom he knew, but the perception in the fleet was that he was an enforcer for the Office of the Chief of Naval Operations. "I stopped through CinCPac Fleet, where I was greeted like a polecat at a beach party, a spy coming in," he said, "just like a guy from Ernie King's staff wearing gray in World War II." He was no longer just a Pacific destroyerman; Hank's future now lay in another direction.

In 1971, Zumwalt made a visit to Europe that included a stop in Norway, where he saw firsthand the vulnerability of NATO's northern flank. With the upsurge of Soviet naval activity, the Norwegians felt very much behind the lines in the Soviet sphere. Zumwalt "stimulated government policy to confirm our use of Iceland for ASW/surveillance aircraft, more frequent NATO naval exercises along the flank, and alliance infrastructure improvements in Norway to show our resolve," said Bagley.

"A proposal for homeporting in the U.K. or Netherlands never got through the American system," he added. When Zumwalt saw that homeporting in northern Europe and Britain was "impracticable," his attention turned to the Mediterranean, Bagley continued. There, the Soviet Black Sea Fleet was increasing in size and power and threatening the political balance in Greece and Turkey. These two NATO allies also feared that the United States would abandon them in the event of a NATO crisis in central Europe. To begin to redress the political balance in a way that was within the budgetary limitations he faced in Washington, Zumwalt decided to homeport a carrier and escorts abroad.

This proved to be yet another contentious issue in which Hank played a visible role in preparing the supporting arguments. Traditional Navy thinking held that it took three ships in inventory to keep one ship deployed. While one ship was in overhaul, a second was in predeployment work-up, and a third was deployed. Overseas homeporting broke that mold. Zumwalt argued that he could increase his naval presence in the Mediterranean and northern Pacific without tapping forces committed to the Vietnam War or an increase in ship construction.

Aviators accepted homeporting a carrier and a destroyer squadron in Japan, because the Atsugi airfield was available for work-ups and training exercises to maintain readiness. In October 1971, Destroyer Squadron Fifteen with six destroyers went to Yokosuka, followed a couple of years later by the carrier *Midway*.

Mediterranean homeporting was not so simple. First, the United States had no infrastructure comparable to its facilities in Japan. Countries in the western Med did not want a carrier, and NATO and U.S. Air Force assets already had filled the airfields in the region. In January 1973, Zumwalt was finally able to homeport a few submarines at the Italian island of La Maddalena between Sardinia and Corsica. In the eastern Med, the political-military factors led only to one conclusion—Greece.

For valid reasons, the aviation community immediately opposed the idea. "The mythology of the day," said Hank, "was that the carriers would operate indefinitely at sea without shore support. The reality was quite different." Athens did not have a counterpart to Atsugi. As a result, the plan had to include the release of U.S. and NATO funds for an airfield where the aviators could maintain their qualifications and where logistics could focus to support the carrier and her air wing. The Navy found a partially constructed Greek airstrip at Megara, some thirty miles west of Athens, but the aviators declined to homeport a carrier in Greece until the field's completion. Further construction required NATO funding, "which was just another ticket for delay."

Homeporting escorts was more straightforward. The Navy opted for Elefsis, a town some twenty miles west of Athens, and began construction immediately on a temporary pier large enough to berth six destroyers and a tender. In the autumn of 1972, the destroyers of Destroyer Squadron Twelve arrived in Athens.

Hank's first tour in the Office of the Chief of Naval Operations was coming to a close. It had been a grueling time for Lucy, who would drive him to the Pentagon from their home in Alexandria every day and then shuttle the children to and from their various schools. "The workload and the hours at the office were extraordinary," he said, "but I had studied at the feet of the masters, Worth Bagley and Jim Doyle, and had learned the most precious of all staff talents: how to express complex issues in 'Dick and Jane' language."

He was eager to return to sea, and, as was his custom, he consulted with his father as to his next move. Lloyd advised him to pursue a unit command. "When you go to be a destroyer squadron commander, you find the challenges of unit command, where you're commanding commanding officers instead of yourself commanding your own ship, are very different, and are the best prep school for further command if you're going to stay competitive for flag rank." Requesting a destroyer squadron, preferably San Diego–based, Hank submitted his "dream card."

In April 1973, Zumwalt appointed Bagley as the four-star commander in chief, U.S. Naval Forces, Europe. In turn, Bagley offered to take Hank to London as his four-stripe executive assistant and aide. "Hank was a harvest of ideas and a good judge of other concepts," Bagley recalled, "a combination that was useful to his seniors and the Navy." While not orders to a unit command in the Pacific, the offer was a shore assignment of the first rank. Hank gratefully accepted and prepared to set his continued eastward professional course. He had arrived in OpNav as a Pacific destroyerman steeped in guns and propulsion. He was leaving to enter the politico-military affairs of NATO and Mediterranean command.

Chapter 31

Introduction to NATO

THE FROCKED CAPTAIN IN SLEEPY HOLLOW

In August 1973, Worth Bagley and Hank Mustin, now a frocked captain, arrived in London. Bagley came to town as an activist to drive Zumwalt's initiatives in the NATO area of operations, in particular the Athens homeporting of Destroyer Squadron Twelve. Having seen firsthand how successfully Zumwalt used a kitchen cabinet to further Project 60, Bagley had asked Hank to help him assemble his own ministaff. Hank recommended three dynamic commanders, Scot McCauley, George Lanman, and Arie Sigmond, and put forward a lieutenant commander, Connie Lautenbacher, his weapons officer on the *Wilson,* to be Bagley's flag lieutenant.

On arrival, Bagley and Hank found the U.S. Naval Forces, Europe, headquarters "a Sleepy Hollow" with "retired-on-active-duty captains who were homesteading over there because they all liked to walk around town with their rolled-up umbrellas and their homburgs." The offices were off Grosvenor Square by the U.S. embassy in the eight-story headquarters building.

Bagley was a workaholic who had the benefit of his own well-appointed family flat on the fourth floor. "This meant that we would work till seven-thirty or eight," said Hank, "then he'd get in the elevator and go upstairs and have a martini, and the rest of us would have to find our way home. Then we'd get in there at six o'clock in the morning, and he'd be there at six-fifteen. He was the most stimulating flag officer I was ever associated with, and it was an enormous challenge to keep up with him." Hank, Lucy, and the children lived several blocks north in an Orchard Court set of quarters that Admiral Bagley had arranged for them.

Bagley and his high-octane staff were in London on a mission to reclaim the NATO flanks. To that end, he had very firm ideas on how the Sixth Fleet would operate in the Mediterranean and what should be done to make Zumwalt's homeporting work. The import of the mission became evident within two months.

On 6 October 1973, Yom Kippur, the Soviet-supplied armies of Egypt and Syria crossed the Suez Canal and assaulted the Golan Heights, routing Israeli positions. After four days of major losses, the Israelis turned the tide of battle. The Soviet Union responded with airlifts to Damascus and Cairo, thanks to overflight rights granted by a NATO ally, Turkey. On 12–13 October, the United States unilaterally launched its own resupply. Without the support of NATO or the logistically critical Spain, replacement fighter aircraft for the Israelis had to fly across the Atlantic to Italian ports. From there, the Sixth Fleet provided security along the way to Israel to ensure that the Soviet Navy would not interfere.

The tail end of that naval support operation was in the eastern Med, where the *Independence* task group had positioned itself south of Crete. On 16 October, the U.S. ships suddenly found themselves shadowed by an unusually large Soviet Navy combatant force. Despite requests, Washington declined to reinforce them. According to Zumwalt, Kissinger, wedded to his notion of détente, prevented Admiral Moorer from sending additional ships eastward.

Five days later, when Israeli forces crossed the Suez Canal and surrounded the Egyptian Third Army, the war assumed a superpower dimension. The Soviet Union responded to Egyptian requests for aid by threatening to send troops. Kissinger thereupon went to Moscow to negotiate a cease-fire. Thinking he had achieved one, he returned to Washington, but the Navy knew the crisis was far from over. The Soviets continued to deploy naval forces to the Med. By 24 October, as cease-fire violations by both sides continued, the Soviet presence had risen to eighty ships, many with substantial antiship cruise missile capabilities. Tensions rose worldwide. On the twenty-fifth, Nixon ordered U.S. forces to Defense Condition 3—a nuclear alert.

This superpower confrontation was eerily reminiscent of the Cuban missile crisis. Politically, however, in 1973 the United States was disadvantaged, almost paralyzed by the fallout from Watergate. More seriously, the nation had neither the nuclear nor the conventional military advantage it had enjoyed in 1962. In London, Bagley and his staff could see the Navy's weakness in the eastern Med. On 26 October, the Soviets began large-scale anticarrier warfare operations against the *Independence* task group. By the end of the month, they had ninety-six warships, including thirty-four surface combatants and twenty-three submarines. "They came out of the Black Sea Fleet and down out of the Northern Fleet," said Hank, "and all of a sudden, we had never before seen—and never since—the concentration of Soviet naval power in the Med."

The Sixth Fleet and the Soviet Mediterranean Fleet were poised for war at sea. This time, the United States blinked, although worsening weather prevented U.S. withdrawal until 30 October. Three days later, the Soviet units began to disperse. Although the crisis abated, the U.S. Navy maintained a heightened readiness until 18 November.

The standoff prompted a realization in Navy circles that a surge deployment to European waters would face a potent Soviet force, including attack submarines already positioned for battle. As such, the crisis validated Zumwalt and Bagley's case that the Soviet Navy was now capable of denying U.S. Navy sea control and consequently its ability to project power.

In the aftermath, Bagley and his staff considered how to exercise solutions to the sea-control questions raised by the Soviet ship deployments. The next few months would introduce Hank to the operational constraints that NATO placed on the U.S. Navy. His focus often was on how to reconcile U.S. rules of engagement with NATO fears that incidents at sea during any naval exercise could lead to a war in Europe.

"One of the NATO issues became rules of engagement," he recalled. "The Central Front people did not want to be drawn into a war with the Soviet Union because two ships shot it out in the Mediterranean. So, they attempted to impose very stringent hostile intent rules on the naval forces." The rules meant essentially that a U.S. unit could not fire a weapon until an enemy fired his. "The people in command of the naval forces disagreed. 'If we see seventy-five Soviet bombers take off and head our way, we're going to shoot them down, and if you guys don't like it, we won't chop our forces to NATO.' That was the Navy position, but SACEur, the Supreme Allied Commander, Europe, was an Army officer, and so the issue festered for years."

While these debates raged, NATO forced on the U.S. Navy very tight rules of engagement for operations against the Soviets. One of the great challenges was the Soviet use of the so-called tattletale, a heavily armed combatant stationed some two thousand yards from a U.S. carrier that provided continuous location information to Soviet submarines and aircraft. Under hostile intent rules, the tattletale could have emptied her magazine of missiles into a carrier before U.S. aircraft, forced to stand off beyond the range of Soviet antiaircraft missiles, could get to a delivery point to fire their weapons against her.

The 1973 crisis and subsequent exercises also proved that the Navy did not have the tactics or weapons, that is, the antiship missiles, to respond to fleet-on-fleet engagements. This was very sobering to both the surface and the aviation communities. For decades, the aviators had assured the surface force that they would sink the enemy before he fired a shot. It was Hank's view that their approach ignored not only the new capabilities of the Soviet Navy but the contemporary rules of engagement in a NATO theater. "As but one example, Soviet air-to-surface missiles outranged all U.S. Navy air-to-ground weapons; analyses showed unacceptable U.S. aircraft attrition if U.S. aircraft were the only means of dealing with the Soviet surface navy."

As Hank attempted to resolve the conundrum that hostile intent presented for any tactical development, he became more aware of the difference between the U.S. and European attitudes to defense planning—and the profound consequences for the Navy. Land powers dominated NATO's European military establishment, and the U.S. Army was the dominant voice in NATO. Per the politics of the U.S. "CinC-doms," the commander in chief of the U.S. European Command would always be Army, and that U.S. general would be NATO's supreme allied commander, Europe. For Army planning purposes, the NATO area of operations was the German Central Front and its two flanks, Norway and the Mediterranean. The Army and the Air Force focused on the battle for Europe; the Navy was left to focus on the flanks, a secondary priority.

Oft unsaid, but accepted by all, NATO was many divisions short on the Central Front. The U.S. deployment in Germany served only as a trip-wire for a controlled escalation. The scenarios that followed from this cynical truth suited the Europeans, who had no intention of fighting another prolonged conventional war on their continent. The NATO strategy accepted that a conventional war would not occur: In every case it would escalate to a nuclear exchange between the Soviet Union and the United States.

The strategy was deterrence: The Soviets would not invade Western Europe because of the threat of a U.S. nuclear response. If deterrence were to fail and the Soviets were to attack, and if NATO started to lose, the alliance would resort to tactical nuclear weapons, thus offsetting the Soviet numerical superiority. "The problem was that the Soviets would respond to 'tactical' nuclear weapons use with strategic nuclear strikes against the United States. . . . In every war game that I played in NATO," said Hank, "when very senior people played themselves, within a very few days, ten days or so, SACEur would always say: 'I need nuclear release authority, because I'm being overwhelmed.'"

On the other hand, if NATO found itself winning a conventional war, the alliance assumption was that the Soviets would be the first to "go nuke." In sum, the various scenarios exercised according to the very flimsy tenets of controlled escalation all had the same end game: global thermonuclear war.

The president obviously could not say to the American people that his strategy in Europe assumed a nuclear exchange between the United States and the Soviet Union. Likewise, the Europeans were not going to say that they did not support the NATO strategy of controlled escalation, because they did not want Europe to be a nuclear battleground.

As Hank dealt with the Europeans and the NATO command structure, he quickly discovered how this unstated reality played in Washington regarding U.S. force requirements. It worked for the Army and the Air Force, but it failed for the Navy, reckoned by her sister services to be at the margins of the action. If the Navy's wartime NATO role was mainly supportive, the Navy Department could not make a convincingly strong argument for the Navy's budget in the Department of Defense.

Zumwalt had attempted to justify naval modernization on the basis that a conventional war in Europe needed long-term resupply and the Navy was thus critical to running convoys nonstop to and from Europe. The NATO commanders, the senior Army and Air Force brass, were telling the office of the secretary of defense privately that, given that all scenarios point to going nuclear, the Navy's case was irrelevant: Don't fund it. Hank determined that to get funding for modernization, the Navy had to find a rationale to be more involved in Europe.

The crisis of 1973 proved the Zumwalt-Bagley thesis and provided that rationale: The strength of the Soviet Navy now required that the United States invest money and time in constructing ships, "as opposed to training an infantryman." The Navy would have to reconfigure its fleet and its combat systems and build "ships that have room in them to grow," said Hank. "That's a very expensive proposition."

To make the Navy more relevant and get the money to do it, Zumwalt needed to make the argument so compelling that service opponents could not reject it. Compelling though it was, the Navy unfortunately failed to get the necessary increases. For Zumwalt, it was a major setback. The vital defense of the Fulda Gap and the European Central Front continued to place ground forces as NATO's highest priority, the case that the Army could convincingly make to the Washington bureaucracy. In addition, the administration in 1974 was following Kissinger to Moscow to negotiate a strategic arms limitation treaty.

Zumwalt no longer was in step with his civilian bosses. In any event, it was time for him to retire. He wanted Bagley as his successor. However, by association, Bagley had become almost as controversial as Zumwalt himself. With Secretary of the Navy John Warner's acceptance, an aviator, James L. Holloway, got the nod, although Zumwalt did succeed in getting Bagley the job as vice chief, with Holloway's support.

The appointment cut short Bagley's time in London. The change was completed on 29 June. Two days later, Gen. George S. Brown, USAF, relieved Moorer as chairman of the Joint Chiefs of Staff. In London, Hank did not want to repeat the staff transition that he experienced when McCain relieved Sharp in Honolulu. He told Bagley that he wanted to go when he did. Having screened for a command at sea, he asked for a destroyer squadron. Bagley offered him Destroyer Squadron Twelve in Athens.

Lucy did not receive the news well. The children were all in school and loving London, getting around independently on buses and in taxis. By this time, they were living in luxury in a posh flat on Portman Square; the flat below them was occupied by Aristotle Onassis's sister. Lucy was not happy about leaving to go to a billet where "they were burning cars."

The unpopularity of the military junta in Greece would be the least of Hank's challenges. With homeporting a centerpiece of Zumwalt's sea-control strategy, Bagley and Hank had made a number of visits to Athens to work with the Greek government and had devoted time to ensure the proper manning and support for the destroyers. Despite their efforts, the ships' performance worsened, putting the whole homeporting concept at risk. Morale had deteriorated to the point that sailors were deserting or committing crimes like robbing Greek taxi drivers. The Navy recognized that a change of leadership at the top of the squadron was immediately in order.

Prior to his assuming command, Hank returned to the States to meet with his Cruiser-Destroyer Force, Atlantic, type commander, Rear Adm. Ralph Stratford Wentworth, compressing the normal six-month pipeline for major command to about a week, thanks to a waiver from Bagley owing to the desperate situation in Athens. Wentworth's orders to him were straightforward: "Square away the squadron and fast."

When Hank reported to Athens in May 1974 as Destroyer Squadron Twelve commander, he was gladly returning to the operational navy. He and Lucy found a house in Kifissia, a quiet village north of Athens. That spring, the Cypriot government was accusing the Greek junta of attempting a coup. Tensions were escalating not only between left and right, but also between NATO allies Greece and Turkey over the Cyprus issue.

Hank's immediate focus was on the material condition of his destroyer squadron. Sure that Admiral Wentworth would not settle for excuses, Hank set himself an ambitious task: to command a squadron that could challenge the Soviets for sea control of the eastern Mediterranean. Given the squadron reports that he had read in London, he had no illusions. "They blamed everybody but themselves," said Hank, "the Bureau of Personnel for not providing enough qualified people, the type commander for not sending them needed spare parts, and even a cement factory in Elefsis for blowing dust on the pier."

On arrival, he went straight to the *Barry,* one of two ships restricted to the pier by the Propulsion Examining Board. He was appalled. "The engineering plant was in a shambles. It was in pieces on the deck plates. When you walked past the after fire room, the smell of pot coming up out of the hatches was enough to give you a high. They had people over the hill—that had been over the hill for months—somewhere in Greece."

To achieve readiness, Hank would have to work his command in stages. He first would tackle the personnel issues by cleaning house and motivating what doers he could find, addressing the material issues along the way.

He started at the top. He summarily relieved the *Barry's* skipper, took command himself, and arranged for Cdr. Greg Streeter, his highly capable former engineer on the *Lawrence,* to be the relief. When Streeter arrived, he worked with him closely to put the ship in order.

Hank was on board every day, driving the process. A former engineering officer himself, he realized that Streeter could solve most of the *Barry's* problems with spare parts. Indeed, such was the case with many of the ships. Hank helped each of his skippers by pressuring Surface Forces Atlantic in Norfolk to expedite the request process and ship them the parts promptly. "My impatience with the responsiveness of the SurfLant staff caused a number of very bluntly worded messages to fill the air."

He also used his authority to reward good performance. Faced with an after engine room in complete disarray, he and Streeter found a willing first class machinist's mate in Ozan Ozkosar. A Turk who was justly afraid to set foot in Greece as the crisis over Cyprus deepened, he chose to remain on the *Barry* and pass the time studying for his exams for promotion. Hank made him a promise: If Ozkosar could get his space through the Propulsion Examining Board inspection, he would see that he made chief machinist's mate in three months. In six months, Ozkosar got his space to pass and not only advanced to chief, but made warrant officer as well. In April 1985, he got his commission as ensign. As Second Fleet commander, Hank presided at the ceremony and administered the oath.

In virtually each ship and each space, he and his captains found like sailors and gave them the recognition and the authority to get the job done. As for the deserters and pot smokers, Hank shipped them home. In 1975, by the end of the annual cycle, the *Barry* was the most improved ship in the fleet, for which it won that year's Arleigh Burke Award for the Atlantic Fleet.

The second ship on PEB restriction was the *Manley*. Although he held her captain responsible for her condition, Hank approached her executive officer, Lt. Cdr. Gene Black, whom he knew to be a very capable officer. If Black got the ship to pass the PEB, Hank promised, he would qualify him for destroyer command; if the ship failed again, he would relieve both Black and his skipper. In no time, Black returned the ship to sea, with the PEB reporting that she was the finest ship of her class inspected to that time.

Turning to the crews, he got help from Teddy Ross, one of his chiefs on the *Wilson*, who had made master chief and after thirty-five years service was scheduled for retirement. By now a good friend, Ross wanted a waiver to remain on active duty. Hank arranged it through Bagley. He sent Ross to the *Gearing*-class destroyer *William M. Wood.*

Finding resistance in the forward fire room from a chief who assumed he was not sufficiently expert in a *Gearing*-class destroyer, Ross challenged him in front of his men for both to put on blindfolds and trace the auxiliary steam line from the number one boiler in the forward bulkhead to the end of the after engine room. "The first guy to finish," barked Ross, "is the one who knows the plant." Before the other chief had left the forward fire room, Ross had finished. News of the contest quickly passed throughout the squadron, winning Ross wide support, even from the chief he had humbled.

To address the trouble that U.S. sailors were causing on liberty, Hank put together a council of senior chiefs, led by Ross, to propose ideas to resolve the morale problem. From this council came a number of projects. The squadron converted a set of shacks at the end of their pier into a movie exchange, where his men were able to see first-run sea prints. Next, they established a slop chute that sold beer and liquor and generated recreation funds for foosball games and shuffleboard. Eventually, they had enough money to build an enlisted club. Men from all the ships came together and built the clubhouse themselves, complete with a bar that had beer on tap and a liquor license. Alongside, they cleared a recreation area where the sailors could throw footballs and baseballs and shoot hoops.

Not surprisingly, Hank found that his men were falling asleep during the routine indoctrination movies that cautioned against all manner of misbehavior. He had just received an autographed photo from John Wayne that his cousin Joe Howard had sent him from San Diego. It reminded him of hearing how Wayne had visited the units in the Mekong Delta and promised the men that he would do anything for them if they ever asked. From Athens, Hank wrote the star a thank you letter, adding his request for a public service announcement in the form of a morale builder for the sailors. Hank included notes for a script. Wayne replied with a two-minute clip. "On comes the Duke, saying, 'Hi, I'm John Wayne. You guys are ambassadors for America, and DesRon Twelve is special.'" The trailer was a hit, and, over time, incidents ashore declined.

As morale increased, Hank increased the emphasis on training. At times, he was unable to take his ships to sea, either because of the political situation in Greece or from a shortage of fuel. To make use of the downtime, he structured a competitive in-port training program. He had the ships do every engineering drill in the type commander's battle efficiency competition, except stopping and locking the shaft. In gunnery, he would drill for gunfire support by conducting procedural exercises, where the gun crews would turn their switches in the proper sequence and dry fire. For communications, the ships would read each others' signal flags from across the pier.

Many ideas for drills came from Ross's chiefs council. A pipe-patching drill that took place on the pier with a small pipe rigged to a high pressure water hose led the senior chiefs to expand such drills into what they called the damage control Olympics. A second drill involving knot tying became the boatswain's mate Olympics. For both competitions, the chiefs would serve as judges. Later in his career, when Hank was the deputy at Surface Forces, Atlantic, he implemented these competitions throughout the force.

Before his squadron could hope to challenge Soviet sea control, Hank needed competent mariners driving his ships. The Atlantic Fleet commander and the commander of the Atlantic cruiser and destroyer force had explicitly told skippers to avoid any bumping incidents at sea, regardless of whether a potential incident involved a Soviet ship or simply a change of station within a formation. Hank's captains were consequently reluctant to have their junior officers conn their ships. Once he felt his destroyers were ready to operate as a squadron, he assembled his skippers to convey the high priority he placed on seamanship. He ordered them to train their junior officers, promising that if a captain did not fully comply, he would give him an unsatisfactory in seamanship on his fitness report.

Hank made a concerted effort to enhance the stature of his commanding officers. Although he rotated his flag through the squadron, changing every three months to allow him to focus on each ship's progress, he was careful to have his own mess. Only his staff would eat at the ship's wardroom. "I did that because I wanted the captain to be able to sit there and tell his own jokes, have his own guys see him sitting at the head of the table, let him pick the movies, and do all the things you want for a captain to raise his image with his junior officers." In the end, and only after his captains requested it, did he dine with them in the wardroom. Hank remembered one of his skippers who requested his presence telling him, "To many of these junior officers, you are the only four-stripe captain they've ever seen up close."

By this time, Destroyer Squadron Twelve was performing to Hank's standard. When other units could not get under way, the squadron undertook their operational commitments. In other instances, when ships that deployed to the Sixth Fleet for some reason were unable to shoot their weapons, Hank saw to it that he got their training firing. Such would be the case, for example, when a skipper was not able to get permission from the French to use their missile range because he was not familiar with the request procedures. Since Rear Adm. Forrest S. Petersen, commander of Task Force 60, often had unused munitions from his quarterly allocation that were in his "use it or lose it" category, he was happy to make them available to Hank, who eagerly stood ready to request it. With that munitions largesse and having the contacts and knowing the drill with respect to France's missile range, Hank was able to work his ships so that each was able to complete an entire year's schedule for the battle efficiency competition in every quarter.

Once his ships were fully operational, he started the serious work on the tactical development that they would need to face the Soviet Navy. On the *Sampson*, he found an operations officer, Lt. Neil Byrne, who had invented a tactical dice game using ship models. Byrne had assembled detailed U.S. and Soviet ship capabilities and called it NavTag for naval tactical game. Hank initiated a series of NavTag games among his ships that evolved so as to enable each ship to exercise virtually all the type commander's tactical notes. When his officers started playing anti-tattletale tactics, they came to the conclusion that carrier air alone was incapable of countering the threat and developed new ways of dealing with it. In no time, the wardrooms became enthusiastic in their overall pursuit of tactical proficiency.

Eager to find ways to overcome the tattletale threat and improve integration of carrier air and surface ship air defense, Admiral Petersen had his aviation squadron commanders participate in the NavTag project. NavTag become so successful as a gaming device that when Hank, as a two-star, became the division director in charge of surface weapons in the Office of the Chief of Naval Operations, he had Byrne automate the game for installation at the Naval Academy and the Naval War College.

On 20 July 1974, the Turks invaded Cyprus, and three days later, the Greek junta fell in Athens. The Sixth Fleet commander, Vice Adm. Frederick "Fox" Turner, fearful of any suggestion to Turkey that the United States was tilting to Greece in the crisis, ordered Destroyer Squadron Twelve to leave Athens. The squadron remained under way for forty-five days.

It was a tense time for Lucy and the children. Greek leftists were bombing American cars in the neighborhood. Having to buy food at the local markets and shuttle the children to schools, Lucy depended on her Greek-American friend, Roula Hunter, for intelligence. "She must have called me three different times while we were there by ourselves and said, 'Lucy, stay in today.' I was so lucky to have her. . . . And really where they were bombing was just a street away from us, and they were blowing up the cars."

At sea, Hank was conducting all manner of routines for which the ships had trained. When the men returned to port in September, Destroyer Squadron Twelve was a different unit, with the highest morale.

While under way, the squadron had observed how the Soviet Navy tried to lay claim to places in international waters that could serve as sanctuaries. "When they'd send their ships into the Med, essentially they'd anchor them," said Hank. "They didn't do very much, unless they came out and put a tattletale on the carrier." The submarines shadowed the U.S. carrier, while the Soviet surface navy went to anchorages, one of which was the island of Kithira, at the southern tip of the Ionian Sea in the approaches to Athens. When Hank reported that a number of Soviet combatants were always anchored there, Turner ordered him to anchor overnight in Kithira every time he returned to Athens, to thwart any Soviet assumption that it was their undisputed preserve.

Into the following year, the squadron continued to improve readiness. In April 1975, Destroyer Squadron Twelve participated in the NATO Sardinia 75, during which Hank learned that Greece, Turkey, and Italy could operate at only a very basic level. "If you had a notion at the time that we were going to be this magnificent integrated force, that was a pretty naive notion." For a start, none of their ships had a Naval Tactical Data System of any kind.

By the summer, Konstantin Karamanlis's government in Athens had taken the position that the United States was responsible for the continued Turkish occupation of northern Cyprus. Withdrawing from military commitments to NATO, Karamanlis finally asked the Navy to leave Greece. When Destroyer Squadron Twelve left at the end of the summer, Turner and Petersen awarded it the Navy Meritorious Unit Commendation. Each of the captains received a Navy Commendation Medal. In the words of both commanders, Destroyer Squadron Twelve was the Med's best destroyer squadron in ten years. "It really just became a plain old leadership matter," said Hank. "When you figure out that you've got a problem, don't blame it on somebody else—fix it."

Hank arranged for his ships to return from the Mediterranean carrying male dependents. His eldest sons, Lloyd and Tom, made the trip on board the *Barry*. The four-week transit included stops at Ville Franche on the French Riviera and Palma de Mallorca in the Balearic Islands. After a port visit to the Navy's facility at Rota on Spain's Atlantic coast, they headed westward to Philadelphia, where they arrived on 20 August.

Preparing for their arrival, Hank asked his chiefs council how they could make the homecoming memorable for the men, many of whom had been overseas for two years. The chiefs discovered that what they most missed were Big Macs. Hank wrote to Ray Kroc, the McDonald's chairman and founder. When the ships arrived in Philadelphia, five huge McDonald's trucks were on the pier waiting for them. In no time, the sailors and their families "mobbed" each one. Said Hank, "It was great."

For the rest of the year, the squadron remained in the Philadelphia Navy Yard as each of the ships cycled through her overhaul. He knew he was going to the Office of the Chief of Naval Operations, so by the beginning of the school year Lucy and the children had returned to their house in Alexandria. Until December, Hank remained with his squadron in the yard aboard the *Sampson,* commuting south on the weekends to be with his family. Before he was relieved, he left his skippers with one last bit of characteristic advice. "You're the captain. You're responsible for the ship, not BuShips [*sic*] or the shipyard trying to keep its workload up. The system will always try to chip away at your authority. Don't let it, because if you let some tech rep usurp your decisions, he can't relieve you of the responsibility for those decisions."

Chapter 32

Driving Surface Warfare

In January 1975, while Hank was in Athens, the Navy amalgamated the cruiser-destroyer forces and the amphibious, service, and mine warfare communities into the Atlantic and Pacific surface commands. With that year's arrival of the surface warfare pin, comparable to the long-familiar aviator wings and submarine dolphins, the surface warfare officer designation defined the community.

Vice Adm. Jim Doyle, the deputy chief of naval operations for surface warfare, now wanted to open opportunities for surface warriors throughout the fleet. He began seeking to expand his control over personnel and requirements to include the amphibious and service force as well as cruisers and destroyers. At the same time, aviators, whose carrier force had been halved by Zumwalt, were desperate for other ship types in which to serve for their deep-draft ship and major command requirements. Under the aviator chiefs of naval operations, they had gotten close to half of the command billets in the amphibious and service forces. A fight for turf was brewing. "Jim Doyle," observed Hank, "was more than equal to the task."

Hank entered the fray in January 1976, when he started his tour as head of the Combat, Support, and Readiness Branch under Doyle, who would call him his "right-hand man on weapon systems and surface navy requirements." The following October, he became head of Fleet Combatants in the Requirements and Readiness Branch for Rear Adm. Bob Morris, the director of the Surface Warfare Division. Morris had long experience in Pacific Fleet destroyers, and Hank was his man to define new surface requirements. As such, he would play a key role in the development of virtually all of the weapons and tactics the Navy would use into the new century.

By this time, Hank had realized two fundamental flaws in Zumwalt's high-low mix concept that called for a fleet composed of a mix of high-technology and cheaper, less capable ships. First, the low-mix sea-control ships could be relevant only if the Navy faced a bona fide blue-water threat. Second, as for the supposedly lower threat environment, the Navy still needed to provide high-mix ships to enable the low-mix ships to survive. Hence, in order for the concept to work, it would need all of its requirement for the more capable high-mix ships, but in the budget wars, it was getting only about half. "Put another way," said Hank, "ships such as the *Oliver Hazard Perry*-class frigate had almost no role in smaller wars against nations with small navies and little or no submarine force."

The surface community understood that the *Charles F. Adams*-class destroyer was inadequate against antiship missiles, particularly long-range antiship missiles. As for the *Spruance*-class, the destroyermen never were happy with it. The concept of single-purpose destroyers operating together enraged them all. The *Spruance* was the largest destroyer ever built, but because of her singular focus on antisubmarine warfare, she had virtually no other weapons on board.

Under Doyle, Hank and his requirements branch converted the *Spruance* hull into the DXG with the Aegis multifunction radar system. Authorized in 1977, the ship ultimately became the *Ticonderoga*-class cruiser in 1980. The early *Spruance* ships were the first destroyers backfitted to receive the vertical launch system. Beginning with the sixth ship, the *Ticonderoga* cruisers also would have the system.

Together, Doyle and Hank began to define the next-generation destroyer to carry the Aegis radar, the DDGX. At the same time, they addressed the lack of power projection capability in the existing destroyer force. They started with a year's study to determine requirements. Doyle gave the task to Rich Fontaine, the new director of the Surface Warfare Division. Fontaine assembled a team including Pete Roane, Ron Tucker, Ted Parker, and Capt. Wayne E. Meyer, whom Hank called "the Rickover of the surface navy's weapons." Meyer had been the project manager for Aegis since 1970. While Fontaine worked on his study, Hank became acting director of surface warfare in December 1977 and thus emerged as the driver of the analyses to support the ship's requirements.

Money was a perennial problem. Into 1978, Hank and his team turned their gaze to the FFG-7 as a prime candidate for cancellation. Under Zumwalt, the Navy's initial response to the Soviet blue-water strategy had been frigate construction. It was one of the few Zumwalt ideas with which Hank did not agree. A single-purpose convoy escort, the single-screw FFG-7 was an operational disaster. If, for whatever reason, the prop would not turn, she was dead in the water. "[The FFG-7] was not effective in a battle group," said Doyle. "We needed multi-mission battle group capable ships with a robust offensive and anti-air warfare capability. There wasn't enough money to do both."

To make the NATO force rationale work, the surface Navy needed more destroyers fully capable of operating with the battle group. Frigates were deploying with the carrier battle groups, but in wartime, they would not have the speed to operate in support of the carrier. The war plan required them to be in Norfolk for convoy and anti-submarine warfare escort duty when the war started, but they would be in the Med escorting carriers. Making the case for their destroyer to Capitol Hill, Hank asked, "Can you imagine Com Sixth Fleet sending half of the fleet home just at the time the Soviets are putting a hundred ships into the Mediterranean? Ridiculous." More importantly, he added, the FFG-7s were designed for open ocean operations, and if they stayed in the Med, they would be sunk.

Senators Margaret Chase Smith of Maine and John Stennis of Mississippi were especially receptive to Hank's case. Keen to preserve their states' shipyards, Bath and Ingalls, respectively, they lent full support to DDGX authorization, given the FFG-7 cancellations. Hank generally found these and other lawmakers more enthusiastic about the new destroyer than the Office of the Secretary of Defense, which felt the Navy was irrelevant to the NATO strategy.

The bitterest fights, however, were within the Navy. The opposition, primarily from the aviation community, was intense. Seeing the expensive Aegis as a competitor for funding for the F-14 Tomcat, the plane that specifically would engage any air threats to the fleet, the aviators were in strong opposition.

In July 1978, Adm. Thomas C. Hayward, another aviator, succeeded Holloway as chief of naval operations. Fresh from a series of Pacific assignments, he was critical of the NATO-first swing strategy that proposed wartime redeployment of Pacific Fleet carriers to the Atlantic. To his mind, the better solution was more carriers, putting him programmatically at odds with the DDGX. "Admiral Hayward did not like the [Fontaine] study or the recommendation for the Aegis system on DDGXs," said Doyle, "primarily because of the cost. He was looking for a smaller ship in displacement and size and a cheaper ship."

Hayward and the aviators saw the DDGX helicopter requirement, for example, as a drain on funding for tailhook aircraft. The director of the Air Warfare Division thus was structuring his budget for the advanced LAMPS III antisubmarine warfare helicopter in such a way that the airframe would never get to sea. Hank devised a scheme whereby his office would accelerate research and development on the avionics by "giving up" funds from FFG-7 for the first airframe buy. He thus put surface warfare's "nose under the tent" for helicopter acquisition, in effect, committing the Air Warfare Division to the program in the out years. The ploy worked.

The second part of the DDGX strategy was to remove the helicopter requirement from the early flights of the DDGX in order not to force more helicopter procurement onto the already strained aviation budget. As a result, the first *Arleigh Burke*–class destroyers would have a landing platform but no hangar or helicopter on board. This work-around meant that Hank had to devise an operational approach to use the LAMPS capability by "hopscotching" helicopters from other ships onto the *Burke* destroyers. Reluctantly, the aviators agreed to the DDGX, despite their additional concern that a Tomahawk strike capability would come at the expense of attack aviation.

This concern generated another set of intense debates. In addition to his drive to put Aegis on as many surface ships as possible, Doyle wanted to change the Navy's sole reliance on the carrier and A-6 Intruder attack aircraft, given his goal to disperse offensive firepower throughout the fleet. Aegis would be the force multiplier for fleet air defense, and the Tomahawk would enable the dispersion of offensive assets to project power from long range.

In the early 1970s, the Navy had to come to terms with the possibility of attack from long-range antiship missiles, a scenario that generated an interest in long-range engagement and by extension long-range land attack. The two programs under way were the Harpoon antiship missile and the longer-range Tomahawk cruise missile to go on surface ships first and then submarines and aircraft. Entering the fleet in small numbers in 1977, the Harpoon was limited in value because of the requirement to marry it to existing surface ship and submarine launching systems that consequently limited its range to about seventy miles.

As first conceived, Tomahawk was to be a submarine-launched, land-attack and antiship cruise missile. It would be low flying, capable of carrying a conventional or nuclear warhead weighing as much as a thousand pounds, with a range of eight hundred to a thousand miles. With a terrain mapping guidance system, the Tomahawk enabled surface ships to do a carrier's job in land attack.

Seeing that the Tomahawk threatened the rationale and continued funding for the Intruder, aviators bitterly opposed the missile. As a result, Hank's team bypassed the program objectives memoranda (POM) budget process and cut several deals with the Defense Advanced Research Projects Agency to provide some funding where it could. For all intents and purposes, the agency was the inventor of digital scene matching, which allowed the terrain mapping to guide the missile to its target.

Hank and his team wanted the Tomahawk to launch from a vertical launching system, as opposed to existing box launchers. While a Tomahawk-capable vertical launching system would involve an expensive ship redesign and lengthened cells for the missile canisters, the flush-deck system would be capable of launching missiles directly from a 122-cell magazine. The box launcher, in contrast, had a smaller eight-cell magazine, required reloading, and was slower and less reliable. Politically, they had to overcome opposition from the Mark 26 launcher lobby, whose system was going into the first seven *Ticonderoga*-class Aegis cruisers, and from the ship's designers and builders, who had to redesign the ships for an unproven launcher and an unproven missile. Hank persevered and had analyses done that proved the need for the Tomahawk in large numbers, if it ever were to complement manned air strikes.

The missile offered a revolutionary land-attack capability for the new destroyer, but Fontaine's requirements study initially could offer no measures of its effectiveness. Hank devised a series of analyses around a carrier air strike against the Soviet Navy facilities at Petropovlovsk in the northwest Pacific, consonant with Hayward's Pacific orientation. He compared the data from aircraft alone against data from the same strike supported by Tomahawks, where the cruise missiles would attack air defenses in advance of the Intruder strikes.

The cost analysis curve compared the cost of the air strike in terms of aircraft attrition and Tomahawk procurement. At one end, the cost of the strike without the Tomahawk was significant because of aircraft attrition. Moving to the other end of the curve, the costs declined as the force increased employment of the missiles. It rose again as the number of missiles increased "after aircraft attrition had bottomed out." Hank's analyses, said Doyle, "enabled us to roll over OSD, Program Analysis and Evaluation, who had taken the position that surface ships only needed the short-range, surface-to-surface Harpoon."

Hayward dismissed the findings, but Capitol Hill did not. Lawmakers eventually put pressure on the Office of the Secretary of Defense to support the program for the DDGX.

The Tomahawk would give the surface Navy the ability to influence events ashore well beyond the range of the 5-inch gun. In the defense of Europe, carrier battle groups in the Northern Atlantic could now strike the Kola Peninsula. From the eastern Mediterranean, naval forces could hold at risk targets in the Soviet Union, something they could not do previously unless carriers were positioned far north in the Adriatic. "With the Tomahawk, there was no aircraft attrition and no potential POWs," said Hank, "which then—as well as now—is a very sensitive and emotional issue." With all of this understanding, the Office of the Secretary of Defense got on board with the program.

The Soviets recognized the tactical nuclear potential of the Tomahawk. During Holloway's tenure as chief of naval operations, the SALT I negotiators had included in the protocol a two-part restriction on the Tomahawk: (1) the Navy could develop but not deploy the missile, and (2) it could not have a range greater than six hundred miles. Doyle and Hank preferred a conventional Tomahawk anyway, better to serve the land-attack scenarios. However, a conventional cruise missile required greater accuracy, making the program much more expensive and complex.

In working the Hill and the Office of the Secretary of Defense with his Petropovlovsk study, Hank knew he had irritated Hayward. He considered the possibility that he would be retired, and thus applied to and was accepted by Harvard Business School. In February 1978, however, Doyle told Hank he was on the flag list for selection to rear admiral and that he wanted him to remain as his division director in charge of all surface Navy weapons.

One of Hank's responsibilities was the incremental modernization of Aegis to get it small enough to go on the *Arleigh Burke* class. Initially intended for cruisers, it had to be shrunk to fit destroyers. Altogether, Hank played a role in introducing such combat systems as the digital computer versions of the Navy Tactical Data System, the Standard II missile, the vertical launch system, battle group antiair warfare (the precursor to the cooperative engagement capability, a communication system that links Navy assets for tracking and targeting), the close-in weapon system, SLQ-32 radar, towed arrays, and the new generation sonar. His division also upgraded the capabilities of amphibious and service force ships, notably the LHA amphibious assault and the AOE fast combat support ships.

Notwithstanding his commitment to introducing high-tech weaponry to the fleet, Hank soon became aware of the challenge of meeting any wartime surge requirement for these weapons. When the Shah of Iran fell in 1979, deposed by the Ayatollah Khomeini, the Navy suddenly faced a threat that U.S. weapons sold to Iran, specifically F-14 Tomcats and Harpoon missiles, could be used against U.S. ships. Hank moved quickly to have the Navy run tests on short-term counters to Harpoon attacks, and chaff was found to be the only quick fix.

When it came time to load chaff rock on ships deploying to the Persian Gulf, however, Hank found that the inventory was not available. He told Doyle it would take $13 million and that he had located some funds but that industry would require eighty weeks to ramp up. Recognizing that chaff was obviously a very simple weapon, Hank was "deeply concerned" about the implications of the Navy's decision to rely on complex, high-tech, precision-guided munitions such as the Harpoon, Tomahawk, and Standard missiles without fully funding both large stockpiles and full life-cycle support costs. "Without adequate inventories on hand at the start of hostilities, these weapons simply would not be delivered in any real-time sense."

The lead time for a Tomahawk at the time was about a year. Hank knew that the program, including support, was far from fully funded. It was, he cautioned, "a prescription for disaster, as the Air Force almost found in Bosnia where they got down to something like only eighty cruise missiles left in their inventory."

Hank's time in the Office of the Chief of Naval Operations was coming to an end. With the Navy poised to introduce a new generation of weapon systems, officers in the fleet now had to develop the tactics to use them. Hank wanted to be among them and sought Doyle's assistance to get him posted to a cruiser-destroyer group, where he could focus on tactical development. At the peak of his influence, Doyle had developed the command screening process for the surface Navy and was able to place his surface flags in the fleet. Regarding Hank as "a tower of strength . . . and a great friend and shipmate," Doyle assigned him command of Cruiser-Destroyer Group Two in Charleston, South Carolina.

Reflecting on his tour with Doyle, Hank considered him as "the most successful director of surface warfare in the last half of the twentieth century." "The powerful surface fleet that constitutes today's Navy," he maintained, "is the direct result of Jim's skill, determination, and ability to prevail in the most difficult of bureaucratic wars. One of my great disappointments was that he did not receive a well-deserved fourth star, probably denied him because he was just too successful."

Chapter 33

Bagging the Carriers

A TWO-STAR IN THE PENALTY BOX

In March 1980, in advance of going to Cruiser-Destroyer Group Two, Hank went to the senior officers ships material readiness course at the Nuclear Power Training Unit in Idaho Falls, Idaho. Rickover had instituted the requirement, since removed, that a senior officer going to any command had to attend his engineering school, "because only he knew how to teach engineering."

Hank maintained that Rickover designed the program for aviators. "It wasn't nuclear training. . . . They tried to teach them alternating current theory without teaching them calculus." Having been chief engineer on two destroyers, he knew most of the material.

In July, Hank arrived in Charleston, a small port geared to the surface navy. Cruiser-Destroyer Group Two had twenty-eight ships—two cruisers, twenty-six destroyers, and a destroyer tender. "I think it was something like the twelfth-largest navy in the world." Welcomed in person by South Carolina's Strom Thurmond, Hank responded to the senator's offer of assistance by asking for help in getting funds for an additional pier. Since these dollars did not appear in the president's budget, Thurmond promptly earmarked a sum in the Navy's military construction account. The vice chief of naval operations was understandably upset, but Hank got his pier.

A couple of weeks after the change of command, Hank went to sea on a fleet exercise in the Caribbean that his predecessor, Rear Adm. Gordon Nagler, had put together around the Harpoon. As he watched Nagler's exercise unfold, Hank could see that the tactics and the procedures essentially were unchanged from those of his time in the *Lawrence* and Destroyer Squadron Twelve. He would bring to his new command a wealth of knowledge about the hardware on which he had been working during his two tours in the Office of the Chief of Naval Operations. These weapon systems were coming into the Navy from the top down, but the operational concepts governing how the fleet would use them had to come from the bottom up. As a cruiser-destroyer group commander, he would develop them. He determined that the next fleet exercise, three months away, would be very different.

Hank was able to make an immediate impact thanks to an extremely high-powered staff and a unit ready to exercise. The Propulsion Examining Board and other innovations had so improved ships' engineering readiness that he did not have to worry about whether they could get under way. He could therefore shift their emphasis to training in combat systems. As he had with Destroyer Squadron Twelve, he told his captains to teach their junior officers ship-handling, regardless of the risk of damage, and he instituted ship-handling and navigation competitions. As before, he put in writing that a skipper could refer to his directives in writing if some junior officer got into trouble handling a ship. He also expanded the boatswain's mate and damage-control Olympics and the in-port training regimen that he had developed as a squadron commander, rolling them into what he called the "surface warfare training week." In the years since his Athens duty, the fleet had introduced more new technology with which to train. Although he was unable to simulate antisubmarine warfare in port, he and his staff devised many ways to use the newest version of the Navy Tactical Data System and its digital links to exercise antiair warfare problems.

Development of antiair warfare and Tomahawk tactics was his highest priority. The Tomahawk, however, was not yet in the fleet. Still needing to conserve fuel, he developed in-port training approaches that involved Tomahawk war gaming and learning how to target, as well as exercising air defense tactics.

Later in 1980, he put together the Navy's first at-sea exercise of Tomahawk tactics. He assembled a six-ship surface group operating with two submarines to conduct a force opposition drill against a carrier battle group that was operating in the Caribbean. While the carrier tried to sink his flagship, his force would try to locate and sink the carrier.

Hank departed from Charleston in Capt. William H. Peerenboom's guided missile cruiser *Wainwright*, accompanied by five ships. The force headed south along the East Coast in electronic silence and lost themselves in one of the merchant routes, as the carrier air wing searched vainly at very long range. In the meantime, Hank's two submarines located the carrier and kept him informed of her position. When the ships reached Tomahawk range, they simulated fire of six missiles on both the carrier's position as reported by the submarines and the position of her electronic signals that his flagship had intercepted. The roll of the dice gave them two hits. Later, they found that the carrier had her planes on deck at the time, "calling to mind the debacle of the Japanese carriers at the Battle of Midway."

Hank sent a message to the Second Fleet commander, Vice Adm. Tom Bigley, detailing the course of the drill and the result. Soon word of the exercise reached the Office of the Chief of Naval Operations. When two officers from Hayward's Office of Legislative Affairs happened to be in Charleston, they met with Hank, who ill-advisedly gave them a copy of his message to Bigley. The message somehow found its way into the hands of a powerful congressional staffer, Tony Battista, the head of research and development for the House Armed Services Committee. At a time when he was vigorously working to get support for aviation programs as opposed to cruise missiles, Admiral Hayward was understandably very sensitive to any evidence of carrier vulnerability and how it might play on the Hill. The leak made him furious, and he and his staff placed blame squarely on Hank. "Lost in the noise was the point that I was trying to make," said Hank. "We had Tomahawk plus aviation at sea, and the Soviets had only their own Tomahawk. Thus, we had a competitive advantage the Soviets could not overcome by building a carrier force."

Although he now faced a chief of naval operations bristling at his apparent disloyalty, Hank had impressed Vice Adm. Bill Small, the Sixth Fleet commander in the Mediterranean. Wanting to get a handle on how to use some of the new weapons moving into the fleet, he had Hank deploy under him for a spring exercise. Hank and his staff located in the carrier *Forrestal* as the fleet's carrier strike force commander, traditionally an aviator's role. "I was the first CruDes commander—blackshoe—to fly his flag in a carrier in the eighties," said Hank. "So, I flew my flag in the *Forrestal,* which really annoyed the aviators. They objected strenuously, but Bill Small—himself an aviator—persisted. Now it's a matter of routine."

Three weeks into the exercise, they got orders to Libyan waters. Libya's President Muammar Qaddafi had said that he would fire on the next U.S. reconnaissance aircraft to fly over the Gulf of Sidra. The *Forrestal*'s air wing was to provide escort for an Air Force RC-130 electronic reconnaissance aircraft operating from Greece. Hank thus had the opportunity to run "one of those rattle-Qaddafi's-cage exercises."

Hank was not satisfied with the hostile intent restrictions that prevented the escorts from engaging or shooting at a Libyan aircraft until it fired at them. Having dealt with this aspect of rules of engagement before, he opted to allow the escorts to fire in advance of an actual shot if the Libyan appeared to be threatening the unarmed plane. He then informed Small and Adm. Ron Hays, the Navy commander in chief in London, that he would proceed on that basis "unless otherwise directed." Both supported him. So empowered, the force crossed Qaddafi's "Line of Death" and entered the gulf. When the RC-130 received a challenge from some Libyan aircraft, the Navy escorts interposed themselves. After some very tense minutes, the Libyans retreated.

After he completed the rest of his deployment, Hank transferred to the *Wainwright* and headed for Charleston. The experience had reinforced his conviction that naval aviation was the dominant element in the struggle for maritime superiority and had formed in him new admiration for aviators. "Command of a carrier," he maintained, "is the most difficult job in the entire military universe."

When he arrived in port, Hank discovered that orders had gone to his relief, a surprise, but within normal rotation times. More disturbing were the rumors of his retirement. Evidently, Hayward believed he had leaked his Bigley memo to Battista intentionally to build a case for more Tomahawk funding. The admiral was not going to tolerate such disloyalty, and he let it be known that he did not have a new job for him.

Later in the summer of 1980, Vice Adm. James "Ace" Lyons, Second Fleet commander, came forth with a timely proposal. Lyons wanted to run a carrier-versus-carrier exercise that would begin when the *Forrestal* departed the Med and the *Dwight D. Eisenhower,* the Navy's newest carrier, was on her way to northern Europe. They would conduct the exercise only with the missile weapons they had—Harpoons. Lyons proposed that Hank, accompanied by his staff, return to the Med via C-5 airlift, board *Forrestal,* and command her battle group. Hank agreed. He would be working the exercise for two senior admirals, Harry D. Train, commander in chief, Atlantic Fleet, and Lyons, who would prove crucial to keeping his career alive.

Hank had his force operate in total electronic silence. He sent his three Harpoon-carrying escorts north to the Greenland–Iceland–U.K. gap. The ships then drifted southerly with the heavy merchant traffic into the central Atlantic. Using electronic deception and not flying any of her own aircraft, the *Forrestal* hid from the *Ike*'s aircraft.

The *Dwight D. Eisenhower* patrols continued looking for a battle group departing the Med. The *Forrestal* and her destroyers scattered and camouflaged singly in heavy merchant traffic. At three o'clock one morning, two of Hank's Harpoon shooters were able to close the carrier undetected and simulate launches from nine miles away, almost point-blank range. The Harpoons found the target carrier and bagged her with her planes on deck and unprepared.

The exercise became another bone of contention with the aviation community. The *Dwight D. Eisenhower* had just entered the fleet, and future funding for additional carriers was at issue. The senior aviators regarded the exercise as inflammatory because it highlighted the vulnerability of the carrier to a determined enemy who was going to employ electronic deception and antiship missiles.

Lyons delayed forwarding the exercise report up the chain. Instead, he returned drafts to Hank for changes that would restate what the missiles hit, the severity of the damage, and how many hours the carrier would be out of action. In the final report, many of Hank's remarks were, nonetheless, deleted.

After this second exercise, the retirement rumors heightened. Hayward reiterated to the commander, Surface Forces, Atlantic, Dave Johnson, Hank's type commander, and Harry Train, the Atlantic Fleet commander, that he did not have a job for him. It was the kiss of death. Johnson arranged with Train to put Hank on his staff until the heat subsided. Forced to acknowledge the support, Hayward yielded and allowed Hank to become Johnson's deputy commander. Although unaware at the time what his mentors were doing on his behalf, Hank knew enough to be cautious in any statements to the public. In February 1982, he reported to Johnson in Norfolk, where he would remain and "lie low" until September.

When Hank arrived at Surface Forces, Atlantic, he decided to work on an issue of which he had long been aware: the need to reorganize the staff to put more emphasis on weapons and tactical development. He wanted an organization that had an assistant chief of staff for combat systems as well as for engineering. After three months, he managed to persuade Johnson to make this change. When he instituted his by now familiar surface warfare training drill, Navy Tactical Data System performance improved, leading to his establishment of NTDS performance standards, a basic for fire control.

"I was trying," said Hank, "to prepare the ground for the introduction of all these significant capabilities that still were just sort of trickling in one by one." During one of his first training drills, he visited one of his squadrons doing a waterfront gunnery exercise involving the new Mark 86 fire control system. The notional targets were Soviet PT boats. Hank observed that his squadron commander was not using a rocking ladder, in particular a down rocking ladder developed under fire in World War II combat at sea, that used a sequence of long and then short shots until ordnance was on target. The Bureau of Ordnance had delivered the Mark 86 without instructions on how to set up a rocking ladder or any other instructions relating to anti-PT boat firing. Hank called the Bureau of Ordnance to complain, only to find that the civilian bureaucrats claimed that the system was "so accurate we don't need it; we shoot to hit"—an impossible claim when firing at a rapidly maneuvering target at a distance with munitions whose time of flight is about a minute. Hank thereupon sent Atlantic surface force units to sea to fire the 86 system until they had developed a series of realistic anti-PT boat tactics involving the use of rocking ladders.

In the spring of 1982, word was out that a submariner, James D. Watkins, would be the new chief of naval operations. Shortly thereafter, Lyons called Hank to tell him a job offer was coming that he would not like but that he should take. Lyons had worked a deal with Secretary of the Navy John Lehman, with the assistance of Train and Johnson. They had persuaded Watkins that Hank should return to Washington as the Navy's inspector general after Watkins relieved Hayward.

In September, Hank became the Navy inspector general. While Watkins took a more hands-off approach, Lehman had definite ideas about the position. When Hank reported for duty, the secretary told him he wanted him to monitor the "big issues—fraud, waste and abuse and the organization in the Navy." He particularly wanted to strengthen the Navy inspector general billet, because he feared it was going to be absorbed by the Office of the Secretary of Defense. Lehman's fears were justified. The Department of Defense had just created its own inspector general.

Hank thus became the principal adviser to the secretary and the chief of naval operations on the Navy's organizational and management structure. To tap more talent, Hank went through the difficult process of creating a reserve unit that he had assigned to his office, with a senior vice president from Westinghouse and the Stanford University's dean of management, along with some chief executive officers and chief financial officers of major corporations. "I went down the list with a couple of trusted agents and picked out the initial bunch of candidates."

Reorienting the inspector general's office to focus on improving some organizational weaknesses, Hank instituted a hotline and procedures to deal with waste, fraud, and abuse and looked at automation of the material command and implementation of internal controls. As inspector general, he had to represent the Navy Department to lawmakers on some hot-button issues. "I had to go over to Congress to defend all this stuff," he said. "Of course, the $600 toilet seats were an accounting device, and everybody knew that. They were lumped in with overhead. But those congressmen didn't want to be confused with the facts—they just wanted headlines and favorable coverage on the TV evening news."

Unhappy about the Naval Audit Service's poor record in recouping monies after audits and the performance of the Naval Investigative Service, he asked Lehman if he would put them both under the inspector general. The suggestion incurred the wrath of the Naval Investigative Service (NIS), and shortly afterward, he found that he was the subject of an investigation. "They couldn't find anything," he said defiantly.

The NIS interest came on the heels of his own thorough displeasure over its overzealous response to an allegation against a prospective commanding officer for flashing. Retired Vice Adm. Doug Katz felt strongly that Hank's handling of the case by itself testified to his consummate integrity as a naval professional.

The case came to Hank's attention via an academy graduate whose classmate had been relieved and assigned to a meaningless billet with no charges or reason other than the NIS telling him that he was under investigation. Hank agreed to look into the matter. He soon found that the classmate, a commander, had been the prospective commanding officer (PCO) for a new construction ship who had been staying in a motel near the shipyard and had been accused by one of the maids as a persistent flasher. Evidently, the NIS had acted on the basis of her testimony alone.

Delving further, Hank found that the accused commander was a jogger who would sometimes take phone calls in his skivvies before showering. Secondly, he learned that the maid was a "local round-heel and really of dubious virtue" who was attempting to get money from an out-of-court settlement. Hank told Dave Winkler in one of his 2001 interviews that the NIS "had caused this guy a terrible, terrible miscarriage with no efforts to follow up. They just put him in this limbo and left him twisting slowly." He was furious, as were other senior admirals when made aware of the case. Hank presented the case to the vice chief of naval operations, Vice Adm. Ron Hays, with the recommendation that he extend him an official apology and a destroyer command in Charleston. Hays made the apology and offered the command, both of which the officer accepted.

A couple of weeks later, Hank consulted with James F. Goodrich, the undersecretary of the Navy, who was also livid. Hank asked for him to put the NIS under the inspector general, thus incurring the retaliatory investigation. In the end, the office of the inspector general never absorbed the NIS or the Audit Service. As for his intervention on the wronged PCO's behalf, Hank told Winkler that it was "one of the things that I'm most proud of to this day."

Similarly, he took pride in righting another wrong done both to Adm. Chester Nimitz and his famous staff cryptologist, Cdr. Joe Rochefort. Hank got John Lehman to give the heretofore unrecognized Rochefort the Distinguished Service Medal for determining explicitly that the Japanese intended to attack Midway. In the 1960s, Nimitz had made the request before he died and was twice declined by various Navy Department bureaucrats. Thanks to Hank, Lehman held an award ceremony for the family in his office where he presented the DSM to Rochefort's son and other family members.

In the spring of 1984, Hank learned that his time in what he called the penalty box would soon be over. News broke that he would be getting his third star. He was going to Norfolk to command the Second Fleet. He would command what had become the most strategically significant of the four fleets in the U.S. Navy. For the next two years, he would play a key operational role in the endgame of the Cold War.

Chapter 34

Commander, Second Fleet

Both John Lehman and Adm. Jim Watkins were confident that Hank Mustin was the right man to implement what they were calling the Maritime Strategy, a forward strategy to fight the carriers into the Norwegian Sea in the event of war in Europe. Hank had been under the lens in Washington for a year, and Lehman was pleased with his no-nonsense performance as inspector general.

As commander, Second Fleet, Hank also would be commander of the Striking Fleet, Atlantic, one of NATO's major subordinate commands. In a 29 May 1984 letter, Adm. Wesley L. McDonald, soon to be his immediate boss as the triple-hatted commander in chief, Atlantic Command and Atlantic Fleet, and NATO supreme allied commander, Atlantic, congratulated him on his selection. McDonald particularly noted how "immensely important" was his "knowledge of Atlantic and Mediterranean operations," as well as the "aggressive and innovative leadership" he would bring to his new command.

Late in the summer, Hank joined the outgoing Second Fleet commander, Vice Adm. Joseph Metcalf, for a fleet exercise in the Caribbean. On the three-day transit south, he rode with Metcalf to observe U.S. workups for ships deploying to the Sixth Fleet and the Med. His thoughts, however, were on NATO, where he would have more clout to implement his operational ideas. Metcalf encouraged him to put his energies into exercising the NATO Striking Fleet, Atlantic, as a credible strike force, instead of just rehearsing his ships for deployment to the Mediterranean.

The change of command was to be on the *Eisenhower*, but a hurricane sent the carrier to sea, and the ceremony moved to the hangar deck of the helicopter assault ship *Nassau*, berthed in Norfolk. In relieving Metcalf, Hank had arrived at the operational pinnacle of his career. At last, he was a fleet commander, a position from which he could implement a lifetime of lessons and fulfill a dream his father had wished for himself. As commander, Second Fleet, he would train and influence the succeeding generation of naval leaders, including a captain, Vern Clark, who would later take the Navy into the next century as chief of naval operations. As commander, Striking Fleet, Atlantic, he would follow his grandfather's wish to have "a voice in the progress of events," and he would find a way to put naval aviation's story on the front pages during a time when Washington's anticarrier forces were once again on the rise.

By the mid-1980s, the Soviets had begun shifting their undersea force to a so-called bastion strategy. Instead of operating their ballistic-missile and attack submarines far afield in the Atlantic, they were restricting them to areas around Murmansk and the Kola Peninsula east of Scandinavia. Thanks in part to the betrayal of Navy spy John Walker, the Soviets knew that the United States could track their ballistic missile submarines. The discovery scared them. The sea-based leg of their strategic deterrent no longer was credible. By withdrawing their submarine force to the bastions, they hoped to ensure the survivability of their boomers.

As the U.S. Navy realized that the Soviet attack boats no longer were deploying in numbers below the Greenland-Iceland-U.K. gap, it concluded that the submarine threat was not a show-stopper for the Atlantic bridge. Hank immediately saw that he would not fight the battle of the Atlantic in the Atlantic; he would fight it in the Norwegian Sea. "Indeed, a succession of SACLants [Supreme Allied Commander, Atlantic] had testified that they had just about one-third of the forces necessary to construct the Atlantic bridge." Even more significant, he saw that the Navy could play far more than just a supporting role in the battle for Europe. It could influence the course of a war on the continent.

Admiral Watkins's developing Maritime Strategy contained a concept whereby the Striking Fleet would fight its way into the Norwegian Sea and then run strikes on the

Soviet naval and military sites in the Kola Peninsula. "It became apparent to me that we couldn't do that," Hank said. "The closer we got to the bastions, the tougher it was." The strategy assumed that Norway still would be in the NATO orbit. He found that assumption somewhat shaky and decided to run it to ground.

Norway in fact was drifting toward neutrality. In a late 1985 visit to the Finnmark border town of Kirkenes, Hank confirmed some of his suspicions. The town square had a large statue of a Red Army soldier, a tribute to the Soviet liberation from the Nazis. Many northern Norwegians were asking him, "Why do you want to bomb the Russians? They're the ones who liberated us."

In addition, the Norwegian government in Oslo faced a hard military truth: The supreme allied commander, Europe, had convened a study concluding that a Soviet armored assault could overrun Norway in three days. The Soviets then would control the Baltic Sea and the entire NATO northern flank, putting at risk all NATO assets on the European Central Front and reducing carrier forces to "charge of the Light Brigade" status. Combined with the Soviet concentration of sea-based strategic nuclear assets, the possibility of a Soviet armored thrust into the northern flank became as compelling as the more familiar scenario that assumed an assault across the Fulda Gap in Germany, assured because of the NATO inability to construct the requisite Atlantic bridge.

Hank saw an opportunity to build an operational concept for the Maritime Strategy whose requirements the Navy could argue successfully in Washington. He took the SACEur study, and together with Dave Perin, who represented the Center for Naval Analyses' Operations Evaluation Group on his staff, worked his own analyses on the defense of the northern flank. The key component, Hank believed, was the Norwegian air order of battle, which would require augmentation by NATO air assets that the allies on European central front could not spare. Perin found that by augmenting Norway with one carrier and air wing, NATO still would lose the land battle, but "if you sent two, suddenly the land campaign became a toss-up, because now, when the Soviet tanks are coming across the frozen tundra, we're picking them off with airborne anti-tank weapons. If you send in three carriers, NATO wins, because of the air." Significantly, for the interservice standpoint, the U.S. Air Force could not bring this sort of air power to bear because north Norway had too few airfields and no plans for additional construction.

From these analyses, Hank fashioned his iteration of the Maritime Strategy. Foremost, in order to counter any threatened three-day Soviet assault to overrun Norway, the carriers had to be in position before a war went hot. "Luckily, with naval forces, you can do that because you don't have to cross any boundaries, no visa required—all that standard navy logic with international waters." He was careful to accentuate the defensive nature of such prepositioning, however. "We're not going to get up there just to strike the Kola Peninsula. We're going to get up there to provide the air power so that NATO can win the land defense of Norway. Big change."

The NATO study had said that it would take the Soviets twelve to fourteen days to mass their tank divisions, so Hank developed a logic based on that time frame to send two Second Fleet carriers and one Sixth Fleet carrier to Norwegian waters. He had to secure support from a number of stakeholders. Opting to treat the problem as a NATO issue, as a NATO major subordinate commander he could work through the alliance and the supreme allied commanders, Europe, and Atlantic, rather than through the Pentagon bureaucracy.

One of Hank's supporters was the U.S. ambassador to Oslo, Robert D. Stuart Jr., who helped to secure the green light from the Norwegians, and the powerful general Bernard W. Rogers, USA, who was in the fifth year of his unprecedented eight-year reign as supreme allied commander, Europe. As such, Rogers was the overall commander of the Sixth Fleet in the Mediterranean. A key issue for him was chopping his Sixth Fleet assets to the Norwegian Sea. Hank was able to persuade him that any action in the Mediterranean paled in comparison to winning the battle of the Atlantic, now more accurately the battle of the Norwegian Sea. NATO commanders thus came to realize that if the U.S. were to reinforce Europe, the only way to do that was to control the Norwegian Sea, and to control that sea required U.S. naval aviation on scene in numbers.

Having made his case, Hank now focused his attention on the matter of making the forward concept work. He immediately reorganized Striking Fleet, Atlantic, to be more of an integrated strike force with principal subordinate commands for the Carrier Striking Force, Antisubmarine Warfare Striking Force, Amphibious Striking Force, and Marine Striking Force. The Navy's Caribbean exercises that previously had simulated operations in the Med now practiced for operations in the Norwegian fjords.

One of his first tasks was to reconfigure the guidelines for exercises in advance of Ocean Safari '85, the following year's major NATO exercise. Ocean Safari ran every other year, alternating with Northern Wedding. It had always focused on the defensive employment of the Striking Fleet in support of convoys across the Atlantic; Northern Wedding focused on amphibious operations in Norway. Hank first insisted that the Striking Fleet not exercise convoy escorting but work offensive operations forward in the Norwegian Sea. Second, he resolved to eliminate the artificial distinction between the two exercises. Strike and amphibious components would be included in both, and into 1985, he worked on the requisite tactics. His partner in these efforts was Lt. Gen. Al Gray, then commander of the Fleet Marine Force, Atlantic. "Al Gray had a better understanding of sea power than ninety percent of our admirals, and he was a no-nonsense combat veteran with an unerring ability to sort out the wheat from the chaff."

Notwithstanding enemy submarines, the primary threat the fleet faced in any operation in the Norwegian Sea was from Soviet naval aviation. Regiment-sized stream raids from the long-range Backfire bombers armed with conventional and nuclear antiship cruise missiles would be the killer in any scenario, if the Soviets had Norway. If the war were to go hot, Hank was proposing virtually to steam into the bastions. Survivability was a real question.

Hank's proposed solution was bold and drew mainly from earlier British amphibious exercises in Norway and, in particular, Royal Navy operations in the 1982 Falklands War. Operating their amphibious force in San Carlos Water, the British found that the high mountains surrounding the water augmented their air defense. The peaks and escarpments provided a radar shadow over the ships, restricting Argentine aircraft's ability to target and thus make successful antiship missile attacks. Hank similarly wanted to preposition his carriers in the Norwegian fjords, where, in the case of Vestfjord just north of the Arctic Circle, the escarpments reached three thousand feet.

First he had to get the up-check from the carrier community that a carrier could indeed conduct flight operations in the fjords. Hank got Wes McDonald to lend him Rear Adm. R. Paul Ilg, an aviator who had just commanded the *Nimitz* and now was McDonald's deputy chief of staff for plans, policy, and intelligence. After scouting the Norwegian fjords, Ilg returned with the up-check.

As for the submarine threat, mining could seal the fjords and be completed in twelve to fourteen days, the time the Soviets would need to reinforce their assault forces in the Kola. Hank would make the conventional deterrent credible, justified as augmentation of the air defense of Norway and therefore within the overall defensive context fundamental to NATO strategy.

His concept pleased all the NATO stakeholders, especially the Norwegians. The British were happy to get a major role in both antisubmarine warfare and the amphibious operation. General Rogers was delighted that for the first time the Navy had proposed a truly effective role for the carriers in a NATO war scenario, and with him on board, the Army followed. Believing that it could handle the air power requirement, the Air Force, however, initially was at odds. Only when Hank proved that Norway had just three airfields in the north, too few to support the necessary surge of U.S. land-based aircraft, did the service concede that U.S. carriers were the only way to offset Soviet air superiority.

Within the Navy, all three Navy unions and the Fleet Marine Force benefited from Hank's approach. All had a role to play, which generated requirements that in turn drove acquisition of attack submarines, carriers and carrier air, and Aegis and Tomahawk, as well as Marine assets.

"The guy that really brought the Maritime Strategy into its own was Hank Mustin," said Adm. Harry Train, McDonald's predecessor as supreme allied commander, Atlantic. "[He] did more than anybody to mature the Maritime Strategy and market it and therefore make it an extremely useful document to procurement people, to our acquisition folks. He felt that that was his role as Second Fleet, to just go in there and take what was given him and make it better."

For Train, the Maritime Strategy was in essence a "procurement strategy." Hank's role would be to make an operational concept work with systems that were in the fleet, but not yet in numbers. When he became commander, Second Fleet, for example, he had only one Aegis ship. To ensure that the surface navy would get more, Hank had to prove they worked and do it with an operational concept built around Aegis.

The first practical challenge was to demonstrate that the carrier could operate aircraft in the restricted space in the fjords. Second, Hank had to prove that radar shadowing was operationally effective. Third, he had to fine-tune his force structure and the rules of engagement, the latter of which involved close liaison with Ambassador Stuart, NATO, and the Norwegians to permit operating U.S. tactical aircraft in the civilian airspace around Vestfjord.

In early 1985, Hank had Second Fleet test the impact of the Aegis system on air defense in a series of three readiness exercises. In ReadEx 1–85, he had no Aegis ships and was able to engage 65 percent of the targets in the outer defense zone at an average distance of 110 nautical miles from the carrier. In ReadEx 3–85, he had no Aegis ship and was able to engage only 50 percent of the targets at one hundred nautical miles. In ReadEx 2–85, however, he had the Aegis cruiser *Yorktown*. With the cruiser, the force was able to engage 80 percent of the targets at two hundred nautical miles, beyond Soviet air-to-surface range. Hank had proved the impact of Aegis in mid-ocean. Now, he had to prove it in the fjords.

On 28 September, Hank began his make-or-break exercise, the seven-week Ocean Safari '85. The exercise was the largest multinational, multiservice operation since World

War II, involving three carriers and the battleship *Iowa,* 166 ships and more than three hundred aircraft from eleven allied nations. Hank flew his flag in the *Nassau.*

The exercise began off the East Coast as the Strike Fleet escorted the convoy across the Atlantic. Detaching two carriers and the *Iowa* to continue with the sealift to the western approaches, Hank, on board the *Nassau,* the carrier *America* with Rear Adm. Dick Dunleavy, and HMS *Illustrious,* led by Rear Adm. Julian Oswald, the British Antisubmarine Warfare Strike Force commander, headed north into the Norwegian Sea. Once the force was in Vestfjord, B-52 bombers dropped Captor mines to seal the fjords, and the *America* began to operate with land-based U.S., U.K., and Norwegian air.

Ocean Safari proved the effectiveness of radar shadowing. Using airborne radars equivalent to the Soviets' best, the "enemy" flew passes at the carriers but could not launch air-to-ground missiles until they were inside their weapons' minimum range. Moreover, they then were within range of the surface-to-air missiles of NATO destroyers and cruisers. Instead of shooting at enemy missiles, the NATO force was shooting at enemy planes. That finding was especially critical in the event the Soviets armed their antiship missiles with tactical nuclear warheads. The longtime goal of "shooting the archer instead of the arrow" was now a reality.

Diplomatically, of course, the location of the force in Norwegian territorial waters complicated the use of tactical nuclear weapons for the Soviets. If they went nuclear against U.S. forces, they would be doing so on the European continent. Thus unable to isolate the conflict at sea, the Soviets could not use tactical nukes.

At the time, Watkins was having to defend Aegis funding to Congress. He asked Hank to write a report that he could enter in the *Congressional Record.* Five days after the conclusion of Ocean Safari, Hank was able to boast, "We have dealt, successfully and repeatedly, with multi-regimental sized air raids in very dirty environments," adding that he had "replicated Soviet air threats and tactics to an unprecedented degree, including raid size, jamming, and chaff." Aegis, he said, "brought *clarity* to the air battle."

His two Aegis cruisers had passed targeting information to non-Aegis ships whose own radars were degraded by clutter and false tracks in the fjords. Hank noted that the *Ticonderoga* had faced fifty-five-knot winds and thirty-foot seas, but throughout, her Aegis had remained operational. Hank asked Watkins for more.

The forward strategy had rules of engagement implications for the sixteen countries of NATO and its commanders, afloat and ashore. Hank worked closely at high levels to sell the strategy to the alliance governments, particularly Norway, but it was not always easy. Critics objected to its presumed offensive nature, which seemingly was at odds with a defensive alliance. Hank, like his father and Oley Sharp, believed a solely defensive strategy could not win a war and that history validated this belief. "You can have an overall defensive strategy, but there must be offensive elements in it."

Watkins had approved the final version of Maritime Strategy in May 1984. After Ocean Safari '85, the U.S. Naval Institute's *Proceedings* published it in January 1986. In its 3 February issue, *Newsweek* ran an article on the Reagan military buildup that included a photo of a swaggering Hank in aviator sunglasses, tossing a challenge to the Soviets. "You're going to be so busy keeping us out of the Kola that if you've got enough forces left over to do something else, be my guest." This quote, which the magazine took out of context from an hour-long interview, "made me sound like [professional footballer and coach] Mike Ditka," Hank said. "I had laid out in detail the rationale for the defense of Norway, but that had not been colorful enough for *Newsweek*." The piece generated wide consternation in Norway to the extent that the parliament, the Storting, held a special session to address the overall issue of Norwegian support to NATO. Only after Hank's staff wired a transcript of the entire interview to the U.S. embassy in Oslo was Ambassador Stuart able to extinguish the fires.

Ocean Safari certainly presented the Soviets with a counterstrike threat. They were nervous about the perceived offensive capability of U.S. naval attack aircraft and Tomahawks to hold hostage their land-based naval aviation and fleet facilities in the Kola Peninsula. In truth, the Tomahawk capability was not yet a reality. For a start, no targeting from the Defense Mapping Agency existed for the region, and with only two Aegis ships, Hank did not have the missile magazine capacity for an effective strike. Moreover, the supreme allied commanders, Europe, and Atlantic, had not yet resolved who had release authority. Hank pushed for resolution of these and other Tomahawk issues until he feared that his credibility was at stake. In an 8 January 1986 letter to Vice Adm. Jerry O. Tuttle, deputy and chief of staff for the commander in chief, U.S. Atlantic Fleet, he wrote, "[T]here is a targeting problem which centers around the inability of theater mission planning centers to plan the numbers of missions required. Until we whip this one, our ability to employ TLAM/C [conventional land attack Tomahawk] in *quick* support of national objectives is zero—and we're sitting on a time bomb here because we can't seem to get started, and yet our Washington colleagues have advertised this as an *in-hand today* capability."

While wearing his Second Fleet commander's hat, Hank's priority was training. He had operational command over Al Gray's Fleet Marine Force, Atlantic, and forces from the three-star type commanders, Robert Dunn, Naval Air Forces Atlantic, Bud Kauderer, Submarine Forces, Atlantic, and Scot McCauley, Surface Forces Atlantic. In addition, he was the direct subordinate of Admiral McDonald as the Commander of Joint Task Force 120, the force that Metcalf led into Grenada in the autumn of 1983. JFT 120 included the 101st Airborne and some forces from Tactical Air Command.

Hank continued his damage-control and boatswain's mate Olympics and the surface warfare training weeks. He also expanded the cruiser-destroyer in-port training that he had instituted for Surface Forces, Atlantic, to include Atlantic submarines and aviation units in tactical development. Linking his units to the relevant training centers at Dam Neck, Virginia, he called the program Battle Force In-Port Training. Said Gray, "Hank was one of the pioneers in exploiting this method of training."

One of his priorities was to institute fleet-level war-gaming for war-at-sea strikes against modern Soviet forces. Heretofore, all of the tactics in the war-at-sea strikes assumed the fleet would know where the enemy was. He chose to start with the opposite assumption and thus began exercising with a combination of search and attack tactics. Knowing that NavTag inventor Neil Byrne had automated his game and put it on a computer, Hank requested and got him assigned to his staff.

As fleet commander, he sought to mix his three type commanders, Kauderer, Dunn and McCauley, plus Gray, into NavTag to dismantle their parochial points of view. In the end, said Hank, they all had fun, built personal friendships, and began to get their communities working as an integrated team. According to Gray, Hank had forged relationships within a year that were "as smooth as I had ever seen them."

Each carrier air group commander had his own set of aviator's war-at-sea tactics for use against Soviet surface combatants, so Hank put all his air group commanders and their staffs together to test their tactics on the NavTag to determine which one the fleet would use. Having determined which was the best, they tested it in free play, and it became the Second Fleet war-at-sea tactic. The aviators loved the approach.

Hank got Kauderer to provide his submarines both to work with surface and carrier forces and to serve as the enemy. He wanted submariners to understand fleet operations, so he also proposed to take a submarine flag officer on every one of his fleet exercises and give him a warfare commander function not related to antisubmarine warfare. On the first trip, he made submariner J. D. Williams the antiair warfare commander on an Aegis ship, ensuring that he had a proper staff. He then made a similar offer to Dunn and put carrier aviators on cruisers. He knew the Navy training establishment was designed to train tactical action officers, "but there was nobody to train the admirals," said Hank. He thus made it his business to train rear admirals to be future fleet commanders.

Hank continued to work on antiair warfare tactics. The aviators argued that they could shoot enemy bombers with existing long-range engagement tactics. That approach, however, required combat air patrol stations hundreds of miles from the carrier, presenting tanking and refueling challenges. The NavTag war games revealed the fundamental problem: Once the combat air patrol aircraft engaged the Backfires and shot their loads of air-to-air missiles, they had to return to the carrier while other aircraft, held in reserve, moved forward to engage. "There is no way to tank weapons," said Hank. "In Vietnam, questions about the fuel capacity of the Seawolf helicopters had become irrelevant. Long before the helos would run short on fuel, they would have expended all of their ordnance and would have to return to rearm, even if almost fully loaded with fuel." Ultimately, he proved that the partnership between the Aegis—with its SPY-1 radar system, which could offset the cycle-time considerations of the E-2C Hawkeye tactical warning and control system aircraft—*and* carrier aircraft was necessary in order to manage the outer-air battle.

Hank also was working on long-range air strikes to highlight the strike capability of the carrier. To that end, he organized an exercise with three carriers off the East Coast and another in the Caribbean to illustrate how four carrier air wings possessed the strike capability of eight hundred B-17s and could deliver ordnance all the way to St. Louis. He then took the results to Capitol Hill to defend the carrier budget line. Thus, an officer that some quarters vilified as "anti-carrier" was now the Navy's point man for generating political support for naval aviation.

On 29 May 1986, when Carl Trost was named chief of naval operations, Hank got the post of deputy chief of naval operations for strategy, plans, and policy. Shortly after the announcement, the Navy gave him an additional assignment to its delegation to the 1986 Incidents at Sea meetings in Moscow. Chairing the delegation was not traditionally a fleet commander's role, but the chief of naval operations felt that Hank's operations in the Norwegian Sea qualified him, especially as he was the incoming deputy chief for strategy, plans, and policy.

Through the 1970s, the Incidents at Sea negotiations fine-tuned a general compliance. In the 1980s, the mood changed. Behind the Soviet strategy to withdraw their ballistic missile submarines into the Barents Sea and the Sea of Okhotsk was the fact that their intercontinental missiles now had greater range. The United States responded by pressing its forward strategy in the Atlantic and the Pacific with freedom-of-navigation operations. Incidents increased correspondingly in both number and intensity.

On 7 June, after traveling through nine time zones, Hank's delegation arrived at the Moscow airport, wearing their blues, to find the city sweltering in a 95-degree heat wave. Hank was exhausted. Meeting him on the tarmac was Vice Adm. Pitr N. Navoytsev, the Soviets' first deputy chief for operations. Well experienced in the negotiations, the old admiral took him straight to the Soviet naval headquarters for their first session and attempted to force him to negotiate.

Navoytsev opened with a statement demanding to know why the U.S. had committed dangerous acts in the Mediterranean that were dragging the world to the brink of nuclear holocaust. He called upon Hank to cease and desist immediately. At issue was the Navy's April strikes on Libya in response to a Berlin disco bombing that killed one and wounded sixty-three U.S. soldiers. Navoytsev challenged him on the raid, and Hank responded that he would do it again. The Soviet also berated him for the Navy's conduct off Lebanon, where tension had prompted U.S. naval commanders to establish keep-out zones around their ships and publish the announcement in the NOTAMs, the notices to airmen.

"Just a minute," Hank replied angrily. Mindful of his intelligence on the Kremlin's recent castigation of a senior Polish naval officer, he countered, "You're not talking to a Polish Admiral. I am a fleet commander in the United States Navy. . . . So if this kind of incident happens again, I'm here to tell you that we'll do the same goddamn thing."

"Thank you very much, Admiral," Navoytsev replied, "I understand your position." Later, he confided to Hank that his statement was actually for the benefit of a KGB member of his own delegation.

Over the course of the next seven days of meetings, the Soviet side complained about simulated attacks by U.S. aircraft at sea and freedom-of-navigation operations off the Kurile Islands, in the approaches to the Sea of Okhotsk, and in the Black Sea. The two sides then determined what had happened in each case, who was at fault, and what could be done to reduce such incidents in the future. Eventually, Hank and Navoytsev developed a good relationship.

While in Moscow, Hank attended the receptions hosted by the two delegations and an embassy party hosted by the U.S. ambassador. Present at the embassy gathering was the editor of *Pravda,* who, smiling, gave Hank a framed cartoon from the paper. The memento depicted Hank wearing a Stetson, sitting on the forecastle of the *Missouri.* In

his hand was a leash at the end of which are dogs with spike collars terrorizing a fleeing Soviet dove of peace.

After returning Stateside, Hank had an important ceremonial duty to perform before
returning to sea for the Northern Wedding exercises in Norway. A number of his units
were participating in July Fourth celebrations, including an international naval review, for
the Statue of Liberty centenary. Flying his flag on board the battleship *Iowa,* Hank hosted
President and Mrs. Ronald Reagan and other VIPs. Later, he and Lucy attended a star-
studded gala performance before the statue. As the event concluded, the weather turned
suddenly cold. VIPs, including Frank Sinatra, raced to the small boat ramp that could
handle only two boats at time in an attempt to jump the queue for the scores of launches
that would return them to Manhattan. According to family lore, Sinatra grew impatient
waiting his turn and ordered his Coast Guard escort to call his launch immediately to the
ramp. Unimpressed by celebrity, Hank in response had his NIS escort order his coxswain
to preempt this effrontery and forthwith place his admiral's barge alongside. Ignoring
Sinatra's indignant remonstrations, Hank, Lucy, and their personal guests boarded and
shoved off, leaving the singer to stew on the makeshift landing.

Northern Wedding exercises began on 29 August and ran until 19 October, with
simultaneous exercising of the amphibious and air defense components of the forward
strategy. Afterward, Lucy joined Hank for two weeks of formal receptions and travel to
cap his fleet command tour. Fittingly, Hank held his change of command in the
Norwegian fjords, with John Lehman presiding. His fleet command at an end, it was
now Hank's time to steel himself for a return to Washington and the high policy politics of the Office of the Chief of Naval Operations.

Chapter 35

The Ops Baron

In October 1986, Hank became deputy chief of naval operations for plans, policy, and operations. He was in effect the chief of naval operations' second on the Joint Chiefs of Staff, a role that found him often interacting with the chairman, the other service chiefs, and their operations deputies. He also was the office's interface with the fleet for operations, which involved him directly with the planning and execution of the 1987 Kuwaiti tanker reflagging, Operation Earnest Will. As well, he was the "keeper" of Navy force structure and force justification, a position that took him to Capitol Hill as part of the annual budget process.

On arrival, Hank's immediate task was to represent the Navy in Joint Staff discussions and decisions on service implementation of the Goldwater-Nichols Act, the latest congressional effort to reorganize the Pentagon. Passed on 1 October, the legislation—among other things in the zero-sum game of Washington—increased the powers of the secretary of defense, the chairman of the Joint Chiefs of Staff, and the war-fighting commanders in chief at the expense of the service secretaries and chiefs. Goldwater-Nichols also established two new specified commands, the Special Operations Command and the Transportation Command.

The Navy was "very, very hard over against" the legislation, Hank observed.

Secretary of the Navy John Lehman regarded Goldwater-Nichols as a threatening over-centralization that stifled dissent. He was especially bothered by the creation of the two new specified commands, seeing them as a product of empire-building by the Army and Air Force. Adm. William J. Crowe, on the other hand, a submariner who had become the chairman of the joint chiefs, was a solid supporter of defense reorganization and Goldwater-Nichols. Hank thus found himself in the middle.

"On all the issues, where you stand depends on where you sit," said Hank. "So, my job was to protect the interest of the service secretary and the service chief in an environment where it was clear that the pendulum was very heavily swinging in the other direction."

In one of his first actions, Hank called a meeting of all the naval officers on the Joint Staff and told them not to forget they were in the Navy. They were to understand the Navy positions and be prepared to defend them. "Also, don't forget that when you finish your joint tour you're going to come back to the Navy," he cautioned. "You don't want to do anything down there that's going to make it tough for the Navy to welcome you back with open arms." When Crowe heard about the speech, he was furious. It was not a good start.

Hank was in a tough spot. Lehman had instructed him to present the Navy position forcefully in any discussion on Goldwater-Nichols. Accepting the inevitability of the special operations and transportation commands, he wanted the Navy to compete for the top billets. When Hank raised the issue, Crowe replied that since the number of four-star billets for each service is fixed, the Navy would have to surrender one of its own four-star billets to nominate an admiral for either post.

Hank took the response to Carl Trost, another submariner who had relieved Watkins as chief of naval operations that July. When he asked which four-star billet Trost was prepared to surrender, he found himself caught in the middle again, because the answer was "none." Trost and Lehman "detested each other, which is a charitable way to put it," said Hank. Moreover, Trost suspected that Hank was "a spy" for Lehman, although Hank maintained that his association with Lehman was not direct but rather through Ace Lyons, who had become commander in chief, Pacific Fleet. Unfortunately, Lyons was also not among Trost's favorites, either. Although Hank's personal relationship with Trost had been good throughout their careers, in the high politics of Washington, Trost clearly did not perceive Hank to be on his team.

As part of Goldwater-Nichols implementation, Hank was also responsible for developing the Navy's plan for joint duty assignments. Meeting the staffing requirements in the new joint commands would prove to be a problem. For example, if the Navy followed congressional direction and fully manned its portion of the headquarters staff at the Special Operations Command, it would have only five SEAL captains available for operational duty. If it did not, the headquarters staff would be 90 percent Army and Air Force. Power was going to the commanders in chief. Hank assured Trost that if the command did not have a solid Navy staff, the Navy would lose, not only operationally but also in Washington's requirements and budget battles. Hank got Trost to agree to increase the number of SEAL billets. He was able to get Coronado's Basic Underwater Demolition School to reduce its attrition rate and to triple the number of SEAL slots for Naval Academy graduates to eighteen.

Hank quickly was finding that the staff in the Office of the Chief of Naval Operations was poorly equipped to handle the Goldwater-Nichols transition. The air, undersea, and surface warfare barons were refusing to assign their best officers to the Joint Staff, but more and more of the real Pentagon action was in that staff. Especially opposed were the aviators and "the nuclear cabal." Trost was very concerned about the policy that required nuclear-qualified officers to qualify as joint specialists to be eligible for flag rank. Under the new policy, officers would have to serve in at least twelve months of joint duty. Heretofore, the only officers Rickover had ever released from his program to joint duty assignments were the "second-string nuclear engineers." The aviation community felt the same way and wanted to keep its A team operating aircraft. "So what was happening was the best officers in the submarine force and naval aviation were the guys who had the most difficult time in making flag, because they were the least likely to be sent off to joint billets."

Crowe gave the Navy a year to solve the problem. Hank was on the selection board for the first flag list that had to implement the new requirements. That year, the board asked for and got a waiver for the first-team nuclear-qualified officers. The following year, however, Crowe refused.

As a work-around, Hank wanted to define many billets as joint. For example, knowing that the commander, Second Fleet, also wore the hat of commander, Joint Task Force 120, he devised a plan to make every Second Fleet staff assignment count as joint. He also found he could send new flag appointees into a year of watch standing at the Pentagon's National Military Command Center, a bona fide joint slot, while they waited for the routine roughly twelve months between selection and actual promotion, governed among other things by vacancies in the flag community.

Politics within the Office of the Chief of Naval Operations and the Secretariat continued to make Hank's life very difficult. As inspector general, he had gotten good advice from retired admiral Robert L. J. Long, who had run the investigation into the 1983 bombing of the Beirut Marine barracks, on how to tread amid the intense personality conflicts. "You're going to have to really be careful not to get identified in the minds of any of the players as being a member of the other camp," Hank recalled Long telling him. "You'd better get a little log and log how much time you spend in office A and office B and office C, and the times better be roughly equal, or somebody's aide is going to finger you." In Hank's case, "A" and "B" were the secretary of the Navy and the chief of naval operations.

Outside the Navy, Hank was able to develop his many harmonious working relationships. While resolving the Goldwater-Nichols transition, he solidified his collaboration with his counterparts in the other services, Air Force lieutenant generals Harley A. Hughes and Michael J. Dugan, Marine lieutenant general Carl E. Mundy Jr., and Army lieutenant generals Bob RisCassi and H. Norman Schwarzkopf. Together, they worked on the joint billet structure, doing "a lot of horse trading" to staff the Unified Command Plan and to justify joint billets for flag eligibility. Later, they addressed a number of operational issues, notably the intelligence gathering and covert submarine operations of the final stages of the Cold War and the new littoral warfare challenges of the Persian Gulf.

Hank also had colleagues from previous duties serving in the White House, notably Capt. Jim Stark on the National Security Council staff, with whom he worked on arms control issues. He also drew on personal relationships he had developed with his NATO commanders, particularly the British. "Whenever an issue came up that involved them and the U.S. Navy, we could handle that right away." When the United States was having a problem getting the British government to approve the Navy's use of Diego Garcia in the Indian Ocean in advance of [operation] Earnest Will, for example, Hank called Admiral Sir Sandy Woodward, who secured approval in two hours. Other contacts that proved helpful were British admirals Sir Julian Oswald, Sir Richard Fitch, Sir Nicholas Hunt, and Sir William Staveley. In addition to the operational issues associated with Persian Gulf operations, they continued to address residual Cold War matters such as coordination of submarine operating areas.

Hank also had ongoing involvement with allied navies through a series of routine navy-to-navy talks with the French, Koreans, Japanese, and British. A persistent issue was foreign military sales. A number of allies wanted equipment transfers that involved sensitive technology, in particular those applicable to submarines. The United States was tightening all its transfers, however, in the wake of the Shah's fall and Iranian Revolution. Hank was very conscious that, in what might become a confused post–Cold War era, U.S. weapons could be used against U.S. forces.

Hank also got the assignment to be the Pentagon's senior military representative to the United Nations. In the course of his duties with that international organization, he immediately became aware of the serious command limitations that would adversely affect any UN military operation. For a start, the secretary general had no line authority over the UN military. Secondly, UN peacekeeping and peace making fell into two separate stovepipes under the Security Council. Most seriously, he found that the UN had no command center. In his reports to Washington, Hank reinforced essentially two points: (1) if the United States were to participate in any UN operation, then it must run it, because the U.S. military had a command center, and (2), any peace-making operation should also run through an appropriate regional organization like NATO. The Clinton administration subsequently ignored his advice in 1993 when it allowed retired admiral Jonathan Howe to serve as the secretary general's special representative for Somalia. According to Hank, he had no real authority. Fortunately, one positive result of that disastrous and tragic episode was the final establishment of a UN command center, as Hank had recommended almost a decade earlier.

On 11 October 1986, President Ronald Reagan and Soviet Communist Party Secretary Gen. Mikhail Gorbachev had their mini-summit in Reykjavik. There, they announced their plan to reduce their ballistic missile forces by 50 percent and to eliminate intermediate-range nuclear missiles in Europe. Suddenly, arms control became yet another brief Hank would have in his portfolio.

Mindful that arms control had an arcane language with nuances of its own, Hank established what he called his "A-team of analysts" to work full-time on the implications that the Strategic Arms Reduction Treaty (START) presented to the Navy. The team functioned at the Center of Naval Analyses under Capt. William A. Owens, later a vice chairman of the Joint Chiefs. Hank also formed a reserve cell, similar to his inspector general unit, to help him deal with congressional staffs that were getting in the mix.

Not surprisingly, the interservice politics within the Pentagon over the future of strategic nuclear weapons assumed "enormous" proportions. The initial infighting was between the Navy and the Air Force. "The Navy's position," said Hank, "was, 'Do not cut the Trident force, because those warheads are survivable. Cut the Air Force.' And the Air Force position was, 'Baloney. Survivability's not an issue. We need a retaliatory command, and NORAD is going to tell us in time to launch. So cut the Navy.' That's essentially what was going on in the Defense Department. The debates dominated the Joint Staff and got very heated down to the counting of warheads." In one notable occasion, after Hank's office presented the CNA study to Air Force Chief of Staff Gen. Larry D. Welch with the finding that the Air Force position "essentially invited a Soviet strategic strike against the continental United States," the result was a "very spirited confrontation" between Hank and the number one Air Force four-star.

With regard to interservice—and for that matter intraservice rivalry—Hank had very definite beliefs. "Parochial views are not part of some insidious scheme to undermine a service chief or colleagues. They are firm views held by powerful people who have the best interest of their service or union at heart. This constant struggle . . . ensure[s] that the cream will rise to the top and that the programs selected, having withstood the firestorm of passionate debate, are ultimately the strongest and therefore the best for the nation."

When Reykjavik also focused attention on the tactical intermediate-range nuclear forces in Europe, the interservice tussle grew to include the Army and its ground-launched cruise missiles. The U.S. Arms Control and Disarmament Agency, with European support, was pushing for an intermediate-range and shorter-range nuclear forces treaty. "That appealed to the Europeans, because it now took you back to Massive Retaliation," said Hank. "It appealed to the Soviets, because it took out a lot of stuff that had caused them problems in Europe. And it appealed to Europe because it was no longer a nuclear battleground. It did not, however, appeal to the U.S. Army, which stood to lose a lot of firepower in Europe."

At this point, interservice squabbling became intense, spilling into conventional force budget allocations. If the Army had to relinquish its tactical nukes, it had to have more tanks, which would only come from Air Force aircraft and Navy carrier accounts. Still geared to fighting the Soviets on the European Central Front, the Army turned to reemphasizing the need for the Navy to provide convoy escort. Its slogan was "ten divisions in ten days in Europe."

Hank responded, making the case that the Navy was responsible for only one-third of the resupply continuum. As such, he would not commit Navy resources to the problem until the Army (1) put money into programs dedicated to getting its matériel by rail to Norfolk and (2) persuaded the allies to fund the NATO infrastructure account for additional networks to transport that matériel from European ports to the Central Front. "NATO's got to build the railroads, and NATO countries haven't done it," said Hank, "because they don't intend to fight a conventional war in Europe." Failure in these two efforts would mean the Army would have to buy vast stockpiles and preposition in Europe, ergo "the Army had two-thirds of the problem." Said Hank, "The whole thing just sort of resulted in a bunch of speeches to the Navy League and the Army Association." Inevitably, defense officials undertook no substantial reallocation of Navy or Air Force funding.

Arms control also had implications for the Navy's forward strategy, because Soviet diplomacy attempted to exploit them by applying the concept of nuclear-weapons-free zones to European waters. Faced with the prospect that START would take intermediate-range weapons out of Europe, the Navy saw a nuclear version of Tomahawk as an offset to that pending loss. Even if the United States took ground-launched cruise missiles out of Europe, it still could have sea-launched cruise missiles. Naturally, the Soviets desired to include sea-launched missiles in the treaty.

Hank hit the stumps campaigning that naval arms should not be part of any intermediate- or shorter-range nuclear forces treaty. Working with Harvard's Samuel P. Huntington of the John F. Kennedy School of Government, he developed a case against the zones, saying they would prevent U.S. attack submarines from operating in the vicinity of the Soviet ballistic missile submarine forces and that they would prevent carrier operations in large areas across the world's oceans. The Soviets could not manage similar deployments of their navy, and they knew, said Hank, that their attack submarines could not operate in numbers off U.S. shores because they had no way to support them. Unable to solve those problems internally, they tried diplomacy.

In an article in the Winter 1988/89 issue of *International Security,* Hank made the Navy's argument against offering sea-launched cruise missiles as a bargaining chip for a larger START agreement. Attack submarines armed with cruise missiles were invulnerable to preemptive attack, he wrote, and the high-tech Tomahawk compelled the Soviets to invest in air defense systems and thus complicated their planning. The Soviet campaign to ban sea-launched cruise missiles was so important, he concluded, because they recognized that the land-attack missile was the United States' asymmetric advantage. "If you let naval arms control become a part of the dialogue," said Hank, "you will be granting the Soviets one of their longest and most dearly held strategic objectives: neutralizing an asymmetrical strength we have and they don't have. And they can do that without firing a shot or spending a dime."

Notwithstanding his tough stance on tactical nuclear weapons at sea, Hank was finding his personal dealings with the Soviet Navy warming. In 1987, it was Washington's turn to host the Incidents at Sea talks. Unlike the Moscow discussions the previous year, the Soviets proved to be very straightforward. Hank raised only two alleged violations; the Soviets, one. Together, they agreed to add a ship-to-ship voice radio channel for communication.

It was Admiral Navoytsev's last year as head of the Soviet delegation. The year before, the Soviets had allowed Hank to be photographed standing before the Kremlin, and Navoytsev now wanted his own photo before the White House. Hank arranged for the shot. In addition, Hank had remembered the old admiral telling him that he was the only person in the world who had commanded both a U.S. and Soviet ship. With some research, Hank found Navoytsev had commanded one of the destroyer escorts that the United States had provided the Soviets at the end of World War II. He got a photo of the ship from the Navy archives and framed it with a brass plate detailing her history. At a small cocktail party at a Washington hotel, he presented the photo to Navoytsev. "This hardened old Soviet sea dog actually cried, he was so touched."

The following June, Hank would attend his third and final Incidents at Sea meeting. *Glasnost* and *perestroika* were loosening Soviet society, and the much improved atmosphere would generate a significant U.S. concession. In late 1987, the United States conducted a series of operations in the northern Pacific that included testing Soviet claims to territorial waters around Kamchatka and a mock air attack on Petropavlovsk. In early 1988, a number of bumping incidents had occurred in the Black Sea as the Navy aggressively exercised freedom of navigation. Hank's Soviet counterparts complained that the commissars were pressuring them to do something or they would cut the navy budget. Hank recommended to Washington that the United States "back off for a while," which it did. Later that summer, the two navies would exchange port visits in Norfolk and Sevastopol, starting a new era in the evolution of the relationship between the two sea services.

Hank was one of a number of senior naval and defense officials in the late 1980s who believed the Soviets had shifted their emphasis from "attack-NATO-conquer-Europe" to economic warfare. "So the focus of their efforts," he said, "was going to be to penetrate the Middle East where the oil is."

The Soviet strategy, Hank believed, was to foment unrest, not necessarily to disrupt the worldwide oil supply but to affect its price. Given the volatility of the ongoing Iran-Iraq war, the epicenter for any potential disruption was the Persian Gulf. Around a Navy toehold in Bahrain, Hank began to plan an increase in naval presence in the Gulf that would be equivalent to the Sixth Fleet in the Med and a part of a "miniature NATO." He thus began to focus on the Middle East.

Hank chose to view the Persian Gulf as a maritime theater. The cornerstone of regional policy was the U.S. commitment to Israel, and with that policy pillar, he knew the Arab countries would not permit the Army and Air Force to introduce large forces, even for exercises. "The only force in town is the Navy," he noted.

The United States was making an unadvertised shift toward Iraq, led by Secretary of Defense Caspar Weinberger, that included providing the Iraqis with targeting information in their war with Iran. Both combatants had been attacking neutral tankers transiting the Gulf, but the Kuwaitis were suffering the most from Iran. "So, we were looking for a way to get the U.S. into the tanker war before the Soviets got in, without obviously tilting the scales in favor of Iraq," said Hank. "My role was to find out whether we could do that, and how we could do that."

By early January 1987, the Kuwaitis were inquiring about leasing ships. When Washington learned that they also had asked the Soviets about leasing, it offered on 7 March to reflag eleven Kuwaiti tankers and provide protection. "The idea really surfaced from a breakfast between Cap [Weinberger] and [Secretary of State] George Schultz. And it turned out that reflagging is pretty easy and is done all the time." As the administration grappled with ramifications raised by Congress, Hank wrestled with the technicalities of reflagging.

U.S. companies routinely reflagged U.S. merchantmen to other countries, but Hank had to work the issue in reverse. "Now those ships have got to conform to U.S. rules and there are expenses associated with that—crew size, OSHA safety standards, a whole baggage of U.S. requirements." The U.S. companies were not happy with the costs, but once the ships bore the U.S. flag, "if someone attacks them, we're going to blast them. And we were looking for reasons to blast Iran."

As Hank was working these issues, on the night of 17 March he got the call from the Navy command center that the frigate *Stark* had been hit and was on fire. An Iraqi Mirage F-1 fighter had fired two Exocet missiles into the ship, killing thirty-seven sailors.

With Admiral Crowe out of town, Hank and the vice chairman, Gen. Robert Herres, USAF, started briefing Congress and President Reagan. While the president's principal advisers were "wringing their hands" over how to handle the political aspects of the incident, Reagan himself was more concerned for the families of the casualties. "Admiral," he asked Hank, "do you think that you could arrange that when the sailors' bodies are returned I could be there to meet them and comfort the families to the degree that I can?" Hank said he would make the arrangements, and he left impressed with Reagan's "ability to identify what was really important as opposed to worrying about how it was going to read on page one of the *Washington Post.*"

Later Hank indeed had to face the relentless probings of the press. According to one retired officer, he handled the press conference about the *Stark* "masterfully." In an 18 May letter, retired captain Bruce G. Stone wrote him, "I've watched a lot of press conferences on a lot of subjects of national importance and I honestly cannot recall one in which a spokesman for the Government was as poised, balanced, sensitive, candid and direct as you were. . . . You did the Navy, yourself, and most important, the officers and men of *Stark* proud." Hank replied, "It was a real damage limiting exercise, but there is no way I was going to second guess—from the sanctity of the Pentagon—a skipper who had almost lost his ship and was putting thirty-seven of his boys into body bags."

Notwithstanding presidential statements that the United States was loosening its rules of engagement, Hank maintained that the rules did not change after the *Stark* attack and had always been in effect. The real problem was one of attitude, but the president's remarks did go a long way toward assuring the Navy of favorable support for any actions taken in self-defense. "My role in that drama was to clarify the rules of engagement for naval commanders." From then on, he had every officer heading for command in the Gulf spend an hour with him.

"The first thing they would always say, these guys were admirals down through commanders, 'We don't understand the rules of engagement.' I'd say, 'Let me clarify them for you. No matter what anybody tells you, your most fundamental responsibility as a commander is for the safety and security of your forces. If you're a skipper of a ship, that's your ship. And so, I expect that you will act that way. And I'm telling you that if your ship ever takes a round and you haven't responded to it before it was fired, you're going to be relieved before the fires are out. Have you got any questions about the rules of engagement?' 'No, sir. That's pretty clear.' And they all went out. And I said, 'Incidentally, I've backed that up in writing. If anything ever happens, you just feel free to quote the rules. Quote me. Say you acted in the way I told you to.'"

Hank recalled that the Navy increased its presence in the Gulf from six to nine ships, with a carrier stationed outside the Strait of Hormuz in the Gulf of Oman to provide air cover.

Just as we found with the war in Vietnam when we had taken the bulk of naval forces away from Europe, we found that despite the Reagan buildup of military and naval forces, we did not have the force to do what we were doing in the Gulf and at the same time take on Qaddafi in the Med. . . . If you guys can't handle a re-flagging operation, a little Mickey Mouse operation in the Gulf, without drawing down on the rest of the world, how are you going to handle two major contingencies? And, of course, we couldn't. We couldn't then, can't now.

Hank worked with the NATO allies in an attempt to get them on board for escorting tankers. The British immediately joined the effort. The French resolutely refused. Constitutional restrictions prevented the Germans from playing a role. The Japanese offered to pay for some of the operations but could not send ships because they were a self-defense force. Beyond these, no other country could provide any useful forces, he said. By mid-1987, however, British, French, Belgian, Dutch, and Italian warships had joined the Americans and Soviets in patrolling the Gulf.

With the coalition forces, "there was an extraordinary level of cooperation, and the interesting thing about it was [that] it was cooperation in a hot war scenario, whereas all the other co-operations were a sort of war-game, or what-if. There wasn't actually shooting."

On 22 July, the Navy escorted its first convoy of reflagged Kuwaiti tankers under Operation Earnest Will. By that time, the multinational force in the Gulf included eleven warships and seventeen supply, patrol, and minesweeping craft. In addition, sixteen ships, including an aircraft carrier and a battleship, remained outside the strait.

Two days into the transit of the Gulf, the reflagged supertanker *Bridgeton* hit a mine. By the end of the month, three tankers had struck mines. Hank had not been able to provide U.S. minesweeping assets. The Navy had virtually no surface ships for that purpose, and, with no carriers in the Gulf, minesweeping helicopters lacked platforms from which to fly.

Hank argued to have the carriers forward in the Gulf, but the aviator Adm. Ron Hays, commander in chief, Pacific Command, who owned the forces, was opposed to the idea. When Riyadh refused to allow the Air Force to use Saudi Arabia as a staging base, Hank saw that the only way to get the needed aviation assets into the Gulf was with Hays's carriers. With support from Gen. George Crist, USMC, commander in chief of Central Command, Hank argued again for sending carriers and the battle-ship *Missouri* into the Gulf, with Aegis ships providing protection. He wanted Crist to have operational command.

Hank was thinking more in joint terms, especially now that Lehman no longer was secretary of the Navy. He did not agree with the Navy position that when the Navy supported a land commander, operational command of the carriers remained with the providing Navy commander in chief. Although his service strongly opposed giving the carriers to Army generals, Hank applied a warrior's logic to argue that not doing so would result in divided command. Subsequently, after his retirement, Hank's views became the norm.

As for Hays, his public line was that operations in the confused waters of the Persian Gulf were restrictive and that the carriers were vulnerable. "I think the real agenda was letting his forces go to CinCCent," said Hank. In the end, Crowe supported Hays, killing the idea in the near term. Later, under Crowe's Army successor Gen. Colin L. Powell, the carriers moved into the Gulf, where they performed admirably in Desert Storm.

Once the surface forces entered the Gulf, they found themselves "escorting these tankers in a very dense littoral environment." Said Hank, "This was what you might call the precursor of the littoral warfare campaign." With some 80 percent of the world's oil passing through the Strait of Hormuz, the great majority of the sea traffic was commer-cial. Adding to the challenge were the crowded commercial airways above.

Joint planners were addressing a combat environment where forces were either "red, white or blue—red being the enemy, blue, us, and white, the neutrals." "How do you sort out shooting at the reds instead of the whites?" Hank asked. The pressure on the destroyer skippers was constant. "The CIA was flying their own little Air Force around and not telling anybody about it, so that the air picture was unmanageable."

Hank outlined a proposed concept of operations. If Iranian missiles, planes, ships, or small craft attacked the tankers or escorts, naval forces would respond directly against the attackers. If the Iranians attacked shore facilities in Kuwait, they would not "con-fine our attacks to just the forces that attacked us, we're going to attack their bases." In particular, Hank was in favor of striking missile sites and the military airfield at the Iranian port of Bandar Abbas, using land-attack Tomahawks. For this purpose, he had pirated all the Tomahawks in the total Navy inventory, some forty weapons, for use in the Gulf. At the time, the Tomahawk had not yet been fired in anger and was operationally untested. Its terrain-following feature was still preprogrammed for strikes against the Soviet Union. In effect, the missile would have to detour substantially from the most direct path to target for its guidance system to acquire reference points. "At the time, we had no idea whether it would work."

Meaningful, sustained power projection required carriers, but Hank's plan "was just too tough for the Joint Chiefs to swallow accordingly." Without them, the tanker war and the reflagging became a frigate and cruiser exercise during which the U.S. and Iran engaged each other into 1988. "So we shot up a couple of fueling stations and sank a couple of PT boats, and that's about it."

As deputy chief of naval operations for plans, policy, and operations, Hank would testify before Congress to support submarines, aircraft carriers, and surface forces. As for in-house, working requirements, he had to determine whether antisubmarine or antiair warfare was a more pressing threat for the Navy and thus where the money would go. His bent, as a surface officer closely aligned with the Aegis program, was to push antiair warfare. Hank felt that spending money on frigates with predominantly open-ocean ASW capabilities and on large numbers of new submarines was a waste. The battle of the Atlantic had passed into history; naval strategy had shifted focus to littoral operational environments. The regional submarine threat was minor. "How much money do you want to spend on shallow-water ASW when you're talking about a country that's got four submarines?" he asked. As the *Stark* attack showed, however, likely adversaries did have large modern air forces. For Hank, the point was clear: During the Zumwalt era, the U.S. needed a sea-control navy, but in the 1990s, it faced no bona fide blue-water opponent. "Sea control was simply not an issue, and the sea control forces were of lower priority than those serving power projection."

After two years as a deputy chief of naval operations, Hank was a candidate for a four-star billet, and he was most qualified for command of the Atlantic Fleet. Hank's chief advocate in his quest for command of the Atlantic Fleet had been Lehman, but on 10 April 1987, Lehman suddenly left office, leaving behind a lot of bad feeling. On 1 May, James H. Webb succeeded him. While Hank also had Webb's support for the billet, the new secretary lacked the political clout to move Hank's name through department channels. Then Webb abruptly resigned in February 1988 over Defense Secretary Frank Carlucci's cancellation of sixteen frigates in the Navy budget. On 28 March, William L. Ball became the administration's third secretary of the Navy. A John Towers man, Ball arrived in the Pentagon in advance of the Texas senator, who expected to become secretary of defense after the 1988 elections.

In the end, Crowe was able to get his favorite, fellow submariner Powell Carter, to be the commander in chief, Atlantic Fleet. With that appointment, all nine Navy four-star slots were filled. When Trost told him he had no place for him to go, Hank had to accept the inevitable. It was time to leave.

When he returned from the Incidents at Sea meetings in Moscow, he learned of a move afoot to place him in a joint four-star billet, commander in chief, Central Command, to relieve General Crist. Leading the charge was Marine Corps Commandant Al Gray, who submitted Hank as his nominee, as opposed to a marine. "When you're a service chief, your first responsibility is to be a joint chief," said Gray, "and contrary to popular opinion, I always tried to do that."

Gray and Hank shared an understanding that the Persian Gulf was a maritime environment where access was vital. "I also felt that Hank had a very keen understanding of aviation and the employment of aviation, and that would play a big role in any of CinCCent's command. He had also an excellent grasp of the employment of Marines coming from the sea and had learned from the exercises that we used to conduct on the East Coast with the Eighty-second Airborne Division and other Army units. So, I thought that he was the best person in the Department of the Navy that we had at that time to nominate for that very important billet."

The Army nominated Norm Schwarzkopf. When the chiefs voted, the Army and Air Force cast their votes for Schwarzkopf, and the Navy and Marine Corps went for Hank. To break the tie, Crowe cast his vote for Hank, and the decision went to Carlucci.

Right away, the Army mounted a public relations campaign for Schwarzkopf, whose photo soon appeared on the front page of the *Washington Post*. More significantly, the service drew on a key ally in the White House. Army Lt. Gen. Colin Powell had been Carlucci's assistant when he was national security adviser and had succeeded him in that position when Carlucci became secretary of defense. He also had served with both Weinberger and Carlucci during their days at the Office of Management and Budget.

As for Hank, the Navy did not mount a similar campaign for his nomination. He received a measure of support from Capitol Hill, notably from Indiana Republican Senator Dan Quayle, at the time a major force on the Senate Armed Services Committee. In a 7 July letter, Quayle wrote Carlucci to express his "strong recommendation" for the nomination. Al Gray continued to be his principal supporter in the Pentagon.

Unfortunately, four days before, the Aegis cruiser *Vincennes* had mistaken Iran Air Flight 655 for an attacking Iranian F-14. She fired two Standard missiles that destroyed the plane and killed 290 civilians. Press reports soon revealed that under a commander widely regarded as "trigger happy," the *Vincennes* had acquired the nickname "Robocruiser."

For Hank's nomination, the timing could not have been worse. The incident was a major embarrassment to the Navy and convenient fodder for Powell, who had long identified himself with policies of military restraint. When Carlucci called the White House to submit Hank's name, Powell responded that the commander in chief of Central Command was going to be an Army general. According to Hank, Powell told his erstwhile boss that he'd "have more trouble than [he could] handle" if he forwarded a Navy nominee to the president. Yielding to pressure, Carlucci submitted Schwarzkopf's name instead, overriding the recommendation of his chiefs.

The game was over. Hank would retire on 1 September 1988. At the Eighth & Eye Barracks, Al Gray hosted a farewell parade that family members, including Lloyd, attended. Addressing marines and guests, the general praised Hank, saying that "the Navy has lost the only admiral who is at heart a marine."

On 15 August, Hank's staff organized and hosted a farewell party, inviting his ship-mates from all ranks to join him aboard the destroyer *Barry* at the Washington Navy Yard. Well-wishers sent messages of support and admiration from across the Navy and the world. "Few will ever come close to matching your record of dedication, integrity, energy, courage, innovation and achievement," wrote retired Rear Adm. Robert B. Rogers. A "flabbergasted" Adm. Sir Julian Oswald wrote, "A service which can manage without you in its highest ranks must indeed be rich in talent. . . . On a more personal note I would just like to say how great it was to work with a real committed fighter—it was never a dull moment and I enjoyed every moment."

Immediately after his retirement in January 1989, Hank went to work for his old friend, Charlie Kaman, at the Kaman Corporation as vice president for international marketing. He represented nationally and internationally the SH-2G Super Seasprite helicopters and other high-tech equipment and services.

In 1992, he became a distinguished fellow at the Center for Naval Analyses. For two years, his work included development of the gunnery improvement program that led to guided projectiles and liberalized Tomahawk targeting. He also served as the only military member on President Clinton's 1992 commission, co-chaired by the

Republican congressman from Iowa, James A. Leach, that studied U.S. military participation in the United Nations, where his views were not shared by the rest of the committee that was composed mainly of academics. In succeeding years, he would make periodic appearances on national television as a "military expert," worked with the director of naval research in the area of communications and network-centric warfare, and was a trustee of the U.S. Naval Academy Foundation.

Throughout the nineties, Lucy was the most visible Mustin in Navy circles by virtue of her work with the Society of Sponsors of the United States Navy. On 3 March 1987, Navy Secretary John Lehman had asked her to sponsor the Aegis guided missile cruiser *Cowpens* at Bath Iron Works. The christening was on 11 March 1989; the commissioning, two years later in Charleston, South Carolina.

The following year, she became the society's treasurer, a position she held for the next three years. After serving as vice president for two more years, she was president of the over six hundred-member organization from 1995 to 1997. During that time, she was present at every one of the dozen or so ship commissionings and a score of christenings. As a sponsor of the *Cowpens* and the second destroyer *Mustin,* she was one of only a dozen women who have sponsored two ships.

Recalling many years later how his appreciation for Hank Mustin dated from their time aboard the *Lawrence,* Adm. Worth Bagley wrote, "I learned close-hand that he had an impeccable character, was highly intelligent, an expert on material and equipment, an instinctive mind for operations, a very effective administrator, good sense in balancing efficiency and economy to achieve the highest possible capability for combat, a reliable and forthright colleague, and a forceful but considerate leader of men. Underlying these exceptional attributes was a moral and physical courage that inspired everyone."

On 12 April 1986, Bath Iron Works held a commissioning for the frigate *Samuel B. Roberts.* Her captain invited Hank Mustin to be the principal speaker. Two years later, as Admiral Trost's operations deputy, Hank had to face the press, seven days after the ship's near-fatal 14 April explosion when she struck a mine in the waters of the Persian Gulf. "We can't speak highly enough for those young fellows who brought us back our ship," he told reporters. Six days later, he wrote personally to her skipper, Cdr. Paul X. Rinn, "You and your crew would not let your ship die, and one has to go back to World War II to find heroism, training and performance like yours. I'm honored to be an Honorary Plankowner in *Samuel B. Roberts.*"

That spring, Hank received an undated letter with a photo from Ben Masdon, a retired quartermaster signalman, prompted by the "Be My Guest" article in *Newsweek*. "I used to think a lot of you back aboard the USS Duncan DDR 874 in 1956 thru 1958," Masdon wrote. "I have [a photo] of you covered with oil when the hose blew out when we were in Japan and refueling. . . ." Unsure whether Hank would remember him, he closed by writing, "Anyway I am very proud of you and to be able to say I knew you."

In a 5 May note, Hank responded with a humility that bespoke his genuine affection for the men and women with whom and for whom he had served in a career that spanned four decades. "Dear Ben, Thanks for your nice letter with the enclosed photo of the great *Duncan* oil spill. I was convinced on that day that I'd never make LTJG. I certainly do remember you. . . . Best of luck to you, shipmate."

Chapter 36

Tom Mustin

SWASHBUCKLING FROM

WARDROOM TO COURTROOM

Thomas Morton Mustin's first memories were of Annapolis at war; he was born on 11 February 1941. "More generally, I remember the fact that all of my parents' friends were naval or Marine officers," he recalled. "What a great group of people to be surrounded with when you're growing up. The older I get, the more lucky I feel I was to be in that environment. I just couldn't have been happier with that whole period of my life, with the exception of the requirement to move every couple of years."

When he was seven, the family moved to Coronado, where they remained for two years. After a series of moves up and down the East Coast, they returned, arriving on Labor Day 1954, just as he was about to enter high school. Lloyd had three consecutive Pacific jobs, enabling Tom to participate fully in the burgeoning postwar California youth culture. When his father drew East Coast duty again in April of his senior year, Tom remained with his cousins Anne and Don Thomas until he graduated in June from Coronado High School.

He did not remember making a decision to go the Naval Academy. "I was never against going. It was just understood by everyone, including me. Every man that I knew, including my brother, had gone. It never occurred to me to do anything else." As a hedge, he applied for an NROTC scholarship and was accepted at California Berkeley and Harvard. If he failed to make the academy, he decided that he would go to

Berkeley. "I guess I was thinking that I wanted to stay in California." In the end, he got a presidential appointment and on 30 June 1958 entered the academy.

When the academic year began, Tom was assigned to Thirteenth Company. His classmates in that company included a disproportionate number of prior enlisted men, many of whom were marines. On the somewhat impressionable seventeen-year-old, these twenty-year-old former corporals and sergeants had a profound impact, reinforcing the example set by the commissioned officers in the Yard.

One marine in the executive department impressed him deeply: Capt. William Groom Leftwich Jr. "I think everyone thought he was a most exemplary guy." In 1970, Leftwich was killed in action in Vietnam, and today, the Marine Corps awards a trophy in his name for outstanding leadership. Tom's plebe-year company commander, Jack Phillips, another marine, also was killed in Vietnam. For a time, Tom gave "very serious thought to taking [his] commission to the Marine Corps."

Tom was not an academic performer at the academy, but he was gifted with a razor-sharp mind, and the pettiness of the "chicken regs" frustrated him to the point where he on occasion considered leaving. "I didn't get on well there at all. I just didn't like it. I think I had a bad attitude about the place. A lot of people did. You know, they kind of pride themselves on the bad attitude," said Tom. The *Lucky Bag*, however, recorded an opposite state of mind, profiling his "easy-going attitude" and "ability to find humor in any situation."

When it came time for service selection in early 1962, Tom's class was equally split across line, aviation, and submarines. Tom had gone to Pensacola for his second-class summer, but aviation was not an option for him. When he took the eye test, the results indicated that he would develop nearsightedness. He had no interest in going into the nuclear submarine program. That left the line community. "What I thought I wanted to do was what my father had done at Guadalcanal, which was slug it out in gunfire with the enemy ships. I think I was the only man Jack at the Naval Academy who didn't know that was never going to happen again."

He asked for a guided missile destroyer. "I certainly wasn't the highest-standing guy in my class to ask for a DDG. When they asked, 'Home port?' I replied, 'San Diego.'" On 24 March, his orders came for the *Hoel,* a guided missile destroyer homeported in San Diego.

The *Hoel* was a new-construction ship in the middle of her fitting-out. On 11 July, Tom reported in Boston after taking his graduation leave in Coronado. After a month of operating out of Boston, the ship sailed independently to San Diego via the Panama Canal.

Tom had become a member of the *Hoel*'s commissioning crew. His assignment was assistant navigator, a role he had loved at the Naval Academy. The duty was a unique opportunity, for he was navigating the ship by taking star sights at night and sun lines by day and plotting them throughout the transit to San Diego. He later navigated the ship across the Pacific. "After about six or eight months, the exec, who was head navigator, persuaded the captain that I could be designated navigator."

On 11 September, the ship arrived in San Diego and spent the next year completing acceptance tests and trials and underway training with antisubmarine rocket (ASROC) and Tartar missile firings. From July through September 1963, she was in the Long Beach Yard for post-shakedown availability. During that year, Tom qualified as officer of the deck under way— "a real feather" in his cap—took the shore bombardment course in Coronado, and cleared for nuclear weapons, specifically the ASROC.

On 17 October, the *Hoel* departed Long Beach for her first Western Pacific deployment as the flagship for the commander of Destroyer Division Twelve. On 6 December, Tom made lieutenant (junior grade). About that time, he became the gunnery assistant. His goal now was to be a DDG weapons officer.

In March 1964, he had to attend crypto school in Kamiseya, Japan. Like his father, he hated the idea of being a duty cryptographer and the laborious mechanical process of decrypting messages. The next month, he began a far more interesting six weeks at Mare Island's Tartar missile officers course. When he finished, he felt he had "a perfect understanding of Tartar missile systems of the day." The ship had a good performance record, but he recalled, "It was a constant struggle to keep those things operational, and they often just didn't function right. It was always a problem getting spare parts. The radars would go down."

In preparation for her 1965 Western Pacific deployment, the *Hoel* took the shore bombardment course at San Clemente. After the marines landed in Vietnam that spring, naval activity offshore increased dramatically. Tom was bitterly disappointed, however, when he arrived on station off Vietnam in April to find that the Navy considered DDGs as too valuable as carrier defenders to put them on the gun line. As a result, the *Hoel* drew plane guard duty for the carriers *Midway* and *Coral Sea* on Yankee Station, "a pretty good way to bore yourself to tears, frankly."

While in the Pacific, Tom received orders to the Postgraduate School and thus did not complete the deployment. "I didn't just get orders out of the blue." The Bureau of Personnel had asked if he wanted to go and offered him the operations analysis curriculum, the only course that interested him. He accepted and in August was in Monterey beginning his studies. On 1 December 1965, he made lieutenant.

The following summer, Tom drew temporary duty in the Pentagon working for his father who was the Joint Staff's director of operations. At the time, the military was wrestling with the air interdiction campaign in Vietnam. While examining classified documents associated with the issue, Tom discovered depictions of the North Vietnamese transportation networks from Hanoi, along the Ho Chi Minh trail and into the South. Intrigued, he copied much of the material and returned to Monterey with the idea that it could form the basis of his thesis research.

His thesis adviser was a young professor, Allan McMasters, who taught network theory, the science of applying math to networks, defined as "nodes connected by arcs." "If you draw a network, and you assign a capacity to each arc," Tom explained, "there are algorithms and formulas that will tell you what is the total capacity of the network, what can get from the beginning of the network to the end, and at what rate it can get there." He proposed using network theory determine how limited resources could reduce the total capacity of the network.

For the purpose of the thesis, his resources were the number of sorties per day that could be launched against the network. The question he wanted to answer was where to apply these strikes to achieve the most reduction in overall network capacity. As his last semester drew to a close, he still had not solved the problem, until one weekend at a Carmel bar the solution came to him. "Just like that. I've never been excited about anything that involves just thinking about something as I was about that. I went home and started putting it on paper, and overnight I had it."

He titled his thesis "Optimal Allocation of Air Strikes for Interdiction of a Transportation Network." "It was the best thesis I ever received in all my years of teaching," said McMasters, adding that he was so impressed that he wrote Tom the glowing reference that he thought got him into law school. McMasters polished the thesis and later published it in *Naval Logistics Quarterly* and the journal of the Operations Research Society of America and presented it at the society's annual meeting.

In his first year at the Postgraduate School, Tom had met a student a year ahead of him in operations analysis by the name of Walsh who received orders to Vietnam to serve in the newly created River Patrol Force. Tom already had discussed riverine duty with his brother and determined to go. While in Washington during the summer of 1966, he had gone to the Bureau of Personnel and asked for orders to river patrol boats "in the face of strenuous advice from my detailer who said, 'You don't want to do this.'" Tom prevailed, and immediately after receiving his master's in operations research/systems analysis, headed for the amphibious base in Coronado. The river patrol boat program included two weeks of language instruction and a survival, evasion, resistance, and escape course. On 23 July, he moved to the Naval Inshore Operations Training Center northeast of San Francisco, where he trained in PBRs until he left for Vietnam. He was impatient with the length and content. "The guys who were teaching it really didn't have much experience. Very few of them had *any* experience, and they didn't know what to prepare for or how."

On 7 September, Tom arrived in-country with orders to be the first operations officer, the number two, for River Section 514, which was forming to operate with new Mark II patrol boats. Unfortunately, the Mark IIs still were under construction in the states, so until April, he would be operating in a number of places for two- to three-month stretches. "I met and worked with a lot of different guys, officers and enlisted." Many of the officers and boat crews were in the later stages of their tours and had known and served with Hank.

Tom's first temporary posting was to River Division 52 in Vinh Long at the top of the Co Chien River. He had no particular title and thus served as a "roving patrol officer." "It was the ideal duty assignment," he recalled, "because I was just on temporary duty to River Section 521, and I was on a patrol, twelve-hour patrol, then I'd come back for eighteen or twenty-four hours, then I'd go on another patrol. I had no other duties. I had no administrative duties." While with the division, Tom cut his teeth on twenty-one combat patrols.

Hearing in mid-October that his boats had arrived, Tom left for Nha Be, a small naval base downriver from Saigon. When he got there, the boats were not yet ready to operate. On the twenty-third, he joined Nha Be's River Division 54 and began running patrols in the Rung Sat Special Zone.

Tom worked with a standard section, ten boats that patrolled two at a time, "the one unassailable point of doctrine." Initially, he was always on board one of the boats, although later, down on the Bassac, he increasingly operated more ashore with South Vietnamese Regional/Popular Forces, or Ruff Puffs. To be more effective, someone had to work directly with the Vietnamese. "And I said, it's gonna be me. So, I had a Vietnamese guy with a radio, and off we'd go through the rice paddies, tree lines and what not, and I'd just keep in touch with the boats, making sure they knew where we were, and where I thought they ought to go, and so on. It was unusual."

His unit quickly improved its intelligence gathering. He particularly relied on the SEALs and two Catholic priests who had outposts on the Bassac. "They preached to their flock, but they also went about armed, and they spoke French. So, I could talk to them in pidgin-French and get intelligence from them."

When he learned where the Viet Cong were going to be or where they had a tax collector making his rounds, he would operate differently. "We'd plan with a Vietnamese liaison guy in the operation where we might just take a two-boat patrol, but we might take four or even six boats and load them up with Ruff Puffs. We'd take two up this canal and two up that canal and let the Ruff Puffs disembark and go shoot the place up, basically. After I thought I'd figured it out pretty well, I'd usually go with the Ruff Puffs."

On 14 December, River Section 535 arrived in Binh Thuy with five Mark IIs. Lt. Jack Doyle was the officer in charge, and by this time Tom was operating with him in his familiar role as "independent contractor." Five days later, he was downriver on the Bassac, operating with four boats in patrol through the canals. Two of his PBRs, along with some Ruff Puffs, had gone up a twenty-meter-wide canal and had come under heavy enemy automatic weapons and B-40 rocket attack. In contact by radio, Tom came to their aid with his two boats and a Seawolf fire team. He ordered air strikes and then led his boats up the narrow canal to deliver follow-up fire and shuttle the Ruff Puffs to the enemy side. For his actions, the Navy awarded him its Commendation Medal with a Combat V, citing his "exemplary initiative, courage under fire, and outstanding professionalism."

A month later, on the night of 31 January 1968, the eve of the Vietnamese lunar new year, Tet, Tom had scheduled a patrol to run from eight in the evening to eight the following morning. Some of the men at Binh Thuy were on their second tour and, knowing the drill, were expecting a pyrotechnic display at midnight. As a chief gunner's mate named Canby told him, "Any guy with a weapon on the Delta, which means every guy, will fire off tracers into the sky, and it will look like a big fireworks show."

Later that night, Tom was on a PBR downriver off the city of Can Tho, his engines cut and his two boats drifting in the hope that he might surprise a contraband-carrying sampan attempting to cross. "At midnight, here come the tracers, but many of them are horizontal." The enemy was unleashing its Tet Offensive. Upriver, the Viet Cong mortared the compound at Binh Thuy and attempted an assault. As dawn broke, Can Tho had "black smoke roiling into the sky." The city was "under siege and under great duress. Everybody scrambled and got boats out onto the river, and we looked for targets of opportunity." Another three weeks of intense activity on the Bassac and elsewhere throughout the Delta and South Vietnam followed.

When the aftershocks of Tet subsided, Tom left for Washington, where from 26 February to 19 March he was on temporary duty with the Army Map Service and Engineer Studies Group. Evidently, someone senior had acquainted the group with his thesis. The unit was working on the same problem and wanted to ask him, "How do we decide where to send the aircraft?" Tom was puzzled. The Pentagon had experts who thought they knew the North Vietnamese's network capacity and the location of roads and bridges. It had others who thought they knew how much they could degrade that capacity with air strikes. The matter was fairly straightforward. "Here's my thesis," he offered, adding that he was in the middle of fighting his own war and had to return to his unit.

When he returned in-country on 7 April, Tom found that River Section 514 had been activated, and his Mark IIs were ready to operate. He would serve with his unit for just a month.

On 3 May, his friend Carl Kollmeyer, the officer in charge of River Section 511, decided to take four PBRs upriver to Chau Doc, just below the Cambodian border. He arrived as two battalions of Viet Cong and North Vietnamese crossed the border, laid siege to the town, and "shot it up pretty good" as part of the May Offensive. Kollmeyer's boat lost power during an engagement and was hit by a 75-mm recoilless rifle, killing him and wounding two of his crew. On 5 May, Tom was awakened at two in the morning with the news that his friend was dead and that he was now officer in charge of 511. His orders were to take four PBRs and get under way for Chau Doc.

By the time they arrived, the assault was substantially over, but Tom remained in the area through 9 May, patrolling and searching for the enemy. Once the situation stabilized, he tied his boats to a makeshift boat ramp on the river in front of a villa. There he discovered that during the initial offensive the Viet Cong had overrun the site, used by a Navy doctor and nurse as part of the area's hearts-and-minds effort. "This nurse, Maggie, who my ops officer ended up marrying, had hidden in a cupboard under the sink. The VC came all through there and then left, and she came back out."

Tom remained as officer in charge of 511 for four months. He and most of his fellow lieutenants had sensed that the higher-ups' idea of intercepting sampans and hoping that one of them was carrying weapons was leading nowhere. As the ones who actually were on the river every day and night, they wanted to experiment with better tactics that had been developing since late 1967. Tom opted to conduct more special operations, when he had the intelligence to enable him to take offensive action. Working with the Vietnamese militia, he would seek to "take the war to the enemy in ways that involve something other than search and seizure." On the other hand, he did not agree with some of the senior-level approaches that had put the PBRs and their crews in harm's way in the hope it would lead to a firefight.

> I was sure thinking, "What are they trying to accomplish?" and I still don't know. "Why do we send a bunch of boats to get into firefights for no apparent purpose?" There developed a mindset in some quarters that a firefight was an end in itself, but I think most of the guys on the river wanted something to show for it besides a few holes in the boat.

In a deeper sense, however, Tom was disheartened by the news emanating from Washington. On 31 March, when President Lyndon Johnson gave his "I shall not seek, nor will I accept" speech and renewed a previous offer to stop the U.S. bombardment of the North, Tom knew instantly that the United States was preparing to cut and run. "I remember that that made me feel, made everyone feel, a lot less enthusiastic about what we were doing."

"The longer I operated," he said, "the more I began to just wonder whether what was really going on was just a partisan war between two competing Vietnamese factions, at least in the Delta. . . . I don't know how ideological either side was. . . . A lot of the things that led to us being able to carry out offensive action was very commercial activity. It was tax-collectors on canals, getting rice or money from sampans coming by."

On 5 July, Tom got orders to the guided missile destroyer *McCain* as the prospective executive officer. His Vietnam completion date would be 4 September. He had told the Navy he wanted a West Coast DDG. "I don't care where it is, in fact, I prefer to be in Southeast Asia." At the time, officers coming from Vietnam were not being reassigned, but, said Tom, "I wanted to go back there."

He had had an exemplary combat record. While with River Sections 514 and 511, he was in twenty-one firefights in his boats and another two firefights ashore. For several of his actions, he received the Bronze Star with V, the Navy Commendation with V, and the Combat Action Ribbon. The River Patrol Force was awarded the Presidential Unit Citation. When he left Vietnam, he had 335 days of combat duty as operations officer, eight months of which was with River Sections 521 and 514. Altogether, he commanded 104 combat patrols and nine ground sweeps.

On 1 September, he returned to the world by way of thirty days' leave in Sydney, Australia.

When Tom arrived Stateside, the *McCain* was undergoing conversion and behind schedule. The Navy canceled his orders and issued him new ones to another DDG, the *Decatur,* homeported in Long Beach. Tom then went to Norfolk for courses in nuclear weapons and antisubmarine warfare and to nearby Dam Neck for another course in Tartar missiles.

On 18 December, he reported in Hong Kong harbor to the *Decatur* as weapons officer. The ship was in the middle of her six-month Western Pacific deployment, where most of the time she was operating in task force air defense and air traffic control for the carriers and their air groups on Yankee Station. From 21 December to 6 January 1969, she was in the Southeast Asia combat zone, at one point on a solo patrol off Sihanoukville in the Gulf of Thailand. In total, Tom booked twenty-one additional days of combat duty.

Although he was pleased to have qualified as command duty officer, Tom found the "combat" unsatisfying. The *Decatur* had only one 5-inch mount. "So, she was forbidden to do shore bombardment, for example, because the 5-inch 54 itself had enough downtime that you could find yourself on the line and unable to shoot," he noted. "You'd crank out ten rounds, and you'd be down for an hour. If you had two guns, at least you could continue to discharge your mission if you were on the gunfire support line, but the ships that only had one, yeah, it was certainly a question in my mind, 'What good are these missiles against a Chinese junk?'" The *Decatur* might have been in the zone, but Tom was not seeing any action as he understood the word.

After visits to Subic Bay and Singapore, the ship returned home, via Australia, New Zealand, and American Samoa, arriving on 26 February. For the next year, she was in and out of Long Beach. In June, Tom took further instruction for ASROC in San Diego. In September, he completed his dream card, writing that he "strongly desired to avoid the Atlantic Fleet" and that he wanted either to be the executive officer of a DD/DDG or in a billet in which he could use his operations analysis. That winter, he made lieutenant commander.

On 10 February 1970, the *Decatur* returned to the Western Pacific for more operations off Vietnam. Between March and July, Tom racked another seventy days in the combat zone, but he was getting restless in the Navy. "I was junior enough that I was thinking about the excitement, or boredom, of the job, as the case might be. I don't know if I ever had that much of the sense of or interest in the big picture." In February, he had requested a command. He wanted to be commanding officer of an ocean minesweeper. The Navy honored his request, assigning him to command the *Force.*

"I know by the time I got those orders, I had notified the appropriate person in the Bureau of Personnel that my intention was to leave the Navy," he said. "I felt I'd done all I wanted to do, and I wanted to do something else. And then up come these orders to command, to which I said, 'No way am I going to submit my resignation while I'm in command.'" To his mind, the gesture would have been "bad form." His sister, Doug, did not believe that he would resign while their father was on active duty.

On 27 July, the day the *Decatur* left Japan for Long Beach, Tom headed to Charleston, South Carolina, for instruction at the mine warfare school. He knew the offer to command the *Force* had been an effort to keep him in the Navy. When he accepted the orders he said to his detailer, "I don't want you to think that this means I will continue to stay in." Nonetheless, for almost a full year, he threw himself into command in the finest Mustin tradition: More than other commanding officers in the division, he insisted that his ensigns qualify as soon as possible as officers of the deck.

As his tour was concluding, the Bureau of Personnel offered him another inducement to stay in the Navy. The Nixon administration required the services to send field grade officers—for the Navy, lieutenant commanders—to positions throughout the executive branch for mutual benefit. Tom was skeptical of the rationale but accepted the offer nonetheless. Orders came on 8 October 1971.

Just prior to his detachment, his division shifted its home port to Guam by way of Wake Island and Kwajalein, where they stopped for fuel. His relief came on board at Kwajalein. The morning after they arrived in Guam, Tom held the change of command. The following day, 10 December, he was on a plane to the States and a posting that had nothing to do with the Navy.

Tom's orders were to the White House's Office of Telecommunications Policy (OTP). He was among a number of military officers working out of uniform for a very young and gifted Clay T. Whitehead, the office's director. A staff of fifty-five essentially supported with analyses the president's telecommunications policy with respect to cable and public broadcasting and Federal Communications Commission regulations. Tom became executive assistant to Walter Hinchman, who subsequently advanced to be an FCC commissioner.

What he knew about telecommunications, he learned on the job, and he began to regard some of the OTP leaders as visionaries. "People will actually do their shopping from their desk and office," Tom recalled a number of them saying. The staff was a combination of bureaucrats, economists, and think-tank academics that included C-SPAN chairman and chief executive officer Brian Lamb, then Whitehead's public affairs officer. The general counsel was eventual Supreme Court Justice Antonin Scalia, who "was very vociferously opposed to regulation of any kind over anything."

OTP opened Tom's eyes to the broader horizons that his abilities afforded him, and it was there that he began to think seriously about a career in law. Until then, he had seen himself as career Navy. "I just wanted to see the world in a different way, I guess. The more it progressed into the twenty-year career, the tougher it would have been to cut the cord."

Hank recalled getting a call about that time from Vice Adm. Dave Bagley, the chief of personnel. "Your brother is the guy who has got the number two fitness report index in his year group," Bagley told him, "that is, he is the second most highly thought-of guy in year group '62. He's a cinch for early selection and flag rank. And it's up to you to keep him in."

Tom, however, had bought his first home, in Georgetown, and was resolved to leave the Navy. He would take the law boards and apply to law school. Once accepted, he would tender his resignation.

In June 1972, the Watergate scandal broke, and by the spring of 1973, when Tom took the boards, "you could pick up the *New York Times* or the *Washington Post,* and every story on the front page would be about legal issues, and I just thought, 'Yeah, I want to know about that stuff.'"

On 21 February, Tom applied for the excess leave program, but the Navy denied his request. On 8 May, he resigned. Years later, he said of his decision, "I guess I had the sense that most of the adventure was over."

The Navy released him with an honorable discharge on 4 September. Twenty-two days later, it unaccountably tried to woo him back by offering him a White House fellowship. Already at Harvard, Tom was not interested, not even in the Naval Reserves. "My whole mind-set was 'When I leave, I'm going to leave it altogether. I don't want to be a reserve officer.'"

Surprisingly, Tom did not enjoy Harvard. "Of the entire Law School faculty, there was one single Republican," he recalled, "the late Philip Areeda. Most of the remainder prided themselves on their antiwar, antimilitary pasts; none ever mentioned military service. Perhaps having Alan Dershowitz as my professor of criminal law colored my thinking." At the end of his first year, he returned to OTP to work in the legal department as a general legal assistant. The following summer, he landed an internship at Latham & Watkins, a prestigious corporate firm in Los Angeles. He did well, and got an offer before returning for his final year at Harvard. "I knew before I got out of law school that I wanted to be a litigator, just for the blood sport aspects of it, really."

The attorneys at Latham "were cutting-edge kind of people, very much a swashbuckling kind of attitude. They preserved that air for quite some time." Arriving in Los Angeles in mid-1976 as a first-year associate, Tom told the firm he wanted to enter the litigation department as soon as possible. Latham had a policy of rotating new associates through every department for at least two years to enable them to make a "more informed judgment." Tom replied, "I've already made my judgment. I'm thirty-five years old, and I want to get started." He was in litigation at the end of a year.

He attacked his new profession with a vengeance, acquiring the nickname "Navy Tom," which eventually shortened to simply "Navy." Initially, he shared a house high above Hollywood in Laurel Canyon with another Navy Vietnam vet who was with the firm. Several years later, he would buy bandleader Artie Shaw's house just to the west on Outpost Drive, ultimately moving into a third in the Hollywood Hills above Sunset Plaza.

His first action was as a junior player in some major uranium antitrust litigation. Latham was representing Gulf Oil, accused of illegally being a member of an international uranium cartel. The case began in late 1978 and ran for three years. "One year, I think I spent six hundred hours on the record in taking depositions, and I was taking depositions from the entire board of directors of Exxon, for example. That was a pretty heady assignment for a young lawyer."

By February 1984, he was a partner and working on the high-profile Fortune 500 cases. In 1991–92, he represented Shell Oil in an action where individual members of the board of directors were accused of misconduct.

By that time, Tom was feeling he had done enough law. It had become repetitive. Moreover, the practice and business of law had changed dramatically. His eighty-nine-member Los Angeles firm had grown to 650 lawyers, with offices in London, New York, Washington, Chicago, San Diego, and San Francisco.

Regarded by the family as a larger-than-life latter-day Hemingway, Tom had an income that allowed him some extravagance. Prompted by his good friend and fellow partner Steve Wilson, Tom embraced big game hunting. In the early 1990s, he and Wilson made two trips to Alaska and one safari in Zambia. He also hunted wild boar in Paso Robles, California, and javelina near Tucson. Among the dozen or so trophies he acquired were a male lion and Cape buffalo. When he finally bought a house in Coronado, he had his sister, Doug, by then an architect, design an extension with high-ceilinged walls to allow the buffalo and other trophies to adorn them. On the custom-made mantelpiece, his lion reclined, a paw draped over the edge.

On New Year's Eve 1994, Tom married Jean Phillips Root in a ceremony at Wilson's Hancock Park mansion in Los Angeles. Their friend Judge Cynthia Holcomb Hall of the Ninth Circuit Court of Appeals presided, reading the service from the 1928 Episcopal Prayer Book. Tom toasted his bride, identifying her as "the first, last, and only woman that I have ever loved." Afterwards, while attempting to cut a prodigious wedding cake with his commissioning sword, he quickly grew impatient and finally proceeded to hack wildly at the pastry. While the scores of family and well-wishers attending may have been nonplused by his performance, his niece, Terry Baldauf Curtin, a Hollywood heavy hitter in her own right, gleefully exclaimed, "For God's sake, Tom, why don't you just take out a gun and shoot it?"

Within a year, he would leave the Los Angeles office to work from San Diego. Before 1994 was out, he had stopped taking new cases and had settled into comfortable Coronado retirement with his bride, surrounded by the Navy and family. Not without irony, he would characterize himself for a new century as a "sportsman/financier."

Appendix

The First USS Mustin

On 20 December 1937 at its yard in Newport News, Virginia, Newport News Shipbuilding & Dry Dock Co. laid down the keel of the first *Mustin* (DD-413). Named after Henry C. Mustin, she was a 1,570-ton *Sims*-class destroyer with four 5-inch 38 single gun mounts. Launching was a year later on 8 December. Her sponsor was Emily Morton Mustin, wife of Henry C. Mustin's eldest son, Lloyd Montague, and the maid of honor was her first cousin Anne Claude Howard. Commissioning was on 16 September 1939, Lt. Cdr. James B. Freeman commanding.

For her first two years of service, the *Mustin* served in the western Atlantic as part of the Neutrality Patrol operations to safeguard allied shipping while Europe was at war. On 7 December 1941, she happened to be in Boston for an overhaul. The following day, she went to sea to rendezvous with the battleships *Idaho* and *Mississippi* and provide escort while they left the Atlantic for duty in the Pacific. After finally completing her overhaul on 3 January 1942, she headed for Pacific duty, arriving in Pearl Harbor on 17 February.

Until 3 April, the *Mustin* escorted convoys between Hawaii and San Francisco. In May, her escort duties took her to Samoa in the South Pacific. When the Japanese attack on Midway appeared imminent, she escorted a merchantman with reinforcements to the island. The Battle of Midway was joined while she was returning to Pearl Harbor.

Two days after she arrived, she returned to sea with Task Force 17 in a fruitless search for Japanese survivors. For the next two months, she was busy training and patrolling in advance of her deployment to the South Pacific and the struggle to secure Guadalcanal.

On 17 August, the *Mustin* departed with TF 17, commanded by Rear Adm. George D. Murray aboard the carrier *Hornet*. Once in the vicinity of Guadalcanal, she operated with her task group covering the southern approaches during the initial fighting there. On 5 October, she earned her first battle star in the strikes against Buin, Faisi, and Tonolai.

On 26 October, the destroyer was with the *Hornet* for the Battle of the Santa Cruz Islands. During the engagement the *Hornet* sustained heavy damage from a coordinated dive-bomber and torpedo-plane attack and had to be abandoned. After the action, the *Mustin* rescued 337 of *Hornet*'s survivors and with her sister ship the *Andersen* had the bitter task of scuttling the doomed carrier. Nine torpedoes and more than four hundred rounds of 5-inch shellfire set the ship fully ablaze but failed to sink her. Only after Japanese destroyers forced the pair to withdraw and fired four 24-inch torpedoes into the blazing hull did the *Hornet* finally sink beneath the surface.

The *Mustin* continued to operate in the Guadalcanal campaign. On 11 November, she was with Rear Adm. Thomas C. Kinkaid's TF 16 and the carrier *Enterprise* for the third battle of Savo Island. In addition to screening and patrolling with heavy ships, she alternated with escorting supply vessels in convoys from Nouméa and Espíritu Santo.

On Christmas Day, the *Mustin* unleashed a shore bombardment against enemy positions on Guadalcanal. After the Japanese withdrew from the island in February 1943, the ship remained until mid-April, guarding carrier air operations, patrolling, and escorting.

Upon her return to Pearl Harbor, the *Mustin* deployed to Adak in support of the Aleutians campaign. On 11 May, she was part of the covering force for the landings on Attu and later patrols northwest of the island until the end of the month. Through the summer, she continued her patrols as a blocking force to any Japanese reinforcement of Kiska. On the night of 25–26 July, her task group engaged a phantom enemy force in what became known as the "Battle of the Pips," where ships fired on false radar returns created by unusual atmospheric conditions. On 15 August, she covered the unopposed American recapture of Kiska.

After a Mare Island overhaul, the *Mustin* returned to Pearl Harbor in late October in advance of the campaign in the Gilbert and Marshall Islands. On 20 November, she participated with Task Force 52 in the assault on Makin in the Gilberts. Then she returned to San Pedro to exercise amphibious operations. In late January 1944, she was in Lahaina Roads, Maui, the staging area for the Marshalls invasion. On 30 January, she was bombarding enemy positions on Wotje. The following day, she was screening cruisers lobbing shells at Kwajalein and joining in the bombardment herself a day later. For the rest of the month, she was escorting different task groups around the atoll and operating off Eniwetok.

In March, the *Mustin* escorted fleet oilers supporting the fast carriers of Task Force 58 during its Central Pacific raids on Palau, Yap, Woleai, and Ulithi in the Carolines. She became part of the Seventh Fleet soon afterwards. In April, she returned to the southwest Pacific to screen carriers in amphibious assaults on Aitape and Hollandia in New Guinea. In May, she continued the operation at Wakde. Continuing operations on and around New Guinea involved escort, patrol, bombardment, and directing fighter aircraft, as one landing after another moved up the coast to wrest the huge island from the enemy. Noemfoor, Sansapor, Mios Woendi, Humboldt Bay, and Biak, all were struck by forces in which the ship was serving.

On 15 September, the *Mustin* served as primary fighter director in the initial assault on Morotai, Netherlands East Indies. On 10 October, after escorting reinforcements from New Guinea, she cleared Humboldt Bay for newly invaded Leyte. Arriving 25 October, the *Mustin* departed the same day, escorting a convoy safely away from the Battle for Leyte Gulf. Escort operations among the major bases of the western Pacific followed as the ship gave distant support to the Philippines operation on 25 November before returning to Leyte Gulf, where she joined the local defense force that two days later came under attack by enemy planes. The ship accounted for three Japanese losses.

In January and February 1945, the *Mustin* took part in the invasion of Luzon and other elements of the recapture of the Philippines. After rehearsals off New Guinea, on 9 January, she sortied for the assault on Luzon. For the next month, she fired in support of land forces, joined in repelling enemy air attack off Lingayen, and made anti-submarine patrols. She continued to operate in the Philippines, aiding in movement of reinforcements, until 2 February, when she made for Guadalcanal. There she served as antisubmarine patrol ship while awaiting the beginning of the rehearsals for the Okinawa operation.

Her task group staged at Ulithi. On 1 April, they arrived off Hagushi Beach, Okinawa, where she screened the transport area as the initial assault was made. For the next four days, she guarded the transports off the beaches by day and during their night retirements, firing on the numerous kamikaze attackers. From 5 to 17 April, the *Mustin* brought a convoy from Saipan and Ulithi, then returned to fire support, radar picket antisubmarine, and antiaircraft duty off Okinawa until 2 May, when she joined the screen of an escort carrier group operating to the southwest of the island.

On 28 May, the *Mustin* left Okinawa for Guam, Pearl Harbor, and Eniwetok. On 18 June, she arrived in San Pedro for a yard overhaul and alterations. Six days before she left, the war ended. After refresher training, she departed for occupation duty in Japan, arriving in Ominato, Honshu, on 16 September 1945.

In 1946, she was in Hawaii preparing for Operation Crossroads, the atomic tests in the Marshall Islands at Bikini Atoll, where in July and August she served as one of the target ships. On 29 August, she was decommissioned and remained at Bikini until taken to Kwajalein. On 18 March 1948, according to the Naval Historical Center, she was destroyed by gunfire and sunk.

For her World War II service, the *Mustin* received 13 battle stars.

(Thanks to *The Dictionary of American Naval Fighting Ships.*)

USS *Mustin* (DDG-89)

The decision to commission a second *Mustin* came in 1999, when on 22 October, Secretary of the Navy Richard J. Danzig announced that the thirty-ninth ship of the *Arleigh Burke*–class Aegis guided-missile destroyer would be the *Mustin* (DDG-89). In this instance, she would honor not just Capt. Henry Croskey Mustin, but also his son Vice Adm. Lloyd Montague Mustin and his grandsons, Vice Adm. Henry Croskey Mustin and Lt. Cdr. Thomas Morton Mustin.

The christening was on 15 December 2001 at the Pascagoula, Mississippi, shipyard of Ingalls Operations, a division of Northrop Grumman Ship Systems. Adm. Vernon E. Clark, chief of naval operations, was the principal speaker at the ceremonies.

Ship sponsors were three Mustin family members: Hank's wife, Lucy Holcomb Mustin, Tom's wife, Jean Phillips Mustin, and their sister-in-law Douglas Mustin St. Denis. Anne Howard Thomas, maid of honor for christening of the first *Mustin,* was matron of honor.

The prospective commanding officer of the ship is Cdr. Ann Phillips, one of only three women in the Navy currently commanding a combatant. The ship was commissioned in July 2003 and is homeported in San Diego.

Congress has currently authorized fifty-eight *Arleigh Burke* destroyers. The *Mustin* is the eighteenth built by Ingalls.

Sibling Careers and the Next Generation

As for Lloyd Mustin's generation, neither of his brothers, Henry Ashmead or Gordon Sinclair, followed him to the Naval Academy. Both had vision impairments that prevented them from passing the physical examination.

Henry went to the University of Virginia and from there into newspaper reporting. For a time, he was with the Washington *Evening Star.* During World War II, Pete Mitscher got him commissioned as an air intelligence officer. He served in the Pacific aboard the carrier *Essex,* where his duty was to brief aviators. After the war, he returned to reporting. He also distinguished himself as a radio broadcaster, for a time working with the Voice of America.

Gordon went to Yale, graduating in 1940 with an engineering degree in chemistry. Through George Murray, he got a commission and a wartime job in the Naval Research Laboratory, where he worked on anticorrosion coatings. After the war, he continued working with the Navy Department as a civilian.

Lloyd's daughter, Douglas Howard Mustin, once characterized her life as a Navy junior as "never quite being in one place long enough to be listed in the phone book." Married to one of her brother Hank's classmates, Laurance Charles Baldauf II, she raised their three children and still found time to develop "her great loves," painting and acting. Her career began in the 1960s and included appearances in film, television, theater, and in over a hundred TV commercials.

In the summer of 1976, Doug and Larry divorced in Coronado. Two years later, she married well-known San Diego architect Dale St. Denis, who later inspired her to pursue architecture in addition to her acting.

In 1989, she enrolled in San Diego's Newschool of Architecture, where she was on the dean's list and was student body president for two years. While a student, she was also editor of *Cartouche,* the school's architectural and design review published for the San Diego design community. In 1994, she graduated cum laude with her bachelor of architecture degree and was voted the outstanding student of design for the academic year, receiving as well the school's design award as best designer.

That year, she became a partner with her husband in St. Denis & St. Denis Architects in San Diego. In addition, she continues her commercial acting and regularly exhibits her painting and photography. In the summer of 2002, she joined the writing staff of *Coronado Lifestyle Magazine*.

Her brother, Hank, was initially unsure whether the next generation of Mustins would continue the family tradition of naval service. His eldest, Lloyd Montague Mustin II, born on 9 February 1959 in Jacksonville, Florida, graduated from St. Stephen's School in Alexandria, Virginia, in 1977. He chose the University of Richmond, where he got his bachelor of science in business in 1981.

"The day he graduated [from Richmond]," Hank said, "he called me up and said, 'Hey, how do I get in the Navy?'" Lloyd entered the OCS program and after getting his commission went to Charleston, South Carolina, to serve on the destroyer *William V. Pratt*. Within a year of reporting, he qualified as a surface warfare officer. True to Mustin tradition, he pursued ordnance and was initially the assistant gunnery officer. He later advanced to gunnery officer and first lieutenant.

Lloyd's calling, however, was to be an entrepreneur. Although he chose to remain in the Naval Reserve, he left active duty in 1988. The following year, he founded XL Associates, Inc., a suburban Maryland services company that within its first few years of existence generated nearly $5 million in annual revenues. In the early nineties, *The Washington Times* Money Section featured him as XL president and one of the national capital's successful entrepreneurs. The firm now has a national client base that includes more than eighteen Fortune 500 companies and government agencies.

Since its founding, Lloyd has expanded the company's operations into areas of engineering services, information technology, and technical management both for government and its prime contractors. His initial contracts were with the Department of Energy. One involved mentoring DOE senior management. A second and still ongoing contract was to conduct operational readiness reviews nationwide across the DOE nuclear complex. XL also works with the Agency for International Development, where it leads a contract to recruit disaster assistance relief teams that deploy worldwide to relieve suffering. With the Department of Agriculture, the firm is re-engineering USDA business processes for worldwide food aid. Lloyd has also recently teamed with Accenture, the management and technology services organization, in an international airport security contract with the new Transportation Security Administration.

In 1995, Lloyd received a masters of science in business with a concentration in finance from The Johns Hopkins University, where he graduated summa cum laude. Three years later, as a Naval Reserve lieutenant commander, he received an award from the Reserve Officers Association as the "Outstanding Junior Officer in the Naval Reserve."

In 1997, Lloyd advanced to commander. After the terrorist attacks of 11 September 2001, the Navy recalled him to active duty. The first military officer to arrive at Site R at Pennsylvania's Raven Rock Mountain, Lloyd took charge of the Office of the Secretary of Defense's Crisis Response Cell, where he worked for Douglas J. Feith, the undersecretary of defense for policy. Site R was on a wartime footing, and while there Lloyd played a critical role to ensure that the site could execute the Continuity of Operations Plan for OSD principals and staff.

Later in the month, he was assigned to the Pentagon, where he trained a team of senior officers to man and operate the OSD Executive Support Center. He served as a watch stander in the National Military Command Center as the OSD Liaison to the Joint Staff Crisis Action Team to "push through" time-critical deployment orders in support of the war in Afghanistan. In recognition of his contributions, he was awarded the Defense Superior Service Medal, an award seldom given to a reservist.

Lloyd's wife, Tracy Proctor Mustin, is also a Naval Reserve commander. After graduating in 1984 magna cum laude from North Carolina State University with a bachelor of science in chemical engineering, she entered the Civil Engineer Corps, where she remained from 1984 to 1991, at one point serving as aide to the chief of civil engineers. "She was the first female commanding officer of a commissioned Seabee Unit," said Hank, and she led more than two hundred unit members located throughout the Northeast.

From 1987 to 1991, Tracy served as a White House social aide for Presidents Reagan and Bush. After leaving active duty in 1991, she went to work as a Department of Energy program manager, working on various environmental management, cleanup, and nuclear material stabilization projects. In 1997, she became a senior technical adviser at DOE, traveling worldwide to assist in negotiations involving the shipment of spent nuclear fuel for disposal in the United States. In 2000, she served as the director of the Office of Transportation, responsible for policy and planning for the unclassified shipment of nuclear material and waste throughout the DOE complex. In 2002, she accepted a position with the National Nuclear Security Administration, where she is now responsible for various programs supporting the International Atomic Energy Agency aimed at ensuring the physical protection of nuclear material around the world.

Lloyd's youngest brother, John Burton Mustin, was born in Coronado, California, on 24 January 1967 and graduated from St. Stephen's in 1985. He attended Virginia

Polytechnic Institute and State University for one year before transferring to the Naval Academy. He graduated in May 1990 with a bachelor of science in systems engineering, with orders to report to the Aegis cruiser *Vincennes* in San Diego following Surface Warfare Officer's School in Coronado. In February 1991, he reported and became the CIC officer prior to his first western Pacific cruise. Qualified as a surface warfare officer and standing the antiair-warfare coordinator watch station for the deployment, John said that he enjoyed the "art" of air warfare and "found repeated documentation in my study materials that were quotes and policies of my recently retired father."

Following forty months aboard the *Vincennes,* John went to Monterey, California, in June 1994 for Postgraduate School, where he earned his master's in operations research. In September 1996, he reported to Newport, Rhode Island, to begin six months of department head school, followed by pipeline training en route to his next tour as the precommissioning operations officer on board the Aegis destroyer *Donald Cook* in construction in Bath, Maine.

Despite a successful tour, John opted not to pursue a naval career. He began his transition from the active Navy by serving temporarily at the Navy Recruiting District, New England, Headquarters in Boston. On 31 December 2000, John served his last day as the last Mustin on active duty as a commissioned officer of the United States Navy. On 1 January 2001, he became a reserve lieutenant commander.

A short while later, he joined Lotus Interworks, a New England–based technology incubator, as vice president of operations, charged with starting companies specializing in web-enabled business solutions. As a reservist, he became the assistant operations officer for the Battle Group Two staff, the reserve unit supporting the Commander, Cruiser Destroyer Group Two—a command previously held by both his grandfather and father. In August 2002, he deployed for two weeks aboard the carrier *George Washington.*

His first cousin, Laurence Charles Baldauf III, Doug's son, also went Navy. Born on 8 August 1958 in Palo Alto, California, Larry spent his childhood in Coronado, graduated from Coronado High School in 1976, and went to UCLA. In 1982, he got his B.A. in industrial design and graphic arts. From there, he chose to follow his father's career and attended Aviation Officer Candidate School in Pensacola. In March 1983, he was commissioned as an ensign and ultimately designated a naval aviator in March 1985.

Larry qualified for tactical jet aviation and initially flew the A-7E Corsair II. In February 1986, he was assigned to the Argonauts, attack squadron VA-147, Carrier Air

Wing 9. That year, he was aboard the carrier *Kitty Hawk* during her around-the-world cruise. The following year, he deployed with the carrier *Nimitz* on a WestPac cruise.

Larry was a qualified landing signal officer, ranked the squadron's number one junior officer and the only junior officer in the air wing to be strike leader qualified. During this period, he received a nomination for the Wesley McDonald Junior Officer of the Year Award and earned two Navy achievement medals for inspirational leadership/tactical expertise and a Navy Commendation medal as a weapons officer and tactical training officer.

In 1988, Larry entered F/A-18 Hornet fighter training as a flight instructor with VFA-125, the "Rough Raiders," the Navy's first strike fighter squadron at Reeves Field, NAS Lemoore, California. In 1991, his peers selected him as an F/A-18 instructor of the year, and with over 580 carrier traps, he won his second Navy Commendation Medal for tactical expertise.

That year in June, he transferred to the reserves, operating in NAS Miramar, California, with the "Fighting Saints," composite fighter squadron VFC-13, the adversary reserve squadron. There, he flew A-4 Superfox and F-18 aircraft and provided advanced air-to-air instruction to fleet replacement pilots training in F-14 and F-18 aircraft.

Entering commercial aviation, he began flying the MD-80 as a first officer with Alaska Airlines. In 1992, he went to American Airlines, where he remained until February 1994. That winter, Larry suffered a serious snowboarding accident that required him to leave both naval and commercial aviation.

In January 1995, he took a position in motion picture marketing with Walt Disney Pictures, at Buena Vista International. In June 1997, he shifted to domestic pictures marketing at Walt Disney Pictures. In early 2000, he became creative director at Fox Searchlight Pictures, where he was responsible for the creation of all theatrical advertising materials. Later that year, he went to the Santa Monica visual effects, commercial post-production, and animation production company Harley's House as its creative director, where he launched its theatrical ad agency and managed work for every major studio in theatrical audio-visual advertising. In 2001, he became vice president for new business development and producer for New Wave Entertainment, one of Hollywood's leading creative services and entertainment companies for digital audio and video creation, production, and post-production.

Larry's cousin, Hank's middle son, Thomas Russell Mustin, has been an anchor/reporter for the Denver CBS affiliate TV station NEWS4 Colorado since January 2002. Born on 18 November 1960 in Monterey, California, he graduated from St. Stephens in 1978 and attended Hampden-Sydney College in southern Virginia, where he was a two-year football letterman before transferring to Virginia Tech in Blacksburg. In 1983, he graduated from Virginia Tech with a bachelor of science degree in economics with a minor in English and then headed to Los Angeles, where he worked for several years in magazine publishing and as an actor, notably in the 1986 film *Star Trek IV: The Voyage Home.* Other acting credits included appearances in the TV series *Melrose Place, LA Law, General Hospital,* and *The Young and the Restless.*

Tom later attended UCLA, where he received a certificate in broadcast journalism in 1995 and began his television news career as an intern at KABC-TV in Los Angeles; that led to his first job in 1996 as a reporter at WVIR-TV in Charlottesville, Virginia. His next move was the following year when he became a weekend anchor and reporter at WLBT-TV in Jackson, Mississippi. While at WLBT-TV, he received a Associated Press award for his half-hour special documentary, "The City Council vs. Capitol Cablevision," and was part of the team that received an award for outstanding coverage of the 1 October 1997 shooting at Pearl High School in Pearl, Mississippi.

In 1998, he joined ABC 45 in Winston-Salem, North Carolina, where, after anchoring the morning show for three months, he became the main anchor for the 6:00 P.M. and 11:00 P.M. broadcasts. He covered many breaking news stories, including 16 September 1999 Hurricane Floyd.

His sister, Katherine Elizabeth Mustin Miller, was born in Philadelphia on 7 December 1961, which she observed was "quite apropos for a Navy Brat." Kay remembered moving ten times while growing up: "1973, London, 6th grade; 1974, Athens, Greece, 7th grade; high school, 1975–1979, St. Agnes." From there, she went to James Madison University in Harrisonburg, Virginia, where she got her bachelors degree in business administration in 1983. She immediately went to work as a search executive for the Springfield, Virginia, executive recruitment firm WSS. In 1984, she became director of physician recruitment for Physician Search of Fairfax, Virginia. In 1992, she went to her present position as physician recruiter for Potomac Hospital in Woodbridge, Virginia.

Her cousin, Corinne Baldauf Lynch, Doug's eldest daughter, was born on 15 March 1957 in Palo Alto, California, before moving with her family to Coronado, where she spent her childhood. In 1975, she graduated from Coronado High School. For over a decade, she was in publishing, both as a freelance writer and as an advertising executive. She held positions with *Los Angeles Magazine,* as manager of national fashion accounts, and at *San Diego Magazine,* as executive vice president and associate publisher.

In July 2002, she joined Media Networks, Inc., a division of Time Inc., as San Diego–area representative. Her responsibility is for creation of strategic advertising packages for thirty-five national magazine titles, including *Time, Newsweek, People, Vanity Fair, Sports Illustrated,* and *Fortune.*

Corinne's younger sister, Terry Baldauf Curtin, was born in Carmel, California, on 17 January 1961. She graduated from Coronado High School in 1979 and went to UCLA, getting her bachelors degree in English literature in 1983. From there, she temped with an agency that placed her in 20th Century Fox, which quickly hired her, thus launching her on a monumentally successful twenty-year career in motion picture promotion.

While at Fox, Terry was in the publicity and promotion department as vice president of field operations/promotions and ultimately as vice president for national publicity. Among the many campaigns she supervised were *Alien 3, Home Alone, Die Hard,* and *Die Hard 2.* In 1992, she went to Morgan Creek Productions as vice president of worldwide publicity and promotion, where she created and implemented the campaign for *Ace Ventura: Pet Detective,* among others.

In 1994, she became senior vice president, worldwide publicity and field promotions, for MGM/UA Distribution Co., where she oversaw publicity campaigns for a number of films including *Get Shorty.* In 1996, she went with Disney, where she was senior vice president for publicity at Buena Vista Pictures Marketing, during which time she also represented Touchstone.

In March 1999, she became executive vice president for publicity at Universal Pictures, promoting such films as *Erin Brockovich* and *Notting Hill.* In January 2002, she conducted a hard-fought campaign on behalf of the Oscar-winning *A Beautiful Mind.* Shortly afterwards, she became head of marketing and distribution at Revolution Studios, the company that released *Black Hawk Down.*

In December 2002, *The Hollywood Reporter*'s eleventh annual Women in Entertainment Power 100 ranked Terry number forty-five.

Source Notes

Much of the primary material for the two sections on Henry Croskey Mustin and Lloyd Montague Mustin originates with the Mustin Family Private Papers, hereafter *MFPP.* The papers are held by Ms. Douglas Mustin St. Denis of Coronado, California, and include newspaper and magazine clips and articles, letters, photographs, scrapbooks, unpublished manuscripts, interviews, service records, reports, etc. Subjects include Henry C. Mustin, Corinne Montague Mustin Murray, George D. Murray, Lloyd Montague Mustin, and Emily Morton Mustin.

INTRODUCTION
Byrne account of Hank Mustin's 1985 Vestfjord press conference from his interview with the author. "Brains" quote in J. J. Clark and Clark G. Reynolds, *Carrier Admiral* (New York: David McKay Company, 1967).

Part 1. The Aviator
In addition to the materials found in the *MFPP,* this section owes a great deal to the Papers of Henry C. Mustin in the Naval Historical Foundation Collection at the Manuscript Division of the Library of Congress, hereafter *PHCM.* Among the significant items in that collection are the many letters from Mustin to his wife, Corinne Montague Mustin.

CHAPTER I. THE ACADEMY YEARS:
A PHILADELPHIAN JOINS THE TIDE

Early Mustin family information comes from the U.S. Naval Institute's Lloyd Montague Mustin oral history, conducted by Dr. John T. Mason Jr., hereafter *Mason,* and unpublished, transcribed reminiscences dating from the early 1990s found in the *MFPP,* hereafter *Reminiscences.* Cruise information and records draw from items held in the Special Collections of the Nimitz Library, U.S. Naval Academy, specifically the *Lucky Bag* 1895 and 1896, the various editions of the *Annual Register of the United States Naval Academy,* Annapolis, Md. (U.S. Government Printing Office, Washington, D.C.) for the class years 1893–96 and the Records of the Office of the Dean of the Academic Board: Records of the U.S. Naval Academy: Record Group 405, National Archives, Entry 62, "Registrations of Candidates to the Academy," and Entry 86, vol. 15, "Academic and Conduct Records." Additional material comes from the fiftieth anniversary commemorative for the Class of 1896 in the *MFPP.* The *Sun* clip was also in the *MFPP.*

CHAPTER 2. AN ENSIGN GOES TO WAR

Orders came from his service records held by the *PHCM.* An explanation for Sampson's erratic behavior, "multiple infarct dementia resulting from a succession of small strokes," can be found in Martin G. Netsky, M.D., and Capt. Edward L. Beach, USN (Ret.), "The Trouble with Admiral Sampson," *Naval History* 9 (November-December 1995): 8–17. The published report on the *Maine* was the *Report of the Naval Court of Inquiry,* aboard the lighthouse tender *Mangrove,* the first day, 21 February 1898 in Havana; "'Projection showing present position of keel and bow of Maine redrawn from draft made by Ens. W.Y.N. Powelson' assisted by divers Olsson, Smith, Rindquist and Schluter, drawn by Naval Cadet H.C. Mustin," in the Special Collections of the Nimitz Library, U.S. Naval Academy. The Sampson quote is from W. A. M. Goode, *With Sampson through the War* (New York: Doubleday & McClure, 1899). Sampson's recommendation is quoted from a newspaper clip in *MFPP.* Mechanical semaphore designs are in *PHCM.* Fiske's mention of Mustin is in Bradley A. Fiske, *From Midshipman to Rear-Admiral* (New York: Century Co., 1919), 341.

CHAPTER 3. COMMAND IN THE PHILIPPINES:
FROM OYSTER TO PIRATE

Mustin commentary from his letters to Corinne in *PHCM.* The dates and detail for his time in the Philippines largely rely on his *Taaleno Journal,* from the gunboat *Taaleno,* dating from 26 September to 13 October 1899, and on the accompanying *Samar Journal,* which covered the period from 14 October 1899 to his last entry on 28 February 1900 in *PHCM.* Much background information on gunboat operations is available in Vernon Leon Williams, *The U.S. Navy in the Philippine Insurrection and Subsequent Native Unrest, 1898–1906* (unpublished dissertation, Texas A&M, 1985). Background information on Mustin's tour in the *Isla de Cuba* can be found in Frederick Lewis Sawyer, *Sons of Gunboats* (Annapolis, Md.: U.S. Naval Institute, 1946).

Testimonials from Hare, Young, McCalla, in both *MFPP* and *PHCM*. Court-martial account in National Archives, RG 125, Records of the Office of the Judge Advocate General (Navy), Proceedings of the General Courts Martial (Board) 1860–1942, Box No. 202, Entry 27, #8821, Case of Ensign Henry C. Mustin. Pedro Cuervas story in his letters to Corinne, in *PHCM*.

CHAPTER 4. THE GUNNER FINDS HIS MASCOTTE

Watson letter in *PHCM*. Alger quote in Elting E. Morison, *Admiral Sims and the Modern American Navy* (New York: Russell and Russell, 1968, 1942). Mustin's comments on his time in the *Culgoa* in his letters to Corinne, in *PHCM*. Oliver letters in *PHCM*. *Culgoa* rescue in *PHCM*. The record of Mustin's relations with Saegmuller is in their correspondence in *PHCM*. The Fiske account is in Fiske, *From Midshipman to Rear-Admiral*. Mustin's fire control memo is in *PHCM*. The account of the social life surrounding the Gun Factory is from the unpublished autobiographical manuscript of Lelia Montague Gordon Barnett in *MFPP* and from Mustin's letters to Corinne in *PHCM*. Family background of the Montagues from newspaper clips in *MFPP*.

CHAPTER 5. WITH THE GREAT WHITE FLEET:
ALMOST BETTER THAN MY HONOR

Account of the Mustins' wedding and honeymoon from Mustin letters to Corinne in *PHCM*. Matthews's description is in Franklin Matthews, *With the Battle Fleet: Cruise of the Sixteen Battleships of the United States Atlantic Fleet from Hampton Roads to the Golden Gate, December, 1907–May, 1908* (New York: B. W. Huebsch, 1908).

CHAPTER 6. INTO THE AIR

Mustin and Reid exploits in newspaper reports are found in *MFPP*. Saegmuller correspondence is in *PHCM*. Mustin/Sims exchange is in *PHCM*. Mustin statements on Philadelphia in news clip are in *MFPP*.

CHAPTER 7. A HIGH TYPE IN VERA CRUZ

Much of the chronology of the operation is available in Mustin/Bristol correspondence in *PHCM* and also in the Papers of Mark L. Bristol in the Naval Historical Foundation Collection of the Manuscript Division of the Library of Congress. Also, Mustin letters to Corinne are in *PHCM*. James B. Connolly account is in *Collier's*, 20 June 1914, available in *MFPP*. Other press accounts in news and magazine clips are in *MFPP*. Mustin's action report, dated 19 May 1914, is in *MFPP*.

CHAPTER 8. A WARRIOR AT WAR WITHIN AND WITHOUT

Mustin aboard the *North Carolina*, from his letters to Corinne in *PHCM*. Archibald D. Turnbull and Clifford L. Lord, *History of United States Naval Aviation* (New Haven, Conn.: Yale University Press, 1949) is an excellent source for early naval aviation history and contains a fair amount of discussion on Mustin's role, as is George van Deurs, *Wings for the Fleet* (Annapolis, Md.: U.S. Naval Institute, 1966). Further material on Mustin can be gleaned from published biographies of early naval aviators, including Towers, Bellinger, Ellyson, and Mitscher, as well as Moffett and Pratt.

CHAPTER 9. RETURNING TO THE GAME

Mustin letters to Corinne in *PHCM*. His 19 August 1917 sea-sled proposal, "Plans for Air Operations against German Naval Bases and Fleet, including a Plan for Air Attack on Essen," in *MFPP*. Further background to the proposal is in his testimony on 18 March 1919 to the General Board, which was looking at air policy for the future, and in a 1980 draft manuscript article, "Mustin's Wonderful Sea Sleds," by Capt. A. L. Raithel Jr. (USN), also in *MFPP*. Towers's recommendation in *PHCM*. Legette rescue in *MFPP* and *PHCM*. Mustin congressional testimony from National Archives. Account of Mustin's role on the Crowell Commission in Charles M. Melhorn, *Two-Block Fox: The Rise of the Aircraft Carrier, 1911–1929* (Annapolis, Md.: U.S. Naval Institute Press, 1974).

CHAPTER 10. AVIATION IN THE PACIFIC

Account of Balboa flight is in his report on material and report on harbors in *MFPP*. Press accounts are also in *MFPP*.

CHAPTER 11. BUAER AND HENRY CROSKEY'S LEGACY

On Mustin's role in BuAer and his relationship to Moffett, see William F. Trimble, *Admiral William A. Moffett: Architect of Naval Aviation* (Washington, D.C.: Smithsonian Institution Press, 1994), and particularly Clark and Reynolds, *Carrier Admiral,* p. 36, on Mustin's promotion of Moffett. Refer to Edward Arpee, *From Frigates to Flat-Tops* (Lake Forest, Ill.: Arpee, 1953), 97, for discussion of the five-year plan. Sims letter in *MFPP*.

PART 2. THE GUN BOSS

The main primary source for this section comes from *Mason*. A second primary source, especially for his career after mid-1964, is in the *Reminiscences* found in the *MFPP*. While this version contains some minor inaccuracies and is at times at variance with information in *Mason,* it does contain some interesting family details not found in the latter.

CHAPTER 12. GROWING UP A NAVY JUNIOR

Press report of Mustin-Murray marriage in *MFPP*. Press accounts of Mustin Field dedication in *MFPP*. Drain, Wilber, and Hall letters in *MFPP*. Murray remarks on 15 May 1928 letter in *MFPP*.

CHAPTER 13. THE ACADEMY YEARS: IT ISN'T LUCK, IT'S SKILL

Cruise information and records, held in the Special Collections of the Nimitz Library, U.S. Naval

Academy, from the *Lucky Bag* 1932, the various editions of the *Annual Register of the United States Naval Academy,* Annapolis, Md. (Washington, D.C.: U.S. Government Printing Office, 1928–32) for the class years 1928–32 and the Records of the Office of the Dean of the Academic Board: Records of the U.S. Naval Academy: Record Group 405, National Archives, Entry 62, "Registrations of Candidates to the Academy" and Entry 86, v. 15, "Academic and Conduct Records" (both available in microfilm). Press accounts of Lloyd's swimming in *MFPP.* Commendation letter in *MFPP.* Moffett letter in *MFPP.*

CHAPTER 14. ON THE ASIATIC STATION:
BY THE SLOP CHUTE ON THE OL' WHANGPOO
Information from *Mason* and oral history in *MFPP.* Additional information from a separate 10 March 1970 interview with Dr. Jack Mason on the subject of Admiral Nimitz in *MFPP.* Swim team results in clips from *The China Press,* Saturday, 19 May 1934, in *MFPP.*

CHAPTER 15. THE MAKING OF A GUN BOSS
Lloyd's thesis, "A Servo-Mechanism for a Rate Follow-Up System," in the MIT Department of Electrical Engineering, 16 May 1940, in *MFPP.* Lloyd's commentary on his thesis was in his *Memorandum for the Record,* 1 January 1971, while he was DASA Director, available in *MFPP.*

CHAPTER 16. FIRST BLOOD ON THE *ATLANTA*
Much of the information on the *Atlanta* originates in Lloyd's diary, found in the *MFPP,* and in a version edited by David Winkler of the Naval Historical Foundation. The diary covers the ship's history from 23 December 1941 to 27 October 1942. Of the postwar works on the night action of 11–12 November 1942 at Guadalcanal, Lloyd regarded the most accurate account as Samuel Eliot Morison, *History of United States Naval Operations in World War II,* vol. 5, *The Struggle for Guadalcanal, August 1942–February 1943* (Boston: Little, Brown and Co., 1947–62). All accounts cross-checked against *Mason* as well as James W. Grace, *The Naval Battle of Guadalcanal: Night Action, 13 November 1942* (Annapolis, Md.: U.S. Naval Institute Press, 1999). Lloyd's Narrative for the Office of Naval Records and Library conducted by a Lt. Porter at the Fire Control School in Anacostia on 3 June 1943 in *MFPP.* Account of Emily's reaction to the *Atlanta's* sinking in interview with Douglas Mustin St. Denis with author. Lloyd's 18 November 1942 damage control report for the *Atlanta's* executive officer, Cdr. C. D. Emory, in *MFPP.* The "cool-headed" quote from William B. McKinney, *Join the Navy and See the World* (Los Angeles: Military Literary Guild, 1990), 45, in *MFPP.* "He doesn't like it" quote from news clips from the *Chicago Tribune* compiled by Edward D. Corboy in his *The Log of the Mighty A* (*U.S.S. Atlanta* 1985 Reunion Association Scrapbook Photocopy), 7. Additional information from an untitled, anonymous unpublished enlisted man's diary of *Atlanta* and Lloyd's 19 April 1986 letter to Ivan Musicant and enclosures in *MFPP.* Newspaper account of Tassafaronga bombardment in *MFPP.* Lloyd's commissioning sword quote said to author.

CHAPTER 17. AT WAR, AT SPEED WITH PETE AND CHING
Mustin quotes from *Mason.*

CHAPTER 18. COMING TO TERMS WITH
THE POSTWAR MISSILE NAVY
Mustin quotes from *Mason.*

CHAPTER 19. FIRST COMMAND: A LOVE YOU COULD TASTE
Mustin quotes from *Mason.*

CHAPTER 20. EARLY EXPOSURE TO PENTAGON
POLITICS: NOTHING BUT LOGIC
Mustin quotes from *Mason.*

CHAPTER 21. A DESTROYERMAN AT HOME IN THE PACIFIC
Mustin quotes from *Mason.*

CHAPTER 22. FROM ARGUS TO BERLIN: AN OPERATIONAL
FLAG OFFICER IN THE STRATEGIC REALM
Another source for the Argus operation was a detailed 11–12 March 1975 interview with
Mustin conducted by John Conrad and Bill Ogle, in the *MFPP.* Hanson W. Baldwin's 19
March 1959 *New York Times* article, in *MFPP.*

CHAPTER 23. OPERATION DOMINIC: SHOOTING SWORDFISH IN A
FISH DESERT
The 4 May 1962 *Time* cover story, "U.S. NUCLEAR TESTING: The Shot Heard Round the World,"
in *MFPP.*

CHAPTER 24. J-3 AND VIETNAM: WRESTLING A FINE ITALIAN HAND
This chapter relies on interviews by Michael Krepon of Johns Hopkins University on 12 and
17 September and 12 October 1973 and *Reminiscences,* both in *MFPP.* Additional material comes
from Neil Sheehan, et al., *The Pentagon Papers: As Published By The New York Times* (New York:
Quadrangle Books, 1971), and Sen. Mike Gravel, ed., *The Pentagon Papers: The Defense Department
History of United States Decisionmaking on Vietnam* (Boston: Beacon Press, 1971–72). McCone quote
in his Memorandum for the Record, Washington, 22 April 1965, 12:34–2:20 P.M., Meeting of the
NSC Executive Committee, 22 Apr 65, Document 269, found in "Increase in U.S. ground forces
in Vietnam and consideration by the U.S. Government of a bombing pause, March 8–May 8,"
from *Foreign Relations of the United States, 1964–1968,* vol. 2, *Vietnam, January–June 1965,*

Department of State Publication 10288 (Washington, D.C.: United States Government Printing Office, 1996). Sharp quote in his *Strategy for Defeat: Vietnam in Retrospect* (San Rafael, Calif.: Presidio Press, 1978).

CHAPTER 25. CAREER'S END AND RETIREMENT: NEVER BETTER

Interview with Larry Baldauf by author. Material also from the *Reminiscences* in the *MFPP.* Additional DASA background information from a publication made available by the Defense Threat Reduction Agency titled *Defense Special Weapons Agency 1947–1997: The First 50 Years of National Service.* Henry A. Mustin quote on Lloyd's reaction to Emily's death to author. John B. Mustin quote from his 1 April 2002 e-mail to author. Lloyd's last quote from conversations with author.

Part 3. The Surface Warriors

Much of this section's material comes from interviews in November and December 2000 with the author and a series of interviews in early 2001 conducted by David Winkler of the Naval Historical Foundation, hereafter *Winkler.* Additional information from the Papers of Hank Mustin, hereafter *PHM.* Among those papers are correspondence, speeches, and newspaper and magazine articles about and by Hank Mustin and official reports.

CHAPTER 26. HANK MUSTIN: CHILDHOOD AND USNA— GROOMING FOR THE A TEAM

Emily Mustin quote from conversations with the author. Cruise information and records, held in the Special Collections of the Nimitz Library, U.S. Naval Academy, from the *Lucky Bag* 1955, the various editions of the *Annual Register of the United States Naval Academy,* Annapolis, Md. (Washington, D.C.: U.S. Government Printing Office, 1952–55) for the class years 1952–55. Webster, Adams, Lucy Holcomb Mustin, and Joseph Bowyer Howard recollections and quotes from interviews with author.

CHAPTER 27. THE YOUNG DESTROYERMAN IN THE CAVALRY

Additional material comes from Webster, Lucy Mustin, and Douglas Mustin St. Denis interviews. Quotes and recollections from Jim Toole from interview with author.

CHAPTER 28. BROWN-WATER OPERATIONS IN VIETNAM: TERRY AND THE PIRATES

Howard material from author's interview. Background to brown-water operations and chronology from Center of Naval Analyses report CRC 284, Victory Daniels and Judith C. Erdheim, *Game Warden* (January 1976) in the *PHM.* Further material from author's interview with Toole. Incident with Tom Harkin from author interview with Douglas Mustin St. Denis. Sharp quote from personal inscription to his and Gen. William C. Westmoreland's *Report on the War in Vietnam [as of 30 June 1968]* (Camp H. M. Smith: 1968) in *PHM*. Moorer quote from interview with author.

CHAPTER 29. ON THE GUN LINE: DESTROYER COMMAND

Material from author and *Winkler.*

CHAPTER 30. FIRST DUTY AT OPNAV:

A POLECAT AT A BEACH PARTY

Zumwalt allegation about Kissinger in Elmo R. Zumwalt Jr., *A Global Military-Political Perspective: Past and Future* (Berkeley: University of California, 1989), p. 27. Connolly quote from Hank in *Winkler.* Bagley quotes from interview with author.

CHAPTER 31. INTRODUCTION TO NATO:

THE FROCKED CAPTAIN IN SLEEPY HOLLOW

Lucy Mustin quotes from her interview with the author.

CHAPTER 32. DRIVING SURFACE WARFARE

Doyle quotes from his interview with author.

CHAPTER 33. BAGGING THE CARRIERS:

A TWO-STAR IN THE PENALTY BOX

Material from author and *Winkler.*

CHAPTER 34. COMMANDER, SECOND FLEET

Adm. Wesley L. McDonald's 29 May 1984 letter in *PHM*. Walker assertion in the U.S. Naval Institute oral history with Adm. Harry D. Train. Hank's 25 October 1985 letter to Watkins in *PHM*. The *Newsweek* 3 February 1986 "Be My Guest" article and Hank's 8 January 1986 letter to Tuttle in *PHM*. Gray quotes in his interview with author.

CHAPTER 35. THE OPS BARON

Retired Captain Bruce G. Stone's 18 May 1986 letter to Hank and Hank's 27 May 1986 reply in *PHM*. Gray quotes in his interview with author. The 7 July 1988 letter from Senator Dan Quayle in *PHM*. Adm. Sir Julian Oswald quote in 8 September 1988 letter in *PHM*. Bagley quote in interview with author. Transcript of 21 April 1988 press conference on the *Roberts* incident in *PHM*. Rinn letter of 27 April 1988 in *PHM*. Ben Masdon undated letter and 5 May 1986 reply in *PHM*.

CHAPTER 36. TOM MUSTIN: SWASHBUCKLING
FROM WARDROOM TO COURTROOM

Most of this material originates from the author's summer 2001 interviews with Tom Mustin and from his personal papers, which include his service record, master's thesis ("Optimal Allocation of Air Strikes for Interdiction of a Transportation Network"), photos, etc. Cruise information and records, held in the Special Collections of the Nimitz Library, U.S. Naval Academy, from the *Lucky Bag* 1962, the various editions of the *Annual Register of the United States Naval Academy*, Annapolis, Md. (Washington, D.C.: U.S. Government Printing Office, 1959–62) for the class years 1959–62. Allan McMasters's quote from telephone interview with author. Combat award citations from Tom Mustin's service record in his personal papers. Hank's recollections in *Winkler*. Wedding account from author.

APPENDIX

Material on the first USS *Mustin* drawn primarily from the *Dictionary of American Naval Fighting Ships* (Washington, D.C.: U.S. Naval Historical Center, 1959–91). Material on Lloyd Montague Mustin's two brothers, Henry Ashmead and Gordon Sinclair, from *Mason*. Material on Douglas Mustin St. Denis and the next generation from author interviews with each, as well as from résumés and curriculi vitae.

Index

About the Author

John Fass Morton has been a defense and homeland security conference director in Washington for the last decade. He is currently director of conferences at King Publishing, publisher of *Defense Week,* and he has served as a contributing editor and journalist for virtually every major defense publication, including the Naval Institute *Proceedings.* Prior assignments include public relations and advertising for several years in New York and in communications and entertainment for nine years in London.